걸프 사태

쿠웨이트, 이라크 및 각국 경제 제재

걸프 사태

쿠웨이트, 이라크 및 각국 경제 제재

| 머리말

  걸프 전쟁은 미국의 주도하에 34개국 연합군 병력이 수행한 전쟁으로, 1990년 8월 이라크의 쿠웨이트 침공 및 합병에 반대하며 발발했다. 미국은 초기부터 파병 외교에 나섰고, 1990년 9월 서울 등에 고위 관리를 파견하며 한국의 동참을 요청했다. 88올림픽 이후 동구권 국교 수립과 유엔 가입 추진 등 적극적인 외교 활동을 펼치는 당시 한국에 있어 이는 미국과 국제사회의 지지를 얻기 위해서라도 피할 수 없는 일이었다. 결국 정부는 91년 1월부터 약 3개월에 걸쳐 국군의료지원단과 공군수송단을 사우디아라비아 및 아랍 에미리트 연합 등에 파병하였고, 군·민간 의료 활동, 병력 수송 임무를 수행했다. 동시에 당시 걸프 지역 8개국에 살던 5천여 명의 교민에게 방독면 등 물자를 제공하고, 특별기 파견 등으로 비상시 대피할 수 있도록 지원했다. 비록 전쟁 부담금과 유가 상승 등 어려움도 있었지만, 걸프전 파병과 군사 외교를 통해 한국은 유엔 가입에 박차를 가할 수 있었고 미국 등 선진 우방국, 아랍권 국가 등과 밀접한 외교 관계를 유지하며 여러 국익을 창출할 수 있었다.

  본 총서는 외교부에서 작성하여 30여 년간 유지한 걸프 사태 관련 자료를 담고 있다. 미국을 비롯한 여러 국가와의 군사 외교 과정, 일일 보고 자료와 기타 정부의 대응 및 조치, 재외동포 철수와 보호, 의료지원단과 수송단 파견 및 지원 과정, 유엔을 포함해 세계 각국에서 수집한 관련 동향 자료, 주변국 지원과 전후복구사업 참여 등 총 48권으로 구성되었다. 전체 분량은 약 2만 4천여 쪽에 이른다.

2024년 3월

한국학술정보(주)

| 일러두기

· 본 총서에 실린 자료는 2022년 4월과 2023년 4월에 각각 공개한 외교문서 4,827권, 76만 여 쪽 가운데 일부를 발췌한 것이다.

· 각 권의 제목과 순서는 공개된 원본을 최대한 반영하였으나, 주제에 따라 일부는 적절히 변경하였다.

· 원본 자료는 A4 판형에 맞게 축소하거나 원본 비율을 유지한 채 A4 페이지 안에 삽입 하였다. 또한 현재 시점에선 공개되지 않아 '공란'이란 표기만 있는 페이지 역시 그대로 실었다.

· 외교부가 공개한 문서 각 권의 첫 페이지에는 '정리 보존 문서 목록'이란 이름으로 기록물 종류, 일자, 명칭, 간단한 내용 등의 정보가 수록되어 있으며, 이를 기준으로 0001번부터 번호가 매겨져 있다. 이는 삭제하지 않고 총서에 그대로 수록하였다.

· 보고서 내용에 관한 더 자세한 정보가 필요하다면, 외교부가 온라인상에 제공하는 『대한 민국 외교사료요약집』 1991년과 1992년 자료를 참조할 수 있다.

| 차례

정리보존문서목록					
기록물종류	일반공문서철	등록번호	2020120211	등록일자	2020-12-28
분류번호	772	국가코드	XF	보존기간	영구
명 칭	걸프사태, 1990-91. 전12권				
생 산 과	북미1과/중동1과	생산년도	1990~1991	담당그룹	
권 차 명	V.1 쿠웨이트, 1990-91				
내용목차					

0001

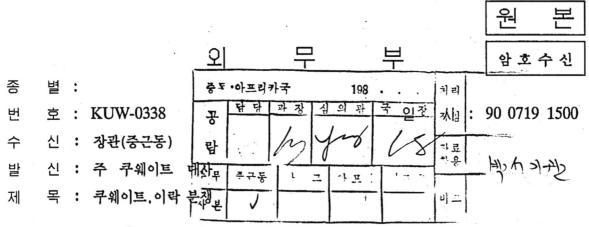

종 별 :

번 호 : KUW-0338

수 신 : 장관(중근동)

발 신 : 주 쿠웨이트 대사

제 목 : 쿠웨이트, 이락 분쟁

1. 이락 정부는 7.17. 쿠웨이트를 공격하는 아래내용의 각서를 아랍연맹 사무총장에게 보냈음.

가. 쿠웨이트는 60 년대 및 70 년대의 협상에도 불구하고 아직 국경이 확정되지 않은 "이락 남부지대"에 이란, 이락전쟁기회를 틈타서 군사, 경찰시설과 더불어 유전을 개발하고 농장을 개간했다. 이런일은 군사적침략에 해당되는 것으로본다. 1988 년 ALGIER 에의 아랍연맹 정상회담에서 동문제 해결을 쿠웨이트에 제의했지만 해결은 회피하고 이러한 시설을 계속 확장하고 있다.

나. 쿠웨이트는 "이락영토에 있는" LEMIELLA 유전에서 그동안 24 억불에 해당하는 원유를 불법 체굴했다. 이금액을 이락에 반납해야한다.

다. 쿠웨이트와 U.A.E 는 OPEC 쿼타를 지키지않고 초과생산해서 원유가격을 폭락시켰다. 이것은 이락을 포함한 아랍 산유국들의 경제를 붕괴시키는 것이며 제국주의 및 시오니즘 정책을 방조하는 군사적 침략행위로 본다.

라. 아랍연맹은 이러한 쿠웨이트의 침략행위를 중지시키기 바란다.

마. 여타 아랍국가들과 함께 쿠웨이트와 U.A.E 가 이.이전때 이락을 지원한것은 사실이나 지원금은 무상증여가 아닌 차관인데 이락이 전쟁을 한 것은 이락만을 위한 것이 아니라 아랍전체 특히 걸프지역을 위한 것이었으므로 차관은 탕감되어야 한다.

2. 이에대해 쿠웨이트는 (NATIONAL COUNCIL) 7.18. 강력한 내용의 반박 성명을 발표했음. 동성명에서 이락의 "THE POLICY OF VIOLENCE, THREATS AND EXTORTION" 을 비난하고 이러한 기도에 굴복하지 않을것이라는 강경한 입장을 밝혔음. 또한 쿠웨이트는 자국 입장 설명과 지지획득을 위하여 SABAH 외무장관은 사우디를 위시한 GCC 국가들을, ABDEL RAHMAN 내각담당장관은 이집트, 수단, 지부티,소말리아, 요르단, 시리아 및 레바논을 방문하기 위하여 AMIR 의 친서를 휴대하고 7.18. 출바하였으며

중아국   장관   차관   1차보   2차보   정문국   청와대   안기부

0002

DHARI ABDALLAH 법무장관은 리비아, 뷔니지아, 알제리아, 모로코, 모리타니아를 방문할 예정임.

3. 이락은 근자에 원유가격하락(평균 14$ BPD)이 OPEC 회원국들 특히 쿠웨이트와 U.A.E 등 걸프만 산유국들의 쿼타 초과생산에 원인이 있다고 비난하고 생산 축소를 요구하면서 원유가격을 25$이상 인상하도록 요구했음. (90.5.30 바그다드 아랍정상회담에서 사담 후세인 대통령 발언)

4. 쿠웨이트의 쿼타는 1.5 백만 배럴인데 실제로는 200 만 배럴을 생산하여온것 같고 주재국은 쿼타증량을 강력히 요구하여 왔음. 그러나 근자의 원유가격 하락과 이락의 입장을 감안한 것으로 생각되는데 1.5 백만 배럴 쿼타생산을 재 확인하고 이의 준수를 천명한 바 있음. 쿠웨이트 정부는 금년 4/4 분기에 가격과 시장상황을 감안하여 쿼타증량을 요구할 예정인 것으로 알려짐.

5. 이러한 상황인데도 이락이 돌연 쿠웨이트에 이러한 조치를 취한 것은 최근 이지역에서 고조되고 있는 긴장상태와 관련 이락이 전비를 확보하려는 노력으로도 볼 수 있으며 쿠웨이트와의 국경을 이락이 원하는대로 해결하고 OPEC 안에서 이락의 쿼타를 증량하여 원유판매 수입을 늘릴수 있는 계기를 마련하려는 종합적인 정책으로 생각되며 양국관계로 보아 쿠웨이트가 이락에 상당한 정도로 양보할 것으로 예상됨. 끝.

(대사-국장)

Iraq Accuses Kuwait of Plot To Steal Oil, Depress Prices

Charge Seen Part of Gulf Power Move by Saddam Hussein

By Caryle Murphy
Washington Post Foreign Service

CAIRO, July 18—Iraq has accused its wartime ally Kuwait of stealing Iraqi oil, building military installations on its territory and reducing its oil income by cooperating with an "imperialist-Zionist plan" to depress oil prices through overproduction.

Iraqi Foreign Minister Tariq Aziz made the charges against the desert sheikdom in a letter to the Arab League made public today. A day earlier, Iraqi President Saddam Hussein charged that some Persian Gulf states had stabbed Iraq in the back "with a poison dagger" by exceeding their oil-production quotas in what he said was a U.S.-led conspiracy to ensure cheap petroleum prices.

Saddam Hussein added ominously that "if words fail to protect Iraqis, something effective must be done to return things to their natural course and return usurped rights to their owners."

The Iraqi outburst is the latest move in what appears to be an aggressive campaign by Saddam Hussein to impose his will on other Arab states, particularly his neighbors in the Arabian Peninsula who are fellow members of the Organization of Petroleum Exporting Countries.

In Washington, a State Department spokesman said the United States remains "strongly committed to supporting the individual and collective self-defense of our friends in the gulf with whom we have deep and longstanding ties," but he declined to say whether the United States would provide Kuwait with military help against an Iraqi attack.

Kuwait, one of the world's major oil producers, convened an emergency session of its National Assembly today to discuss the Iraqi threats. Saad Abdullah Sabah, the crown prince and prime minister, told the assembly that the government viewed the situation as critical.

Foreign Minister Sabah Ahmed Sabah left the closed meeting, saying he was flying to Saudi Arabia and other gulf states "to inform them about Kuwait's position on the Iraqi note." Two other top-level emissaries were sent to other Arab states.

Kuwait's swift and public response appears to indicate it is taking the Iraqi threats seriously. Western diplomats reached by phone in Kuwait said they were unable to tell if the government expects an Iraqi military attack, but one added that Kuwait, squeezed between Saudi Arabia and Iraq, does "feel threatened."

Aziz's nine-page letter, delivered to the Arab League Monday and broadcast today by Iraq's state-run radio, also attacked the United Arab Emirates for exceeding its oil-production quota. Baghdad has charged repeatedly that overproduction by Kuwait and the Emirates has caused oil prices to slide from $21 to $16 a barrel in the last seven months.

Iraq's charges took many observers by surprise, since just last week Kuwait and the Emirates, under Iraqi and Saudi pressure, agreed to stop exceeding their quotas in preparation for an OPEC meeting next week in Geneva. After Iraq's accusations today, officials in both countries said they would abide by that agreement.

Some oil market analysts suggested that Iraq's threats might be designed to set the stage for it to demand even higher oil price targets than those proposed for discussion at the coming OPEC session.

During Iraq's eight-year war with Iran, Kuwait and other gulf states provided Baghdad with arms and an estimated $30 billion in loans and credits, largely because they saw a greater threat in Iran's revolutionary Islamic regime. But with the war over, they are watching Saddam Hussein's aggressive bid for Arab leadership with some trepidation, Western diplomats said.

In Kuwait's case, Iraq has refused repeatedly to discuss a longstanding border dispute or publicly disavow territorial claims on the Kuwaiti islands of Bubiyan and Warba, diplomatic sources in Kuwait said.

The gulf states' fears over Saddam Hussein's intentions have grown just as their decade-long concerns about Iran's attempts to export its revolution are fading in the wake of conciliatory diplomacy from Tehran.

Last week, Iranian Foreign Minister Ali Akbar Velayati concluded what both sides called a successful visit to Kuwait, capping a months-long reconciliation. The two countries recently agreed to restore maritime traffic and air links, and Iran, which already has an ambassador in Kuwait, has accepted Kuwait's designated envoy to Tehran, officials said.

In renewing ties with Iran, Kuwait is reverting to its historical strategy of protecting itself by playing off its two large northern neighbors against each other, Western diplomats in Kuwait said.

Aziz's letter alleged that Kuwait began to "steal" oil worth $2.4 billion from Iraqi fields shortly after the outbreak of the gulf war. He said Kuwait then began "flooding the world oil market . . . causing a double harm for Iraq: weakening its economy at a time when it was in great need of revenues and stealing its wealth."

Aziz also complained that Kuwait and the Emirates had declined to cancel Iraq's war debts.

On Tuesday, Saddam Hussein said the sharp drop in oil prices in the first half of 1990, which cost Iraq $14 billion in revenue, was the result of a U.S.-planned "subversive policy" intended to "secure the flow of oil . . . at the cheapest prices."

During the gulf war, Washington provided Kuwait with naval protection, and five Kuwaiti vessels still sail under the U.S. flag. Washington said the operation was aimed at deflecting Iranian aggression, but some Western diplomats in Kuwait said it also has served, especially since the end of the war, to keep hostile Iraqi designs against Kuwait in check.

長官報告事項

報告畢

1990. 7 . 20.
中東.아프리카局
中近東課(24   )

題目 : 이라크, 쿠웨이트間 産油紛爭

이라크와 쿠웨이트間 産油 紛爭이 激化되고 있는바, 關聯事項을 다음과 같이 報告 드립니다.

---

1. 狀 況

이라크 및 쿠웨이트는 산유분쟁 관련, 각기 상호 강경 비난 및 아랍연맹 중재를 촉구

○ 이라크측 : - 쿠웨이트의 이라크 영토 불법점령 및 석유채굴에 의한 재산손실 야기(24억불 상당) 주장

   - 쿠웨이트의 산유정책이 이라크 경제를 파괴하고, 아랍권의 힘을 약화시키고 있음을 규탄

   - 후세인 대통령의 대쿠웨이트 비난 연설 및 아랍연맹에 동 타결 촉구 서한 발송(7.17)

○ 쿠웨이트측 : - 이라크의 쿠웨이트 영토 침입 및 영내 서유 채굴 주장으로 역 공격

   - 아랍연맹에 중지요청 긴급서한 발송 및 각료 3명 파견, 반이라크 외교활동 모색 (7.18)

앙교제	90년 2월 20일	담 당	과 장	심 의 관	국 장	차관보	차 관	장 관
		舞	郑	앙				人

0005

2. 背景

최근 쿠웨이트등 걸프만 산유국의 원유 초과 생산에 대한 이라크 불만 고조

○ 쿠웨이트 등의 원유 생산량 쿼타 불 준수로 유가 하락 촉진

○ 최근 유가 침체로 이라크 재정 압박 가중

3. 分析 및 評價

○ 이라크 국내정치 불안에 대한 국민의 관심을 국외로 돌리려는 책략

- 후세인의 종신 대통령제에 의한 장기 집권 기도

○ 쿠웨이트와의 국경분쟁 및 유가문제 관련 이라크에 유리한 입지 확보 의도

- OPEC 회의 제시 유가보다 높은 유가 요구 관철 목표

- 쿠웨이트에 대한 군사적 압력

○ 최근 쿠웨이트, 이란관계 강화 움직임에 대한 이라크의 견제

○ 아랍권 주도국으로서 이라크의 걸프역내 영향력 실증 의도

4. 展望

○ 산유분쟁으로 양국관계 악화가 예상되나, 결국 이라크 요구에 쿠웨이트의 상당한 양보 가능성이 큼. 끝.

0006

관리
번호 90/626

외 무 부

종 별 :

번 호 : UNW-1365　　　　　　　　　일 시 : 90 0720 1850

수 신 : 장관(중동,국연,기정)

발 신 : 주 유엔 대사

제 목 : 이락-쿠웨이트 유전 분쟁(자료응신 제 14호)

　　금 7.20 권참사관이 유엔사무국 직원으로부터 입수한 표제 분쟁관련 쿠웨이트 AL SABAH 부수상겸 외무장관 명의의 유엔 사무총장앞 7.19 자 서한요지를 아래 보고함(쿠웨이트는 동서한의 사본을 안보리 의장에게도 통보하였음).

　　1. 쿠웨이트는 이락 정부로부터 7.15 자 각서를 접수하였음. 이락측 각서는아래와 같은 근거없는 주장과 비난을 포함하고 있음.

　　0 쿠웨이트가 세계시장에서 원유가격을 인하시키고 있음.

　　0 쿠웨이트가 이락내 AL REMAELA 유전으로부터 이락 원유를 도굴하고있음.

　　0 쿠웨이트가 상기 행동으로 이락에 대해 군사침략에 상응하는 중대한 경제적 손실을 끼쳤음.

　　0 상기 쿠웨트의 행동은 사전음모된 것이며 외국세력과 공동으로 획책한 결과임.

　　0 쿠웨이트가 국경문제 해결 노력을 지연시키고있음.

　　2. 상기 이락의 주장은 모두 사실을 왜곡한 근거없는 주장임. 이락측 각서는 근거없는 침범의 시정을 요구하고있는바 동 각서의 위협적 성격을 지적코자함.

　　3. 이락측 각서는 이락-이란 중동전 종결이래 동지역에 긴장을 새로이 불러들이고 있음. 쿠웨이트는 선린우호정책, 평화공존, 대화의 원칙에 입각하여 이락과의 문제를 해결코자하며 유엔 헌장의 목적과 원칙 준수를 재확약함. 추후 사태진전을 통보하겠음. 끝

　　(대사 현홍주-국장)

　　예고:90.12.31 일반

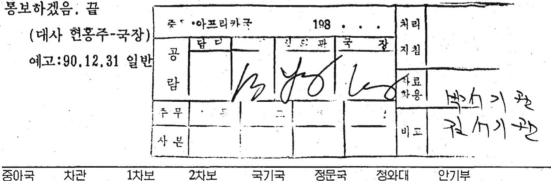

중아국　　차관　　1차보　　2차보　　국기국　　정문국　　정와대　　안기부

0007

PAGE 1　　　　　　　　　　　　　　　　　　　90.07.21　08:50

　　　　　　　　　　　　　　　　　　　　　외신 2과 통제관 CW

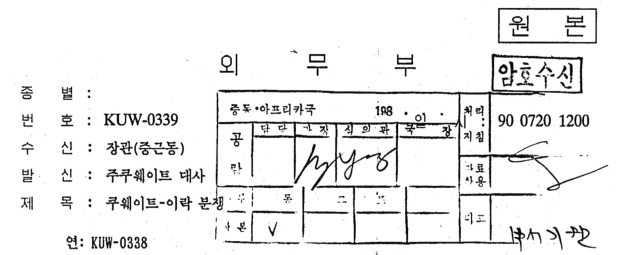

종 별 :

번 호 : KUW-0339

수 신 : 장관(중근동)

발 신 : 주쿠웨이트 대사

제 목 : 쿠웨이트-이락 분쟁

연: KUW-0338

1. 쿠웨이트 정부는 7.19.에 아랍연맹 사무총장에게 이락 각서에 대한 반박각서를 보내고 그것을 회원국 정부에 배포해 줄것을 요청했음.

2. 쿠웨이트 정부 각서의 주요내용

가. 이락- 이란 전쟁중 이락에 대한 원조사실과 쿠웨이트의 희생강조-쿠웨이트가 얼마나 아랍의 공동이익에 봉사했는지 강조

나. 쿠웨이트가 이락영토를 침탈했다는 주장 반박(FALSIFICATION OF REALITY AND FACTS)

다. LEMEILLA(RUMAILAH)유전은 이락영토가 아닌 쿠웨이트 영토에 있음. 오히려 이락이 이지역에서 채유작업을 계속하고 있으면서 쿠웨이트에 심각한 해를끼치고 있음

라. 국제원유가격 폭락은 쿠웨이트에 책임이 없음. 국제적인 경제상황의 결과임.

마. 쿠웨이트-이락 국경선 결정(DEMARCATION)을 위하여 아랍연맹 조정위원회(ARAB LEAGUE ARBITRATION PANEL) 구성을 제의함.

3. 이락의 "돌연한" 행동에 대하여 KUWAIT TIMES 발행인 ALYAN(쿠웨이트 신문협회 회장)은 "이락이 무력행사를 할것으로 보지않으며 채무탕감을 목적으로하면서 동시에 점점 어려워지는 정치상황에서 국민들의 관심을 밖으로 돌리기 위한 국내정치 술책"으로 본다고 7.19. 본직과 파키스탄대사와 함께만난 자리에서말했음. 한편 본직이 7.18.에 AL-OMANI 석유부차관 서리를 방문했을때 그는 1.5 백만의 OPEC 산유쿼타를 준수할것이라는 점을 강조하였음.

4. 당지 영국대사에 의하면(7.19) 쿠웨이트는 유엔안보리 상임이사국들에게자기입장을 개별적으로 설명하고 지지를 요청했다고 함. 7.18.에 미국무부 대변인이 "WE REMAIN STRONGLY COMMITTED TO SUPPORTING THE INDIVIDUAL

중아국   차관   1차보   2차보   정문국   외연원   청와대   안기부

AND COLLECTIVE SELF DEFENCE OF OUR FRIENDS IN THE GULF ..."라 이문제관련
논평한것은이에대한 대답이라고 하고 영국도 비슷한 입장을 밝히게 될 것이라고 함.
끝.

　　(대사-국장)

162
U BX   WO210   19-07 004
02 27 23 68 08 87

^^KUWAIT-IRAQ, 1ST LD-WRITETHRU,0485<
^EDS: UPDATES WITH KUWAIT CALLING FOR DEMARCATION OF ITS BORDER
WITH IRAQ<
^BY NABILA MEGALLI=
^ASSOCIATED PRESS WRITER=
        MANAMA, BAHRAIN (AP) - KUWAIT URGED THE ARAB LEAGUE THURSDAY TO
HELP DEMARCATE ITS BORDER WITH IRAQ, TRYING TO DEFUSE TENSION OVER
BAGHDAD'S ACCUSATIONS THAT IT HAD STOLEN OIL WORTH 2.4 BILLION
DOLLARS.
        THE APPEAL WAS MADE IN A MEMORANDUM SENT TO THE ARAB LEAGUE
HEADQUARTERS IN TUNIS, TUNISIA, AS KUWAITI OFFICIALS FANNED OUT
ACROSS THE MIDDLE EAST TRYING TO BUILD SUPPORT FOR THE TINY EMIRATE
AGAINST THE IRAQI ALLEGATIONS.
        THE MEMORANDUM, REPORTED BY THE KUWAIT NEWS AGENCY, SUGGESTED
THE FORMATION OF AN AD HOC COMMITTEE TO ''RESOLVE THE DEMARCATION OF
THE BORDER BETWEEN KUWAIT AND IRAQ ON THE BASES OF TREATIES AND
EXISTING DOCUMENTS.''
        IT WAS SIGNED BY KUWAITI FOREIGN MINISTER SHEIKH SABAH AL-AHMED,
WHO VISITED SEVERAL GULF COUNTRIES WEDNESDAY.
        AFTER SAUDI ARABIA AND BAHRAIN, SHEIK SABAH MOVED TO QATAR. HE
ALSO WAS EXPECTED TO VISIT OMAN AND THE UNITED ARAB EMIRATES.
TOGETHER WITH KUWAIT, THE FIVE GULF COUNTRIES FORM THE GULF
COOPERATION COUNCIL.
        SHEIK SABAH, WHO ALSO IS DEPUTY PRIME MINISTER, TOLD THE ARAB
LEAGUE THAT KUWAIT WANTS A BORDER DEMARCATION AGREEMENT OUT OF
''KEENNESS TO END THIS IMPORTANT QUESTION WITH IRAQ.''
        ''KUWAIT HAS CONTINUOUSLY SOUGHT TO DEMARCATE THE BORDER BETWEEN
THE TWO COUNTRIES AND END OUTSTANDING PROBLEMS. BUT IRAQ ALWAYS
REJECTED PUTTING AN END TO THIS QUESTION,'' HE SAID.
        THE BORDER DISPUTE HAS DRAGGED ON SINCE KUWAIT'S INDEPENDENCE
FROM BRITAIN IN 1961. THE THEN-IRAQI GOVERNMENT OF GEN. ABDUL KARIM
KASSEM REFUSED TO RECOGNIZE KUWAIT AND THE EMIRATE CALLED IN BRITISH
TROOPS FOR PROTECTION.
        KASSEM WAS DEPOSED IN A FEBRUARY 1963 COUP BY THE BAATH ARAB
SOCIALIST PARTY, WHICH INSISTED KUWAIT WAS PART OF IRAQ.
        IN THE MEMORANDUM, SHEIK SABAH EXPRESSED ''EXTREME SURPRISE'' AT
THE IRAQI ALLEGATIONS, AND CALLED THEM ''DISTORTIONS OF FACTS.''
        ''IRAQ HAS A RICH RECORD OF VIOLATIONS OF KUWAITI TERRITORY, A
RECORD SUPPORTED BY FACTS,'' SABAH SAID.
        HE SAID KUWAIT WAS PRODUCING OIL FROM FIELDS ''WELL WITHIN ITS
TERRITORY.'' IRAQ CONTENDED THAT KUWAIT STOLE 2.4 BILLION DOLLARS
WORTH OF OIL FROM THE RUMAILAH FIELD, BUT SABAH SAID PART OF THE
FIELD IS ON KUWAITI SOIL.
        ON WEDNESDAY, IRAQ ALSO ACCUSED KUWAIT AND THE UNITED ARAB
EMIRATES OF CAUSING A RECENT SLUMP IN OIL PRICES BY PRODUCING FAR IN
EXCESS OF THEIR OPEC QUOTAS.
        IRAQI PRESIDENT SADDAM HUSSEIN CLAIMED THE PRICE SLUMP HAS COST
BAGHDAD 14 BILLION DOLLARS IN LOST REVENUE. HE WARNED THAT IRAQ
WOULD RETALIATE, WITH FORCE IF NECESSARY, IF KUWAIT AND THE U.A.E.
CONTINUED TO FLOUT PRODUCTION QUOTAS DESIGNED TO BOLSTER PRICES.
        HIS FOREIGN MINISTER, TARIQ AZIZ, ACCUSED THE GULF STATES OF
ECONOMIC SABOTAGE AIMED AT WEAKENING IRAQ.
        AZIZ, IN A LETTER SENT TO THE 21-MEMBER ARAB LEAGUE, CHARGED
KUWAIT'S ACTIONS WERE TANTAMOUNT ''TO MILITARY AGGRESSION.''
^MORE<

AP-TK-19-07-90 1637GMT<

WASHINGTON, JULY 20, REUTER - U.S. OFFICIALS BELIEVE TENSION BETWEEN IRAQ AND KUWAIT IS UNLIKELY TO ERUPT INTO WAR, BUT SAY THE POSSIBILITY OF AN ATTACK BY BAGHDAD CANNOT BE RULED OUT.

+OUR ASSESSMENT IS THAT (IRAQI PRESIDENT) SADDAM HUSSEIN IS UNLIKELY TO TAKE MILITARY ACTION IN THE GULF, AT LEAST IN THE SHORT TERM. BUT HE IS UNPREDICTABLE. HE HAS HIS OWN AGENDA AND HIS OWN OBJECTIVES,+ SAID ONE BUSH ADMINISTRATION OFFICIAL. .

+I DON'T BELIEVE THEY WILL TAKE IMMINENT MILITARY ACTION,+ SAID ANOTHER. +BUT IN THE LONGER TERM, YOU CAN'T RULE IT OUT.+

HUSSEIN THIS WEEK ACCUSED UNIDENTIFIED GULF STATES OF COLLUDING WITH WASHINGTON TO OVERPRODUCE OIL AND DRIVE DOWN WORLD PRICES, HITTING IRAQ'S WAR-TORN OIL ECONOMY.

KUWAIT AND THE UNITED ARAB EMIRATES WERE LATER SINGLED OUT BY IRAQ IN A LETTER THE GOVERNMENT SENT TO THE ARAB LEAGUE. IT ACCUSED KUWAIT OF STEALING OIL FROM IRAQ'S SOUTHERN RUMEILA FIELD AND OF AGGRESSION AGAINST ITS TERRITORY -- AN APPARENT REFERENCE TO DISPUTED BORDER AREAS.

THE BUSH ADMINISTRATION HAS MAINTAINED DIPLOMATIC AND ECONOMIC RELATIONS WITH IRAQ DESPITE OPPOSITION IN CONGRESS, AND WAS CERTAIN TO COME UNDER EVEN MORE PRESSURE TO CURTAIL U.S.-IRAQI TIES AFTER THE THREAT.

+WE WANT TO ENGAGE HUSSEIN IN DIALOGUE. BUT STATEMENTS LIKE THESE JUST UNDERCUT OUR EFFORTS,+ SAID THE FIRST U.S. OFFICIAL.

CRITICS OF IRAQ HAVE CALLED FOR SANCTIONS TO PUNISH HUSSEIN FOR HIS USE OF POISON GAS AGAINST KURDISH CIVILIANS AND A HUMAN RIGHTS RECORD DESCRIBED BY THE STATE DEPARTMENT AS +ABYSMAL+.
MORE

NNNN
!
ZS YKD633

200909 :BC-IRAQ-AMERICAN (SCHEDULED)=1.1 WASHINGTON:
THEY ARE ALSO WORRIED ABOUT IRAQI ATTEMPTS TO ACQUIRE NUCLEAR WEAPONS AND HUSSEIN'S WARNINGS THAT HE WOULD UNLEASH CHEMICAL WEAPONS AGAINST ISRAEL IF IT ATTACKED AN ARAB STATE.

OFFICIALS SAID HUSSEIN, WHO LAUNCHED AN EIGHT-YEAR WAR BY ATTACKING IRAN IN 1980, HAD DUAL MOTIVES FOR HIS LATEST MOVE.

HE COULD WANT THE GULF STATES TO WRITE OFF PART OR ALL OF IRAQ'S HUGE DEBTS TO THEM, ACCRUED DURING THE GULF WAR AND ESTIMATED AT AS MUCH AS 60 BILLION DOLLARS.

IRAQ, RUSHING TO RECONSTRUCT ITS ECONOMY, HAS DEFAULTED ON SEVERAL INTERNATIONAL LOANS AND HAS A POOR CREDIT RATING.

IN ITS LETTER TO THE ARAB LEAGUE, IRAQ CALLED FOR AN ARAB +MARSHALL PLAN+ SIMILAR TO THE U.S.-SPONSORED PLAN WHICH RESCUED THE ECONOMIES OF WESTERN EUROPE AFTER WORLD WAR TWO.

ECONOMICS ASIDE, HUSSEIN HAS LONG HAD AMBITIONS TO ESTABLISH HIS PREEMINENCE IN THE GULF AND THE ARAB WORLD.

+NOBODY KNOWS FOR SURE WHAT GOES ON IN THE MIND OF THIS MAN. HE WANTS TO ESTABLISH IRAQI HEGEMONY OVER THE GULF. IF IT IS NECESSARY TO USE FORCE TO DRIVE THE POINT HOME, IT IS POSSIBLE HE COULD DECIDE TO DO THAT,+ SAID MARTIN INDYK, DIRECTOR OF THE WASHINGTON INSTITUTE FOR NEAR EAST POLICY.

OFFICIALS SAID HUSSEIN WAS LIKELY TO WIN ARAB AGREEMENT TO MAINTAIN OIL QUOTAS AND COULD WIN OTHER ECONOMIC CONCESSIONS.

+GULF STATES HAVE TRADITIONALLY BOUGHT THEIR WAY OUT OF TROUBLE,+ SAID ONE. +ONE ASSUMES THEY WILL DO SO AGAIN.+

INDYK AGREED: +A WEAK STATE IN THE POSITION OF THE KUWAITIS FACED WITH A STRONG NEIGHBOUR SEEKS TO APPEASE TO THE EXTENT IT CAN. IF THAT GETS TOO DANGEROUS, THEY WILL COME RUNNING FOR HELP TO THE UNITED STATES.+

0011

11

외 무 부

종 별 :

번 호 : KUW-0356

일 시 : 90 0730 1300

수 신 : 장관(중근동,기정)

발 신 : 주 쿠웨이트 대사

제 목 : 쿠웨이트.이락 분쟁

연: KUW-0350

1. 쿠웨이트. 이락 간의 분쟁해결을 위한 회담이 주재국의 SAAD 국무총리와 EZZAT IBRAHIM 이락 혁명위원회 부위장간에 7.31. 부터 젯다에서 개최될 예정이라함.

2. PLO 의 ARAFAT 의장이 쿠.이 양국간의 분쟁해결을 돕기위해 7.29. 주재국을 방문하였으며 HUSSEIN 요르단왕은 7.29. 이락을 방문한 후에 주재국을 방문할 예정이라함.

3. 쿠웨이트 외무부측 (차관) 은 금 7.30. 오전에 유엔안보리 상임이사국 대사들을 불러 JEDDAH 회담에 대한 쿠웨이트 입장을 설명했음. 쿠웨이트는 국경문제는 "협상대상이 아니"라는 입장을 강조했다고 함.

(대사-국장)

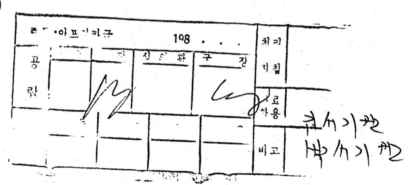

중아국   차관   1차보   정룬국   정와대   안기부

0012

외 무 부

종 별 : 긴 급

번 호 : KUW-0360

일 시 : 90 0802 0630

수 신 : 장관(중근동,기정,노동부,건설부)

발 신 : 주 쿠웨이트 대사

제 목 : 쿠웨이트.이락 분쟁

1. 쿠웨이트 SHEIKH SAAD 수상은 사우디아라비아 젯다에서 7.31.(화) IZZATIBRHIM 이락 혁명위원회 부의장과 회담후 8.1. 귀국하였음.

2. 회담내용이나 결과에 대하여는 쿠웨이트 정부당국의 발표가 없으나, SAAD 수상이 예상보다 일찍 귀국한것으로 보아 양측간의 합의가 이루어진것 같지 아니함. 쿠웨이트 국영통신 (KUNA)는 SAAD 수상이 8.1. 귀국하였으며 앞으로 이락과 모든분쟁에 대하여 협의하기를 쿠웨이트는 희망한다는 보도만 하였음.

3. 8.2. 05:40 현재 당지에서 청취한 영국 BBC 방송은 협상이 결렬 되었으며 쿠.이락 국경에서 충돌이 발생하였다고 간단히 보도한바 있음.

4. 06:30 현재 상황은 정부 라디오, TV 에 일체 "국경충돌"에 관한 보도나 언급이 없으나 라디오는 계속해서 애국적인 노래와 시구를 방송하고 있으며 시내 중심가에 대한 교통은 차단되고 무장군인이 교통통제 하고 있으며 군병력이동 추럭이 간간히 눈에띠고 있는 생태임. 또한 05:30 경부터 원거리 (쿠.이락 국경쪽) 에서 간간히 포성소리같은 소리가 들리는 상태임. 이시간 현재 정부당국과 일체접촉이 되지않아 더 자세한 파악이 어려운바 수시 보고 위게임. 끝.

(대사 소병용-장관)

중아국	장관	차관	1차보	2차보	정문국	영교국	청와대	안기부
건설부	노동부							

외 무 부

종 별 : 지 급

번 호 : KUW-0361　　　　　　　　일　시 : 90 0802 0700

수 신 : 장관(중근동, 영사)

발 신 : 주 .쿠웨이트 대사

제 목 : 쿠.이락 분쟁(2)

연: KUW-0360

1. 연호 금새벽 06:00 경 미대사관에 연락하여 상황 확인코자 한바 이락측이 쿠웨이트를 공격한 것은 사실이나 아직 자세한 상황은 입수되지 않음.

2. 당관에서는 이러한 사태에 따라 한인회장과 기타 교민조직을 통해서 교민들에게 통보하고 외출자제등 조치를취함.

끝.

(대사-국장)

중아국	장관	차관	1차보	2차보	정문국	영교국	청와대	안기부

0014

PAGE 1

90.08.02　14:05

외신 2과　통제관 DH

외 무 부

종 별 : 긴 급

번 호 : KUW-0362   일 시 : 90 0802 0710

수 신 : 장관(중근동, 영사, 영재, 기정, 노동부장관, 건설부장관)

발 신 : 주 쿠웨이트 대사

제 목 : 쿠. 이락 분쟁(3)

　　　연 : KUW-0360

　　1. 연호사태에 따라 우리나라 건설업체 작업현장 (현대건설 4 개) 을 점검하였는바, 안전에 이상이 없음.

　　2. 현대건설이 작업하고 있는 4 개작업현장중 이락과의 국경에 자하라 송전설로 건설현장 (한국인 74 명) 은 쿠웨이트 당국이 잡업장 봉로를 봉쇄하였으며 인원을 CAMP 로 철수 대기시키고 있으며 유사시 시내에 있는 담수화현장 (쿠레스) 으로 철수준비를 완료함. 타 현장도 작업장외에 출입을 일체금지시키고 CAMP 내의 작업만 계속중임.

　　3. 당관에서는 각 작업현장에 대해서 비상연락망 유지, 비상시 철수 계획 점검 대기토록 하였고 지사의 봉제하에 각 현장별로 안전보호 기구를 설치. 운영중임. 끝.

　　(대사 소병용-국장)

중아국	장관	차관	1차보	2차보	정문국	영고국	영고국	청와대
안기부	건설부	노동부						

외 무 부

종 별 : 긴 급

번 호 : KUW-0363

일 시 : 90 0802 0750

수 신 : 장관(중근동,기정)

발 신 : 주 쿠웨이트 대사

제 목 : 쿠.이락 분쟁(4)

연: KUW-0360,0361,0362

1. 05:30-06:00 경 국경쪽에서 비교적 자주들리던 포성으로 생각되는 폭발음과 06:00 전후 간헐적으로 들려오던 시내 중심가의 총격소리는 그이후 이상은 현재까지 들리지 않고 있는것으로 보아 일단 충돌사태는 소강국면을 유지하고 있는것 같음. 그러나 미국 CNN 은 07:50 경 "이락 탱크 350 대가 쿠웨이트로 남진중이다" 라고 보도하였음.

2. 07:50 현재 쿠웨이트 시내 상황은 왕궁을 중심으로한 시내 중심가에 출입을 완전히 봉제하고 있는 이외에는 비교적 긴박한 분위기는 아님.

3. 미확인 정보 (시내거주 교민등) 에 의하면 왕궁경비 경찰과 일부 군복 부대 (군인인지 여부 미확인) 간에 총격전이 06:00 경 있었다고 하며 이시간 현재는 왕궁을 원래 경비하던 경찰대 대신 군인들이 경비하고 있다고 함. 이정보를 확인하기 위하여 왕국지역에 접근을 시도중이나 불가능한 상태인데 만일 이것이 사실이라면 어떤 내부 변란 가능성도 있을수 있음.

5. 사태진전 및 상황 계속 파악토록 노력하여 보고 드리겠음. 끝.

(대사 소병용-장관)

중아국 노동부	장관	차관	1차보	2차보	정문국	영교국	안기부	건설부

외 무 부

종 별 : 긴 급

번 호 : KUW-0364

일 시 : 90 0802 0840

수 신 : 장관(중근동,기정)

발 신 : 주 쿠웨이트 대사

제 목 : 쿠.이락 분쟁(5)

연: KUW-0360,361,362,363

1. 왕궁지역 사태파악을 위하여 현장에 나갔던 당관 직원 보고에 의하면 08:10 경 왕궁지역으로 부터 3KM 짐도 지점까지 접근하였을 적에 도로 통제요원이 진출을 저지하고 "전방에 이락군이 있으므로 못 간다"고 하였다함. 연호에서 보고드린 군복집단이 이락군 특공침투부대일 가능성도 있으나 아직 사태는 불분명함. 한편 아직 미확인 정보이나 이락군이 쿠웨이트 시내에 침투하여 방송국과 공항등을 장악하고 있다고 하는바 이시간현재 공항은 폐쇄되었으며 방송은 여전히 음악만 계속하고 있음.

2. 왕궁과 같은 경내에 있는 외무부는 전혀 전화를 받지않고 있음. 끝.

(대사 소병용-장관)

중아국	장관	차관	1차보	2차보	정문국	영교국	청와대	안기부
건설부	노동부							

PAGE 1

종 별 : 긴 급

번 호 : KUW-0367

일 시 : 90 0802 0940

수 신 : 장관(중근동, 영재)

발 신 : 주 쿠웨이트 대사

제 목 : 쿠웨이트, 이락 분쟁(6)

연: KUW-0362

금일 현재 당지거주 아국인은 공관원, 부역관직원, 한국학교교사와 그가족 39 명, 주재상사원 및 그가족 38 명, 건설회사 임직원 및 근로자 319 명, 일반거류교민 252 명, 게 648 명임을 참고로 보고하며 당지시간 09:30 현재 이상없음. 끝.

(대사-국장)

중아국   차관   2차보   정문국   영교국   안기부

0018

PAGE 1

90.08.02   17:15

외신 2과   통제관 DH

24   걸프 사태 쿠웨이트, 이라크 및 각국 경제 제재

외 무 부

종 별 : 긴 급

번 호 : KUW-0368

일 시 : 90 0802 1010

수 신 : 장관(중근동,정일,기정)

발 신 : 주 쿠웨이트 대사

제 목 : 쿠웨이트,이락 분쟁(7)

연: KUW-0360

1. 10:00 현재 이락군 탱크수십대 (교민이 목격 확인) 가 쿠웨이트 외곽지대를 통과하여 중심지로 이동중이겨 왕궁과 그리고 왕궁으로 부터 약 500M 반경내 지역에서 연기가 부분적으로 올라오고 있는 것으로 보아 다시 전부가 일어나고 있는것 같음.

2. 이시간 현재 쿠웨이트 국방부를 이락군이 공격중임이 확인되었으며 당 대사관으로 부터 국방부청사쪽으로 약 2KM 지점에서 연기가 올라오고 있으나 총격음은 들리지 않고 있음.

3. 전반적으로는 왕궁, 국방부등 중요거점에서 충돌이 있는것 같으나 도심 (왕궁) 에서 약 15KM 떨어진 당 대사관 지역은 자동차 교통량이 평소의 절반이하 정도로 줄어들고 간헐적으로 쿠웨이트군 장갑차가 통과하는 것 이외에는 다른 긴박한 분위기는 없음.

4. 은행과 주요상가는 폐점되고 있고 주민들은 식료품, 특히 물을 구입하기 위하여 일부 식료품점에 장사진을 치고 있는 상황임.

5. 일부 미확인 정보에 의하면 쿠웨이트 왕이 연금을 당하고 있고 정부가 붕괴되었다고 하나, 공식적으로 확인된 바는 없고 쿠웨이트 라듸오는 10:00 시에 국민들의 항쟁을 촉구하고 아랍국가들에 대하여 원조를 요청하는 메시지를 방송 하였음. 끝.

(대사-국장)

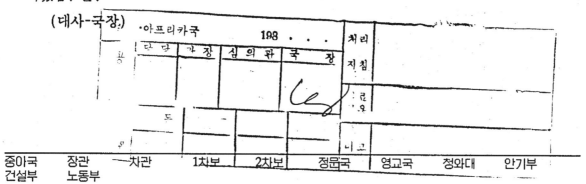

PAGE 1

발 신 전 보

WKU-0168   900802 1834 **EZ**

번   호 : _____   종별 : _____

수   신 : 주 쿠웨이트   대사 . *총영사*

발   신 : 장   관   (중근동)

제   목 : 이라크, 쿠웨이트 침공

1. 표제 관련, 외신 보도 내용을 아래와 같이 통보하니 참고 바람.

o 8.2. 새벽 2시 이라크군, 쿠웨이트를 전격 침공, 탱크를 앞세우고 수시간
　　만에 수도 쿠웨이트 청사 점령

o 이라크군이 쿠웨이트 왕궁 포위 및 쿠웨이트 영공 봉쇄 (공항이 폭격당해 폐쇄)

o 350 여대의 이라크군 탱크가 쿠웨이트 시내 진입

o 이라크 후세인 대통령이 이끄는 혁명 평의회는 성명을 통해 쿠웨이트
　　정부는 전복 됐으며, 이라크의 쿠웨이트 침공은 자유 쿠웨이트 임시정부의
　　요청에 의해 이루어진 것이라고 함

o 동 평의회는 또한 이라크군은 사태 정상화 여부에 따라 수일 또는 수주내
　　철수할 것이라 함

2. 상기 관련, 동 사태를 예의 주시하고 관련사항 수시 지급 보고 바람.

끝.

1990. 12. 31. 에 예고문에
의거 일반문서로 재 분류됨.

(중동아프리카국장   이 두 복)

0020

외 무 부

종   별 : 긴 급

번   호 : KUW-0371   일   시 : 90 0802 1230

수   신 : 장관(중근동,정일,기정)

발   신 : 주 쿠웨이트 대사

제   목 : 쿠웨이트.이락분쟁(8)

연: KUW-0360

1 11:40 현재 이락군은 시내 중심부 일원을 사실상 장악하였으며 쉐라본호텔에 사령부를 설치하였음. 다만 시가지를 장악하는 과정에서 쿠웨이트측의 무력저항은 없었던 것으로 파악되었음.

2. 한편 이락측은 10:40 경에 GUN-SHIP 헬리콥터 20 여대가 저공비행하면서 몇군데 군사목표물에 소형 폭팔물을 부하하였고 12:00 경에는 이락 전폭기가 왕궁을 로켓트로 공격한 것으로 보아 아직도 쿠웨이트측은 계속 저항하고 있는것으로 보임.

3. 쿠웨이트 외무부의 한 간부직원에 의하면 오늘 아침 08:00 경 외무부에 출근할때 이미 외무부(왕궁경내에 있음)가 이락군에 점거되어 있었다고 하며 쿠웨이트 내부의 불만세력들이 봉기하여 왕궁을 이락군 침입전에 점거하였다는 소문에 대하여는 확인할수 없다고 말하였음. 동 간부는 또한 설령 불만세력들이 이락과 시간을 맞추어 습격하여 점령하였다 하더라도 아직 그러한 단체나 지도자 또는 이른바 신정부 공표가 없는 것으로 보아 불확실한 사정이라고 말함.

4. 쿠웨이트에는 인구 200 만중에 약 30 퍼센트만 쿠웨이트일뿐 나머지는 외국인인데다 이들중 상당한수가 이락사람이며 또한 쿠웨이트 시민중에도 이락계가 다수 있는점을 고려하면 이락이 침공전에 내부"봉기"를 연출했을 가능성도 있음.

5. 방송, 신문, 봉신등이 중단되어 이번사태에 대한 외국으로 부터의 뉴스가 두절된 상태이어서 이부분에 대한 정확한 파악은 어려우나 CNN 방송등에 기초한 정보에 의하면 미국이 유엔 안보리를 소집요청하고 또한 항모 이동등 군사적 개입움직임을 보이고 있는 속에서 이락측은 쿠웨이트에 대하여 "석유값 손실금" 배상등 휴전 조건을 제시하고 있다고 함. 앞에말한 외무부간부에 의하면 현재 카이로에서 열리고 있는 GIC 외무장관 회의에서나 아랍연맹 회원국들로부터 전혀

중아국   장관   차관   1차보   2차보   정문국   영교국   청와대   안기부
건설부   노동부

쿠웨이트의 자원호소에 대한 반응이 없다고 하는바, 이러한 상황속에서 쿠웨이트와 이락간에 군사력 상관관계로 볼때 미국등 외부의 군사적인 개입이 없다면 쿠웨이트로서는 군사적으로 저항을 계속하기는 불가능할 것이므로 이락측의 요구를대폭 수락하는 쪽으로 사태를 종결지울수 밖에 없을것 같음.

6. 최근에 OPEC 기준가격을 21 불로 인상하고 쿠웨이트와 U.A.E 를 포함한 GULF 산유국들의 산유량 하향조정등으로 이미 상승국면으로 돌아선 국제원유가격이 이번 사태로 인하여 등귀 할것으로 염려되므로 원유소비국으로서는 긴밀한 관찰이 요망되며 이문제에 대한 당지의 반향은 추보하겠음. 끝.

   (대사-국장)

외 무 부

종 별 : 긴 급

번 호 : KUW-0373   일 시 : 90 0802 1530

수 신 : 장관(중근동,정일,기정동문)

발 신 : 주 쿠웨이트 대사

제 목 : 쿠웨이트,이락 분쟁(9)

　　　연: KUW-0371

　　1. CNN 과 BBC 방송에 의하면 JABER 국왕이 사우디로 탈출하였다고 하는데 당지에서 아직 확인할수는 없음. 한편 바그다드 방송은 JABER 국왕의 쿠웨이트 정부는 붕괴되었으며 조만간 총선으로 새정부가 구성될 것이라는 취지로 말하고 있는바, 이러한 사실들은 당지 정부기관, 모든 언론매체 등이 다 폐쇄된 상황에서 확인이 되고 있지 않음. 몇몇 대사관과 계속접촉중이나 아직 상황은 불확실함. 영국과 미국대사관은 오전부터 전화 통화가 되지않고 있는데 전화선이 차단된 것으로 추정됨. 그러나 쿠웨이트 라듸오는 오후 3시현재 계속 음악방송만 하면서 간헐적으로 "JABER 국왕과 SAAD 수상의 영도하에 분기할것"을 호소하는 간단한 메시지를 반복하고 있으며 텔레비전 방송은 15:20 경 부터 보도(ANNOUNCEMENTS)없이 음악과 함께 JABER 국왕과 SAAD 수상사진과 과거의 독립기념행사등 애국적인 행사기록 필름을 보여주고 있어서 쿠웨이트와 이락간에 타협가능성이 생긴것이 아닌가하는 추측을 가능하게 하고 있지만 확실한 평가를 할수있는 자료는 없음.

　　2. 쿠웨이트시 중심지역은 기보고한 바와같이 이락군대의 장악하에 평온이 유지되고 있으나 외곽의 쿠웨이트 군시설 거점지역에서는 아직도 산발적인 전투가 계속되고 있음. 끝.

　　　(대사-국장)

중아국	장관	차관	1차보	2차보	정문국	청와대	안기부

0023

외 무 부

종   별 : 긴 급

번   호 : KUW-0374

일   시 : 90 0802 1600

수   신 : 장관(중근동,정일,기정동문)

발   신 : 주 쿠웨이트 대사

제   목 : 쿠웨이트.이락 분쟁(10)

    연: KUW-0372

    1. 쿠웨이트 국방부와 경찰사관학교등 주요시설지대로 부터 약 2KM 떨어진 지역(리까이)에 우리교민 약 20 세대가 거주중인데 정오경부터 일단 중지되었던 전부가 주요시설지대에서 오후 3 시 30 분경 재개되고 포탄 3 발이 교민 거주지역에 약 5 분 간격으로 아파트 공지에 떨어졌음.

    2. 이러한 사태발전에 따라 당관에서는 그지역 교민들에게 가능하면 일단 대사관으로 철수하도록 지시 하였는바, 우선 대사관까지 약 20KM 거리에 자동차 봉행가능성 여부를 점검하여 문제가 있으면 거주지역 아파트내에 지하층으로 우선 집단대피하도록 조치중임.

    3. 경찰사관학교등 지역의 전부는 치열한 전부는 아닌 산발적인 총격전이며위의 아파트 지역에 떨어진 포탄은 동지역 거주자의 관찰에 의하면 살상용포탄이 아니고 일종의 공포탄 (낙하지점에 폭팔흔적이 없고 연기와 폭발음만 크게나는종류라고 함) 이라고 함으로 당장에 위급한 상황은 아니라고 생각되나 이러한 공포탄을 사격하는 의도가 공포분위기 조성으로 쿠웨이트측에 저항의지를 꺾을려고 하는것인지 아니면 본격적인 사격을 위한 예비적 단계인지는 불확실하나 그아파트 지역에 군시설도 없고 또 방위병력도 배치되지 아니한 민간거주지역인 것으로 보아 전자의 경우가 아닌가 생각됨. 끝.

    (대사-국장)

중아국	장관	차관	1차보	2차보	정문국	상황실	청와대	안기부
안기부								

0024

90.08.03   00:05

외신 2과 통제관 CN

외 무 부

종 별 : 지 급

번 호 : KUW-0378　　　　　　　　　일 시 : 90 0802 2100

수 신 : 장관(중근동,정일,기정동문)

발 신 : 주 쿠웨이트 대사

제 목 : 쿠웨이트.이락 사태(13)

1. 21:00 현재 쿠웨이트시 및 외곽지역에서 일체 총격소리는 없으며 도심지역을 포함한 대부분의 지역에 가로등과 신호등이 켜져 있는 상태이며 간헐적으로 차량도 봉행하고 있음.

2. 이락군대는 쿠웨이트시 주변의 해안지대에 탱크와 보병들을 배치하고 있어서 바다로 부터의 공격에 대비하고 있는 형국을 보이고 있음.

3. 쿠웨이트 라듸오는 쿠웨이트 영토밖에서 같은 주파수로 방송하는 것으로 추정되는데 20:30 분경에 "JABER 국왕의 대변인"이 다음과 같은 발표를 하였음.

　- JABER 국왕은 SAFE PLACE 에 안전하게 있음.

　- 미국의 부시대통령이 이락의 철수를 강력하게 촉구하고 있음.

　- 미국정부는 미국에 있는 쿠웨이트와 이락정부 예금을 동결하였음.

　- 소련은 대이락 무기공급을 중단하고 이락의 철수를 촉구하였음.

　- 아랍연맹에서는 해결책을 토의중임.

　- 미항공모함이 걸프만으로 이동중임. 끝.

　(대사-국장)

중아국	장관	차관	1차보	2차보	정문국	정와대	안기부

0025

외 무 부

종 별 : 긴 급

번 호 : KUW-0381　　　　　　　　　　　　일 시 : 90 0803 0800

수 신 : 장 관(신일,중근동)

발 신 : 주 쿠웨이트 대사

제 목 : 통신회선 불통

　　주재국의 국제전화 및 텔렉스가 06:30 부터 두절되었으니 주이라크 대사관을 통하여 중계토록 조치바람.끝
　　(대사 소병용-외신관리관)

신일　　　신이　**중아국 / 차보　안기부**

외 무 부

종 별 : 긴 급

번 호 : BGW-0408　　　　　　　　　　　　일 시 : 90 0803 0800

수 신 : 장 관(신일,중근동)

발 신 : 주 이라크 대사

제 목 : TLX 회선 개봉

　　　주재국의 텔렉스가 금일 아침부터 개봉되었음을 보고함.끝
　　　(대사 최봉름-외신관리관)

외 무 부

종 별 : 긴 급

번 호 : KUW-0379　　　　　　　　　일 시 : 90 0803 0600

수 신 : 장 관(중근동, 영재, 정일, 기정)

발 신 : 주 쿠웨이트 대사

제 목 : 쿠웨이트. 이라크사태(14호)

　　　대: WKU-0170

　　　대: KUW-0375

　　　교민및 근로자 피해상황

　　　1. 현대건설 미귀환 3명은 이시간 현재 귀환치 않았음

　　　2. 이라크군측에 억류된 1명에 대해서는 억류현장에 접근하였으나, 확인 되지않고
있으며 금일중 재차 확인토록 노력중임

　　　3. 송전선로 공사 현장 소속 2명에 대해서는 현장접근이 곤란하여 현재로서는
확인에 어려움이 있으나 가능한한 계속 추적하여, 보고토록 하겠음

　　　4. 기타 교민들로부터는 피해상황은 보고된것은 없으며 당관에서 교민 밀집지역에
전화로 확인한바 피해 상황없음

　　　5. 리까이지역 한세대가 대사관에서 임시체재중임 (리까이 지역은 8.2 밤 21:30
현재 포경 및 총격은 없으며 현재까지 평온함). 끝

　　　(대사 소병용-국장)

중동·아프리카국			198 . . .	처리 지침	
공람	담당	과장	심의관	국장	자료 거용
				ら	
소무 사본	동	그	프	ᄀ	비고

중아국　　차관　　1차보　　정문국　　영교국　　정와대　　안기부　　乙차보

0028

PAGE 1　　　　　　　　　　　　　　　　　　　90.08.03　　15:08 WG

外信 1과　통제관

외 무 부

종 별 : 긴 급

번 호 : KUW-0380　　　　　　　　　　　일 시 : 90 0803 0630

수 신 : 장 관(중근동,영재,정일,기정)

발 신 : 주 쿠웨이트 대사

제 목 : 쿠웨이트.이라크사태(15호)

　　연: KUW-0378

　　연호 이후 시내는 평온을 유지했으나 금일 06:15부터 공관에서도 확실히 들을수 있는 포성과 기관총성 (15 KM 정도 떨어진 SHUAIKH항구지역과 국방부청사 부근으로 추정됨)이 크게나기 시작하였음.상황 추보하겠음.끝

　　(대사 소병용-국장)

	중도·아프리카국		193 . . .		처리 지침	
공	담당	과장	심의관	국 장		
					자료 활용	
	등		그			
본					비고	

중아국　차관　1차보　정문국　영교국　안기부　乙차보

0029

발 신 전 보

번   호 : WKU-0173   900803 1613 ER   종별 :

수   신 : 주 쿠웨이트   대사 / 총영사

발   신 : 장 관   (중근동)

제   목 : 이라크, 쿠웨이트 사태 상황

표제 관련사항을 별첨과 같이 통보하니 업무에 참고 바람.

첨   부 : 사태 상황 . 끝.

(중동아프리카국장   이 두 복)

1990. 11. 31. 에 예고문에
의거 일반문서로 재 분류됨.

앙 고 재	1990년 4월 03일 중근동	기안자	과 장	국 장	차 관	장 관		보안통제	외신과통제
		박창호							

0030

외 무 부

종   별 : 긴 급

번   호 : KUW-0384   일   시 : 90 0803 1130

수   신 : 장관(중근동,영재,정일,기정)

발   신 : 주쿠웨이트대사

제   목 : 쿠웨이트.이라크사태(17호)

    연: KUW-0381

    1. 연호 포격 상황은 07:00경에 끝나고 그시간이후보고시간(11:00)까지 평온한 상태임

    2.쿠웨이트측의 저항은 완전히 제압된것같고전지역을 이라크군이 장악하고 있는것으로 보임

    ,3.따라서   외부의   물리적인   관여가   없는한심각한   전부행위가 쿠웨이트내에서재발될것같지는 않음.쉐라톤호텔을 중심으로시내중심에 배치된 이라크 군대는 전부태세배치는 않임.점령지 관리국면으로변환된것같이 관찰되었음.끝

    (대사 소병용-국장)

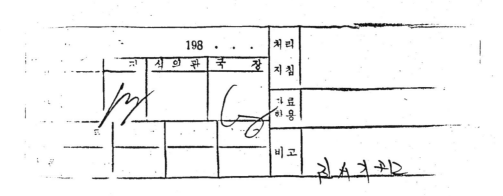

중아국   정문국   영교국   안기부

PAGE 1   0031

외 무 부

종 별 : 긴 급

번 호 : KUW-0385　　　　　　　　　일 시 : 90 0803 1300

수 신 : 장관(중근동, 영재, 정일, 기정)

발 신 : 주쿠웨이트대사

제 목 : 쿠웨이트, 이라크사태(18호)

연: KUW-0384

1. 13:00 현재 전반적으로 긴장된 분위기이며이라크군차량의 이동과 일부지역의 군대의집결현상은 있으나 기본적으로 평온한 상태가계속되고있음

2. 이라크군의 집결지점 부근의 교민들은 만일에대비하여 대사관으로 일단 대피하도록 조치하여보고시간 현재 50여명 정도가 도착하여 있음.

3. 보고한대로 전문 발송이 쉽지 아니한 사정이나상황보고를 계속하겠음.끝

(대사 소병용-국장)

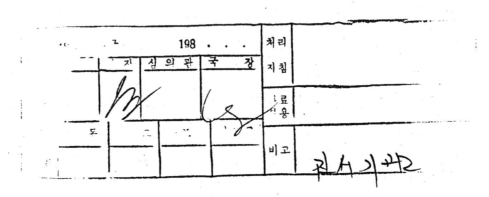

외 무 부

종 별 : 긴급

번 호 : KUW-0386

일 시 : 90 0803 1700

수 신 : 장관(중근동, 영재, 정일, 신일, 기정동문), 노동부장관, 건설부장관

발 신 : 주 쿠웨이트 대사

제 목 : 쿠웨이트, 이락 사태(19호)

1. 16:30 분 현재 전반적으로 평온한 상태가 유지되고 있음.

2. 쿠웨이트 TV 는 오전 6 시경부터 이락측 방송이 나오고 있는데 음악방송만 나오고 있고 간헐적으로 쿠웨이트 임시정부를 지지하라는 메시지를 반복하고 있으나 실제 임시정부 구성에 대해서는 발표가 없음.

3. 현대건설 3 명에 대해서는 보고시각 현재 소식없음.

4. 대사관에는 교민 76 명이 대피중인바 이들의 거주구역이 현재로서는 평온 하나 부근에 이락군이 주둔하고 있어 전투가 재개될경우 위험이 클것으로 생각 되어 대사관에서 8.4 일 까지 대피하고 8.4. 일 상황을 보아 귀가또는 계속 대피조치로 할 계획임. 기타 다른 구역에 사는 교포들은 각각 자택에 대피하도록 조치중임.

5. 당관의 TELEX 가 연결이 아니되어 주이락 대사관경유 소통을 하였던바 16:00 경부터 현대건설지점과 본사사이에 단속적으로나마 교신 가능하게되어 이보고는 이 채널을 이용한것임. 따라서 당관에 대한 전문은 먼저 이 현대채널이용 가능성을 서울에서 검토해서 이 회선이 가능한 경우 일차적으로 이 회선을 이용 하여 주시기 바람. 아니면 이락대사관 경유 타전하여 주시기 바람. 끝.

(대사-국장)

중아국	차관	1차보	정문국	신일	영교국	청와대	안기부	건설부	상영식
노동부									

0033

PAGE 1

90.08.04   01:30

외신 2과. 통제관 DH

외 무 부

종 별 :

번 호 : KUW-0388   일 시 : 90 0803 1915

수 신 : 장관(중근동,정일,기정동문)

발 신 : 주 쿠웨이트 대사

제 목 : 쿠웨이트.이락 사태(21호)

진서기관

1. 은행이 폐쇄되어있고 식료품점과 주요소도 대부분 폐점되어 있으며 일부 잠간씩 문을 여는 상점의 경우도 물품 (특히 물) 이 없어서 곤란한 사정이며 이러한 상태가 수일 더 지속되면 심각한 식료품문제가 염려되고 있음.

2. 또한 미 확인 정보이나 쿠웨이트 남방 50KM 거리에 있는 쿠웨이트 정유및 섬유화확 공업지대인 아흐마디와 슈와이바 지역은 아직 쿠웨이트군이 장악하고 있다고 하는데 만일 이것이 사실이고 이락군이 이 시설들을 만일 점령하기 위해서 전투가 벌어지면 정유시설과 발전시설들이 손상을 받을 가능성이 많고 그에 따라 쿠웨이트시 지역에 단전되어 심각한 어려움이 염려됨을 참고로 보고함. 끝.

(대사-국장)

중아국 노동부	장관	차관	1차보	2차보	정문국	영교국	안기부	건설부

외 무 부

번 호 : KUW-0389   일 시 : 90 0803 2010

수 신 : 장관(중근동,정일,기정동문)

발 신 : 주 쿠웨이트 대사

제 목 : 쿠웨이트.이락 사태 (22호)

　　　쿠웨이트 임시정부 명의로 8.3. 20:00 시에 즉각 통행금지와 외국인 내국인 출국정지를 포고문으로 발표했음. 끝.

　　　　(대사-국장)

중아국	장관	차관	1차보	2차보	정문국	영교국	정와대	안기부
건설부	노동부							

원 본

외 무 부

종 별 : 긴급

번 호 : KUW-0387

일 시 : 90 0803 1900

수 신 : 장관(중근동,정일,기정동문)

발 신 : 주 쿠웨이트 대사

제 목 : 쿠웨이트.이락 사태(20호)

1. 기 보고한대로 쿠웨이트시는 총격전은 없는 비교적 조용한 상태가 유지되고 있으나 이락군이 해안선과 쿠웨이트시의 주요지역에 계속 증강되고 또한 쿠웨이트시 남쪽으로 병력이 증파되고 있는것 같음.

2. 현재 쿠웨이트시 상황은 쿠웨이트 군경의 무력저항은 완전히 제압되어 이락군의 통제가 확립된 상태로 보여지므로 이미 보고드린데로 외부의 무력간섭이 없으면 다시 쿠웨이트시에서 전투가 일어날것 같지는 않을것으로 생각됨.

3. 만일 외부의 무력간섭이 있을경우는 이락측이 기왕에 공언하고 있는 바대로 쿠웨이트를 주전장으로 삼을 것이므로 심각한 피해를 예상할수 있음.

제반징후로 보아 그럴 가능성은 많지않다고 보지만 만일에 대비하여 일본 (거류민, 체류자 200 여명) 불란서 (체류자 미상) 등 이락과 관계가 좋은 우방국들과 함께 이락측에 대하여 만일의 경우 피난구조 항공기를 보내는 문제를 가능하면 협의하는 일을 검토해 주실것을 건의함. 끝.

(대사-국장)

예고:90.12.31 일반

1990. 12. 51. 애 예고문에 의거 일반문서로 재 분류됨.

| 중아국 | 장관 | 차관 | 1차보 | 2차보 | 정문국 | 영고국 | 청와대 | 안기부 |
| 건설부 | 노동부 | | | | | | | |

외 무 부

종 별 :

번 호 : KUW-0390   일 시 : 90 0804 0730

수 신 : 장관(중근동,정일,기정동문),노동부장관,건설부장관

발 신 : 주 쿠웨이트 대사

제 목 : 쿠웨이트,이락 사태(23호)

연: KUW-0386

교민및 근로자 안전상황

1. 07:00 현재 연호 현대건설 근로자 3 명으로 부터는 연락이 없으며 소재가 확인되지 않고 있음.

2. 자하라 송전선로 공사현장의 2 명(조준택, 노재항)에 관하여는 8.3. 현대건설 자하라 근로자 숙소에서 인원을 현장에 보내서 확인하였는데 자재 창고 상주경비원 태국인 3 명도 없었고 현대근로자 2 명도 현장에 없었다고 함. 현장에는 어떤 인명불상사가 있었던 흔적은 전혀 없었다고 하고 이들 근로자 2 명이 8.2. 아침에 타고 현장으로 떠난 자동차도 없었다고 함. 현장의 비축식료품과 자동차 부품등의 일부자재가 없어졌다고 함.

3. 이에따라 현대 자하라 숙소 직원들이 자하라에서 계속 이들의 소재를 수소문 중이고 병원등에도 확인중이나 보고시각 현재 소재가 확인되지 않고 있음. 끝.

(대사-국장)

746-3323
현대건설 총무부

중아국	장관	차관	1차보	정문국	청와대	안기부	건설부	노동부

PAGE 1

외 무 부

종 별 : 긴급

번 호 : KUW-0392

일 시 : 90 0804 0950

수 신 : 장관(중근동,정일,기정동문)

발 신 : 주 쿠웨이트 대사

제 목 : 쿠웨이트.이락 사태(24호)

연 : KUW-0386

1. 대사관에 대피했던 교민들은 일단 귀가시키고 각각 집에서 외출을 삼가하는등 안전조치를 취하면서 대기토록 하였음.

2. 8.4. 09:30 현재까지 전반적인 상황은 산발적으로 기관총등 총격이 있으나 전반적으로 긴장속에 조용한 상태가 계속되고 있음. 이락군대의 차량이동 활동은 매우 활발한 편임. 끝.

(대사-국장)

중아국 노동부	장관	차관	1차보	2차보	정문국	정와대	안기부	건설부

WBG-0192 발신 90080 1528 전 보

WKU -0180

번 호 : ~~WNR 0231 900804 4521 ER~~   종별 : ~~WUK 4297~~

수 신 : 주   수신처 참조~~대사. 총영사~~

발 신 : 장 관   (중근동)

제 목 : 쿠웨이트 사태

1. 중동아 국장은 8.4: 11:00 주한 이라크 대사대리(Burhan Ghazal)를 외무부로 불러 면담하였는바 요지 아래 통보함.

가. 최근 이라크 군대에 의한 쿠웨이트 영토 내에서의 군사적 행동과 관련한 걸프 지역내의 사태 진전에 관하여 아국 정부의 우려를 전달

나. 쿠웨이트 및 이라크내 체류중인 모든 아국인의 신변 안전 및 보호를 위해 이라크 정부가 최선의 조치를 취하여 줄것을 요청하고, 특히 쿠웨이트에서 실종된 아국 근로자 3명의 소재 확인과 석방을 요구 ~~하였음.~~

다. Ghazal 대사대리는 한국 정부의 입장과 한국 근로자 신변 안전에 대한 최선의 조치를 본국 정부에 즉시 보고 하겠으며, 한국인 근로자 3명의 신변 관련, 소식을 접하는대로 가능한 한 8.6. (월) 까지 알려 주겠다고 말하였음.

2. 상기 관련, 보도자료로서 국내 언론에 배포하였으니 참고 바람.

3. 동 대사대리는 8.5. (일) 이라크 군대가 쿠웨이트로 부터 철수할 것이며 8.5. 카이로 긴급 아랍 정상 회담에 후세인 대통령이 참석할 가능성도 있는등 사태가 정상화 될 것이므로 모든 문제가 잘 해결될 것이라고 말하였음.

1990. 12. 31. 에 예고문에 의거 일반문서로 재 분류됨.

(중동아국장 이 두 복)

예 고 : 90.12.31. 일반

수신처 : 이라크, 쿠웨이트 대사

보 안 통 제

앙고재		기안자성명		과 장		국 장		차 관	장 관
90년 8월 4일	홍은동					가결			

외신과통제

0039

외 무 부

종 별 : 긴 급

번 호 : KUW-0393

일 시 : 90 0804 1040

수 신 : 장관(중근동,정일,기정동문)

발 신 : 주 쿠웨이트 대사

제 목 : 쿠웨이트.이락 사태(25호)

1. 쿠웨이트 텔레비젼은 8.4. 10:05 분에 다음과 같은내용의 소위 쿠웨이트 임시정부(INDEPENDENT INTERIM GOVERNMENT) 발표문을 보도하였음.

(원 보도문은 아랍어)

ANNOUNCEMENT:

AS THE SITUATION IS NOW SETTLED AND AFTER ARRANGEMENTS WITH IRAQI GOVERNMENT, WE AGREED THAT IRAQ STARTS TO WITHDRAW ITS TROOPS IN ACCORDANCE WITH A TIME SCHEDULE STARTING FROM SUNDAY, AUGUST 5, 1990.

OLD GOVERNMENT IS OVER FOR EVER. WE WILL BEAT ANY FOREIGN ATTACK STRONGLY AND THE BRAVE IRAQI PEOPLE WILL BE NEAR US FOR HELP IN CASE OF ANY FOREIGN ATTACK.

KUWAIT ENTERIM

INDEPENDENT GOVERNMENT

2. 기왕에 보고한데로 쿠웨이트 임시정부는 상금도 정부지도자나 구성원에 대한 발표는 없는것으로 보아 위의 발표는 실제로는 이락당국(이락군)의 발표문임. 끝.

(대사-국장)

중아국	장관	차관	1차보	2차보	정문국	정와대	안기부

0040

PAGE 1

90.08.04   17:55

외신 2과 통제관 EZ

외　무　부

종　별 : 긴 급

번　호 : KUW-0394

일　시 : 90 0804 1115

수　신 : 장관(중근동,정일,기정동문)

발　신 : 주 쿠웨이트 대사

제　목 : 쿠웨이트,이락 사태(26호)

　　　연: KUW-0388

　　아흐마디와 슈와이바 지역은 지역상황을 탐문한 결과 이지역에서도 쿠웨이트군의
저항이 없고 이락군이 완전히 장악하고 있다고 함을 참고로 보고함. 끝.

　　　(대사-국장)

중아국　　장관　　차관　　1차보　　2차보　　정문국　　청와대　　안기부

외 무 부

관리
번호 90/755

종 별 : 긴급

번 호 : KUW-0397   일 시 : 90 0804 1400

수 신 : 장관(중근동,정일,기정동문)

발 신 : 주 쿠웨이트 대사

제 목 : 쿠웨이트.이락 사태(27호)

1. 쿠웨이트시 외곽의 해안도로에 포진.배치된 이락 탱크등과 병력이 정오경부터 상당부분 다른곳으로 이동하여 13:00 시 현재 소수병력과 탱크가 잔류하고 있음. 탱크와 병력이 이동한 것이 철수하는 것과 관련된 것인지는 알수 없음.

2. 소위 쿠웨이트 임시정부를 조직하고자 하는 이락의 노력은 아직 동임시정부의 구성원등 실체가 발표되고 있지 아니한 것으로 보아 쿠웨이트인들의 협력거부로 성공못하고 있는것 같음.

3. 이락측이 소위 쿠웨이트 임시정부 이름으로 내일(8.5)부터 철수한다고 발표는 했으나 쿠웨이트 새정부를 세우지 못하고 철수한다는 것은 그들이 반대하는 JABER 왕정부의 복귀를 의미하는 것이 될것이므로 이락으로서는 외부압력과 쿠웨이트인들의 비협력 저항사이에 어려운 입장에 빠져 있을 것이므로 발표된데로 철수를 하게될지는 확실치 않다고 봄.

4. 한편 이락방향으로 이동하는 차량이나 탱크가 많이 보이고 도심지에서 이락병사들에 의한 상점약탈, 부녀자들에 대한 공격사례가 오늘 아침부터 발생하고 있는점 등으로 보아 이락군 내부에서 철수한다는 결정이 있고 이것이 일반 병사들에게도 알려져 있는 상태가 아닌가 해석됨. 또한 쿠웨이트 사람들에 의한 이락병사들에 대한 공격과 이락군인들에 의한 쿠웨이트인 총살사례등을 목격교민이 대사관에 보고해 온바 있음.

5. 위 사항사태에 따라 당관에서는 교민들에게 특별히 주의를 당부하고 있음. 끝.

(대사-국장)

예고:90.12.31 일반

19 90 12. 31. 애 예고문에 의거 일반문서로 재 분류됨.

중아국	장관	차관	1차보	2차보	정문국	청와대	안기부

0042

외 무 부

종 별 : 긴 급

번 호 : KUW-0400

일 시 : 90 0804 1740

수 신 : 장관(중근동,정일,기정동문)

발 신 : 주 쿠웨이트 대사

제 목 : 쿠웨이트.이락 사태(29호)

연: KUW-0389, KUW-0397

1. 현재 상황은 지금까지는 군사적인 제압작전에 치중해 왔기때문에 민간인들에 대한 통제가 비교적 허술했는데 점점 통행통제, 검문검색, 가택수색(이락측이 지목하는 쿠웨이트인 색출 및 저격자 수색등)이 강화되고 있고 전화도 지역에따라 또 시간에따라 단속적으로 불통되는등 불안한 분위기가 조성되고 있음.

2. 통행금지는 포고되었으되 시간, 지역등 상세한 내용의 발표가 없어서 원칙으로 말하면 24 시간 통금으로 해석되는데 실제로는 주간에는 민감한 구역을 제외하고는 비교적 제한없이 그리고 야간(초저녁)에도 통행이 허용되어 왔는데 1 항의 사정전개에 따라 통행차량도 점차줄어들고 있음.

3. 따라서 공관원들의 이동도 신변안전을 생각하여 가능한한 최소한으로 조정 관리하고저 함에 따라 보고전문 발송도 부득이 자주할수 없게 될것임을 양해해 주시기 바람. 끝.

(대사 소병용-차관)

예고:90.12.31 일반

199?. 12.31 . 애 예고문애
의거 일반문서로 재 분류됨.

중아국   장관   차관   1차보   2차보   정문국   청와대   안기부

원 본

외 무 부

종 별 : **긴 급**

번 호 : KUW-0401   일 시 : 90 0805 0630

수 신 : 장관(중근동,정일,기정동문)

발 신 : 주 쿠웨이트 대사

제 목 : 쿠웨이트 사태(30호)

연: KUW-0393

쿠웨이트 임시정부 각료 발표

1. 이른바 쿠웨이트 임시정부는 수상등 각료 9 명을 8.4. 20:40 경 TV 에 보도했음. 구성은 수상겸 국방장관겸 내무장관 알라 훗세인 알리 대령, 외무장관왈리드 싸우드 무함마드 압둘라 중령 이외에 7 명인바 내각전체의 명단은 성명철자등을 확인하여 추후 보고드리겠음.(TV 는 아랍어로 보도하였음)

2. 당관이 접촉한 쿠웨이트 인사 설명으로는 이들은 모두 쿠웨이트 사람이 아니고 현역 이락군인인것 같다함.

3. 또한 쿠웨이트 임시정부 군대인 "POPULAR ARMY 또는 아랍국제군"에 이락군인 10 만명이 지원했다고 보도하였음.

4. 이러한 조치는 쿠웨이트를 실제적으로 병합. 통치한다는 것으로 보아야 될것같음. 철수운운 하는 문제도 외형상으로 "철수"하는 형식을 보일지는 모르지만 실제로는 대부분의 군대를 쿠웨이트 군대라는 이름으로 계속 주둔시키게 될것으로 보임.

5. 앞으로 이"정부"에서 주재대사들을 소집하거나 개별적으로 초치할 가능성에 대비해야 할것인데 그럴때 어떻게 대응해야 할지 미리 검토하여 주실것을 건의함. 끝.

(대사-국장)

예고: 90.12.31 일반

1990. 12. 31. 에 예고문에
의거 일반문서로 재 분류됨.

중아국	장관	차관	1차보	2차보	정문국	영교국	청와대	안기부
건설부	노동부							

0044

90.08.05   13:48
외신 2과 통제관 DH

외 무 부

종 별 :

번 호 : KUW-0402   일 시 : 90 0805 0840

수 신 : 장관(중근동,정일,기정동문)

발 신 : 주 쿠웨이트 대사

제 목 : 쿠웨이트사태(31)

연 KUW-0401

각료 명단(영문 철자는 음역임)

- COLONEL ALAA' HUSSAIN ALI

PRIME MINISTER, GENERAL OF ARMY, MINISTER OF DEFENCE AND ACTING MINISTER OF INTERIOR.

- LIEUTENANT COLONEL WALEED SAOUD MOHAMED ABDULLAH

MINISTER OF OIL ACTING MINISTER OF FINANCE.

- MAJOR FADEL HAIDER AL-WAFEEKI

MINISTER OF INFORMATION ACTING MINISTER OF COMMUNITIONS.

- MAJOR MISHAL SAAD AL-HADAB

MINISTER OF PUBLIC HEALTH HOUSING AFFAIRS.

- LIEUTENANT COLONEL HUSSAIN ALI SULAIMAN

MINISTER OF SOCIAL AFFAIRS LABOUR, ACTING MINISTER OF PUBLIC WORKS.

- MAJOR NASER MANOOUR AL-MANDEEL

MINISTER OF EDUCATION ACTING MINISTER OF HIGH EDUCATION.

- MAJOR ESSAM ABDUL-MAJEED HUSSAIN

MINISTER OF JUSTICE LEGAL AFFAIRS, ACTING MINISTER OF AWQAF AFFAIRS ISLAMIC AFFAIRS.

- MAJOR YACOUB MOHAMED SHALLAL

MINISTER OF ELECTRICITY, PLANNING TRADE. 끝

(대사-국장)

중아국   차관   1차보   정문국   정와대   안기부

0045

PAGE 1   90.08.05   18:15

외신 2과 통제관 DH

관리 번호	90 /1233

외 무 부

종 별 : 지 급

번 호 : KUW-0405

일 시 : 90 0805 1030

수 신 : 장관(중동아프리카국장)

발 신 : 주 쿠웨이트 대사

제 목 : 쿠웨이트 사태

연: KUW-0397

연호의 4 항 내용은 일반적인것 처럼 과장 보도되면 곤란하니 특별히 보안(언론에) 부탁드림. 끝.

(대사-국장)

예고:90.12.31 까지

1990. 12. 31. 애 예고문에
의거 일반문서로 재 분류됨.

중아국

외 무 부

종 별 : 긴급

번 호 : KUW-0407

시 : 90 0805 1700

수 신 : 장 관(중근동, 영재, 정일, 기정)

발 신 : 주 쿠웨이트 대사

제 목 : 이라크-쿠웨이트 사태(33호)

1. 쿠웨이트시에는 정규군이 중요 지점에만 배치되어 있고 전반적으로는 "민병"(정부군인지 불명)이 배치 되었는데 중동에서 흔한 모습의 무장인들로서 정규군과 달리 무질서하게 행동하고 있어 아주 치안상태가 위험한 상황으로 변해 가고 있음

2. 교민들의 상점등이 약탈당하는 일들이 늘어나고 "가택수색"도 당하고 있는 실정임.

3. 치안상태 악화로 취약지역 주민들을 대사관으로 대피시키고 있음. 끝

(대사 소병용-국장)

예고:90.12.31.까지

1990. 12. 31. 애 예고문에
의거 일반문서로 재 분류됨.

중아국	장관	차관	1차보	2차보	정문국	영교국	정와대	안기부

PAGE 1

0047

90.08.06   18:50

외신 2과 통제관 DL

외 무 부

종 별 :

번 호 : KUW-0408

수 신 : 장관(중동아국장 이두복)

발 신 : 주 쿠웨이트 대사

제 목 : 업연

일 시 : 90 0805 1700

보낸 서비스 참고만 하십시요. 센세이셔널하게 보도되면 이곳에서 곤란할듯해서 그런 것이니 실제 상황은 꽤 심각함. 끝

예고:독후파기

중아국

0048

PAGE 1

90.08.06   05:18

외신 2과 통제관 CF

54   걸프 사태 쿠웨이트, 이라크 및 각국 경제 제재

관리 번호	90/1235

외 무 부

종 별 :

번 호 : KUW-0409

일 시 : 90 0805 1700

수 신 : 장관(중근동,정일,기정)

발 신 : 주 쿠웨이트 대사

제 목 : 이라크-쿠웨이트사태(34호)

"임시정부"외무장관은 다음요지의 성명을 발표함

이라크에 제재 조치를 하는 나라들에 대하여는 쿠웨이트와 이라크 양국 그들의 생명과 경제에 관계가 있으므로 외교관계를 단절하고 대사관의 폐쇄를 포함한 제반 조치를 취할것임.끝

(대사 소병용-국장)

예고:90.12.31

1996. 12. 31. 에 예고문에 의거 일반문서로 재 분류됨.

중아국	장관	차관	1차보	2차보	정문국	정와대	안기부

PAGE 1

90.08.06 05:07 0049

외신 2과 통제관 CF

외　무　부

종　별 : 긴 급

번　호 : KUW-0411　　　　　　　　　　　일　시 : 90 0806 1030

수　신 : 장 관(중근동, 영재, 정일, 기정)

발　신 : 주 쿠웨이트대사

제　목 : 이라크-쿠웨이트사태(35호)

　8.5일 쿠웨이트 TV 는 쿠웨이트정부의 요청에 따라 이라크에 거주하는 쿠웨이트인, 아랍인 및 외국인들이 이라크에 거주하도록 허락하였다고 보도했는데 기보고한 외국인 이동 과도 관련이 있는 주목할 내용이라고 생각됨. 끝

　(대사 소병용-국장)

중아국　1차보　정문국　영교국　안기부

0050

PAGE 1

| 관리
번호 | PO/785 |

	분류번호	보존기간

발 신 전 보

WKU-0190   900807 1829   ER

번   호 : _____   종별 : _____

수   신 : 주 쿠웨이트   대사. /총영사

발   신 : 장 관   (중근동)

제   목 : 쿠웨이트 사태

대 : KUW-0401

대호 5항 관련, 단체 또는 개별 초치 경우 신정부 관련 명시적 승인을
표시하지 않는한 정부 승인은 않되는 것이 국제적 관례인바, 오해받는 일이
없도록 우방 공관 태도를 관찰 전화 대처 바람. 끝.

적절히 하회각을 보내는등

(중동아프리카국   이 두 복)

예 고 : 90.12.31. 일반

1990. 12. 31. 애 예고문에
의거 일반문서로 재 분류됨.

		보 안 통 제	

앙 고 재	90년 8월 7일 중근동과	기안자 성명		과 장		국 장 전결		차 관	장 관		외신과통제

0051

외 무 부

종 별 : 지 급

번 호 : KUW-0415　　　　　　　　　일 시 : 90 0807 1130

수 신 : 장관(중근동,신일)

발 신 : 주쿠웨이트대사

제 목 : 전문수발

　　통신소통에 어려움을 감안해서 꼭 필요한 전문만 발송 중계하고 암호화
필요부분만축소하여 별도 타전바람.끝
　　(대사 소병용-국장)

중아국　　신일
　✔

PAGE 1　　　　　　　　　　　　　　　　　　90.08.08　　01:56 DP

　　　　　　　　　　　　　　　　　　　　외신 1과 통제관

　　　　　　　　　0052

외 무 부

종 별 : 긴급

번 호 : KUW-0456 일 시 : 90 0817 2130

수 신 : 장관(중근동,정일,기정,노동부)

발 신 : 주쿠웨이트 대사

제 목 : 쿠웨이트사태

현재의상황을 아래보고함.

1. 치안상태

-도심 및 일부교외지역에 정체불명의 무장괴한 또는 군인들이 가택침입, 약탈행위 감행계속

-최근에는 쿠웨이트인의 사보타쥬나 저항등이 산발적으로 발생하고있어 야간에는 총격전이 자주일어나고 특별히 지난 2 일간에는 비교적 도심에서 거리가있는 대사관과 관저지역에서도 총격전이 있었으며 어제(8.17) 총격에서는 유탄이대사관건물에도 떨어졌음.

-많은수의 쿠웨이트인 및 외국인들이 철수 또는 피난하여 시내의 교통량도 평소의 25% 이내로 전반적으로 적막하고 불안한 분위기임.

-이락군인들이 시내에서 많이 철수한데 비해 민병대들과 이락경찰들이 많이배치됨

-초기 10 일동안에 거의 공개적으로 이락측이 대형트럭등으로 식량이나 기타 귀중품들을 이미 많이 약탈, 반출했고 한국인상점들도 많이있는 도심 상가지대는 완전히 황폐화하여 동공상태임.

-앞으로 치안문제는 전반적으로 더나빠질것 같음.

2. 쿠웨이트인 말살정책: 이락은 쿠웨이트를 최단기간내에 비쿠웨이트화 즉쿠웨이트의 IDENTITY 를 말소코자 하는듯 쿠웨이트인에 대한 공포정책을 써서 다수 쿠웨이트인을 국외도피 또는이락으로 강제 압송중임

-FAHD 왕자관련 국방장관등 다수의 쿠웨이트지도층 인사들을 이미 살해한것같음. 이에의하면 800 명 이상의 지도층 인사가 살해되었다고 함

-다수의 빈민층 이락인들이 집단으로 유입되고 있는데 이라크가 종국에는 쿠웨이트로 부터 군사적인 철수를 한다해도 쿠웨이트를 사실상 장악할수있도록

중아국 장관 차관 1차보 2차보 정문국 영교국 정와대 안기부
노동부 대책반

0053

PAGE 1 90.08.18 17:42

외신 2과 통제관 CD

인구구성변질 정책을 실시하는듯함

　3. 쿠웨이트에 대한 손상은 사회적, 경제적, 인구면에서 심층적이고 치명적인 것으로 철수후에도 원상회복에는 상당한 어려움이 있을것 같음. 이상 보도용제건의함,끝

　(대사-국장)

　예고: 90.12.31일반

외 무 부

종 별 : 긴 급

번 호 : KUW-0469

일 시 : 90 0820 1030

수 신 : 장관(중근동,기정)

발 신 : 주쿠웨이트 대사

제 목 : 상황보고

8.20 새벽부터 오전에 걸쳐 탱크, 대포등 중무기가 많이 사우디쪽으로 이동하고있음. 이란국경에서 오는 증강조치인지, 어떤 군사행동 준비를 의미하는지주목됨.

(대사-국장)

90.12.31. 일반

중아국   장관   차관   1차보   2차보   정문국   청와대   안기부   대책반

외 무 부

종 별 : 지 급

번 호 : SBW-0606   일 시 : 91 0227 1500

수 신 : 장관(중일,미북,국방,기정)

발 신 : 주 사우디대사대리

제 목 : 쿠웨이트 정부입장발표

사담의 쿠웨이트로부터의 이라크 철군발표와 관련, 당지 TAIF 소재 임시정부 관방담당 국무장관은 2.26 기자들에게 쿠웨이트 정부 입장을 다음과같이 밝혔음

-사담의 철군발표는 또하나의 책략임

-사담은 단지 자신의 목숨만을 구하려고 노력하고 있음

-쿠웨이트 정부는 완전하고 무조건적인 철군과 12개의 유엔 안보리 결의안 이행이외의 어떤것도 받아들이지 않을 것임

-사담은 확실한 원칙에 따른 안정된 정책비젼이 결여되어 있음, 사담은 매일 입장을 바꾸고 있음

-지금까지 이란,쿠웨이트 및 이라크에 대해 취한 행동은 아무런 의미가 없음

현재까지 쿠웨이트에 들어간 JABER AL-SABAH 국왕 측근들은 없음

(대사대리 박명준-국장)

중아국	장관	차관	1차보	2차보	미주국	정문국	정와대	총리실
안기부	국방부	대책반						

0056

91.02.27   22:11 DA

외신 1과 통제관

정 리 보 존 문 서 목 록					
기록물종류	일반공문서철	등록번호	2020120212	등록일자	2020-12-28
분류번호	772	국가코드	XF	보존기간	영구
명 칭	걸프사태, 1990-91. 전12권				
생 산 과	북미1과/중동1과	생산년도	1990~1991	담당그룹	
권 차 명	V.2 이라크, 1990-91				
내용목차					

0001

원 본

외 무 부

종 별 : 지급
번 호 : BGW-0361
수 신 : 장관(중근동) 사본:주쿠웨이트대사
발 신 : 주 이라크 대사
제 목 : 이라크, 쿠웨이트 분쟁

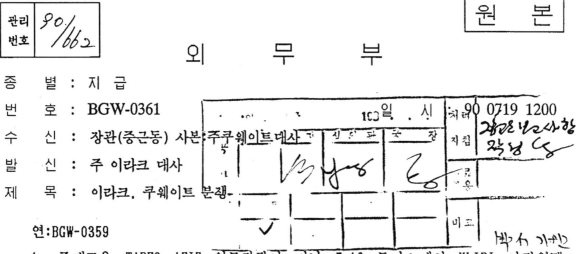

연:BGW-0359

1. 주재국은 TAREQ AZIZ 외무장관이 지난 7.16 튜니스에서 KLIBI 아랍연맹 사무총장에게 전달한 메시지 내용을 7.18 전국 TV, 라디오를 통하여 대대적으로 보도하였는바, 동 요지는 다음과같음

- 이라크, 쿠웨이트 간에는 과거 식민지 시대부터의 국경분쟁이 있었는바, 쿠웨이트는 이라크가 이.이전에 몰두한 틈을이용, 이라크 영토를 불법점령, 군사,석유생산시설 농장을 세웠으며, 지난 알제리 아랍 정상회의시 이라크측의 협상제의에 대해 무성의한 지연 전술로 일관해옴.

- 최근 쿠웨이트와 UAE 는 고의적인 석유 과잉 생산을 통해 유가하락을 초래, 아랍산유국 및 이라크에 심대한 손해를 끼쳤으며, 87-90 년간 유가하락으로 인한 아랍산유국의 경제적 손실(OPEC 책정가 배럴당 18 불 기준)은 250 억불에 달함

- 쿠웨이트는 이.이전 기간중 이라크 남부 RUMAILA 유전을 불법 채굴,80-90년간 24 억불의 부상 수입을 올림.

- 쿠웨이트 및 UAE 의 정책은 이라크 경제를 파괴하고 이라크와아랍권의 힘을 약화시키려는 이스라엘및제국주의 국가의 음모의 일환이며, 특히 쿠웨이트의 DUAL AGGRESSION(이라크영토 불법점령및경제파괴)은 이라크에대한 군사적공격 행위와 다를바가 없음.

- 이라크는 쿠웨이트와 UAE 를 강력히 규탄하며, 아랍제국이 상기 양국의 반아랍적인 정책 중단을 위하여 여론을고취하여 줄것을 촉구함. 또한 이라크는 쿠웨이트가 이라크 석유를 불법채국하여 올린 부당수입(24 억불0을 반환받을 권리가 있음을 분명히 하는바임

- 이라크의 대아랍국 부채와 관련, 이라크가 이.이전 초기(80-82)에 쿠웨이트 UAE

중아국   장관   차관   1차보   2차보   정문국   청와대   안기부

PAGE 1

를 포함 아랍걸프국가들로부터 무이자 재정지원을 받은것은 사실이지만 이는 이라크 전비총액(1,020 억불)의 극히 일부에 불과하며, 이라크가 아랍걸프국가들의 영토방위와 번영을 위하여 막대한 희생을 치루고 이라크의 전쟁기간중 석유 수출공백으로 주변 산유국들이 1,060 억불에 달하는 이득을 올린점을 감안할때 상기 재정지원의 상당부분이 아직도 이라크가 갚아야할 외채로 남아 있다는것은 부당함. 제 2 차 세계대전후 미국의 대유럽 원조사례에 비추어 아랍국가들은 대이라크 외채를 탕감해 주어야할뿐 아니라 마샬플랜과 같은 범 아랍원조계획을 마련해야 마땅할것임.

2. 관찰및 평가

가. 상기 AZIZ 외무장관 메시지는 7.17 후세인대통령의 연설에 이어 쿠웨이트 및 UAE 에 대한 주재국의 제 2 차 공개비난인바, 동내용에서 쿠웨이트에 공격의 촛점을 맞추어 유가문제뿐 아니라 국경분쟁, 이라크 석유 불법채굴등 이라크-쿠웨이트 양국간 문제를 주로 다루었다는점이 특기할만한 사실임. 특히, 후세인대통령의 연설에서 이라크의 이익 보호를위한"효과적인 조치"를 경고한점과표제 메시지에서 쿠웨이트의 정책이"이라크에 대한 군사적 공격행위"와 마찬가지라고 언급한것은 쿠웨이트에 군사적 압력을 가하기위한것으로 분석됨.

나. 주재국이 대쿠웨이트 압력을 강화하고 있는것은 유가문제와 국경분쟁등 현안문제의 힘을 통한 해결을 모색함과 아울러, 최근 VELAYATI 이란외무장관의 쿠웨이트 방문을 계기로한 양국간 관계강화 움직임(테헤란-쿠웨이트 항공편 재개등)을 견제하려는 의미도있는것으로 보임.

다. 또한, 주재국은 이.이전 이후 역대최대의 군사강국으로 부상 90.5 바그다드 아랍정상회의의 개최등 아랍권의 패권을 지속적으로 추구하고 있는바, 금번대 쿠웨이트 공세에는 군사력에 기초한 주재국의 영향력을 역내에 실증하기위한 의도가 있는것으로 분석됨(이와관련, 금번사태가 주재국이 이러한 견지에서 쿠웨이트를 가장 적절한 대상으로 오래전에 선택한데 따른것이며 대 쿠웨이트 압력은 지난 2 월 쿠웨이트 걸프컵 축구대회시 UDAI HUSSEIN (후세인대통령 장남, 축구협회회장) 이 주도한 이라크팀 철수 결정에서부터 이미 시작되었다는 일부의 분석도 있음)

라. 본건관련, 이라크의 압도적인 군사력과 GCC 의 공동방위 체제 미성숙및 이라크와 불가침조약을 체결한 사우디의 개입 가능성 불투명, 그리고 여타 제 3국의 실질적 지원확보의 어려움등을 감안할때, 쿠웨이트로서는 결국 이라크의 요구에 상당한 양보를할 가능성이 큰것으로 전망됨. 끝

(대사 최봉틈-차관)
예고:90.12.31

0004

White House Blocks Furnace Export to Iraq

By MICHAEL WINES
Special to The New York Times

WASHINGTON, July 19 — The White House moved today to block the shipment of three advanced industrial furnaces to Iraq because of concern that they will be used on nuclear weapons-related projects.

The decision, requiring the New Jersey maker of the furnaces to seek a Federal export license, effectively overrides an earlier ruling by the Commerce Department. It came after the Pentagon and a bloc of Republican senators urged President Bush to keep the furnaces out of Iraqi military hands.

Had the White House not acted, a temporary ban on their export, imposed by the Customs Service last month, would have expired on Friday.

The action settles for now what has been billed as a test of the Bush Administration's commitment to stop the proliferation of weapons-related technology to developing nations in unstable regions like the Middle East.

The Pentagon and some Congressional experts believe that Iraq planned to use the furnaces to cast titanium and other exotic metals for use in ballistic missiles, and perhaps as components of nuclear weapons. Iraq has maintained that it wants the furnaces to make lightweight artificial arms and legs, largely for wounded veterans of its long war with Iran.

Government officials said today that they were persuaded to block delivery of the furnaces, at least temporarily, because of solid evidence that they were bound for an Iraqi military complex south of Baghdad.

A team of technical experts from the Pentagon, the Energy Department and other agencies will review the design specifications of the furnaces within the next week to determine conclusively whether they have advanced military uses.

U.S. Authorized Sales

Consarc Corporation of Rancocas, N. J., the maker of the furnaces, received permission from the Commerce Department last year to sell the devices to Iraq after concluding that they were not covered by international agreements regulating the sale of advanced military technologies to developing nations.

That decision is now under review but it has not been changed.

Instead, the Commerce Department informed Consarc today that it would require a validated export license for the furnaces because of new information that their designated user, the Iraqi Ministry of Industry and Military Industrialization, was engaged in "nuclear activities."

Decision at White House

Senior Government officials said the decision to block the sale was reached at the White House.

Raymond Roberts, the president of Consarc, acknowledged receiving the letter and said that his company "will be working constructively with the Government to allay any legitimate national security concerns."

Iraq has a vigorous campaign under way to become a regional military power. It launched a crude three-stage missile last year, and President Sadaam Hussein has boasted that he has the ability to deliver chemical weapons to Israel. Experts say Iraq is working to develop nuclear

Officials at the Pentagon and in Congress had argued vigorously since late June that the export of the furnace should be blocked. The campaign grew as the Iraqi President made more threats against neighboring countries this week.

In a meeting with President Bush, Senator Arlen Specter, Republican from Pennsylvania, urged that the sale of the furnaces be halted and that other Federal assistance to Iraq, including $500 million in loan guarantees from the Commodity Credit Corporation, be withheld until Iraq moderated its belligerency.

Senator Specter, who met with President Hussein in Iraq earlier this year, called the Iraqi military campaign "extremely serious."

He urged President Mr. Bush to press United States concerns about the Middle East situation directly with President Hussein.

배 포 처	장 관 실	차 관 실	一 차 보	二 차 보	기 획 실	의 전 장	아 주 국	미 주 국	구 주 국	중 아 국	국 기 국	경 제 국	통 상 국	경 문 국	영 교 국	종 무 과	감 사 관	공 보 관	외 연 원	청 와 대	총 리 실	안 기 부	부 처
	✓	✓	✓							◯			2					ㅗ	/				

11 매 임

Persian Gulf Crisis Swells As Iraqi Gets New Title

By Caryle Murphy
Washington Post Foreign Service

CAIRO, July 19-Iraqi President Saddam Hussein, pressing his campaign to become the pre-eminent leader in the Arab world, won approval today from Iraq's compliant parliament for a revised constitution that would make him president for life in a legislative vote later this year.

The new demonstration of the Iraqi leader's unchallenged authority in Baghdad came on the heels of a series of ominous public threats by Saddam Hussein against Kuwait and other Persian Gulf states that sent the worried Kuwaitis in search of diplomatic support and drew a strong reaction from U.S. officials.

The crisis flared earlier this week when Iraq accused Kuwait—its former ally in the eight-year Persian Gulf War with Iran—of stealing Iraqi oil, encroaching on its territory and conniving with the United States to depress oil prices, an outburst seen by many gulf analysts as the latest use by Saddam Hussein of bellicose rhetoric in his effort to dominate regional politics.

The Iraqi leader, who last spring threatened to "burn half of Israel" with chemical weapons if the Jewish state launched an attack, also warned certain unnamed oil-producing rivals in a radio address Tuesday that "Iraqis will not forget the saying that cutting necks is better that cutting the means of living."

Kuwait fought back today with its own accusations against Baghdad, but also asked for Arab League mediation as Kuwaiti diplomats fanned out across the Middle East to seek backing against their belligerent northern neighbor.

In Washington, Defense Secretary Richard B. Cheney said today that the U.S. commitment to come to Kuwait's defense if it is at-

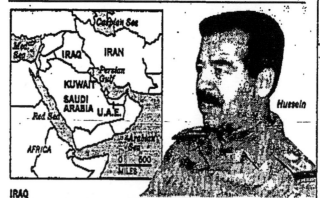

RISING TENSIONS IN THE MIDDLE EAST

IRAQ
President Saddam Hussein, already an absolute ruler, reaffirmed his hold on power by having the rubber-stamp Parliament make him President for Life. Hussein and his government have lashed out at neighboring countries recently, escalating tensions in the region.

KUWAIT
The oil-rich nation has launched a diplomatic offensive to counter Iraqi charges that it violated a common border and pumped billions of dollars worth of oil from Iraqi fields. Kuwait also has been harshly criticized by Hussein for contributing to lower oil prices by exceeding OPEC production levels.

UNITED ARAB EMIRATES
The federation of seven sheikdoms also has been criticized by Hussein for contributing to depressed oil prices.

SAUDI ARABIA
Saudi officials, worried that escalating rhetoric out of Iraq could disrupt next week's OPEC conference on production and pricing, are encouraging a cooling of tensions.

SOURCE: Associated Press

Compiled by James Schwartz

BY MICHAEL DREW—THE WASHINGTON POST

1568-1

July 20, 1990
WP

0006

tacked remains in force, but a former U.S. envoy in the Persian Gulf said the U.S. commitment has always been stated as protection "against the spillover from the Iran-Iraq war" and does not address aggression growing out of the current oil and territorial dispute between Baghdad and Kuwait.

Asked if a general U.S. pledge to come to Kuwait's aid still applied, Cheney said: "Those commitments haven't changed." He would not speculate, however, on how the United States might respond if Iraq moved to seize Kuwaiti territory. "We have got a lot of friends in the Persian Gulf," Cheney said, "nations we have historic relationships with . . . [and] obviously we take very seriously any threat that would put at risk U.S. interests or U.S. friends in the region." And he added, "We've demonstrated in recent years that we have, in fact, a good ability to respond and to do something about it."

To emphasize the U.S. commitment to the Arab gulf states, Cheney asserted that the large U.S. naval deployment to protect Kuwaiti oil tankers flying the American flag "was one of the more successful applications of military power in the post-war period."

Saddam Hussein's campaign of threat and intimidation has heightened tensions in the gulf to the highest level since a U.N.-sponsored cease-fire halted the bloody Iran-Iraq conflict two years ago. "This is not just someone wanting a leading role, but someone trying to establish paramountcy and dominance," said one U.S. gulf analyst in Washington. "This is what all small states in the region feared and thought wouldn't happen. Saddam does not like someone stand-

ing up to him, so he has resorted to outrageous accusations. He wants free rein—a bigger quota for oil production, or to curtail production and push prices up. He is gambling."

In his radio speech Tuesday, Saddam Hussein accused unnamed gulf states of stabbing Iraq in the back with "a poison dagger" by exceeding their OPEC oil-production quotas, thus forcing down oil prices to favor the United States. He added that "if words fail to protect Iraqis, something effective must be done to return things to their natural course."

The next day, Iraqi media made public a letter from Foreign Minister Tariq Aziz to the Arab League in which he bitterly accused Kuwait by name of stealing $2.4 billion worth of Iraqi oil, building military installations on Iraqi territory and refusing to forego Iraq's wartime debts. Iraq's newspapers added fuel to the volatile atmosphere today, one with a giant headline reading "Kuwait Steals From Us," and another commenting in an editorial: "We have been too patient with the violations of Kuwait."

In its message today to the Arab League, Kuwait responded with a charge that "Iraq has a rich record in its violations of Kuwait territory, i.e. record backed by facts." The Kuwaiti note asserted also that Iraq is digging oil wells on Kuwaiti territory and had refused repeatedly to settle a long-standing border dispute between the two countries.

Saudi Arabia's King Fahd telephoned Saddam Hussein and Kuwait's ruling emir, Sheik Jabir Ahmed Sabah, to cool emotions, and Arab League secretary general Chadli Klibi will fly to Kuwait Friday to attempt to mediate the dispute, news agencies reported.

But while Saddam Hussein's regional ambitions may play a central role in Iraq's latest saber-rattling, many Middle East experts say that growing difficulties in Iraq's hard-pressed economy may be the prime motive for the verbal assault on Kuwait, a fellow member of the 13-nation Organization of Petroleum Exporting Countries.

Iraq, which has the world's second-largest oil reserves, had been banking on high oil prices this year to finance its ambitious postwar reconstruction and military programs, and to pay off interest on an estimated $40 billion in war

loans from Japan and West European countries."

At the moment, it is having trouble finding new sources of credit and is struggling to contain inflation and create jobs so that it can demobilize part of its armed forces, which remain at a wartime level of about 1 million, Baghdad-based diplomats have said.

But lower than expected world demand for oil, combined with a market glut—partially generated by overproduction by Kuwait and the United Arab Emirates—has caused a steep slide in OPEC oil prices from $21 a barrel last year to $15 currently. If prices do not rebound significantly, Iraq's oil revenues, short of a miracle, are going to be extremely depressed," and this could spell disaster" for Baghdad in light of its development plans, said Keith McLachlan, an Iraqi expert at London's School of Oriental and African Studies. "I think this really has to be the motive pushing the Iraqis," McLachlan said, echoing assessments by other experts.

But Iraq's decision to make a public issue of its border dispute with Kuwait, which has been simmering in private, could cause unforeseen problems, McLachlan said. "The thing has begun because of oil and a revenue problem, but it might develop into something of a Frankenstein monster with a political dimension."

Saddam Hussein is not the first Iraqi ruler to make territorial threats against Kuwait, whose independence in 1961 was followed by an Iraqi claim of sovereignty over all Kuwaiti territory and oil wealth. At that time, Britain responded by landing troops in Kuwait and sending naval forces into the Persian Gulf until the Iraqis backed down.

Approval of the Iraqi leader's new status as president for life came during a three-day session of Iraq's 250-member assembly, which is dominated by Saddam Hussein's Baath Arab Party. Saddam Hussein, 54, had promised political reforms—including a multiparty system, a free press and the first free elections since Iraq became a republic in 1958—but today's action indicated that the leadership has reneged on the pledge.

Staff writers Patrick E. Tyler and Nora Boustany contributed to this article in Washington.

1518-2

July 2
'99
Wf

0007

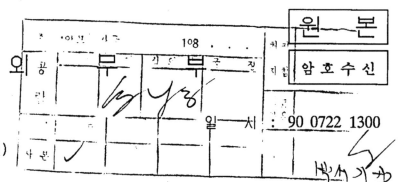

1. 주재국은 7.21 쿠웨이트 정부가 아랍국가 또는 아랍연맹을 통한 중재를 포기하고 이라크-쿠웨이트 분쟁을 유엔안보리 및 유엔사무총장에 호소 이를 국제화시키려 하고 있다고 비난함.

이라크# 정부소식통은 쿠웨이트가 아랍제국에 특사를 파견, 자신의 설득력없는 입장을 설명하려고 노력하고 있으며 또한 지역분쟁에 외세를 개입시키려고하고있는바, 이는 제국주의적 음모라고 맹렬히 비난함.

2. 사우디의 SAAD AL-FAISAL 외상이 7.21 주재국을 방문, 훗세인 대통령에게사우디 국왕의 멧세지를 전달한바, 이는 최근 이라크-쿠웨이트 분쟁에 대한 사우디의 입장 및 중재노력에 관련된것으로 추측되고 있으며 또한 훗세인 대통령은최근 요르단, 예멘및 이집트 국가원수와 접촉을 가졌음.

3. 7.22 자 AL-TAHAWRA 지는 7.21 당지 쿠웨이트 대사의 미국대사 방문을 보도하고 이는 외세와 협력하려는 쿠웨이트 정부의 정책을 보여주는것이라고 함.

4. 7.21 자 당지 바그다드 옵서버지는 아지즈 외상이 아랍연맹에 보낸 멧세지와 관련, 이라크-쿠웨이트 분쟁에 대하여 다음과같이 논평함.

-쿠웨이트를 비롯한 걸프국가의 영토보전과 안전보장을 위한 8 년간의 전쟁에서 이라크는 심대한 인적, 물적 희생을 감수하였으나, 전쟁으로 인하여 경제적어려움을 겪고있는 이라크에 대하여 가장먼저 경제적 지원을 했어야할이웃 쿠웨이트는 지원은 커녕, 저유가 정책을 취하므로 이라크에 심대한 경제적손실을 주고있음.

-전쟁후 쿠웨이트는 무이자 차관을 이라크에 제공하였으나, 이것조차 82 년에 중단하고 오히려 이라크 영토내에 있는 유전을 채굴, 수백만본의 석유를 판매했고 지금은 막대한 석유수출잉여금을 투자 동이자수입이 수십억불에 달하고 있으므로 유가에 개의치 않음. 쿠웨이트 저유가정책은 정치적, 경제적으로 이라크를

중아국   장관   차관   1차보   2차보   정문국   청와대   안기부

0008

저해하려는데서 기인함.

  -유가문제는 이라크의 생사문제로서, 저유가 정책 지지 제국은 그에대한 값비싼 대가를 치룰것임.끝

  (대사 최봉름-국장)

  예고:접수후 일반

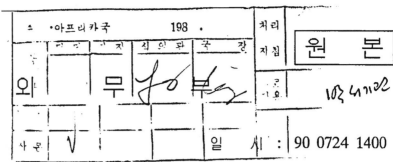

1. 이라크,쿠웨이트 제의 거부

-주재국 아지즈외상은 7.24 쿠웨이트가 유엔사무총장에게 보낸 메로랜덤(7.18)에서 언급한 국경분쟁 해결을 위한 아랍위원회 설치 제의를 거부하면서 아랍간 국경분쟁은 당사국간에 해결되어야할 문제라고 주장함

-동 외상은 이라크-쿠웨이트간의 역사는 어느 아랍국가보다 양국 국민이 더 잘알고 있다고 강조하고, 쿠웨이트 지도자들이 문제를 외세의 개입에 맡기므로 사태를 위기로 끌고가고 있다고 비난함

2. 아지즈 외상, 아랍연맹 사무총장에게 제2차 서한발송

가. 쿠웨이트 정부가 7.18 아랍연맹에 보낸 메로랜덤에 대응하여 아지즈외상이 7.21 아랍연맹사무총장에게 보낸 서한을 발표한바, 동 서한에서 쿠웨이트 주장을 조목별로 반박하고 이는 날조된것이며 사실을 은폐하기 위한 말장난에 불과하다고 반격함.

나. 서한요지

-7.15 자 서한에 쿠웨이트가 놀라움을 표시하였다한데 대하여, 이라크가 전쟁에전념하고있는 동안 쿠웨이트는 의도적이며 점진적으로 이라크 영토를 침해하고 석유자원을 탈취하는등 위해를 가해왔음

-양국간 협력이 진행되고 있었다는 쿠웨이트 주장은 근거없으며, 협력을 회피하고 지연시켜왔음. 대쿠웨이트 수자원 공급관련 사업및 쿠웨이트-바스라 직행 항공료 개설 지연등이 그 예임.

-이라크가 국경확정을 거부해왔다는 것은 날조된것이며, 영토및 해상 국경협정을오히려 쿠웨이트가 회피하고 지연시킴. 이라크와 사우디 및 요르단과의 국경문제는쿠웨이트와의 국경문제와 전적으로 다름

-쿠웨이트 정부는 문제를 국제화 시키고 있으며, 미국의 힘에 의존하려고 하고

중아국   1차보   정문국   안기부

0010

있음.

　3.무바락 이집트대통령 방이

　무바락이집트 대통령은 7.24 주재국을 방문, 훗세인 대통령과 일련의 회담을 가진바, 이라크-쿠웨이트 분쟁등 최근의 아랍사태진전 및 양국 공동관심사에 대한 협의를 가짐.

　4.특사파견

　훗세인대통령은　　　　　　　　　　　　　　　　　　7.24
카타르,바레인,모로코,뷰니지아,수단,모리타니아,지브티,소말리아등　　아랍제국에 특사를 파견, 최근 아랍사태등에 관련된 대통령 친서를 전달함.끝

　(대사 최봉름-국장)

외 무 부

종 별 :

번 호 : BGW-0389

수 신 : 장관(중근동,정일)

발 신 : 주이라크대사

제 목 : 정세보고(응신자료 51호)

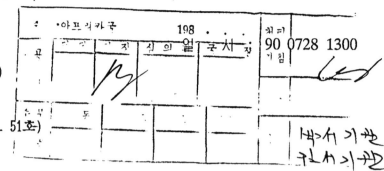

1. OPEC 회의결과 반응

주재국은 90년 하반기 OPEC QUOTA 확정(22.5백만B/D) 과 유가의 바렐당 미불 21로 인상 합의한 금번 제네바 OPEC 회의 결과에 만족을 표명함. AL-CHALABI 이라크 석유상은 금번 회의가 OPEC 의 단결과 그의 권리를 회복한 역사적인것으로, 이는 이라크-사우디의 공동 노력의 결실이라고 말함. 또한 당지언론은 금번 OPEC 합의는 이라크의 승리이며, OPEC 가 과거 5년동안 하지못한것을 훗세인대통령이 수주만에 성취시켰다고 보도 함.

2. 이라크-쿠웨이트 회담합의

-이라크 정부대변인은 7.27 이집트 무바락대통령의 양국 순방 중재노력에 응하여 이라크-쿠웨이트간 분쟁해결을 위하여 사우디의 젯다에서 이라크의 IBRAHIM 혁명지도위 부의장과 쿠웨이트의 AL-SABAH 수상간의 회담 개최에 동의하였다고 발표함.

-동 대변인은 회의에 참석할 쿠웨이트 수상은 이라크에 가한 손해와 침략(HARM AND AGGRESSION)을 제거하고, 이라크의 합법적 권리를 만족시킬 준비가 되어있어야 한다고 촉구하고, '쿠웨이트는 어떠한 위협이나 BLACKMAIL 에도 굴복하지 않을것' 이라는 쿠웨이트 수상의 발언에 언급, 이라크는 위협이나 협박을 하지 않았으며 이라크에게 가해 진 손해와 침략을 솔직히 말하였을 뿐이라고 반박함.끝

(대사 최봉름-국장)

중아국   정문국   안기부

0012

PAGE 1   90.07.28   19:47 CG

외신 1과 통제관

외 무 부

종 별 : 긴 급

번 호 : BGW-0399

일 시 : 90 0802 1000

수 신 : 장 관(중근동, 정일, 건설부)

발 신 : 주 이라크 대사

제 목 : 이라크-쿠웨이트분쟁(응신 재무 53호)

1. 쿠웨이트 혁명 및 KLHL 국경 긴장사태에 관하여 주재국은 8.1.08:00 시 현사태를 다음과 같이 방송보도함

가. 이라크 전군에 경계령을 내림

나. 쿠웨이트 임시혁명위는 이라크 정부에 지지를 요청하였으며, 이라크 군대는 쿠웨이트 혁명을 지지함

이라크 혁명지도위는 쿠웨이트 임시혁명위의 지지를 위하여 외세의 개입을 우려하여 국경에 이라크 군대를 파견하였음

이라크 군대는 사태가 안정되고, 쿠웨이트 임시혁명위의 철수 요청이 있을때까지 국경에 주둔할 것임

다. 모든 이라크 국민의 해외여행을 중단시키고 계속 방송에 귀를 기울려줄 것을 요청함

2. 한편 당지에 진출해있는 건설업체 (현대, 삼성, 한양, 정우, 남광, 대림, 동아등)근로자 및 체류교민 약 700여명은 현재 아무런 이상이 없으며, 정상적인 업무에 종사하고 있음. 끝

(대사 최봉름-국장)

중아국   차관   1차보   2차보   국기국   정문국   정와대   총리실   안기부
건설부

0013

PAGE 1   90.08.02   15:41 WG

외신 1과 통제관

관리
번호 90/
1210

	분류번호	보존기간

발 신 전 보

WBG-0182   900802 1654 DY   종별: 긴급

번   호 : _____

수   신 : 주 이라크   대사.(총영사)

발   신 : 장 관 (중근동)

제   목 : 이라크, 쿠웨이트 침공

표제 사태 관련, 8.2.자 ~~로이타, AP 통신와~~ 이라크 혁명 평의회 성명
영문 TEXT 긴급 입수 송부 바라며, 동 사태 관련 귀관 평가 아울러 보고 바람. 끝.

(중동아프리카국장   이 두 복)

		보 안 통 제					
앙 고 재 일 90년8월2일 중근동	기안자 성명 乙		과 장	국 장 전결	차 관	장 관	

외신과통제

0014

외 무 부

종 별 : 긴 급

번 호 : BGW-0401 　　　　　　　　　　일 　시 : 90 0802 1100

수 신 : 장관(중근동,정일) 사본:주쿠웨이트대사:본부중계필

발 신 : 주 이라크 대사

제 목 : 이라크-쿠웨이트 사태(응신자료 54호)

　　　연:BGW-0399

　　1. 현사태관련 8.2 10:00 시 방송을 통하여 이라크정부는 아래와같이 발표함.

　　가. 전국경 봉쇄

　　나. 모든항공기의 이착륙금지

　　다. 전 장교는 단위 부대별로 집결하고, 61-66 년생 사이의 전 예비군 소집 통고

　　2. 주재국은 현 사태진전에 대하여 구체적 언급이 없으며, 이라크군의 쿠웨이트 국경 집결이외에 쿠웨이트의 침공 여부에 대하여 언급을 하지않고있음

　　3. 본 사태관련, 주쿠웨이트, 주미 및 주 유엔대사등의 보고 사본을 당관에 송부해주시기 건의함. 끝

　　(대사 최봉름-국장)　　　검토필(1991. 6.30)

　　예고:90.12.31 까지

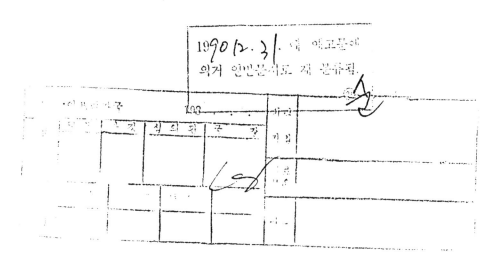

1990 12. 31. 예고문에 의거 일반문서로 재 분류됨

중아국　　장관　　차관　　1차보　　2차보　　정문국　　영교국　　정와대　　안기부
건설부　　노동부

0015

PAGE 1 　　　　　　　　　　　　　　　　　　　90.08.02　17:22
　　　　　　　　　　　　　　　　　　　　　　　외신 2과　통제관 DH

외 무 부

종 별 : 긴 급

번 호 : BGW-0404   일 시 : 90 0802 1500

수 신 : 장관(중근동,정일,기정)

발 신 : 주이라크대사

제 목 : 이라크-쿠웨이트 분쟁

연: BGW-0401

1. 대호 이라크 혁명지도위(RCC) 가 8.2.08:00방송(아랍어)을 통하여 발표한 내용 요지는다음과같음.(동 TEXT 는 당관에서 요약번역한것임)

THE KUWAITI TEMPORARY REVOLUTION ASKED THE GOVERNMENT OFTHE REPUBLIC OF IRAQ TO SUPPORT THEM, THE RCC RESPONDED TO THEIR WISH AND COOPERATE WITH THEM BY SENDING THE IRAQI ARMED FORCES TO STAY ON THE BOARDERS, FEARING FROM ANY FOREIGNINTERFERENCE, THE IRAQI ARMED FORCES WILL STAY IN KUWAIT'S BOARDERS UNTIL EVRYTHING IS SETTLED, AND IF THE KUWAITI TEMPORARY REVOLUTION ASKED TO WITHDRAW FROM ITS BOARDER.

2. 최근황, 금번 사태를 전후하여 주재국이 취한일련의 조치는 다음과같음

가. 7.31 주재국은 이스라엘의 공격 가능성에 대하여 새롭게 경고하면서 이라크를 공격할시 반드시 보복할것임을 천명함

나. 8.1(ASHOOR 종교휴일)이라크 국민들에게 이스라엘 침공에 대비, 긴급시 대피준비를 하고 방송에 귀를 기우리도록함

다. 방송을 통한 정부발표(이라크 국민의 해외여행금지, 국경봉쇄, 공항폐쇄, 예비군동원, 군편제등)이외에 사태진전에 관하여 일체보도가 없으며, 정규방송을 중단하고 계속정부발표 사항만을 반복함

라. 바그다드 시내는 종전과 마찬가지로 평온을 유지하고 있음

마. 8.2.14:40 이라크 방송은 쿠웨이트 임시 혁명군 발표를 인용, JABER 왕정은붕괴되고 혁명이 성공하였으며, 전 왕정하에 이라크에 가한 위해 및 양국 국경분쟁은 해결될 것이라고 보도함

바. 15:00 시 방송은 쿠웨이트 임시혁명군이 이라크. 형제에게 지원을 요청하고이에

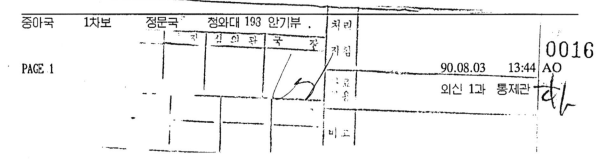

PAGE 1

응하여 군대를 쿠웨이트에 파견하였으며, 쿠웨이트를 방어하기위해 온 이라크 형제와 협력하도록 쿠웨이트 국민에게 요청하였다고 보도함. 또한방송은 쿠웨이트외세의 개입이 있을경우 이라크의 지원을 요청하였다함.끝

　　(대사 최봉름-국장)

외 무 부

종 별 : 긴급

번 호 : BGW-0405

일 시 : 90 0802 1600

수 신 : 장관(중근동)

발 신 : 주 이라크 대사

제 목 : 쿠웨이트,이라크 분쟁

연:BGW-0404

표제관련, 당관의 관찰및 평가를 다음 보고함

1. 이라크, 쿠웨이트분쟁 젯다협상 결렬에 불만을 느낀 이라크는 소위"쿠웨이트 임시혁명위"지원요청에 따라 이라크군을 국경에 파견했다고하였으나 치밀한사전계획(90.7 초 탱크 300 대,3 만명 국경배치설)하에 요소에 특공대를 침투,쿠웨이트 왕정을 전복하고 동침공의 명분을 은폐, 동혁명위 명의 포고령을 당지에서 발표하고있음

2. 금번사태에도 주재국 외무성간부와의 접촉이 불가능하며 대외교단 BRIEFING 도 없었음

3.B.O.PU(8.2 자)TOP 기사로"IRAQI-KUWAITI TALKS ON DISPUTE END WITH NO AGREEMENT"제하, HAMMADI 부수상은 쿠웨이트측의 신중함의 결여로 합의에 이르지 못했다고한 점으로보아 강경책이 아니고서는 소기의 목적을 달성할수 없다고판단, 계획된 실력행사를 단행한것으로 보임

4. 쿠웨이트왕정이 이라크군 무력지원하에 붕괴된 사실은 이라크로서는 득보다 실이더클것으로 평가됨. 즉, 사우디를 위시한 GCC 제국의 불안을 가중시키고 ACC 의 일원인 에집트의 입장을 난처하게 할뿐아니라, 최근 타결 가능성을 보이고있던 이.이 평화회담진행에도 큰 영향을 미칠것이며, 무력침공으로인한 국제사회의 비난을 면할수없고 아랍연맹제국의 단결을 자처해온 이라크의 위신추락으로 아랍의 세력균형이 재편성될것으로 분석됨. 끝

(대사 최봉름-차관)

예고:90.12.31

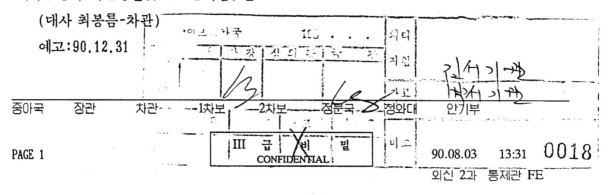

중아국　　장관　　　차관　　1차보　　2차보　　정문국　　청와대　　안기부

III 급 비 밀　　　비고　　　90.08.03　　13:31　　0018
CONFIDENTIAL

외신 2과　통제관 FE

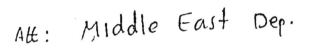

Att: Middle East Dep.

A STATEMENT

BY

THE REVOLUTION COMMAND COUNCIL

ISSUED ON AUGUST 2, 1990

The Revolution Command Council of the Republic of Iraq issued a statement, hereunder, the resume of the said statement ;

As everybody knows that the whole Arab world is united in its stand against treason and to defend itself against outsiders, but the Kuwaiti Ruler and his supporters stayed aside from the said principles, and particularly the principles that are supervising relations among the Arab states.

A revolution has taken place by the Kuwaitis themselves in which they toppled the Ruler of Kuwait and the clique surrounding him. These in charge of the revolution in Kuwait formed a free and interim government which asked the Iraqi government to extend its support to implement peace and security for the Kuwaiti people.

The Revolution Command Council of the Republic of Iraq responded to the Kuwaiti interim government's demand and saying that we will withdraw as soon as the situation comes to normal and upr 'he request by the Kuwaiti government. This will take no more than a few days or weeks.

The Revolution Command Council said that the whole Iraqi people with its military forces and popular army will stand beside Kuwait, and will defend it against any invasion or aggr 'on.

0019

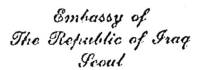

Embassy of
The Republic of Iraq
Seoul

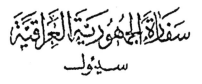

The position of the Government of the Republic of Iraq
on the recent development in Kuwait is as follows :

1. The events currently occuring in Kuwait are an internal
affair with which Iraq has no relation.

2. The Interim Free Government has asked Iraqi Government to
extend assistance for the maintenance of law and order
with a view to sparing the people of Kuwait any harm.
The Iraqi Government has decided to extend the assistance
requested on the basis of this consideration and non
other.

3. The Iraqi Government vigorously reaffirms that Iraq har-
bours no special objectives in Kuwait and is desirous of
establishing relations of fraternity and good neighbour-
liness with it.

4. It is up to the people of Kuwait themselves to determine
in the end their own affairs. The Iraqi forces will be
withdrawn as soon as the situation is settled down and as
soon as the Free Government of Kuwait has so wished. We
hope that this will be a matter of a few days or a few
weeks at the latest.

5. We reject any foreign interference in the current events.
Such interference will only aggravate the situation.

Iraq looks forward to seeing the situation restored
back to normal in Kuwait quickly and by the people of Kuwait
themselves without any foreign interference.

0020

관리 번호 90/1219

외 무 부

종 별 :

번 호 : BGW-0412

수 신 : 장관(중근동,정일) 사본:쿠웨이트대사

발 신 : 주 이라크 대사

제 목 : 이라크-쿠웨이트사태(응신자료 55호)

일 시 : 90 0803 1130

1. 이라크 정부는 동사태에 대하여 혁명지도위(RCC)COMMUNIQUE 를 봉하여 쿠웨이트 혁명은 성공적으로 이루어졌으며, AL-JABIR 왕정은 붕괴되었다고 발표함

-RCC COMMUNIQUE 는 쿠웨이트의 새정부 (주재국은 INTRIM FREE GOVERNMENT OF KUWAIT 로 표현)는 외세 침공에 대항하여 이라크에 군사원조를 요청하였으며, 이라크는 이에 대응하여 군대를 파견하였다고 발표함

-동 COMMUNIQUE 는 쿠웨이트가 자신의 문제를 스스로 결정하도록 맡겨두고, 사태가 정상화되면 군대를 철수시킬것이며, 그시기는 아마 수일내지 수주일내가 될것이라고 말함

-한편 주재국은 대통령 포고령에 따라 예비군 동원령을 내리고, 이라크 전역을 5 개 작전지역으로 편제하는 한편,8.2.10:00 시를 기하여 지상 국경및 영공을 폐쇄함

2. 주재국은 또한 소위 쿠웨이트 임시자유정부의 성명을 인용, 쿠웨이트 사태 및 동향을 다음과같이 보도함

-새임시정부는 AL-JABIR 국왕의 왕정을 축출하고 의회를 해산함으로 쿠웨이트의 정부 및 의회의 모든 권력을 인수하였으며, 안정이 회복되면 정부형태를 결정하게될 의회 선거를 실시하게될것임

-새정부는 AL-JABIR 왕정이 횡령한 막대한 재산을 쿠웨이트와 아랍국가........쿠웨이트 국민에게 공정하게 배분할 것임

-새정부 지도자들(특정인 명시없음)은 예상되는 외세의 개입을 막기위해 이라크에 도움을 요청하였음

-쿠웨이트는 무기한 봉금실시, 해상, 육상및 영공의 봉쇄와 함께 잠정적으로 쿠웨이트에 있는 내.외국인의 출입을 금지하는 조치를 취함

-현쿠웨이트 UN 대표및 아랍연맹대표는 더이상 쿠웨이트 정부를 대표하지 않으며

중아국   정문국

0021

타국가는 이들과 접촉하지 않도록 경고하고, 새정부에 의해 공식적으로 인정되지않은 쿠웨이트 대표의 약속은 이행되지 않을것임

3. 이라크정부는 부시미대통령이 취한 미국내의 이라크 자산 동결 조치를 비난하고, 이에대응하여 이라크의 대미 채무 지불을 동결한다고 8.2. 발표함. 재무장관대리는 미국이 이라크 자산동결 조치를 철회할때까지 대미 채무지불을 중지할것이라고 말하고, 경제협력관계가 악화되지는 않을것임을 시사함

4. 주재국 최근 동정

-당지 8.2 자 언론에는 동 사태에 대한 보도가 전혀 없었으며, 8.3 자 B.O. 지에는 REVOLUTION IN KUWAIT 제목하에 쿠웨이트 혁명정부의 성명 및 정부 성명만 보도하였을뿐, 외신 또는 국제사회의 반응 및 논평은 일체 게재하지 않고있음

-8.2 방송, TV 는 정규방송을 중단하고, 대통령 찬양과 군대 전부 장면을 방영하면서 중간에 정부발표문을 반복 보도함.(제 2 방송-영. 불어 포함 중단)

-이라크와 쿠웨이트는 같은 길을 가는 형제라고 말하면서 새 쿠웨이트 혁명정부를 적극 지지하는 관제집회를 바그다드및 지방도시에서 개최함.

-이라크 시민들에게 이스라엘 침공에 대비하여 대피준비를 하도록 알려주고있는등 평온을 유지하는 가운데 긴장감을 느낄수 있음. 끝

(대사 최봉름-국장)

예고:90.12.31

외 무 부

종 별 : 지 급

번 호 : BGW-0416   일 시 : 90 0804 0900

수 신 : 장 관(중근동,정일,기정,건설부,사본: 주쿠웨이트대사)

발 신 : 주 이라크 대사

제 목 : 이라크 군대 철수발표(응신자료 56호)

    주재국 방송은 8.4. 00:10 INTRIM FREE GOVERNMENT OF KUWAIT 의 요청에 따라 8.5(일)부터 이라크 군대가 쿠웨이트 영토에서 철수를 시작할것이라고 보도함. 이라크 군대의 철수 이유는 쿠웨이트 사태가 안정되었기 때문이라 하며, 동 내용이 반복 방송되고 있음. 끝

    (대사 최봉름-국장)

중아국	차관	1차보	2차보	정문국	안기부	건설부

wku → @sp.oh

PAGE 1   90.08.04   15:59 BB 0023

외신 1과 통제관

관리 90/
번호 1240

외 무 부

종 별 : 지 급

번 호 : BGW-0417   일 시 : 90 0804 1130

수 신 : 장관(중근동,정일,기정)

발 신 : 주 이라크 대사

제 목 : 이라크군 철수발표관련(응신자료 57호)

연: BGW-0416

1. 연호 이라크가 8.4 쿠웨이트로부터 이라크군 철수를 발표하면서도 AL-JABIR 국왕 및 왕족의 복귀는 허용하지 않겠다는 조건을 내걸고 있으며, 쿠웨이트 혁명정부 및 이라크군의 안전상태가 보장되는 조건하에서 철수할것으로 알려지고 있음

2. 동 이라크군 긴급 철수 이면에는 카이로 아랍외상회의에서 이라크 침공이 아랍제국의 지지를 받지 못했고, 특히 미.쏘 비난과 기타국제사회의 비난때문에 철수 시사를 한것으로 관측됨

3. 당지 보도는 요르단만이 아랍문제 대한 외세 개입 경고등 이라크에 호의적인 태도를 보였을뿐, ACC 회원국인 이집트, 예멘의 지지조차 얻지 못하고있는것으로 풀이됨. 끝

(대사 최봉름-국장)

예고:90.12.31

중아국   장관   차관   1차보   2차보   정문국   청와대   안기부

0024

외 무 부

종 별 : 지급

번 호 : BGW-0418

수 신 : 장관(중근동,정일,기정)

발 신 : 주 이라크 대사

제 목 : 사태관련 주재국동정(응신자료 58호)

일 시 : 90 0804 1130

쿠웨이트 침공사태와 관련 최근 주재국 사회변동 목격사항을 다음 보고함

1. 바그다드시내 큰호텔에서는 미.영. 불 서방외국인에 한해 예약을 환영하면서 기타 제 3 국 부숙자는 모두 퇴거 조치를 취하고있는바, 이는 이스라엘이나 미국보복 공격에 대비하는 인상임.

2. 바그다드시 주민에 대해서 도시외곽거주 연고자 거주지 또는 도시 외곽소재 호텔등으로 주재국인을 소개시키는 작업을 전개하고 있는바 이도 동보복 공격에 대응하는 조치로 보임

3. 주재국 각종 사회단체를 동원 쿠웨이트 침공을 지지하는 집회를 각지역및 기관별로 전개, 연대성을 고취하고있음

4. 금번 침공관련, 주재국 인테리계층의 반응은 냉담하며 이스라엘을 앞세운 미국의 군사적 보복을 두려워하고 있음을 엿볼수 있었으나, 8.4 철수 발표후 환영, 안도하는 기색임

5. 시내요소에 군.경을 증강배치 불심검문을 강화하고 당관을 포함 서방 제국대사관 출입자에 대해 크게 주목하고있음. 끝

(대사 최봉름-국장)

예고:90.12.31

중아국	장관	차관	1차보	2차보	정문국	정와대	안기부

외 무 부

종 별 : 지급

번 호 : BGW-0419   일 시 : 90 0804 1130

수 신 : 장관(중근동,정일,기정) (사본:주쿠웨이트대사-중계필)

발 신 : 주 이라크대사

제 목 : 이라크-쿠웨이트 사태(응신자료 59호)

　　1. 동 사태관련, 8.3 훗세인 요르단국왕이 주재국 방문하고, 또한 혁명지도위 IBRAHIM 부의장이 사우디를, RAMADHAN 제1 부수상이 예멘을 방문,(HAMADHI 부수상은 아랍연맹회의 참석을 위해 8.2 부터 카이로 방문중)한바, 이는 ACC 제국에 이라크 조치에 대한 설명과 사태 추이에 대한 협의를 위한것으로 관측됨

　　2. 특히 IBRAHIM 의 사우디방문 이유는 이라크 군대의 사우디 국경집결설을 직접 부인, 해명하기위한 것으로 사료되는바, 이라크는 공식적으로 동 군대의 사우디 국경집결설을 부인하고 이는 악의적이며 조작된것이라고 말함. 정부대변인은 이라크 군대의 쿠웨이트 진입은 쿠웨이트 혁명정부의 요청에 의한 것이라고 반복하고, 이라크와 사우디 및 다른 아랍국가와의 관계는 이라크-쿠웨이트 관계와 전혀 다르다고 설명함.

　　3. 동 사태관련 훗세인대통령이 8.5 젯다회의에 참석할것이라고 외신보도가 있으나, 이에 대해 현지에서의 공식 발표는 없음

　　4. 주재국은 8.3 집권 바스당 이름으로 성명을 발표, 쿠웨이트 사태는 국내문제이며 이라크 군대 진입은 걸프 및 인도양 함대에 동원령을 내리고 있는 미국이 쿠웨이트 사태에 개입하는것을 막기위한 조치였다고 말함

　　4. 동사태관련, 주재국 국회 8.4 긴급 소집함. 끝.

　　(대사 최봉름-국장)

　　예고:90.12.31

∨

중아국	장관	차관	1차보	2차보	정문국	청와대	안기부

0026

외 무 부

관리
번호 90/1238

종 별 : 지 급

번 호 : BGW-0421   일 시 : 90 0804 1340

수 신 : 장관(중근동,정일,기정) 사본:주쿠웨이트대사 ─관계됨

발 신 : 주 이라크대사

제 목 : 이라크.쿠웨이트 사태(응신자료 60호)

    1. 8.4 당지방송은 KUWAITI INTRIM REVOLUTION COMMUNIQUE NO.7 발표를 인용,
쿠웨이트 임시혁명위는 정규군을 지원하는 의용군(POPULAR ARMY)을 창설하기로
결정하였으며, 어떤 아랍국가 국민이라도 동의용병 참가희망시 수락할 것이라고
보도함

    2. 상기 의용군 창설결정은 8.5 이라크군의 철군시사와 결부된것으로, 쿠웨이트
임시혁명위가 소위 혁명후 3 일이 경과하였음에도 불구하고 동혁명 지도자조차 발표치
못하고 있는점을 미루어 이라크군 철수후 신뢰정권을 유지함에 있어 이라크군이
의용군으로 배후에서 조종토록 하는 방안을 강구하고 있는것으로 분석됨. 끝

    (대사 최봉름-국장)

    예고:90.12.31

중아국   장관   차관   1차보   2차보   정문국   청와대   안기부

0027

PAGE 1   90.08.04   19:26

                                                외신 2과 통제관 EZ

외 무 부

종 별 : 지 급

번 호 : BGW-0427

일 시 : 90 0805 1330

수 신 : 장관(중근동,정일)사본:주쿠웨이트대사

발 신 : 주이라크대사

제 목 : 이라크-쿠웨이트사태(응신자료 61호)

1. 쿠웨이트 임시혁명정부 조각발표

가. 8.4 쿠웨이트 임시혁명정부는 수상등 9명의 내각명단을 발표한바, 동명단은 아래와같음. (B.O.지등 당지 전언론보도)

- PRIME MINISTER AND COMMANDER-IN-CHIEF OF KUWAIT'S ARMEDFORCES,MINISTER OFDEFENCE AND ACTING MINISTER OFINTERIOR:COLONEL ALA HUSSEIN ALI

-FOREING MINISTER : LT.COLONEL WALID SAUD MOHAMMED ABDULLAH

-MINISTER OF OIL AND ACTING MINISTER OF FINANCE:LT.COLONELFUAD HUSSEIN AHMED

-MINISTER OF INFORMATION AND ACTINF MINISTER OFCOMMUNICATIONS:MAJOR FADHIL HAIDER AL-WAFIQI

-MINISTER OF PUBLIC HEALTH AND MINISTER OF HOUSING:MAJORMISHIL SAD AL-HADAB

-MINISTER OF LABOUR AND SOCIAL AFFAIRS AND ACTING MINISTEROF PUBLIC WORLD:MAJOR HUSSEIN ALI DEHAIMAN AL-SHAMMARI

-MINISTER OF EDUCATION AND ACTING MINISTER OF HIGHEREDUCATION:MAJOR NASSER MANSOUR AL-MANDEEL

-MINISTER OF JUSTICE AND LEGAL AFFAIRS AND ACTING MINISTEROF AWQAF AND ISLAMIC AFFAIRS:MAJOR ISSAM ABDUL MAJID HUSSEIN

-MINISTER OF TRADE,PLANNING AND ELECTRICITY:MAJOR YACOUBNMOHAMMED SHALLAL

나. 신임수상은 이라크의 즉각 지원에 대해 훗세인 대통령에게 감사의 전문을 보냄과 동시에, 쿠웨이트와 이라크는 이라크군의 단계적철수에 합의하였으며, 국경문제등에 관해서도 즉각 회담을 가질 준비가 되어있다고 말함.

중아국   1차보   정문국   청와대   안기부

0028

PAGE 1

90.08.05   20:40 AO

외신 1과 통제관

다.쿠웨이트 신정부의 첫포고는 대령 이상의 모든 현역군인을 퇴역시키는 조치를 취함

2.한편 쿠웨이트 POPULAR ARMY 창설과 관련하여 13만여명의 이라크인이 쿠웨이트 혁명을 지원하기위하여 자원하였다고함

3.캐로 아랍외상회의에 참석후 8.4 귀국한 HAMMADI 부수상은 이라크군대의 쿠웨이트 철수결의안은 전적으로 무효라고 말하면서, 동 결의안은 아랍연맹 헌장에 규정한 전원일치가 아니기때문에 법적 효력이 없고 또한 쿠웨이트 왕정이 붕괴되었으므로 실질적 의미가 없다고 말함

4.에멘공화국의 SALEH 대통령은 8.4 주재국방문, 훗세인대통령과 회담을 가진바, SALEH 대통령은 이라크 군대의 철수를 결정한 훗세인대통령에게 사의를 표하였으나, 이라크조치에 대한 지지발표는 없었음.끝

(대사 최봉름-국장)

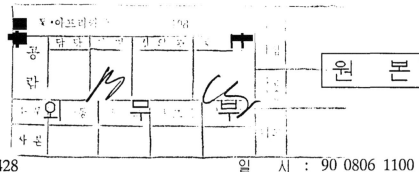

종 별 :

번 호 : BGW-0428

일 시 : 90 0806 1100

수 신 : 장 관 (중근동,정일,기정)

발 신 : 주 이라크 대사

제 목 : 이라크-쿠웨이트사태 (62호)

1. 이라크군 철수개시

-이라크군은 8.5 08:00 시부터 쿠웨이트로부터 단계적인 철수를 시작하였으며 8.7 에는 더많은 군대가 철수하게 될것이라고 이라크군 대변인이 발표함. 이라크군 철수는 쿠웨이트 사태가 평정됨에 따라 쿠임정의 요청에 따른 것이라고 말하면서도 철군 규모나 시한에 대한 언급은 없음

-철군이 단계적임을 전제로 하고 있으므로 가까운 시일내에 전면 철군은 기대하기 어려우며, 철군에 대한 보충으로 쿠웨이트 POPULAR ARMY (이라크 징집의 용군 투입)가 참가함으로 실질적으로 이라크는 쿠웨이트를 계속 장악할 것으로 판단됨

2. 이라크군 증강발표 혁명지도위는 8.5 외세의 개입이나 적대 행위에 단호히 대응할 것임을 경고하고, 새로 11개사단의 보강을 발표함. 새로운 11개 사단은 1개 기갑사단, 1개 기계화사단, 9개 보병사단이 될것이라함

3. 한편, 쿠웨이트 임시정부 외상의 발표를 인용, 다음과 같이 경고함

-쿠웨이트 및 이라크에 응징조치를 취하려는 국가들은 자국민과 그들의 재산이 쿠웨이트에 있다는 사실을 인식해야하며, 이들 국가의 침공시 대응방법을 강구할것임

-이라크 형제국과의 합의하에 쿠웨이트 국민이나 외국인드 이유를 불문하고 언제든지 육상을 통해 이라크로 가는것을 허용함.

-쿠임정은 쿠웨이트에 대해 적대적 태도를 보이는 국가와 외교단절및 대사관 폐쇄를 고려하고 있으며, 이들중 부패한 아랍국가도 포함됨

4. RAMADHAN 제1부수상 터키방문

8.5 터키를 방문 귀국한 RAMADHAN 제1부수상은 OZAL 대통령과의 회담에서 터키는 금번 사태에 대하여 중립을 유지할 것이라고 말한 것으로 보도됨. 동 부수상은 또한 쿠웨이트에 대한 침공은 이라크에 대한 침공으로 간주되며, 쿠웨이트 방어는

중아국 1차보 정문국 안기부

PAGE 1

90.08.07 02:29 FC

외신 1과 통제관

0030

바그다드를 방어하는 만큼 중요하게 생각한다고 말함

    5. 훗세인대통령은 금번사태와 관련, 쏘련및 중국 지도자에게 서한을 보냈다고 보도됨

    6. 훗세인대통령은 8.4 수단, 지브티, 카타르, 바레인, 리비아, 모리타니아, 알제리아, 튜니지아에 특사를 파견, 대통령 친서를 전달함.끝

    (대사 최봉름-국장)

외 무 부

종 별 :

번 호 : BGW-0431   일 시 : 90 0806 1400

수 신 : 장 관 (이두복 중동국장)

발 신 : 주 쿠웨이트 대사 (바그다드 경유)

제 목 : 업연

전문은 당관에 암호가 꼭 필요한 것만 보내고 나머지는 평문으로 해 주시기바람.끝

중아국

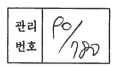

외　무　부

원　본

종　별 : 긴 급

번　호 : BGW-0434

일　시 : 90 0806 1000

수　신 : 장 관(중근동,정일,영재,기정)

발　신 : 주 이라크 대사

제　목 : 전황보고

　　1. 당지 주재국 언론은 이라크군의 쿠웨이트 철수를 보도하고 있으나 이는 사실이 아닌것으로 대부분의 외국인들이 믿고있음. 당관 권공사가 탐문한바 이라크 주력부대는 상금 철수치 않았으며 작전상 이라크 정규군이 새로히 모병한 의용군 (징집)과 현지 교대 한다고함. 이로 인해 당지 체류 외국인들의 인심이 크게 동요하고 있으며 특히 미국정부는 자국민의 최단시일 빠른 방법으로 출국을 권유하고 있다고 함

　　2. 한편 이라크군은 쿠웨이트에서 억류한 외국인 1,500 여명 (대부분의 미국인)을 이라크로 호송하여 시내 SHERATON HOTEL 등에 분산 보호하고 있는바, 이는 미국의 공격에 대비한 인질의 효과 및 미국 공격의 억제 효과를 노리고 있다함.

　　3. 또한 이라크의 터키 통과원유 파이프라인은 상금 절단되지 않고 있으나 미국 국방상의 사우디 방문으로 터키및 사우디 통과 원유라인이 절단될것으로 확실히 예견하고 있음

　　4. 당지 체류 미국인들의 이라크 철수계획은 사이프러스 기지에서 진행될 가능성이 있다고 하며 시기는 미측의 부분적 군사행동 직전에 단행 될것이라는 미확인 루머가 있음

　　5. 주재국 국제공항은 상금 개통되지 않고 있는바 8.6 부쉬대통령의 대주재국 강성 발언으로 인해 이라크 정부의 태도가 더욱 강경 일변도로 태도를 전환함에 따라 공항 폐쇄 조치는 더욱 장기화될 조짐으로 보임.끝

　　(대사 최봉름-차관)

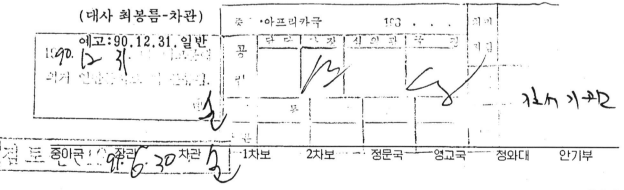

예고:90.12.31. 일반

PAGE 1

90.08.07　15:27 0033

외신 2과 통제관 DL

외 무 부

종 별 : 지 급

번 호 : BGW-0436   일 시 : 90 0807 1000

수 신 : 장 관(중근동,정일,기정)

발 신 : 주 이라크대사

제 목 : 훗세인대통령,미국개입 경고(응신자료 63호)

1. 훗세인대통령 8.6 당지 미국대사대리를 초치,걸프지역에 미국이 개입하지 말라고경고함

동 대통령은 걸프지역의 안전을 위태롭게 할미국의 행동에 대하여 경고하면서,이라크는 어떠한 압력이나 위협에 대항하여 희생할 각오가 되어 있다고 말함.동 대통령은 또한 이라크군의 사우디 국경 집결설에 대해,이를 부인하면서 이라크는 사우디와 형제 관계를 유지하고 있으며 양국은 국내문제 불간섭을 포함하는 불가침조약에 서명한 국가임을 상기시키면서,사우디의 안전은 이라크의 안보와 불가분의 관계에 있음을 강조함

2. 훗세인대통령은 8.6 이례적으로 외무성을 방문하고 외무성직원들을 격려함.끝
(대사 최봉름-국장)

중아국   1차보   정문국   안기부

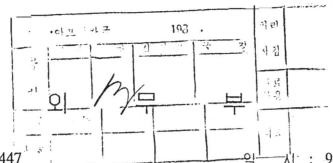

종   별 : 지 급

번   호 : BGW-0447   일   시 : 90 0808 1100

수   신 : 장 관 (중근동,정일,기정) 사본: 주쿠웨이트대사

발   신 : 주 이라크대사

제   목 : 이라크-쿠웨이트 사태 (응신자료 64호)

1. 훗세인 대통령, 쿠웨이트 임시정부 수상 접견

-쿠웨이트 임시정부의 ALA HUSSEIN ALI 수상은 8.7 훗세인 대통령을 면담하고, 혁명을 위하여 이라크군이 지원해 준데 대하여 감사를 표시함. 동수상은 제국주의의 꼭두각시인 전왕정의 전복은 쿠웨이트 국민이 기다렸던 것이라고 말하면서, 쿠웨이트와 이라크는 같은 운명으로 혁명초부터 외세를 막기위해 이라크의 보호를 요청한것은 당연하다고 부언함.

-이에대해 훗세인 대통령은 쿠웨이트에 진정한 주체성을 회복한 ALI 수상을 찬양하면서, 동수상에게 아랍영토를 침해하려는 어떠한 기도에도 단호히 대처할 것임을 확약함

2. 훗세인대통령 전쿠웨이트 왕정비난

8.8 이.이 전 승리 2주년을 기념하여 이라크 및 아랍국민에게 보내는 서한에서훗세인 대통령은 쿠웨이트 혁명을 찬양하면서, 국민을 탄압하고 재산을 강탈해간 전왕정은 쿠웨이트뿐만 아니라 모든 아랍국가에게 해를 입혔다고 말함.

3. 쿠웨이트 공화제선포

-쿠웨이트는 8.7 공화국을 선포 하였다고 쿠웨이트 임정 발표를 인용 보도함.

-한편 8.7 당지 보도는 쿠웨이트 신정부 수상의 발표를 인용, 쿠웨이트와 이라크 디나의 환율을 동등하게 적용한다고 발표함

4. 쿠웨이트에 대한 수출면세 조치

이라크 정부는 쿠웨이트에 수출되는 과일, 채소에 대하여 수출허가 및 관세를면제한다고 발표함. 무역성 대변인은 모든 수출업자 들에게 신속히 수출하도록촉구하였다고 말함. 끝

(대사 최봉름-국장)

√

중아국	차관	1차보	2차보	정문국	안기부

PAGE 1

90.08.08   21:05 DA

외신 1과 통제관   0035

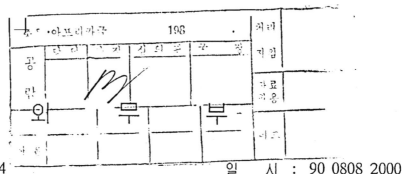

종 별 : 긴 급

번 호 : BGW-0454

일 시 : 90 0808 2000

수 신 : 장관(중근동,정일,기정) 사본:주쿠웨이트대사

발 신 : 주이라크대사

제 목 : 이라크. 쿠웨이트 합병발표

1. 금 8.8.18:30 현재 TV, 라디오방송을 통하여 이라크와 쿠웨이트가 합병하였다고 발표하고 간간이 시내에서 축포소리가 들리고 있음.

2. 동 쿠웨이트 자유임시정부에 포고및 R.C.C. 의 성명은 다음과같음.

A PROCLAMATION BY KUWAIT INTERIM FREE GOVDRNMENT TO THELEADERSHIP OF IRAQ:THE GENOUROUS PEOPLE OF IRAQ,DEARBROTHERS

,WHEN THE UPRISING TOOK PLACE IN KUWAIT,THE GOAL BFIT(AIM)WAS NOT TO OVERTHROW THE PREVIOUS REGIME BUT IT ISTHE HISTORICAL POINT AND AIM,TO CORRECT WHAT THE IMPERALISMHAS DONE,WHEN THEY DEPART KUWAIT FROM IRAQ,KUWAIT IS A PARTOF IRAQ,AS ALL KNEW THAT.

THE IMPERALISM BROUGHT AL-SUBAH AND MAKE THEM RULING KUWAITIN ORDER TO COOPERATE WITH THEM AGAINST THE ARAB NATION ANDTO WEAK THE ARAB NATION THROUGH AL-SUBAH FAMILY.

THE KUWAITI GOVERNMENT DECIDED TO CALL UPON THE PEOPLE OFIRAQ AND THEIR HERRO SADDAM HUSSEIN TO AGREE THAT KUWAIT TORETURN TO ITS HOME(GREAT IRAQ)

R.C.C.ANNOUNCEMENT

WITH RESPONSE TO THE KUWAITI GOVERNMENT,THE R.C.C.DECIDEDTHAT THE PART OF IRAQ(KUWAIT)TO RETURN TO IRAQ FOR EVER ANDALL THE LAWS AND APPLIED IN IRAQ WILL BE APPLIED ON IT.끝

(대사 최봉름-국장)

중아국   1차보   정문국   청와대   안기부

PAGE 1

90.08.09   01:23 DN

외신 1과 통제관   0036

외 무 부

종 별 : 긴 급

번 호 : BGW-0456   일 시 : 90 0809 1100

수 신 : 장 관 (중근동,정일,기정) 사본: 주쿠웨이트대사 (직송필)

발 신 : 주 이라크 대사

제 목 : 이라크.쿠웨이트 합병

    연: BGW-0454

    1. 8.8 이라크의 쿠웨이트 합병 선언후 소집된 국회 및 바스당 간부회의에서 훗세인대봉령은 쿠웨이트 임시정부의 합병요청을 수락하면서 이결정을 방해하는 자는 패배와 굴욕만 당할뿐이라고 경고함. 대봉령은 이 합병결정은 역사적 전환점으로 쿠웨이트가 원래의 소속으로 귀속되는 것이며, 이라크는 침략자도 아니며, 침략할 의사도 없다고 말함. 대봉령은 또한 이제 이라크와 쿠웨이트는 한국민 한나라이며, 하나의미래를 가지는 정상상태로 돌아갈 것으로 이 역사적 순간을 방해하려는 자는 패배가있을 뿐이며, 이결정에 대한 어떠한 타협도 배제함

    2. 8.8 대봉령 포고로 ALA HUSSEIN ALI 쿠웨이트 임시정부 수상을 이라크 부수상으로 임명되었음을 발표함. 또한 R.C.C 는 쿠웨이트 임시정부 각료 8명을 각료급의대봉령 보좌관 (ADVISOR) 으로 임명함.끝

    (대사 최봉름-국장)

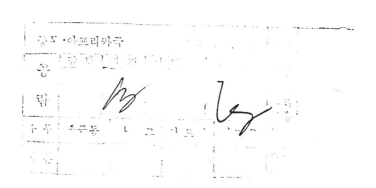

중아국   1차보   정문국   안기부   청와대

PAGE 1   90.08.09   17:02 FC 0037
                                                외신 1과 통제관

외 무 부

종 별 : 긴 급

번 호 : BGW-0464

일 시 : 90 0810 1100

수 신 : 장관(중근동,정일,기정)

발 신 : 주이라크대사

제 목 : 이라크-쿠웨이트사태(66호)

1.주재국, 쿠웨이트의 재정 COMMITMENT 준수ˇ 이라크는 8.9 쿠웨이트 합병후 쿠웨이트의 경제 및 재정에 관한 COMMITMENT 를 준수할것 이라고 발표함.

R.C.C 성명은 국가나 개인, 공공기관 및 개인회사에 대한 쿠웨이트의 모든 경제및 재정에 관한 COMMITMENT 를 완전히 준수하며, 이라크의 주권, 안보 및 국익에상충되지 않은한 쿠웨이트의 채권, 채무에 대해서도 적용된다고 말함

2.라마단 제1부수상 카이로향발

RAMADHAN 제1부수상은 AZIZ 부수상겸 외상, HAMMADI 부수상등을 대동, 긴급 아랍 정상회의에 참석차 8.9 카이로로 향발함. 제1부수상은 향발에 앞선 회견에서 이라크는 외세의 침략에 대해 대대적으로 보복할것이라고 말하면서, 외세 특히 미국에대항해서 아랍 지도자들이 공동입장을 취하여 주도록 촉구함.끝

(대사 최봉름-국장)

중아국   차관   1차보   정문국   안기부   청와대

PAGE 1

90.08.10   16:47 FA 0038

외신 1과 통제관

100 걸프 사태 쿠웨이트, 이라크 및 각국 경제 제재

외　무　부

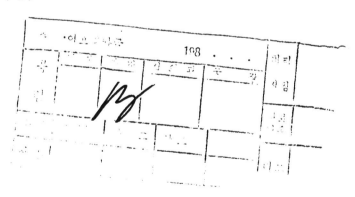

종　별 : 긴급

번　호 : BGW-0473　　　　　　　　　　　일　시 : 90 0811 1000

수　신 : 장 관 (중근동,정일,기정)

발　신 : 주 이라크 대사

제　목 : 훗세인 대통령 성전 선포(67호)

1. 훗세인 대통령은 8.10밤 전국라디오, TV 를 통한 연설에서 성지 MECCA 를 수호하고 신성한 아랍영토를 더럽히고 있는 외세의 총칼을 몰아내기위해 전아랍국민이 궐기할것을 촉 구함. 대통령은 이전쟁은 아랍이 기아와 가난,굴욕에서 벗어나기위한 해방전쟁이며,외세로 부터 아랍이 권리를 찾기위한 전쟁으로 아랍은 부패한 지도자들이 있을땅이 아니라고 선언함

2. 대통령은 또한 사우디가 미국에 군사기지를 제공키로한 조치는 의도적이고, 반이라크 행위로 이라크에 대한 침략의도를 분명히 했다고 말하면서,사우디 지도자들은수치스럽고 불명예스러운 행동을 하므로 그들 국민과 아랍을 조롱하였을 뿐만아니라,모하메드의 무덤이 있는 성지 메카와 신성한 아랍영토를 외세의 총칼아래둠으로 아랍및 이스람 국민에게 도전하고 있다고말함

3. 한편 이라크 전사회단체는 만약 미국이 이라크를 공격한다면 아랍영토 내외를불문하고 전세계에있는 미국의 INTEREST 를 공격하라고 아랍국민에게 호소함.끝

(대사 최봉름-국장)

중아국　정문국　안기부

PAGE 1

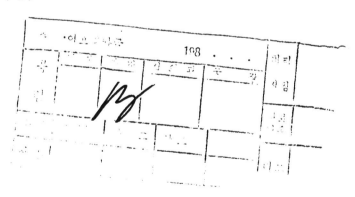

외 무 부

종 별 : 긴 급

번 호 : BGW-0477 　　　　　　　　　　　일 시 : 90 0811 1200

수 신 : 장 관 (중근동,정일,기정)

발 신 : 주 이라크 대사

제 목 : 이라크-쿠웨이트사태(69호)

　　1. 이라크 대화거부

　　-카이로 아랍정상회의에 참석한 라마단 제1부수상은 미국 및 서방국가군대가 걸프지역에 주둔하고있는한 이라크는 걸프위기 해결을 위한 논의를 거부하며, 정상회담 결의안은 이라크 및 몇몇 다른 아랍국가와의 협의(CONSULTATION) 가 없었으므로 수락을 거부 한다고 밝힘

　　-동　　　　　　부수상은　　　　　　정상회담을　　　　　　전후하여 알제리아,지부티,리비아,오만,수단,이집트,요르단 국가원수와 접촉을 가졌다고 보도됨

　　2. 당지 8.11 B.O 지에 의하면, 수만명의 아랍지원자들이 걸프에 전쟁이 일어난다면 이라크를 위해 자진해서 싸울것이라 보도하고, 40,000여명의 요르단인과 사우디 체류 2,000여명의 예멘인들이 이에 동참하고 있다고함

　　3. 훗세인 대통령은 8.10 연설에서 이집트 및 걸프만에 있는 아랍국민들에게 외국함대가 스에즈운하 및 홀므즈 해협을 봉과하지 못하도록 촉구함. 끝

　　(대사 최봉름-국장)

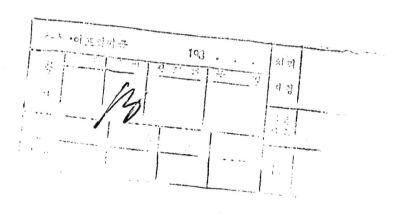

중아국　　정문국　　안기부

PAGE 1 　　　　　　　　　　　　　　　　　　　　90.08.11　　19:00　D0040

　　　　　　　　　　　　　　　　　　　　　　外信 1과 통제관

외 무 부

종 별 : 긴 급

번 호 : BGW-0483   일 시 : 90 0812 1100

수 신 : 장관(중근동,정일,기정)

발 신 : 주이라크대사

제 목 : 이라크-쿠웨이트사태(70호)

1. 홋세인 대통령은 8.11 RCC 및 바스당 합동회의를 주재하고,카이로 아랍정상회의 결과에 대하여 검토함

-동 회의에서 결의안은 다수의 지지를 받지못하였뿐만 아니라 그방법이 불법적이었으며, 아랍연맹국가중 9개국이 이라크를 지지하고 9개국은 반대하였으며,레바논,지브티,소말리아의 대표는 인정할수 없다고 언급함

-정상회의 참석후 8.11 귀국한 라마단 제1부수상은 동회의에서 토의에 앞서 먼저 사우디에서 외국군대의 철수를 요구하였으며,이라크는 공격에 대응할 힘이 있으며침략자는 후회하게 될것이라고 말하였다고 밝힘

2. 8.11 이라크 전역에서 반사우디 및 반이집트 군중집회가 있었으며,특히 사우디 대사관앞 시위에서 이라크 침략을 위해 외국군대를 끌어들이고 신성한 이스람 성지를 더럽히고있다고 비난함

3. 이라크는 8.11 오후 사우디 대공포가 사우디 상공을 비행중인 2대의 이라크 정찰기를 향해 발포하였다는 AFP 보도를 부인하고,이라크 전투기가 사우디 영공을출격한 사실이 없다고 말함

4. RCC 는 8.11 발표한 포고를 통해 식품의 매점매석, 암거래행위를 국가안보를위협하는 사보타쥐로 간주, 사형에 처하게될것 이라고함.끝

(대사 최봉름-국장)

종   별 : 긴 급

번   호 : BGW-0488   일   시 : 90 0813 0930

수   신 : 장 관(중근동,정일,기정)

발   신 : 주 이라크 대사

제   목 : 훗세인 대통령, 중동에서의 전 외국군 철수요구(71호)

훗세인대통령은 8.12 중동에서의 모든 점령군의 즉각적인 철수등 현사태와 관련한 새로운 방안을 제시한 바, 동 제의내용을 아래 보고함

①. 점령지에서의 이스라엘의 즉각적이고, 무조건의 철수와 시리아의 레바논에서의 철수및 이라크.이란간 철수

이러한 원칙하에 이라크의 쿠웨이트에서의 철수도 고려될것이며, 이라크에 대해 유엔안보리가 취한 제제조치는 모든 점령국에게 똑같이 적용되어야 함

②.미국 및 다른나라 군대의 사우디에서의 즉각적인 철수를 요구함.

사우디   주둔군은   아랍군대로   대체되어야   하며,   동   군대의 규모,국적,임무,주둔지역등은   유엔   후원하에   이라크,사우디간의   합의에   따라 결정되어야 함.

③.이라크에 대한 모든 제재 결의는 즉각 해제되어야 함.

우리의 제의에 대하여 미국 및 그동맹국들이 수락하지 않는다면, 우리는 강력히 저항할것임. 끝

(대사 최봉름-국장)

| 중아국 | 차관 | 1차보 | 2차보 | 정문국 | 안기부 | 통상국 |

외 무 부

종 별 : 긴 급

번 호 : BGW-0490   일 시 : 90 0813 1200

수 신 : 장 관(중근동,정일,기정)

발 신 : 주 이라크 대사

제 목 : 이라크-쿠웨이트 사태(72호)

1. AZIZ 외상은 8.12 기자회견에서 이라크는 최악의 사태에 대비하고 있으며, 침략에 따른 최악의 가능성도 고려하고 있다고 말함.

-동 외상은 이라크에 대한 침략 가능성은 크나 이라크는 이를 물리칠것이며, 미국및 그동맹국은 이라크가 이를 두려워할 나라가 아님을 알아야함

-아랍군대를 사우디에 파견하기로한 카이로 정상회담 결의는 이라크에 대한 미국의 침략구실을 준것으로, 전원일치의 합의가 없는 동 결의안은 무효임

-동결의안은 이집트의 무바락 대통령이 만든 시나리오에 불과하며, 동 결의안에반대한 국가에 대하여 이야기할 기회도 주지 않았음

- ACC 장래문제에 대해 이야기 하는것은 아직 시기상조이나, '반이라크 제국주의자의 음모에 가담하고 있는 이집트 정권과 어떻게 협력할수 있는가'라고 반문함.

-이라크에 있는 모든 외국인은 안전하며, 외국인을 보호하기 위한 임시 예방 조치를 취하고 있음

2. 훗세인 대통령은 8.12 성전에서의 여성의 경제적 역할을 강조하고, 가게비용을 줄이고 식품의 사제기를 자제하여 줄것을 이라크 전여성에게 호소함. 끝

(대사 최봉름-국장)

중아국   차관   1차보   2차보   통상국   정문국   안기부   대책반

0043

PAGE 1   90.08.13   18:34 BB

외신 1과 통제관

외 무 부

종 별 : 긴 급

번 호 : BGW-0498

일 시 : 90 0814 1000

수 신 : 장 관(중근동,정일,기정)

발 신 : 주 이라크 대사

제 목 : 이라크-쿠웨이트사태(73호)

1. AZIZ 외상은 훗세인 대통령의 8.12 제의에 대한 미국의 즉각적인 거부에 대하여, 이스라엘의 팔레스타인 및 아랍영토 점령에는 침묵을 지키면서, 이라크에 대해 불공정한 제재조치를 결의한 것은 지역및 국제문제 처리에 있어서 미국의 2중적 태도를 보여준것이라고 비난하고, 이라크가 사우디에 대해 공격태세를 갖추가 있다는 주장을 다시한번 부인함.

2. 주재국 정부는 8.13 터키를 공격할 준비를하고 있다는 보도를 완강히 부인하고, 이는 반이라크 국제음로라고 말함. 한편 HAMDOUN 외무차관은 당지주재 터키대사를 외무성으로 초치, 터키 전부기가 북부 이라크 영공을 침범한데 대한 항의 각서를 진달하고 터키전부기가 이라크 영공 5 KM 까지 침부하였다고 말함

3. 이라크 중앙은행은 8.13 이라크와 쿠웨이트 디나는 모든 상거래나 정부기관에서 폭같이 취급될 것이라고 발표함

4. 주재국은 아랍연맹본부를 뷰니스에서 카이로로 옮기는 것을 반대한다고 아지즈외상이 밝힘.끝

(대사 최봉름-국장)

중아국   차관   1차보   2차보   정문국   안기부   통상국   대책반

90.08.14   15:43 WG   0044

외신 1과 통제관

외 무 부

종 별 : 지 급

번 호 : BGW-0519   일 시 : 90 0816 1630

수 신 : 장 관(중근동,정일)

발 신 : 주 이라크 대사

제 목 : 이라크 대이란 평화제의(응신자료 75호)

1. 훗세인 대통의 8.15 대이란 평화제의에 대하여 이란측은 환영을 표시하였다고 하면서, 이라크는 동제의에 대한 호의의 표시로 일방적으로 8.17 부터 국경에서의 이라크 군대철수 개시와 함께 수천명의 이란포로를 석방할것 이라고 발표함

2. 동평화제의 수락으로 이.이 국경에 배치된 이라크의 30 사단 병력이 사우디 국경으로 이동배치가 가능하게 되었다고 보도됨

3. 본 이.이 평화협상 타결은 이라크의 쿠웨이트 침공이전에 합의한바 있으며 구체합의를 위한 실무회담을 거쳐 8.16 종결 발표한것임. 따라서 이라크 정부는 대이란 관계를 거의 전부 양보하는 조건으로 종결한후 쿠웨이트 침공을 감행한 것으로 평가됨. 끝

(대사 최봉름-국장)

예고:90.12.31.까지

1990.12.31. 에 예고문에 의거
일반문서로 재분류됨

중아국 대책반	장관	차관	1차보	2차보	통상국	정문국	청와대	안기부
PAGE 1	공람	통상국	접수일	담 당	과 장	국 장	차관보	차 관	장 관

담 당 | 과 장 | 국 장 | 차관보 | 차 관 | 장 관

✓

90.08.17   00:30 0045
외신 2과 통제관 DL

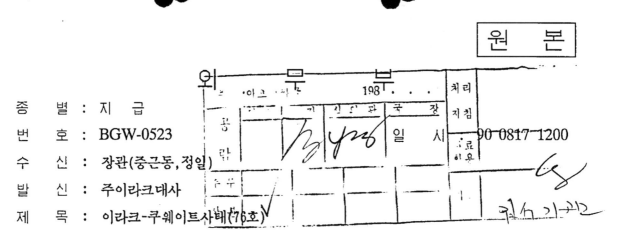

종　별 : 지　급
번　호 : BGW-0523
수　신 : 장관(중근동,정일)
발　신 : 주이라크대사
제　목 : 이라크-쿠웨이트사태(76호)

　　1.훗세인대통령의 부시미대통령에게 공개서한 발송
　　훗세인대통령은 8.16 전국 방송을 통하여 부시미대통령에게 보내는 공개서한을 발표하면서, '거짓말쟁이는 내가 아니고, 부시대통령이 거짓말하고 사실을 왜곡하고 있다'고 맹렬히 비난한바, 동 공개서한 요지아래 보고함
　　-나는 젯다회담때까지 쿠웨이트에 무력을 사용하지 않겠다고 무바락대통령에게 약속하지않았으며, 회담 실패후까지도 무력사용을 하지않았음
　　-미국을 위해 봉사하고, 미국의 명령에 복종하는 아랍지도자들은 아랍인을 대표할수없다.
　　-부시는 그의 침략군이 패배한다면 자신의 위치를 잃게될 것임
　　-쿠웨이트로부터 이라크군의 철수를 강요하기 위해 사우디에 미군을 투입하고 있다고하는데, 만약 이라크가 남미에있는 미군철수를 요구한다면 어떻게 대답하겠는가
　　-아랍및 이스람국민들은 믿음과 성지, 그리고 국민의 명예를 지키기위해 모든 희생을 감수할 것이며, 미국은 패배할 것임
　　2.이란포로 석방개시
　　주재국 대통령실은 금 8.17 2,000명의 이란포로를 석방할 것이며, 장기억류자가 우선적으로 석방될 것이라고 발표함. 당지 ICRC 대표는 2,000명의 일괄 석방처리에 어려움이 있으며 하루 1,000명 정도의 석방수속이 가능하다고 말하고있음
　　3.훗세인대통령은 8.16 군사령관회의를 주재하고 8.17부터 5일이내 점령한 이란영토에서의 이라크군 철수계획에 관하여 협의함.
　　4.이라크공군은 8.17 성지를 점령하기위해 참가하고 있는 모든 외국조종사들에게 이라크영공을 침해하면 격추될 것이라고 경고함.
　　5.주재국 정부대변인은 바그다드가 비상사태하에있으며, 탱크및 장갑차가 거리에

중아국　　1차보　　2차보　　　정문국　　안기부　　　대책반

0046

90.08.17　　21:14 CG
외신 1과　통제관

주둔해있고 군부대가 정부청사에 포진되어있다는 쏘련 TASS 통신 보도를
전적으로부인함. 당관 관찰로는 바그다드시가 비상사태하에 있으나 탱크가 정부청사를
점령하고 있지는 않음.끝

   (대사 최봉름-국장)

외 무 부

종 별 : 지 급
번 호 : BGW-0530
일 시 : 90 0818 1100
수 신 : 장 관 (중근동,정일)
발 신 : 주 이라크 대사
제 목 : 전쟁포로 송환 (77호)

　　　이라크는 8.17 이란군 포로 1,000명을 이라크 북부모슬에서 바그다드경우,
KHOSRAWI 국경을 통하여 이란측에 인도함. 이라크당국은 앞으로 매일 2,000명씩
송환하기를바라고 있으나 현 19명의 ICRC 대표로서는 동인원의 송환절차를 처리하는데
어려움이 있어 당분간 매일 1,000명씩 송환하게 될것이라 함. 이에 대응하여
이란당국도 이라크 포로 1진을 이라크에 송한하기 위해 국경지대로 인도되었다고
말하고 있으나 석방될 포로규모에 대해서는 언급이 없음.끝

　　　(대사 최봉름-국장)

중아국　　1차보　　　정문국　　안기부　　대책반　통상국　2차실　차관

0048
90.08.18　　18:24 FC

외신 1과 통제관

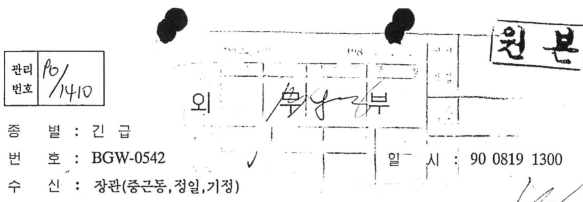

외   무 상 랑 부

종   별 : 긴 급

번   호 : BGW-0542   일   시 : 90 0819 1300

수   신 : 장관(중근동,정일,기정)

발   신 : 주 이라크 대사

제   목 : 체류외국인 인질화(78호)

1. 외국인에대한 식량공급 제환

-주재국은 이라크에 대한 봉쇄조치로 인하여 야기된 식량부족등 고통을 체류외국인도 이라크국민과 똑같이 감사하여야한다고 말함

-노동사회성은 8.18 성명을 발표, 이라크체류 외국인및 전세계 인권단체에 식량확보를위한 봉쇄조치 해제를 요구하면서, 식량과 의약품이 반이라크 무기로 사용되고있다고 비난함. 동 성명은 또한 식량배급의 우선순위는 군인과 근로자들에게 두게될것이며 외국인에 대한 특별배려는 없을것이라고 말함

2. 국회의장의 외국인 인질화 발언

가. 주재국 SALEH 국회의장은 8.17 성명을 통해 이라크가 침략전쟁의 위협하에 있는한 이라크에 적대행위를 하고있는 국가의 국민들은 그대로 이라크에 남아있어야 할것이라고 천명함. 동 의장은 서구는 역사상 전례없이 이라크 국민들을 아사시키려는 전쟁을 시작하려 하고있다고하고 이라크가 전쟁의 위협을 받고있는한, 침략국가 국민들을 억류하기로 하였으며, 이러한 조치는 침략의 위험이 제거된다는 확실한 보장이 있을때까지 유효할것이라고 말함

3. 평가

동 국회의장의 성명은 이라크 국민의 이름으로 발표된바, 아직정부의 공식입장 표명은 없으나, 동의장 발언으로 외국인에 대한 일질화 방침은 명백히 들어났음. 이는 체류외국인에대한 식량공급 제한과 함께 서방에 대한 최후의 저항무기로서 만약 이라크에 대한 침략이 감행될경우 외국인에 대한 신변에 위해가 가해질 가능성도 배제할수 없을것으로 보여짐.끝

(대사 최봉름-국장)

예고:90.12.31

중아국	장관	차관	1차보	2차보	정문국	청와대	안기부	대책반

PAGE 1   90.08.19   23:28   0049

발 신 전 보

분류번호	보존기간

WBG-0294   900820 1643 FA

번   호 :

종별 :

수   신 : 주   수신처 참조 대사.총영사

WSB -0341	WAE -0170
WYM -0184	WIR -0278
WTU -0386	WCA -0303

발   신 : 장   관   (중근동)

제   목 : 이라크.쿠웨이트 사태

　　　　1. 이라크측이 서방국민의 인질 가능성을 공언하고 다국적 지상군 배치 및 해안 봉쇄망 구축으로 양측의 전부 배치가 완료된 것으로 걸프 사태는 새로운 국면을 맞고 있는 것으로 분석됨. (8.20 자 동아일보는 "미.중동 전면전 불가피" 라는 썬데이 타임쓰 기사를 전재함)

　　　　2. 이러한 군사 대치 상황에서 이라크측이 취할 가능성이 있는 선택 (OPTION)을 중심으로 향후 단기 전망을 주재국 정부 포함 다각적으로 파악 보고 바람. 끝.

　　　　　　　　　　　　　　　　　(중동아프리카국장　　이 두 복)

수신처 : 주 이라크, 사우디, UAE, 예멘, 이란, 터키 대사
　　　　　주 카이로 총영사

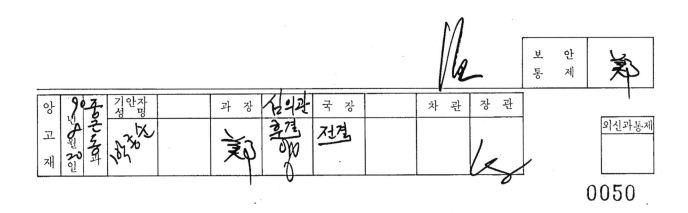

0050

외 무 부

종 별 : 지급

번 호 : BGW-0547   일 시 : 90 0820 1100

수 신 : 장관(중근동,정일)

발 신 : 주 이라크 대사

제 목 : 훗세인대통령,외국인인질화선어(79호)

1. 훗세인 대통령은 8.19 이라크 및 쿠웨이트에 체류하고있는 외국인에게 보낸 공개 서한에서 걸프 지역에서의 미국등 서방군대의 철수와 이라크에 대한 봉쇄 해제를 제의하면서, 이제의가 수락 된다면 외국인은 즉시 출국이 허용 될것이라고 발표함. 동 대통령은 또한 이라크는 사우디를 공격하지 않을 것이며, 사우디도 이라크를 공격하지 않는다는 안보리 보장을 요구하면서, 외국 군대의 사우디 철수일정은 사우디 군사 개입에 소요된 시한을 초과해서는 안된다는 조건을 제시함

2. 동 대통령은 동 서한은 "이라크 국민들은 이라크에 대한 위해가 제거될때 까지 외국인을 억류하기로 결정 하였다는" 8.17 국회의장 성명을 공식화한것으로 상기 제의가 수락된다면 자신의 헌법상의 권한을 사용하여 외국인이 이라크를 떠날수 있도록 하겠다고 강조함. 끝

(대사 최봉름-국장)

예고:90.12.31

1990.12.31. 에 예고문에 의거
일반문서로 재분류됨

중아국   차관   1차보   2차보   통상국   정문국   정와대   안기부   대책반

외 무 부

종 별 : 긴 급

번 호 : BGW-0549　　　　　　　　　　일 시 : 90 0820 1300

수 신 : 장관(중근동,정일,기정)

발 신 : 주이라크대사

제 목 : 이라크-쿠웨이트사태(80호)

1. 쿠웨이트 체류외국인 집결 명령

주재국 내무성은 8.19 쿠웨이트에 체류하고있는 서방국가 및 호주국민들에게 HYATTREGENCY,MERIDIAN,INTERNATIONAL 호텔에 집결하도록 요구하였다고 발표함. 동내무성 대변인은 이러한 조치는 외국인의 안전을 위한 것으로, 이에 응하지 않은 동국적외국인들은 적대적인 ELEMENTS에 의해 생길 위험에 대해 전적으로 책임을져야할 것이라고 경고함

2. 일부 서방국가 국민의 출국허용

주재국 SALEH 국회의장은 8.19 걸프지역에 군대를 파견하지않고 또 무기를 공급하지않은 국가인 오지리,스웨덴,스위스,핀랜드,폴투갈 국민에 대하여는 우호의 표시로출국을 허용키로 하였다고 발표함.

동의장은 또한 앞으로 식량,의약품및 일반상품의 대이라크 수출제재 조치에 대한 태도여하에 따라 추가로 일부 국가국민의 출국을 허용하게될 것이라고 밝힘

3. 쿠웨이트 전왕정 가족 재산압류

RCC 는 쿠웨이트 전왕정의 가족및 각료들의 동산,부동산등 일체의 재산을 압류하였다고 발표함. RCC 포고는 63명의 전왕정 가족및 각료들의 재산압류에는 이라크(쿠웨이트) 국내외에있는 모든 재산이 포함된다고함. 끝

(대사 최봉름-국장)

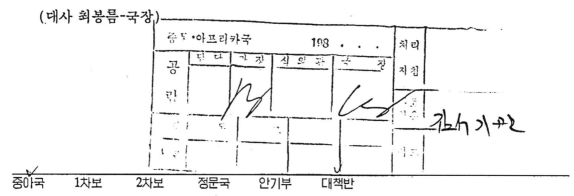

| 중아국 | 1차보 | 2차보 | 정문국 | 안기부 | 대책반 |

외 무 부

종 별 : 긴 급

번 호 : BGW-0558

수 신 : 장관(중근동,정일)

발 신 : 주 이라크 대사

제 목 : 외국인 인질화(81호)

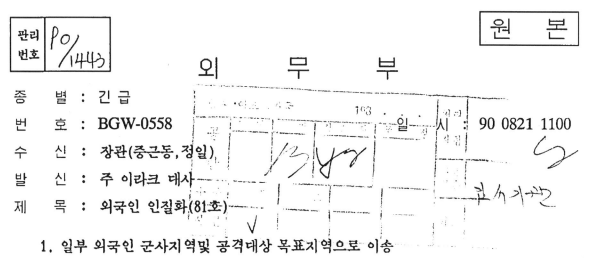

일 시 : 90 0821 1100

1. 일부 외국인 군사지역및 공격대상 목표지역으로 이송

-주재국 국회는 8.20 일부 외국인들이 군사지역 또는 공격목표의 대상이 되는 군사시설및 기타 중요시설지역으로 이송되었다고 발표함. 그러나 동 외국인의수자나 국적에 관하여는 전혀 언급이 없음

-SALEH 국회의장은 이라크에 억류되어있는 외국인은 이라크 국민의 보호하에 안전하며, 억류기간이 장기간되지 않기를 바란다고 부언하면서, 2 차대전중 미국이 10 만명의 일본인을 일본의 공격으로부터 보호하기위해 수용소에 억류시킨사실을 상기시킴

2. 외국인에 대한 은신처 제공 엄금 명령

-이라크 정부는 외국인에게 은신처를 제공하는 사람은 국적을 불문하고 엄벌에 처할것이라고 발표함

-내무성은 8.20 성명에서 이라크에 입국한 모든 외국인은 주소및 방문목적을 신고해야하며, 관계당국에 신고하지 않고 은신처를 제공해주는것은 위법이며,이법은 이라크는 물론 쿠웨이트에도 적용된다고 발표함

3. 한편 국회는 걸프지역에 군대를 파견하지 않기로 결정한 아르헨티나 정부에 대한 감사의 표시로 아르헨티나 국민의 출국을 허용한다고 발표함

4. 주재국 외무성은 8.19 전외교단에 대하여 출국을 허용한다고 말한바있으나, 현재까지 동 방침에 대한 외무성 공식발표는 없고, 국가에 따라 출국을 제한할것으로 보임.따라서 상황변화에따라 아국외교단의 출국도 다시 제한할 가능성 을 배제할수 없으며, 8.20 현재 사실상 미국외교관의 출국을 허용치않고 있는것으로 탐문됨. 끝

(대사 최봉름-국장)

예고:90.12.31

중아국 대책반	장관	차관	1차보	2차보	정문국	영고국	청와대	안기부

0053

Embassy of
The Republic of Iraq
Seoul

NO. 28-90   # PRESS RELEASE   *22/8/1990*

IRAQ READY TO TALK TO U.S.,
SAYS FOREIGN MINISTER

Iraqi Deputy Premier and Foreign Minister Mr. Tareq Aziz told a news conference in the Jordanian capital of Amman on Tuesday, August 21st, 1990, Baghdad was offering to hold talks with the United States on the Gulf crisis.

"We are ready to discuss the situation in the Gulf and other situations... If they are ready to talk, we are ready to talk." Aziz said.

"We told the U.S. Charge d'Affaires yesterday evening, 'we are ready to talk to you, if you want'," Mr. Aziz said. He did not say if the United States had responded.

Aziz said Americans and some Westerners hosted by Iraq were not hostages but guests of the Iraqi people who could contribute to a peaceful solution to the crisis.

"They are not hostages. I am sorry Mr. Bush used this word for the situation of those people." he said.

"We would like to keep them as guests for a while to live with our people and they might contribute to a great cause, that is peace, to prevent the belligerent policy of the United States."

Aziz said there was no need for the United States to send troops to Saudi Arabia, because Iraq was not going to attack.

"There is no aggression and we are ready to provide guarantees on a bilateral basis or under the Arab League." he said.

"This deployment of U.S. forces aims at waging a war of aggression against Iraq which would be faced by a brave Iraqi counter-aggression." he added.

"The Iraqi people will not yield to U.S. pressure. We will fight and the fight will be bloody to us and to them. If the U.S. commits this crime, it will be the gravest in history and in American history," he said.

"So if a number of people can contribute, then they are not hostages. We have not asked for money. We are hosting them with families in Iraq." Mr. Aziz said.

The Iraqi Foreign Minister is on a visit to Jordan, during which he met King Hussein and Foreign Minister Marwan Qassem.

Mr. Aziz on Tuesday delivered a letter from President Hussein to the Jordanian Monarch dealing with bilateral relations and the latest developments in the region.

0054

Embassy of
The Republic of Iraq
Seoul

سَفَارَةُ الجُمهُورِيَّةِ العِرَاقِيَّةِ
سِيؤُل

NO. 29-90   PRESS RELEASE   22/8/1990

PRESIDENT SADDAM HUSSEIN, ON TUESDAY (AUGUST 21, 1990) ADDRESSED AN OPEN LETTER TO THE U.S. PRESIDENT GEORGE BUSH.

PRESIDENT SADDAM HUSSEIN HAS SAID ONCE AGAIN THE AMERICAN PRESIDENT BUSH ADDRESSES THE AMERICANS BY TWISTING THE WORDS AND CONCEALING THE MOTIVES OR PART OF THEM, AND MIXING THE CAUSES WITH THE RESULTS.

IN HIS ADDRESS ON TUESDAY (AUGUST 21, 1990) BEFORE THE AMERICAN VETERANS HE HAS TACKLED THE SUBJECT OF THE AMERICANS PRESENT IN IRAQ AND CONCENTRATED ON CONSIDERING THEM HOSTAGES DESPITE THAT THE STATEMENTS VOICED BY THE IRAQIS HAVE CLARIFIED WITHOUT ANY DOUBT THAT THE AMERICANS HERE ARE A RESULT OF A REAL AGGRESSION THAT THE BEFELL THE ARAB NATION AND IRAQ, AND THAT THE PARTIES CARRYING OUT THIS AGGRESSION IS PRESIDENT BUSH HIMSELF AND HIS ALLY THATCHER.

IF THE AGGRESSION HAS NOT TAKEN PLACE AND PRESIDENT BUSH HAS CONSIDERED THE INTEREST OF THE AMERICAN PEOPLE AND THE AMERICAN CITIZEN PRACTICALLY, THERE WILL HAVE NOT HAPPENED NEITHER TO THE AMERICAN NOR TO OTHERS WHAT HAS ACTUALLY OCCURRED.

NONTHELESS WHAT HAS HAPPENED TO THEM UP TILL NOW IS THE MORE MODERATE FORMULA OF DEALING THAT HAD BEEN DICTATED UNDER FORCED CIRCUMSTANCES EVEN ACCORDING TO THE AMERICAN CALCULATIONS THEMSELVES, HOW IS THAT?

PRESIDENT BUSH KNOWS, OR I PRESUME HE KNOWS, THAT AMERICA DURING THE WORLD WAR II HAS RETAINED TENS OF THOUSANDS OF ITS AMERICAN NATIONALS MERELY BECAUSE THEY WERE OF JAPANESE DESCENT. AND IN THIS ACT THE U.S HAS DEPENDED ON THE RULE OF AVOIDING THE BIGGER HARM BY THE LESSER OR SMALLER ONE.

IF THIS PRECEDENT WAS PRESENT AND REGISTERED IN THE U.S RECORD BESIDES OTHERS CONTAINED IN THE HUMAN RECORD, DOES NOT THAT BE CONSIDERED A KIND OF RACIAL DISCRIMINATION WHEN CONSIDERING WHAT IS PERMITTED FOR OTHER STATES, INCLUDING AMERICA, NOT TO BE ALLOWED FOR THE ARABS INCLUDING THE IRAQIS? HOWEVER, WHAT HAS HAPPENED WAS ONE OF THE FORCED FORMS NOT A CHOICE FROM AMONG MANY OPTIONS, AND WE ARE FEELING SORRY FOR ITS HAPPENING.

NON-ALLOWING SOME FOREIGNERS TO TRAVEL IS NOT TAKEN OUT OF REVENGE BUT TO STAVE OFF A CRIME OF AGGRESSION PRESIDENT BUSH INTENDS TO COMMIT AGAINST THE PEOPLE OF IRAQ AFTER HIS CRIME OF OCCUPYING THE LAND OF MECCA AND THE SHRINE OF THE PROPHET.

0055

AND WOULD THIS CRIME HAVE BEEN COMMITTED A BIG CATASTROPHE WOULD HAVE BEFALLEN NOT ONLY THE REGION BUT RATHER THE WORLD.

2

PRESIDENT SADDAM HUSSEIN FURTHER SAID THEN PRESIDENT BUSH
MAINTAINS TO SPEAK ABOUT THE OUTLAWS AND COMPARES,BY A CLEAR
IMPLICATION, OF HIS PURPOSE, BETWEEN IRAQ AND THE MAN REPRESENTING IT
AND HITLER, FORGETTING THAT ALL THESE DESCRIPTIONS ARE FIT TO BE
APPLIED TO HIM BECAUSE IRAQ DID NOT DESPATCH ITS FLEETS AND WAR
PLANES TO LAUNCH AN AGGRESSION ON AMERICA AND EUROPE AND THAT
PRESIDENT BUSH AND THOSE WHO FOLLOWED HIM TO THE ABYSS ARE THEMSELVES
WHO HAVE SENT THEIR NAVY VESSELS AND WARPLANES AND HAVE COME AS
INVADERS TO OUR REGION WITH THE OBJECTIVE OF MURDERING OUR PEOPLE AND
ROBBING THEIR HUMANITY AFTER DESECRATING THEIR SANCTITIES.

PRESIDENT HUSSEIN QUESTIONS IN HIS LETTER WHETHER THERE IS ANY
DOUBT REGARDING IDENTICALITY OF THESE DESCRIPTIONS WITH THOSE OF
BUSH'S WHEN HE ENDEAVOURS TO IGNITE A WAR THAT WOULD SET THE WHOLE
WORLD ABLAZE.

ARE THERE MORE PROVING INDICATIONS THAN HIS DISREGARD OF ALL
INITAITIVES AND RESOLUTIONS THAT WE HAVE PUT FORWARD WHETHER WITH
REGARD TO THE ESSENCE OF THE PROBLEM OR REGARDING THE SUBJECT OF THE
FOREIGNERS WHO CONSTITUTE AN OUTCOME OF THE ORIGINAL PROBLEM?

IT IS OF MISCONDUCT AND RATHER LACK OF WISDOM AND JUDGEMENT THAT
THE WHITE HOUSE REJECTS OUR INITIATIVE ON AUGUST 12, 1990 JUST A FEW
HOURS AFTER ITS BROADCAST ON THE AIR AND BEFORE PRESIDENT BUSH
BOTHERS HIMSELF TO SEND FOR THE OFFICIAL TEXT AS PRECAUTION THAT THE
TRANSLATION MIGHT BE INACCURATE OR SOME SENTENCES WERE RATHER
INCOMPLETE,FOR ANY TECHNICAL REASON, IS THIS PERMISSIBLE MR PRESIDENT
OF THE UNITED STATES OF AMERICA?

HE WHO WANTS NOT TO BE DESCRIBED BY HISTORY WITH THE BAD
DESCRIPTIONS OF HITLER MUST CAREFULLY SEARCH FOR OPPORTUNITIES OF
PEACE AND NOT HASTEN ARRANGEMENTS OF THE WAR AND WHAT WE HAVE
PROPOSED IN OUR INITIATIVE ON AUGSUT 12, 1990 AND IN OUR MESSAGE TO
THE FOREIGN FAMILIES WHOM THE NATIONAL ASSEMBLY HAS DECIDED TO HOST,
CONSTITUTE THE APPARENT PATH TO HIM WHO WANTS TO BE EXCLUDED FROM THE
BAD DESCRIPTIONS OF HITLER.

PRESIDENT SADDAM HUSSEIN HAS FURTHER SAID WE ARE KEEN TO ADHERE
TO ALL CHARACTERISTICS OF AFFECTION AND PEACE THAT THE WORLD NATIONS
YEARN FOR WHILE AT THE SAME TIME IN WHICH WE DEFEND, WITHOUT ANY FEAR
FROM A TYRANT OR ARROGANT AGGRESSOR, PRINCIPLES OF OUR RELIGION, OUR
SANCTITIES AND THE HONOUR OF THE HOMELAND AND THE NATION AND EVEN
VALUES OF ALL HUMANITY.

PRESIDENT HUSSEIN HAS MAINTAINED THAT IT HAS BECOME CLEAR THAT
SAYING THAT THE AMERICAN TROOPS HAVE COME HERE TO DEFEND SAUDIA IS
SOMETHING THAT CANNOT STAND FIRM BEFORE THE FACTS CONTRADICTING IT
BECAUSE THE ACTUAL REALITY CONFIRMS THAT IRAQ HAS NO INTENTION OF
AGGRESSION AGAINST ANYBODY INCLUDING SAUDIA. AS FOR SAYING THAT YOUR
TROOPS HAVE COME HERE TO DEFEND AMERICAN INTERESTS, YOU KNOW WELL
THAT THE ARABS, INCLUDING IRAQ, ARE NOT AGAINST THE LEGITIMATE
INTERESTS WHETHER THEY WERE FOR THE ENTIRE WEST OR AMERICA. YOU ALSO
KNOW THAT PROSPERITY AND TECHNICAL AND SCIENTIFIC PROGRESS AND
DEVELOPMENT AND ITS FLOURISHMENT CANNOT BE ACHIEVED, AS THE ARABS
HOPE, WITHOUT TRANSACTION WITH THE WEST.

0056

TO ACHIEVE THIS END THEY (ARABS) HAVE TO SELL THEIR OIL AND THE
MAIN OIL·MARKET IS EUROPE, AMERICA IN ADDITION TO JAPAN. I PRESUME
THAT PRESIDENT BUSH KNOWS, FOR INSTANCE, THAT IRAQ SELLS ONE THIRD OF
ITS OIL TO AMERICA UP TILL AUGUST 2, 1990 AND THAT IRAQ WAS AGAINST
THE FEVER OF THE RISE IN PRICES THAT HAPPENED IN 1973, AND WE HAVE
DOCUMENTS THAT PROVE THIS.

AT ALL EVENTS, THE ARABS, INCLUDING IRAQ, WANT TO SELL THEIR OIL
FOR ALL WHAT WE HAVE MENTIONED OF PURPOSES, AND NOT TO DRINK IT OR
FREEZE IT. IRAQ'S POSSESSION OF 20 PER CENT OR LESS OR MORE OF THE
WORLD OIL DOES NOT CANCEL WHAT WE HAVE REFERRED TO OF PRINCIPLES. AND
IF THE PARTY THAT POSSESS OIL SHOULD BE BOYCOTTED BY THE WORLD IT IS
MORE LIKELY, AND FOR SAME REASON THAT THE WORLD SHOULD BOYCOTT
AMERICA AND THE GOVERNMENT OF SAUDIA, MOREOVER IS IT NOT FOOD MORE
VITAL FOR MAN THAT OIL? WE ANSWER BY (YES), IT IS BY ALL HUMANITARIAN
CRITERIA MORE VITAL THAN OIL AND THAT MAN WITHOUT FOOD CANNOT LIVE..
IF PRESIDENT BUSH'S MEASUREMENTS IN BOYCOTTING, ENMITY, WAR AND
BLOCKADE TO BE APPLIED ON IRAQ FOR MERELY IT IS GOING TO BECOME, OR
IT IS NOW POSSESSING 20 PER CENT OF THE WORLD OIL THOSE MEASUREMENTS
AND CRITERIA SHOULD BE APPLIED WITH ALL ITS MEANINGS TO WHOM WHO
POSSESSES THE SAME PERCENTAGE OR MORE OF FOOD, IN THE FOREMOST OF
WHICH ARE GRAINS AND THEN THE STAND REQUIRED FROM THE WORLD IS TO BE
AGAINST AMERICA, AND AUSTRALIA IN THE FIRST PLACE. BUT IF USA'S
INTERESTS HAVE BEEN REDUCED AND SHRUNK FROM THE STANDPOINT OF BUSH
TILL THEY HAVE BECOME CONFINED TO THE CORNER OF THE RELATIONSHIP
BETWEEN BUSH AND FAHD AND WHAT IS BETWEEN IT, OF EXCHANGE OF INTERESTS
THAT PRECEDED PRESIDENT BUSH'S ASSUMPTION OF PRESIDENCY AND
ACCOMPANIED HIS ELECTIONS, AND HAVE SO STRAINED TILL IT HAS BECOME NO
LONGER ABLE TO SEE WHAT THERE SHOULD BE GOOD AND POSITIVE RELATIONS
WITH A BIG AND GREAT NATION BUT WITH JABIR AL-AHMED (CROESUS OF
KUWAIT) AND HIS CLIQUE, WHO IS INABLE EVEN TO CONSTRUCT ONE USEFUL
SENTENCE IN HIS SPEECH AND WHO WAS, AND THOSE ALIKE, THE SOURCE OF
REPROACH ON THE ARABS, AND INDICATION OF THEIR BACKWARDNESS BY THE
WEST, THEN WHAT AN EVIL THING YOU DO. AND BEFORE I CONCLUDE MY LETTER
I HAVE TO SAY THAT THE SOURCE OF COMPETENCE, MR BUSH, CANNOT BE IN
THE VOLUME OF ARMIES AND THE TECHNOLOGICAL SUPERIORITY AND NEITHER BY
YOUR ALLIANCE WITH THOSE WHO BETRAYED THEIR NATION AND PEOPLE. THE
SOURCE OF STRENGTH LIES WITH THOSE WHO ARE RIGHTEOUS AND AT ALL
EVENTS GOD IS MIGHTIER AND MORE POWERFUL THAN ALL, AND THAT AMERICA
AS WE HAVE·SAID, ON A FORMER OCCASION, WOULD NOT HAVE BECOME A
SUPERPOWER·WITHOUT BEING INFLUENCIAL IN THE WORLD AND IN ORDER TO BE
INFLUENTIAL IT SHOULD AND EVEN MUST RESPECT FREEDOM OF PEOPLES AND
OPTIONS OF NATIONS AND SHOULD RESPECT SANCTITIES OF THE OTHERS AND
THEIR FEELINGS.

IF YOUR DISREGARD OF THIS CONTINUES I WARN AGAINST THE OUTCOMES,
AND I WOULD PUT DOWN HERE FOR HISTORY THAT YOUR CONTINUATION IN THIS
PURSUIT WOULD AMERICA DESCEND FROM THE STATURE WHERE IT IS NOW AND
MANY OPPORTUNITIES WILL BE LOSE FOR IT. AND AT ANY RATE WHETHER YOU
RUSHED TO THE WAR OR BOYCOTT, YOU WILL BE THE LOSSERS AND BE DEFEATED
WHILE WE WILL BE, WITH THE HELP OF GOD, VICTORIOUS.

0057

외 무 부

종 별 : 긴 급

번 호 : BGW-0568   일 시 : 90 0822 1130

수 신 : 장 관(중근동,정일,기정)

발 신 : 주 이라크 대사

제 목 : 이라크-쿠웨이트 사태(82호)

1. 훗세인 대통령, 외국인 인질화 부인

훗세인 대통령은 8.21 부시 미 대통령에게 보낸 공개서한에서 이라크 출국이 금지되고 있는 외국인은 인질아니며, 외국인의 이라크 억류는 이라크가 당면하고 있는 침략전쟁을 막는데 기여하고 있다고 강변함

2. 아지즈 외상, 미국과의 대화용의 표명

-아지즈 외상은 8.21 요르단의 암만 방문중 기자회견에서 이라크는 현사태에 관하여 미국과 대화할 용의가 있다고 밝히면서 그러나, 이라크는 미국의 압력에 굴복하지 않을것이며 우리는 싸울것이고 이 싸움은 우리뿐만 아니라 미국도 피를 흘리게 될것이라고 말함

-동 외상은 또한 이라크에 억류된 서방 외국인은 인질이 아니며, 현위기를 해결하는데 도움이 될수 있는 이라크의 손님으로 그들을 가족처럼 대하고 있다고 말함.끝

(대사 최봉름-국장)

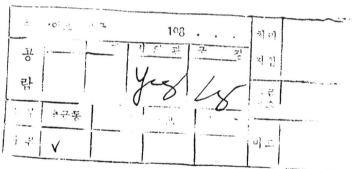

중아국   1차보   미주국   통상국   정문국   안기부   대책반

외 무 부

종 별 : 긴 급

번 호 : BGW-0570　　　　　　　　　　일 시 : 90 0823 1130

수 신 : 장 관(중근동,정일,기정) 사본:주쿠웨이트대사

발 신 : 주 이라크 대사

제 목 : 이라크-쿠웨이트 사태(83호)

　　1. 주재국은 매일 1편씩 바그다드-쿠웨이트간 이라크 항공을 운항 시키고 있음이 이라크 항공을 통하여 확인됨. 이에관한 공식보도는 없었음.(운항시간은 매일 11:00 바그다드 출발 및 도착임)

　　2. 주재국 국회는 8.22 일부 일본 및 프랑스 국민에 대하여 출국을 허용키로 하였다고 발표하고, 이는 이들 국가가 미국의 반 이라크 입장을 추종하지 못하도록 하고 또한 다른 국가들도 이라크에 대한 적대적 행동을 못하도록 하기 위한 호의적인 표시라고 말함

　　3. 주재국 ABDUL SAEED 보건장관은 8.22. WHO, FAO, UNICEF 에 멧세지를 송부하고, 자국에 대한 경제봉쇄 해제를 호소하면서 기아와 질병이 만연될 위험성에 있으며, 특히 어린이와 노약자의 생명을 위협하게 될것이라고 경고함. 끝

　　(대사 최봉름-국장)

중아국　　1차보　　미주국　　통상국　　정문국　　안기부　　대책반

0059

PAGE 1

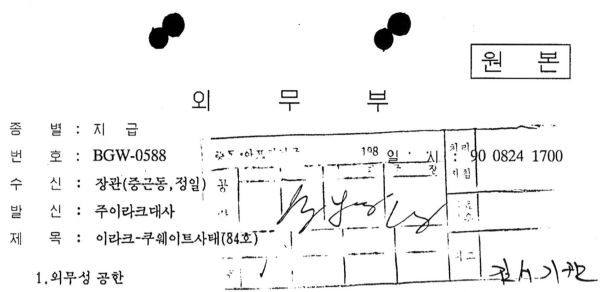

외 무 부

종 별 : 지 급

번 호 : BGW-0588

수 신 : 장관(중근동,정일) 꽁

발 신 : 주이라크대사

제 목 : 이라크-쿠웨이트사태(84호)

1.외무성 공한

주재국외무성은 8.23. 당지 외교단에 보낸 공한을봉하여,외교특권이없는 사람들이외교관차량을이용하여 탈출하지 못하도록 당지 외교관들에게 신분증제시등에 협조하여 줄것을 요청하여왔음

2.훗세인대통령,무바락 대통령에게 멧세지발송

-훗세인대통령은 8.23 저녁 무바락이집트 대통령의 멧세지에대한 회신을 공개발표하 면서,쿠웨이트로부터의 철수에 관해 YES나 NO 를 대답하기 이전에 대화할 용의가있다고 천명하고, 아랍은 한국가이며 대서양에서 아랍걸프만에 이르기까지 하나의 조국임을 입증하는역사적 사실을 설명함

-동 대통령은 이어 쿠웨이트 전국왕의 개인재산은 600억불이고,사우디 국왕의 재산은180억불이나 이재산은 모두 미국이나 서구에 예치되어있음을 무바락대통령에게환 기시킴

3.훗세인대통령 억류 영국인 가족방문

훗세인대통령은 8.23 이라크내 주요시설물에 억류되어있는 일부 영국인 가족들을방문하고, 이들의 이라크내 억류는 전쟁 억제를위한것이므로 이들을 편안하고 잘대우해 주도록지시하였다함. 끝

(대사 최봉름-국장)

중아국   정문국 차관 1차 2차 미주국 대책반 통상국 안기부

0060

90.08.24   23:26 CT

외신 1과 통제관

외 무 부

종   별 : 지   급

번   호 : BGW-0604

수   신 : 장관(중근동,정일)

발   신 : 주이라크대사

제   목 : 발트하임 오지리대통령 방문(85호)

일   시 : 90 0826 1100

1. 발트하임 오지리대통령은 MOCK 외상등을 대동하고 8.25 주재국을 방문, 훗세인대통령과 현사태 진전에 관한 일련의 회담을 가졌으며, 발트하임 대통령은 자국 국민의 출국 허용에 대해 특히 감사를 표함.

2. 발트하임 대통령은 8.2 이라크의 쿠웨이트 침공후 요르단국왕, 예멘대통령에 이어 3번째로 주재국을 방문하는 외국원수로서, 공항영접시 주재국의 전고위인사가 출영하는등 주재국은 큰의미를 부여하고 있는것으로 보임

3. 발트하임-훗세인회담 내용에 관하여는 구체적인 발표가 없었음.

4. 훗세인대통령의 오지리 언론인과의 회견 내용요지는 다음과같음.

-미국이 공격한다면 시작은 있으나 끝이없는 시체의 행렬을 이룰것임

-미국은 그들이 원하는것은 무엇이든지할 수 있다는 생각을 버려야함.

-미국의 이스람 성지 점령은 범죄행위임.

-유엔사무총장의 이라크 방문은 언제든지 환영함.끝

(대사 최봉름-국장)

| 총여국 | 차관 | 1차보 | 통상국 | 정문국 | 안기부 | 미국롱 대략바닥 | 0061 |

PAGE 1

90.08.26   16:16 DN

외신 1과 통제관

외 무 부

종 별 : 긴 급

번 호 : BGW-0605   일 시 : 90 0826 1100

수 신 : 장관(중근동,기정)

발 신 : 주이라크대사

제 목 : 이라크-쿠웨이트 사태

1. 이라크정부는 8.25 쿠웨이트에 있는 대사관의 폐쇄를 거부하는 국가의 외교관가족에 대하여는 인도적인 견지에서 출국을 허용하나, 동외교관에 한해서는 이라크의 결정에 따를때까지 출국을 금지한다고 발표함. 정부대변인은 대부분의 국가가 쿠웨이트에 있는 대사관 폐쇄 결정에 따르고 있다고 말하면서, 이결정은 확고한것임을 강조함. 그러나 어느국가가 폐쇄 결정에 응하였는지 또는 응치하지 않았는지에 대해서는 현재까지 공식 발표가 없음.

2. RCC 는 8.25 외국인을 숨겨주는 자는 간첩죄로 사형에 처하게 될것이라는 포고를 발표함

3. 아지즈 외상은 8.25 유엔안보리 결의에 대해 이는 단순히 미국의 결의에 불과하며 놀라운 일이아니라고 논평함

4. 알제리아 GHAZALI 외상은 8.25 주재국을 방문, 훗세인대통령에게 이라크와 연대감을 표시하는 알제리아 대통령의 멧세지를 전달하였다고 보도됨. 끝

(대사 최봉름-국장)

중아국   차관   통상국   정문국   안기부   대책반

1차보   미주국
2차보

0062

PAGE 1   90.08.26   16:20 DN

외신 1과 통제관

Embassy of
The Republic of Iraq
Seoul

سفارة الجمهورية العراقية
سيئول

NO. 35-90

PRESS RELEASE

27/8/1990

THE REAL HOSTAGES

0063

The presence of foreign nationals in Iraq has been decided by the National Assembly as one of the options that could keep off a war of aggression against Iraq. Their presence has been viewed by Iraqi people as a means to prevent a disastrous war, whose consequences would negatively reflect not only on the Gulf region but also on the whole world.

As President Saddam Hussein told a group of British nationals on Thursday, their presence in Iraq would help the achievement of peace. Each one of those nationals would be contributing to peace, and would even regard themselves as peace heroes in the future.

Iraq has stressed that the foreign nationals staying here are guests of the people of this country. They will be enjoying all respect and will be treated as guests, not "hostages" as the US Administration has claimed.

However, the United States has been creating as many pretexts as it can come up with to justify its aggression against Iraq and intentions to reinforce its occupation of the Arab Gulf region.

It may be true that the presence of foreign nationals in Iraq has been associated with a feeling of bitter experience, yet this bitter feeling is equally sensed by Iraq. Iraq regrets the precautions it has to take to safeguard its sovereignty from a vicious aggression waged by the United States and some of its allies.

The decision to ban some foreigners, especially nationals of states hostile to Iraq, has been considered useful in spare bloodshed. This in itself is a humanitarian objective. The presence of hundreds or thousands of foreigners in the country as a measure for ensuring safety for all would probably help keep the cannons of war silent. Foreigners in Iraq will surely be safe and, besides them, more than 18 million people will enjoy the same safety as all human beings would wish.

The foreigners here are not hostages and will never be so. This is a fact that the US Administration and all other countries are well aware of.

This issue is merely one facet of the anti-Iraq campaign in the West. The US and Britain, in particular, have long been seeking any possible means to try to distort the image of Iraq and its people. They have tried to portray Iraq as a "lawless and terrorist" state which "seeks power and aggression." But the actions taken by the US Administration and British government have proved beyond doubt that they, not Iraq, are terrorists and aggressors.

US President George Bush and his closet ally British Prime Minister Margaret Thatcher, both with their proteges in the region and their foster child Israel have been seeking all possible channels to undermine a nation and destroy its people only because this people refused to submit to enslavement.

Bush and Thatcher have been captive of their own schemings and have put themselves, set their own will, in a very critical situation, which all peace-loving peoples of the world wonder about. If there are any hostages to be talked about, it should be Bush and Thatcher. They are hostage to their own designs. They should find a way out for themselves, or be helped to extricate themselves from their involvement in evil undertakings.

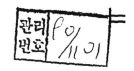

발 신 선 보

분류번호	보존기간

번 호 : WBG-0377   900829 1615 DP   종별 : 지급

수 신 : 주 이라크 대사. 쏭영써/

발 신 : 장 관 (중근동)

제 목 : 미국의 대 이라크 외교적 제재 조치

1. 미국무부는 8.27. 외교단에 대한 정례 브리핑을 통해 발표한 인원감축, 여행제한등 주 미 주재 이라크 대사관에 대한 외교적 제재 조치 내용을 아래와 같아 통보함. ~~명사 우방국이~~ → 이 우방국도 동초라고 12을 으려생기되었으로

가. 제재 조치 내용:

- 이라크 공관원 36명 추방(현 55명에서 19명으로 감축), 또한 이라크가 쿠웨이트 잔류 미국 공관원에 대해 제한을 가할 경우 재차 9명으로 감축 (주 이라크 미국 공관원과 동일 인원)

- 이라크 공관원의 활동 범위를 공관으로부터 반경 25마일로 제한

- 이라크 대사관의 학생 및 소위 인도적 필요를 위한 자금 사용 통제

- 이라크인에 대한 비자 통제(민간인에 대한 비자발급시 신원조회 실시 포함)

- 이라크 외교관에 대한 복수비자를 단수비자로 변경

- 이라크 대사관의 구매관 및 상무관 추방

나. 강조사항:

~~아울러 미국무부는 쿠웨이트 내에 공관을 유지하고 있는 아국을 포함한~~

2. ~~여타 국가에 대해서도 상기와 유사한 조치를 취하여 줄것을 요청 하였는바, 아국으로서는 공관원 및 동 조치에 효응할 경우 근로자들의 신변 안전에 중대한/위해가 초래될 가능성이 들을 교려 있으므로~~ 우선 사태 발전을 관망하면서 여타 우방국들의 자국 주재 이라크 공관원 들에 대한 외교적 제재 조치 동향을 예의 주시, 추후 적절히 대처해 나갈 예정이니 임을 참고 바람. 끝. 차관이관

예고: 90.12.31 일반

19**90**.12.31. 에 예고문에 의거 일반(등성동아갭 라카국장 이 두 복)

보 안 통 제	🖊

앙고재	90년8월28일	중근동과	기안자성명 박규옥	과 장 🖊	심의관 양	국 장 전결	차 관	장 관

외신과통제

0064

외 무 부

종 별 : 긴 급

번 호 : BGW-0631

일 시 : 90 0829 1030

수 신 : 장 관(중근동,정일,기정)

발 신 : 주 이라크 대사

제 목 : 이라크-쿠웨이트사태(87호)

1. 주재국 아지즈외상은 8.28 이집트등의 요청에의한 8.30 카이로 아랍연맹 외상회의 소집은 전원일치의 합의를 얻지 못하였으므로 무효라고 주장하고, 동회의 개최 목적이 아랍권을 분열시키고, 미국 및 NATO 군의 아랍주둔을 합법화하려는 기도라고 비난함

2. 훗세인 대통령은 8.29 자로 이라크에 억류되어 있는 모든 부녀자에게 출국을 허용 하도록 명령하였다고 8.28 RCC 대변인이 발표함.끝

(대사 최봉름-국장)

중아국	차관	1차보	2차보	미주국	통상국	정문국	안기부	대책반

0065

PAGE 1

90.08.29 16:58 WG

외신 1과 통제관

외 무 부

종　별 : 지　급

번　호 : BGW-0642　　　　　　　　　　일　시 : 90 0830 1130

수　신 : 장　관(중근동,정일,기정)

발　신 : 주　이라크　대사

제　목 : 이라크-쿠웨이트사태(88호)

1.시리아에 친이라크 시위 발생 8.30 자 당지 '바그다드옵서버)지는 지난 주말 시리아의 이라크 국경지방에서 친이라크 시위가 발생, 시리아군의 진압과정에서 수십명이사망 하였다고 외교 및 정보소식봉을 인용보도한바, 기사 요지 아래와같음

- 시위는 아사드 대봉령의 반이라크 정책에 대한항의로서 일어났으며, 시리아는 1,100 명의 군대를 사우디에 파견하고 있음

- 시위는 82년이래 시리아 최악의 정치적 불안이며 아사드에 대한 중대한 위기임

- 시위대는 이라크와 접경한 동부지역을 시리아와 분리, 이라크와의 통합을 주장 하였다함

2.부시미대봉령에 대한 반박성명

부시미대봉령의 8.28 이라크와의 대화 가능성 배제발언에 대하여 주재국 정부 대변인은 8.29 부시대봉령이 대화의 전제조건을 두는것은 스스로의 모순을 드러낸 것이며, 그의 비타협성과 미국의 패권중의 정책을 은폐하기 위한 것이라고 비난함

3.필리핀의 MANGLAPUS 외상이 8.29 주재국을 방문하였으며, 미국의 전대봉령 후보 JESSE JACKSON이 주재국 방문차 8.29 당지에 도착함.끝

(대사 최봉름-국장)

중아국　　1차보　　2차보　　미주국　　통상국　　정문국　　안기부　　대책반

0006

PAGE 1　　　　　　　　　　　　　　　　　　90.08.30　17:33 WG

외신 1과　통제관

외 무 부

종 별 : 긴 급

번 호 : BGW-0648

일 시 : 90 0831 1000

수 신 : 장관(중근동,정일,기정)

발 신 : 주이라크대사

제 목 : 이라크-쿠웨이트사태(89호)

　1.훗세인대통령 기자회견

　훗세인대통령은 8.29 CBS-TV 와의 회견에서미국과 대화를 가질 용의가 있으나,쿠웨이트철수에 대한 협상은 강력히 부인한바, 8.31자 당지 B.G 지에 게재된 회견요지 아래 보고함

　-미국에 비밀 협상을 제의한 사실이없으며,쿠웨이트는 이라크의 일부이지 미국의일부가아니기 때문에 협상할 필요가 없음

　-쿠웨이트 철수에 대한 대가로 일부 섬과주요유전의 하나를 요구하였다는 보도는근거없음

　-이라크는 미국의 군사행동에 대비하고있으나 전쟁을 원치않음

　-출국금지된 외국인은 이라크의 손님이지 인질은아님.

　그러나 인도적 차원에서 부녀자의 출국을허용토록함

　-이스라엘의 아랍영토 점령은 합법이고,이라크가 원래의 쿠웨이트 땅을 회복한것은 불법이라는 부시의 생각은 모순됨

　2.이라크 공군사령관은 8.30 만약 전쟁이일어난다면 이라크는 사우디및 이스라엘을공격할것이라고 경고함.끝

　(대사 최봉름-국장)

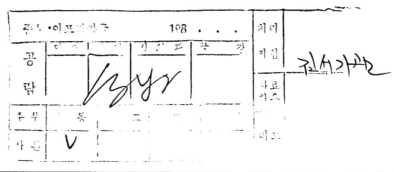

중아국　　정문국　　안기부

외 무 부

종 별 : 지급

번 호 : BGW-0670

수 신 : 장관(중근동)

발 신 : 주 이라크 대사

제 목 : 주재국 일상생활동정

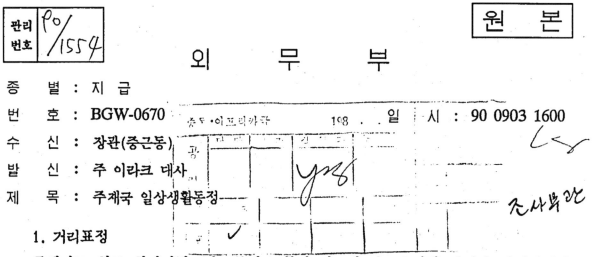

일 시 : 90 0903 1600

1. 거리표정

쿠웨이트 침공 한달이된 오늘 주재국 특히 바그다드는 초기의 팽대한 긴장감이나 한가한 거리 모습과는 달리 쿠웨이트로부터 철수한 제 3 국인의 대거 유입과 일부 피난하였던 주민들이 다시 돌아옴으로서 거리에 많은 사람이 북쩍거리는등 외형상 정상적인 분위기를 되찾고있음. 이러한 분위기는 쿠웨이트 병합의 기정사실화와 함께 일부 억류된 부녀자의 출국허용, 외국기자입국 허용, 유엔사무총장-아지즈외상 회담등을 인하여 긴박감이 다소 완화되는듯하나, 미국등 다국적군의 군사행동 가능성에 대한 의구심과 공포감은 여전 상존하고 있는듯함

2. 생필품 부족

주재국에 대한 경제봉쇄 조치로 쌀, 빵, 고기, 계란, 밀가루, 설탕등 주요식품에 대한 배급제(가구당 판매량제한)를 실시함으로 식량부족에 대비한 장기태세에 들어감. 가게마다 배급을 받기위해 긴 행렬로 기다리는 모습을 볼수있으나, 사회주의 경제체제와 8 년전쟁을 경험한 국민들에게 큰충격이나 혼란은 볼수없으며, 오늘의 어려운 상황을 체념속에 담당하게 받아드리고 있는 모습임

3. 국민여론

현지도체제에대한 일체의 비판이 금지되고, 신문.방송등 언론매체가 강력히 통제된 정보사회에서 국민들은 침묵을 지키고 있음. 쿠웨이트 병합에 대하여 대부분 환영과 쾌감을 느끼고 있으나, 8 년 전쟁의 고통과 최근 송환된 포로의 비참한 모습을 보고 대부분의 국민들은 전쟁에 염증을 느끼고 있다는 인상임.끝

(대사최봉름-국장)

예고:90.12.31

중아국	장관	차관	1차보	2차보	통상국	청와대	안기부	대책반

0068

90.09.03   23:28
외신 2과 통제관 DO

외 무 부

종 별 : 지 급

번 호 : BGW-0672

일 시 : 90 0904 1030

수 신 : 장관(중근동,정일,기정)

발 신 : 주 이라크 대사

제 목 : 이라크-팔레스타인 관계

　　1. 8.2 사태이후 PLO 의 아라파트 의장이 3 차에 걸쳐 주재국을 방문하였으며 9.2 에는 팔레스타인 해방인민전선(PFLP)의 GEROGE HABASH 사무총장이 주재국을 방문, 훗세인 대통령및 라마단 제 1 부수상과 면담함.HABASH 는 9.3 기자회견에서 현사태는 아랍국가에 대한 제국주의 및 시오니즘의 음모로서 8.12 훗세인대통령 제의는 미국의도를 시험하는것이 될것이라고 말함

　　2. 당지 B.O. 지는 9.4 암만발 AP 를 인용, 아랍걸프국가와 이집트가 훗세인 대통령을 지지하는 팔레스타인인을 추방하고있으며, 특히 카타르정부는 반이라크집회 참석을 거부한 P 국민의회 의원및 P 대사관원을 추방하였다고 보도하면서, 걸프국가에서 추방된 P 국민이 당면한 경제문제는 궁극적으로 이라크의 도움으로 해결되기를 희망한다는 PLO 관리의 말을 인용보도함

　　3. 평가

　　주재국은 P 문제에 주도적인 입장을 취하여온바, 합병후 쿠웨이트에 체류하고있던 제 3 국인의 대량 탈출에 따른 인적공백을 P 국민을 받아들임으로서 합병의 정당성과함께 P 문제 해결이라는 2 중의 효과를 기도할 가능성이 없지않는것으로 보임.끝

　　(대사 최봉름-국장)

　　예고:90.12.31

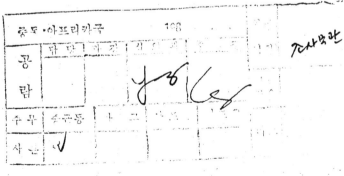

중아국	장관	차관	1차보	2차보	정문국	청와대	안기부	대책반

외　무　부

종　별 :

번　호 : BGW-0673　　　　　　　　　　　일　시 : 90 0904 1030

수　신 : 장　관(중근동,공보)

발　신 : 주　이라크　대사

제　목 : 외국기자　입국

　　　주재국 문공성은 9.2 현재 230명 이상의 외국기자가 입국, 취재중에 있으며 이들의 취재를 위하여 모든 편의를 제공해 주고 있다고 발표함. 문공성은 또한 180명 이상의 외국기자가 입국신청을 하고있으나, 신청하는 모든 기자들을 수용할수 있는 시설이 부족하다고 밝히고 입국을 위하여 대기중인 기자들을 위하여 5일이상 체류중인 기자들은 출국하여 줄것을 호소함. 끝

　　　(대사 최봉름-국장)

중아국　　공보

외 무 부

종 별 : 지 급

번 호 : BGW-0681

일 시 : 90 0905 0930

수 신 : 장 관(중근동,정일,기정)

발 신 : 주 이라크 대사

제 목 : 경제봉쇄에 따른 식량난(90호)

1. 외무성 대변인은 9.4 많은 나라들이 이라크에 체류하고 있는 자국민들에게 긴급식량을 보내려 하고 있으나 미국은 이를 막고 있다고 말하고, 이러한 식량수입 금지 상태하에서 식량부족으로 야기되는 외국인이 고통에 대하여 이라크는 책임을 지지 않을것이라고 발표함

2. 이라크 정부는 9.3 이라크에 많은 자국민이 체류하고 있는 국가들에 대하여 식량확보를 위한 긴급조치를 취하도록 촉구하였으며, 아지즈 외상도 ICRC 의장과의 면담에서 이라크 체류 외국인에 대한 식량공급과 관련하여 필요한 조치를 취하도록 협조를 요청함

3. 한편 당지 9.4 B.O. 지에 의하면 불란서 외무성은 이라크에 대한 식량및 의약품 수송방법에 대하여 연구하고 있으며, 유엔 안보리의 경제제재 조치는 인도적 견지에서 식량등 필수품은 제외된다고 말한것으로 보도함. 끝

(대사 최봉름-국장)

중동·아프리카국		198 . . .		처리
공람	담당	과장	심의관	국 장	지침
					자료 활용
주무 사본	중근동	나 그	아프1	아프2	비고
√					

중아국   1차보   2차보   미주국   통상국   정문국   안기부   대책반

PAGE 1

0071

90.09.05   16:57 BB

외신 1과 통제관

걸프사태, 1990-91. 전12권 (V.2 이라크, 1990-91)   133

외 무 부

종 별 : 지 급

번 호 : BGW-0711

일 시 : 90 0911 1200

수 신 : 장관(중근동,정일,기정)

발 신 : 주 이라크대사

제 목 : 제 3세계 석유 무료공급 제의(91호)

훗세인 대통령은 9.10 제 3세계 지도자및 국민에게 보내는 공개서한을 통하여이라크는 제 3세계에 석유를 무료로 공급할 준비가 되어있으며, 필요한 석유량및 석유 종류를 명시한 요청서를 보내줄것을 제의함

동 대통령은 동 제의에서 이라크가 석유를 수송할수 없으므로, 석유를 요청한국가에서 자신의 비용으로 운송수단을 준비하여야 할것임을 덧붙임.

대통령은 또한 석유 무료공급 결정은 현사태에 대한 태도 여하에 상관이 없으며, 아랍문제에 대한 제 3세계의 지지에 대한 감사의 표시임을 강조함. 끝

(대사 최봉름-국장)

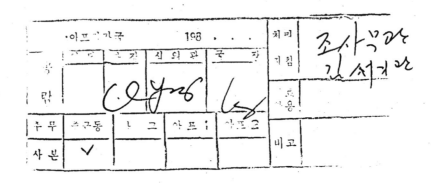

중아국   동자부   2차보   1차보   정문국   안기부   대책반

0072

PAGE 1

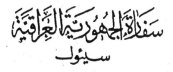

Embassy of
The Republic of Iraq
Seoul

Press Release

NO. 42/90   11/9/1990

TEXT OF THE MESSAGE OF PRESIDENT SADDAM HUSSEIN

TO THE LEADERS AND PEOPLES OF THIRD WORLD COUNTRIES

10 SEPTEMBER 1990

Leaders and Peoples of the Third World Countries,

Peace be upon you,

The big and developed countries in describing you and us as
third world countries did not intend to describe the gap
that separates between us and them in the scientific and
technological aspects and the level and degree of economic
development in general, of which the colonialist countries
which form their world were responsible in the first place.
But, by describing our world as third world, they intend to
limit the human degree that they decided to grant us in the
level of their dealing with us and their approach towards
us.

Such is their real behaviour in dealing with everybody.
Therefore, it should not come as a surprise to you, Brothers,
when the big and developed countries do not give much concern
to your issues, problems and human affairs in every measure
or decision they take.

Proceeding from this fact, those who decided to invade oil
countries in the Middle East and insulted Moslem sanctuities
by occupying the land of Najd and Hijaz did not ask nor did
they provide an answer to the harm they would bring about to
third world countries as a result of their despicable act.

While oil monopolies are still drawing filthy profit from
this crisis, they left third world countries meddle into
trouble with their crisis as a consequence of an increase in
oil prices following their crime to the point that the third
world cannot endure, should oil become scarce or less than
needed.

There is no doubt at all that you would get only the surplus
left by the big and the most developed countries even if you
suffer from major disasters.

On the basis of this judgement, and from the spirit of

0073

brotherhood and solidarity with you, we and our Arab Nation, which share with you the same situation and fate, have become the target for America, Zionism and their satellite imperialist countries and those influenced by them.

On this basis also, we offered our solidarity to you under all previous conditions and situations we called for the alleviation of some of your burden at the Non-Aligned Conference convened in Havana in 1979 . Iraq at that time was faithful to its call when it decided to waive the differences risen from increased oil prices to the third world countries which had purchased oil from Iraq. The countries which were benefitted from that should still remember that generous initiative.

Proceeding from this appreciation, and from the feeling of brotherly solidarity with you, and in recognition of your fair stance towards the fateful Arab issues, mainly the question of Palestine, we announce today that we are still your brothers and share with you the same destiny.

We, therefore, declare now that we are prepared to supply those third world countries with their need of Iraqi oil free of charge. Those who are desirous to be included in such arrangement, on the assumption that these arrangements are not covered by the U.S. boycott, as they do not involve any sale or purchase, should send their applications indicating the quantity and type of oils they need, Should it prove impossible for us to transport the oil in our tankers, they have to make their own arrangement at their own expense.

Brothers,

In taking such decision we are prompted by a principled and moral commitment to ease some of your burden and to demonstrate solidarity with you at a time when we are able to perform such a role. Such a decision is not related to, and shall not be affected by any of your decisions and attitudes towards the current crisis. This is because we respect the opinion of countries and peoples and admit that each has its own appreciation and position. We do not assume that there should be conformity with opinion towards all issues. That will bolster the ties of friendship and fraternity.

We shall not take a stand emerging from a difference in viewpoints or divergence in considerations and information. We take such a stand only when an imperialist country attempts to impose its own position on us by force as an expression of their non-respect complex for the third world countries and peoples and from their failure to feel human equality and consideration towards those countries and peoples.

Our greetings to you and to all oppressed and poor peoples. May God's peace, mercy and blessings be upon you.

God is the supporter of good intention.

Your Brother

Saddam Hussein

20 Safar 1411 A.H.

10 September 1990 A.D.

0074

Press Release

التاريخ : ١٩٩٠/٩/١١   الرقـــم : ٤٢

نص رسالة السيد الرئيس القائد صدام حسين

الـــــى

قادة وشعوب بلـدان العالـم الثـالث

بســم اللـــه الرحمـن الـرحيــم

ايها الاخوة والاصدقاء قادة وشعوب بلدان العالم الثالث المحتـرميــن •

السلام عليــــكم :

ان الدول الكبرى والمتطورة ارادت في وصفنا معكم ووصفها بالعالم الثالث ليس وصف الفجوة التـــي تفصلنا عنكم ، في الجوانب العلمية والتقنية ومستوى التطور الاقتصادي ودرجته بعامة مما كانت الدول الاستعمارية التي تشكل اساس عالمهم مسؤولة عنه بالدرجة الاولى وانما ارادوا من وصف عالمنا بالعالم الثالث تحديد الدرجة الانسانية التي قرروا ان يمنحوها لنا في مستوى تعاملهم معنا ونظرتهم الينـــا وهذا هو سلوكهم وتعاملهم الفعلي مع الجميع ، ولذلك لاتستغربوا ، ايها الاخوة ، عندما لاتضــــع لكم الدول الكبرى والمتطورة نسب اهتمام لقضاياكم ومشاكلكم وانسانيتكم في كل اجراء او قرار يتخذونه وعلى هذا الاساس ايضا فان الذين قرروا غزو بلد البترول في الشرق الاوسط واهانوا مقدسات المسلمين عندما احتلوا ارض نجد والحجاز ، لم يسألوا ولم يجيبوا على مايصيب بلدان العالم الثالث مـــن اذى جراء فعلهم المشين هذا ، وفي الوقت الذي راحت فيه الشركات الاحتكارية النفطيه تغرف الارباح الحرام جراء هذه الازمة ، تركوا بلدان العالم الثالث تتخبط بازماتها بسبب ازدياد اسعار البتـرول نتيجة جريمتهم ، زيادة لايقوى اقتصاد العالم الثالث على استيعابها ، واذا ماعز البترول او تناقص عن الحاجة ، فلا نشك مطلقا بانكم لن تحصلوا من البترول الا على ماهو فائض عن حاجة الكبـــار والدول الاكثر تطورا حتى لو اصابتكم الكوارث الكبرى • وانطلاقا من هذا التقدير ، ومن روحيـــة

0075 الاخوة والتضامن معكم ، نحن وامتنا العربية التي هي جزء من حالكم ومصيركم ، استهدفتها اميركا والصهيونية والدول الامبريالية السائرة في ركابها والمتأثرة بهما ، وانطلاقا من هذا الحال ايضا وتضامنا

معكم في كل الظروف والاحوال السابقة ، دعونا الى التخفيف عن كاهلكم في مؤتمر عدم الانحيـاز الذي انعقد في هافانا سنة ١٩٧٩ ، وكان العراق يومها وفيا لدعوته يوم تنازل عن فروقات اسعـار البترول للدول التي كانت قد اشترت البترول منه من بلدان العالم الثالث ، وان الدول التي شملناها بذلك لابد وانها مازالت تتذكر تلك المبادرة الكريمة ، وانطلاقا من هذا التقدير والشعور الاخـوي التضامني معكم ، وتقديرا لمواقفكم المنصفة في قضايا العرب المصيرية وفي المقدمة منها قضية فلسطيـن نعلن اليوم اننا اخوة لكم ، واننا واياكم في مصير واحد ، ولذلك فاننا نعلن الان استعدادنـا لتزويد المحتاجين من بلدان العالم الثالث ببترول العراق من غير ثمـن .

فعلى من يرغب بمثل هذه الترتيبات التي نفترض بانها غير مشمولة بالمقاطعة الامريكية لانها لاتنطوي على بيع وشراء ، نقول فان من يرغب في ذلك عليه ان يتقدم الينا بطلباته مبينا الكمية والانـواع الذي ...

فعليه تدبير ذلك على حسابه الخاص ، ،

ايها الاخوان .. اننا عندما نتخذ هذا القرار فان الاساس هو الاساس المبدأي والاخلاقي للتخفيـف عن كاهلكم والتضامن معكم في وقت نحن قادرون فيه على اداء مثل هذا الدور ، وان هذا الموقـف لم ولن يرتبط بنوايا او قرار اي منكم وموقفه من الازمة الحالية ، ذلم لاننا نحترم رأي الدول والشعوب ونعرف لاي منهما تقديره وموقفه واننا لانفترض التطابق في كل القضايا لترتبط عرى الصداقة والاخـوة ولا نزعل من اختلاف المواقف على اساس اختلاف زوايا النظر او التباين في المعطيات والمعلومات واننا لنزعل فقط عندما يحاول من يحاول من الدول الامبريالية فرض مواقفهم علينا بالقوه تعبيرا عن عقدة عدم احترامهم لبلدان ولشعوب العالم الثالث وعدم الشعور ازاءها بالمساواة والتقدير الانسانييـن .

تحياتنا لكم والى كل الشعوب المظلومة والفقيره والسلام عليكم ورحمة الله وبركاته ...

والله من وراء القصـد .

صـدام حسيـن

٢٠ / صفـــــر: ١٤١١هـ

١٠/ ايلـــــول/ ١٩٩٠م

٠٠٧٦

Embassy of
The Republic of Iraq
Seoul

سفارة الجمهورية العراقية
سيول

NO. 46-90   # Press Release   15/9/1990

STATEMENT

IRAQI Spokesman denied, categorically, what was circu-
lated by French and Dutch authorities, that IRAQI troops had
penetrated the headquarters of the previous diplomatic missions in the province of Kuwait.   The Spokesman said that
there are strict instruction for not entering these places,
though they are no more diplomatic missions as of August 24,
1990.   The Spokesman clarifies that the IRAQ authorities is
binding itself delicately towards this matter, to preserve
certain consideration, and not in accordance with Vienna
Agreement, because Vienna Agreement does not cover the previous missions in the province of Kuwait. IRAQ, strictly implements this Agreement towards the accredited missions in
it.

0077

*Embassy of
The Republic of Iraq
Seoul*

No. 130-90

Dear Sir,

Enclosed, herewith, please find the text of the letter dated September 4th, 1990, sent from H.E. Tariq Aziz, Deputy Prime Minister, Minister of Foreign Affairs to Ministers of Foreign Affairs of the Nations.

The letter including many historical facts concerning current events taking place in Arab Gulf.

Please accept my best regards.

Press Attache
Embassy of the Republic of Iraq

S E O U L, September 18th, 1990

0078

Greetings

Amidst the developments witnessed in the Arab Gulf region, I find it necessary and useful to present some of the facts which I believe will help you to understand the background to the events that have occured in this region.

Iraq, is known to have always been a political entity and the seat of many states throughout millenia. It has always been a coastal state and a major trading centre. The small village established some two centuries ago on the banks of the Arab Gulf under the name of "Kuwait", an Iraqi term for "a small settlement of people", had remained throughout the nineteenth century and up to the First World War, an Iraqi Qadhas' (district) belonging to the province of Basrah. Under Ottoman administrative law, Kuwait was an integral part of Iraq, subject to the Province of Basrah.

In 1897, the governor of Basrah, Muhsin Pasha, informed the Sheikh of Kuwait, Mubarak al-Sabah, of the Sultan's decree appointing him as Qa'im-Maqam (district administrator) of the Qadhaa' of Kuwait, a district of the Province of Basrah. By then, Mubarak had been instigated by the British to kill his two elder brothers, Mohammed and Jarrah, who had opposed the British plan to turn Kuwait into an entity under British dominance.

In 1899, Britain goaded Mubarak al-Sabah into signing a secret agreement under which the British were to provide him with protection even though he was a vassal of the Ottoman Empire and, accordingly, had no authority to sign any international accord. The agreement was therefore strongly rejected by the Ottoman Sultan, which forced Mubarak to retreat and declare his allegiance and subordination to the Ottoman Sublime Porte in 1901.

Britain never ceased these attempts, but continued to establish bases in various parts of the Arab Gulf in order to consolidate its colonial grip over this region, the strategic importance of which had increased both militarily and politically, within the framework of the competition with the Ottoman Empire, and economically as it constituted an important trade route and was known by the British to contain vast oil reserves. In order to secure the interests of the British Empire by weakening all major states in the region, Britain focused its influence on Kuwait and drew artificial boundaries as they did later, together with their French ally, in the Sykes-Picot Agreement of 1917. By so

- 1 -

doing   Britain pernitiously severed a part of Iraq in a manner that deprived a country ancient in its civilization, and great in its land and population,   of its natural access to the waters of the Arab Gulf, the access which it had possessed throughout history.

It was   through such artificial colonial machinations   that an   artificial entity, called Kuwait, was founded for the first time in history   under British domination and given artificial boundaries which have no historical   or geographical foundations.

Since its establishment in 1921,   the State of Iraq has refused to accept this artificial entity.   All successive Iraqi governments continued to demand the return of this severed part of Iraq and historical and geographical justice be done to Iraq to guarantee its commercial and economic interests   and provide it with the requirements necessary for the defence of its national security. This was the position adopted by successive Iraqi governments, despite the fact that the Iraqi regime at the time was closely linked to Britain.

Britain had also vigorously opposed any project which would bring the one people of Iraq   and Kuwait   close together and in coastout contact with   each other.   The project to provide Kuwait with water from Shatt al-Arab, the Kuwait railway project, the project to establish an Iraqi port in Kuwait City were all rejected.   These projects continued to meet with British procrastination and/or outright   rejection   throughout the period   from the early 1920s   to the   early 1960s.

Then Britain consistently pressurized Iraq into accepting   the fait accompli.   When the British government forced the Prime Minister of Iraq in 1932 to exchange letters   with the British Commissioner in Baghdad,   regarding the demarcation   of the boundaries   on the basis of the draft agreement proposed   between the Ottoman and British governments, the agreement which had remained unsigned   because of the outbreak   of the world war I,   the Iraqi House of Representatives refused, in its capacity as the country's legislative authority,   to ratify the said letters.

During the 1930s,   popular demand increased   for the return of Kuwait to Iraq.   The national press adopted those demands and began supporting them articles and historical document affirming the inevitable return of Kuwait to Iraq. In 1933, the British Political Representative in Kuwait, Colonel Dickson, warnen, in his letters to the British Political Resident in the Gulf, against any approachment between the people in Kuwait and Iraq, and called for their separation.

0080

- 2 -

142 걸프 사태 쿠웨이트, 이라크 및 각국 경제 제재

In 1940, the ruler of Kuwait replaced the Iraqi administration of the post office in Kuwait with British staff. In 1949, the Iraqi school curricula applied in Kuwaiti schools were replaced by Egyptian curricula.

King Ghazi, the second monarch of Iraq, supported enthusiastically the necessity of the unification of Kuwait with Iraq. He expressed his desire to visit Kuwait in return to an earlier visit made to Iraq by Sheikh Ahmed al-Sabah in 1932. Britain, however, did not encourage the visit, and endeavored to prevent Iraq and Kuwait from reaching any agreement.

In April 1938, Mr. Tawfiq al-Suwaidi, Iraq's then Foreign Minister, inform ed the British ambassador in Baghdad, Mr. Peterson, that; "the Anglo-Ottoman Agreement of 1913 had recognized Kuwait as a district belonging to the province of Basrah, and since sovereignty over Basrah had been reliquished by the Ottomans to the state of Iraq, then that sovereignty should be extend to include Kuwait as provided for in the agreement of 1913. Iraq, therefore, does not recognize any change in the status of Kuwait."

The Iraqi popular demand for the return of Kuwait to Iraq was met with wide favourable response from the population in Kuwait. The Kuwaiti youth took an active part in the call for Kuwaiti unification with Iraq. In May 1938, a group of "free Kuwaitis" submitted a petition to the Iraqi Government inviting Iraq to help them achieve their aspirations regarding the return of Kuwait to Iraq. To this end, a "national coalition" was established to call upon Ahmed al-Sabah, the Sheikh of Kuwait to set up a legislative council representing the free people of Kuwait. He was forced to accept this demand, but when members of the new Council expressed their demand for the return of Kuwait to Iraq. The Council's demand displeased the ruler of Kuwait and he disolved the Council on 21 December 1938, and waged a campaign of arrest and oppression against its members.

Nevertheless, the free people of Kuwait continued to demand the return of Kuwait to Iraq. They sent many telegrams to pitition King Ghazi. One of those telegrams, which was broadcast on Baghdad radio on 7 March 1939, called upon King Ghazi to intervene, saying "Our history confirms the integration of Kuwait with Iraq. We shall live and die under the Iraqi flag. Ghazi! help your brothers in Kuwait!"

The situation escalated into a sweeping uprising led by the youth of Kuwait against the authorities on 10 March 1939. The ruler of Kuwait had to re-

- 3 -

걸프사태, 1990-91. 전12권 (V.2 이라크, 1990-91) 143

sort to armed force to disperse the youth, a great number of whom he then arrested and imprisoned.

King Ghazi tried to intervene in order to secure the release of the prisoners. He warned the Sheikh of Kuwait against the continued harassment and imprisonment of the "free Kuwaitis". In consequence, King Ghazi and the then Iraqi Government were subjected to intensified British pressure to desist from Iraqi demands for the integration of Kuwait. To this end, ambassador Peterson had several secret meetings with King Ghazi shortly before latter's sudden death, in an attempt to press him to give up the claims to Kuwait. King Ghazi was killed in a mysterious accident on 5 April 1939, giving every reason to believe that Britain was behind his death because of his strong advocacy of the return of Kuwait to Iraq.

Following the assasination of King Ghazi, Britain's collaborators seized power in the country. Then, with the outbreak of the Second World War and the following years, Iraq and the region witnessed a series of successive changes and developments including the creation of Israel, the Arab-Israeli war and the revolution in Egypt. All these developments gave the British colonialists the pretext to concentrate their influence in Kuwait while severing its political and human links with Iraq.

On 9 March 1956, while, Sellwyn Llyod, the British Foreign Secretary was on a visit to Baghdad attending a consultative meeting of the Permenant Council of the Baghdad Pact, Prime Minister Nouri al-Said of Iraq raised the subject of accession of Kuwait to the Arab Union which was being formed at the time. Llyod promised to put the matter before the British cabinet. Britain's reply, which was delivered via the British ambassador in Baghdad, Michael Wright, was that Britain was prepared to grant Kuwait independence, and Kuwait would have the freedom to decide the question of joining the Union. In order to present Britain with a fait accompli, Iraq dispatched Deputy Prime Minister, Tawfaq al-Suwaidi, in April 1957, to Shtura in Lebanon, where Sheikh Abdullah al-Salim al-Sabah was staying, in order to negotiate with him about the necessity of Kuwait's accession to the Union which was to be established. That effort, however, did not produce any positive result.

Early in 1958, Prime Minister Nouri al-Said of Iraq submitted to the Baghdad Pact the necessity of the integration of Kuwait with Iraq, at a meeting attended by the representatives of Turkey, Iran, and Pakistan along with the US

- 4 -

0082

Secretary of State, John Foster Dulles, who attended the meeting as an observer.

No success was achieved at that meeting because of Britain's persistent objection. Following the establishment of the Arab Union between Iraq and Jordan on 14 February 1958, King Faisal II, joined by Prime Minister Nouri al-Said and the Foreign Minister of the new Union, Tawfiq al-Suwaidi, raised the issue of unity with Kuwait once again with the British Foreign Secretary Mr. Sellwyn Llyod. The British, however, still rejected the Iraqi position.

When Abdullah al-Salim al-Sabah, the Sheikh of Kuwait, visited Baghdad on 10 May 1958, King Faisal II and Prime Minister Nouri al-Said, raised with him the issue of Kuwait's entry to the Arab Union. The Sheikh of Kuwait responded by saying that he had to consult the British and seek cheir advice on the matter.

On 5 June 1958, the Government of the Union presented a confidential note to the British Embassy in Baghdad proposing the accession of Kuwait to the Arab Union. The note stated that

> The land of Kuwait had, from the point of view of international law, been under the sovereignty of the Ottoman Empire, as a qadhaa' (district) belonging to the province of Basrah. This sovereignty had never been subject to doubt or dispute from the point of view of either the local authorities in Kuwait or the British Government. Indeed, the latter had recognized this fact in the Anglo-Turkish Agreement signed in London on 29 July 1913, which stated, in article 6, the right of the Sheikh of Kuwait to exercise his authority invested in him as an Ottoman district administrator subordinate to the Province of Basrah.

As a result of this, the Iraqi Government and the Government of the Arab Union became convinced that Britain was behind the obstacles preventing the achievement of this objective. This generated tension in Iraqi-British relations and led Iraq to intensify its efforts and increase its pressure upon Britain. An official note was prepared by the Iraqi Government to be published on 12 July 1958, with documented evidence supporting the necessity of Kuwait's entry into the Arab Union. But the British ambassador requested that the publication of that note be postponed and conveyed to Foreign Minister Tawfiq al-Suwaidi Britain's approval, in principle, of the idea of the entry of Kuwait into the Arab Union, provided that the details of the matter be discussed at a meeting which was set to be held in London, on 24 July 1958, between the Prime Minister and the Foreign Minister of the Arab Union, on the one hand and their British counterparts. On the other the meeting, however, did not take place because of the Iraqi Revolution on 14 July 1958.

In 1961, Britain decided to grant the artificial entity of Kuwait what it called "independence", a decision which prompted the then Prime Minister of Iraq to declare, in a press conference on 25 June 1961, that Iraq considered Kuwait an integral part of its territory and that Iraq does not recognize the special relationship agreement between Britain and Kuwait which the Sheikh of Kuwait, Abdulla al-Salim al-Sabah, had signed with Colonel M.J. Mead, the British Political Resident in the Gulf, on 19 June 1961. Following that declaration, Britain deployed its armed forces in the area to confront Iraq and protect its new creattion, the so-called "State of Kuwait."

Had it not been for the mistake made by Iraq's Foreign Minister at the time, Hashim Jawad, when he withdrew in angry protest from the meeting of the Arab League Council, which was considering the entry of the so-called "State of Kuwait" into the League of Arab States, thereby allowing a decision to be adopted, on 20 July 1961, to accept Kuwait as a member of the Arab League, this artificial entity would have remained outside the League; and hence out of the international organizations, as the admission of a new member to the League of Arab States is subject to a unanimous vote of approval.

The Iraqi Foreign Ministry issued statement on 21 July 1961, declaring that Iraq considered decision No. 35-1777, accepting Kuwait as a member of the League of Arab States, to be a flagrant violation of the League's Charter which stipulated that such a decision could only be adopted by unanimity. Iraq also declared the said decision to be null and void and made clear its position that Kuwait would remain an integral part of its territory and that Iraq would not abandon its endeavours to restore this part by all legitimate means.

The Government of the former regime in Kuwait also failed in its efforts between 1961 and late 1963 to be granted membership in the United Nations.

Following the downfall of the political regime which ruled Iraq between July 1958 and February 1963, the Prime Minister of the former Government of Ku-

- 6 -

wait visited Baghdad in circumstances of political confusion and instability in Iraq. A joint comminique was issued on the basis of the correspondence of 1932. However, the National Council of Revolutionary Command (NCRC), the highest Iraqi legislative authority according to the interim constitution of 1963, did not ratify that comminique.

This historical review shows that none of the successive governments of Iraq has accepted the severence of the Kuwaiti part from the land of Iraq or signed a border treaty with the artificial entity created therein. No constitutional law has ever been promulgated to describe the border.

Such was the situation prevailing in Iraq by the time the Revolution of 17 -30 July 1968. The revolutionary government leading Iraq since that date has been keen, under instruction from President Saddam Hussein, to settle this issue in a manner that would secure for Iraq a reasonable measure of its historical rights and remove at least a limited part of the injustice done to it since the beginning of the century.

During the 1970s, Iraq was the party that took the initiative in approaching the former rulers of Kuwait to find such a settlement. But those rulers, encouraged by their foreign allies, insited that Iraq accept the measures imposed by British colonialism. The Foreign Minister of Iraq visited Kuwait City a number of times in 1972 and 1973 to discuss this issue. The Interior Minister, too, visited Kuwait for the same purpose on 16 May 1978, several committees were formed without achieving any results.

This chapter on the discussions of this issue was put aside following the outbreak of the Iran-Iraq war. Immediately after the liberation of Faw, however, and while attending the Algiers Arab Summit, I took the initiative in informing the Foreign Minister of the fromer regime in Kuwait of our genuine desire to settle the border issue. We were astonished, when there was no prompt response from the regime and we had to wait until early July 1988, when the Foreign Minister of the former regime visited Iraq to agree that the subject be discussed by the two Foreign Ministers.

The talks between the two sides were delayed becaues of my preoccupation with the Iraq-Iran negotiations following the ceasefire. The President of Iraq decided to send the vice-Chairman of the Revolution Command Council, Mr. Izzat Ibrahim to Kuwait city, on 6 December 1988, to urge the former regime there to resume the talks. It was agreed that our RCC Vice-Chairman would represent our

0085

side while the Crown Prince of the former regime would represent theirs.

The visit of Vice–Chairman Ibrahim was returned by Sa'ad al_Abdullah on 6 February 1689, but it was clear that he was not prepared to consider conceding even the minimum of Iraq's legitimate demands.

On 27 March 1989, Sa'ad al–Usaimi, the Minister of State for External Affairs of the former regime, visited Baghdad and officially proposed that the talks on this issue be postponed. During the visit made by the Sheikh of Kuwait to Baghdad in September 1989, President Saddam Hussein proposed to him that the border talks be resumed. It was agreed that the matter be pursued between Deputy Prime Minister Sa'doun Hammadi and the Foreign Minister of the former regime. Dr. Hammadi visited Kuwait city on 19 November 1989 to discuss the subject. The Foreign Minister of the former regime did not reciprocate the visit until February 1990.

It ought to be mentioned here that the former rulers of Kuwait had in fact exploited the situation throughout the period during which the settlement of this issue remained pending. They exploited Iraq's internal and regional preoccupations, the last and most pressing of which being the Iran–Iraq war which lasted eight years.   They expanded northwards, setting up police-posts, military installations, farms and oil rigs. In 1963, for instance, the check–point for crossing from Kuwait to Basrah was a place called al–Miltaa' where passports were stamped. But during the time in which Iraq was preoccupied with internal and regional problems,   this check–point was gradually moved up to a place more than seventy kilometers to the north of al–Mitlaa' to present Iraq with a fait accompli.

Dear Colleague,

As to the political and economic aspects of the issue, I wish to point out the following;

In February 1990, President Saddam Hussein delivered a speech at the Amman Summit in which he warned against the continued presence of the US navy in the Arab Gulf, now that the war between Iraq and Iran had come to an end. President

- 8 -

0086

Hussein stated that :

The continued US presence in the Gulf is due to the fact that the Gulf, in view of the developments witnessed in international politics and in the prospect of the oil market and of the increasing need for oil by the United States, Europe, Japan, and perhaps even the Soviet Union, has become the most important spot in the region. Indeed it may have become the most important spot in the whole world. The country therefore, that succeeds in wielding the biggest share of influence over the region, through the Arab Gulf and its oil, will secure to itself an unchallenged supremacy as a superpower. This means that unless the people of the Gulf and all the Arabs are aware, the Gulf region will become subject to the will of the United States. The situation may get to the point where, if the debilitation and unawarenes continue the United States will try to dictate the level of oil and gas production for each country, the amount sold to this or that country, and the price at which it is to be sold, all accordance with the special interests of the United States and regardless of the interests of others.

Following the President's speech, a feverish campaign was launched against Iraq by US and other Zionist-influenced circles in the West. It soon became clear that those circles intended to corner Iraq politically and in the information media in preperation for a military strike to be implemented by Israel to destroy Iraq's military power which those circles considered to upset the strategic balance in the region, and which previously in Israel's favour.

The price of oil, at the time of the President's speech in Amman was somewhere between $18 and $21 per barrel. Immediately afterwards we saw the rulers of Kuwait, supported by those of the Emirates, suddenly announced their demand for an increase in their OPEC quotas. Before waiting for the matter to be discussed in OPEC, they proceeded to flood the oil market through overproduction, bringing about a sharp fall in prices and rapid decline in Iraq's already debilitated revenues. The price of oil went down to $11 per barrel, which meant a reduction of several billion dollars in Iraq's income, at a time when the country was encountering the very heavy economic burden left by the coasts of the war.

– 9 –

0087

Iraq sought to draw attention, by diplomatic means and through bilateral contacts, to the destructive consequences its economy because of this policy. Iraq dispatched envoys to Kuwait, the Emirates, Saudi Arabia and other countries; but all was to no avail.

At the Baghdad Arab Summit Conference, which was held over the period 28-30 May 1990, President Saddam Hussein, in the presence of all the leaders, warned against this policy during a closed session on 30 May 1990. The President said ;

War occurs sometimes through soldiers and damage is inficted by explosives killings or coup attempts: at other times it occurs through economic means... to those who do not intend to wage war against Iraq, I say that this is a kind of war against Iraq.

The befhaviour of the former rulers of Kuwait and of the Emirates, however didnot change. They continued to flood the market with oil and to destablize the oil prices. Iraq again took the initiative, late in June 1990, in sending Deputy Prime Minister Sa'doun Hammadi to deliver letters from President Saddam Hussein to King Fahd, Jabir al-Ahmed and Sheikh Zayid. Iraq proposed that a summit meeting be held amongst the four parties (Iraq, Saudi Arabia, the Emirates and Kuwait), with a view to arriving at an acceptable settlement of the problem. King Fahd, however, and both the former ruler of Kuwait and the ruler of the Emirates, evaded such a meeting and accepted instead that the meeting should be on the level of oil ministers. The four oil ministers met on 10 July 1990, and the Saudi, Kuwaiti and Emirate ministers pretended to accept a return to the level of production as agreed in OPEC quotas.

No sooner had the meeting ended than the oil minister of the former regime in Kuwait announced that his regime would again demand an increase in its share in October next. This was meant to sabotage the positive results of the meeting in order to continue the conspiracy to destroy the Iraqi economy.

In his national address of 16 July 1990, President Saddam Hussein reiterated his warning against the new type of conspiracy being perpetrated against Iraq through certain Arab quarters. The President said;

Because the people of Iraq, who have suffered this deliberate injust-

- 10 -

0088

ice, have enough faith in their right to self-defence and the defence of their rights, they shall never forget the saying: "Rather heads be cut off, than sustenance." If words fail to provide protection, then decisive action must be taken to restore the usurped rights to their owners.

President Hussein pointed out in that same address that the loss incurred by Iraq, since the beginning of the slump in oil prices from $28 to $11 per barrel, had amounted to $14 billion. All this was due to the policy of flooding the world market with cheap oil which in turn replenished the strategic reserves of the United States whose need for imported oil had already witnessed a marked increase in recent times. This policy caused huge damage to the national economy and was a treacherous stab in the back for Iraq.

For, although Iraq emerged victorious from a very long and costly war, it was burdened with huge debts which had to be repaid. Iraq had also to continue its development plans and provide food for its people' who had endured much and sacrificed the flower of its youth in defending its national and pan-Arab security and in protecting the Gulf region from advancing the Iranian danger.

Prior to that, His Excellency the president had voiced a clear warning on 9 July 1990, when he received Mr. Hisham Nazir, the Saudi oil minister to whom the President said :

I shall not allow myself to accept for the people of Iraq to go hungery and for the women of Iraq to go naked of need.

On 15 July 1990, I delivered a detailed note to the Secretary-General of the League of Arab States in Tunis, a note substantiated by facts and figures confirming the involvement of the former rulers of Kuwait in the conspiracy to destroy the economy of Iraq, and exposing their delibrate and incessant violations, over the years, of the rights and vital interests of Iraq.

Amongst the things pointed out in that note, copies of which were sent to you through our diplomatic channels, was the following;

The aggression of government of Kuwait, against Iraq has been two-fold; by encroaching upon our territories and oilfields, and by steal

- 11 -

0089

ing our national wealth, such action is tantamount to military aggression. The Kuwaiti government's deliberate attempts bring down the Iraqi economy is an aggression no smaller, in its consequences, than a military aggression.

Following President Hussein's address of 16 July 1990 and my note of 15 July 1990 to the Secretary-General of the Arab League, a number of Arab leaders intervened to help resolve this issue. It was agreed that a meeting be held on 30 July 1990 in Jeddah between His Excellency the Vice-Chairman of the Revolution Command Council and the Crown Prince of the former regime of Kuwait.

Many true Arabs who were eager to see an acceptable settlement being achieved, expected the rulers of Kuwait would in that meeting abandon their arrogance, intransigence and their attempts to harm Iraq. The behaviour of the delegation of the Kuwaiti regime during the meeting was marked, however, by their prevarication, procrastination and a flagrant denial of Iraq's obvious and legitimate rights.

Thus the conclusion was confirmed that the former regime in Kuwait was bent on perpetrating its design to destroy the Iraqi economy and destabilize its political system. It is inconceivable, that such a small regime could entertain the perpetration of a conspiracy of this dimension against a big and strong country like Iraq without being supported by a great power. That power was the United States of America.

This dangerous conspiracy against Iraq led us to extend military assistance to the young revolutionaries of Kuwait in their uprising on 2 August 1990. On the following day, His Majesty King Hussein of the Hashimite Kingdom of Jordan, visited Iraq and informed President Saddam Hussein that he had made intensified contacts with a number of Arab leaders, and that there was a proposal for a small summit to be held in Jeddah on the 4th or 5th of August and attended by Iraq, Jordan, Egypt, Yemen and Saudi Arabia. President Saddam Hussein accepted the idea of this summit which was also confirmed during the visit made to Iraq on 4 August 1990, by His Excellency Mr. Ali Abdullah Saleh, President of the Republic of Yemen.

This summit, which was to be held during the evening of Saturday, the 4th of August, or on Sunday the 5th, did not take place because of the intervention of the United States of America. On the very day for which the Arab Summit

- 12 -

0090

had been scheduled, President Bush asked his Defence Secretary to visit Saudi Arabia seeking the King's approval for US forces to be invited to Saudi Arabia. The US Defence Secretary arrived in Jeddah in the morning of 6 August and the US forces began entering Saudi Arabia on 7 August, the very next day. The speed with which the operation was started confirms two basic facts. The first, is that there was already a US military plan to ensure US domination of the Gulf region, (This has been confirmed by former US officials including Zbigniew Brzezinski), and this was the right time for its implementation. The second fact is that the United States deliberately aborted an Arab solution to the problem as was planned for the Summit to be held in Jeddah on 5 August 1990.

One day after the arrival of the US forces in Saudi Arabia, the government of Egypt proposed, on 8 August, that an Emergency Arab Summit Conference be held in Cairo. The call for this summit was made without prior consultation with Iraq at least ascertain whether President Saddam Hussein would be able to go to Cairo. Neither did we receive an official invitation from the host country nor from the Secretariat of the League of Arab States as required by the regular proceedures.

Despite this aberrant behavior on the part of the Egyptian Government, an Iraqi delegation went to Cairo, headed by RCC member and First-Deputy Prime Minister Mr. Taha Yassin Ramadhan and including two other RCC members, DPM and Foreign Minister Tariq Aziz and DPM Dr. Sa'doun Hammadi. On arrival in Cairo, the Iraqi delegation requested a meeting with President Mubarak. During the meeting, the Egyptian President assured the head of the Iraqi delegation that the objective of the summit was to conduct a "dialogue". Before the openning session on the next day, and prior to any consultation being conducted amongst the leaders present, the member-states of the Gulf Cooperation Council, along with Egypt and other states, presented a paper supporting the Saudi invitation to the US forces to Saudi Arabia and calling on other Arab states to send forces there too. This created resentment amongst the other leaders attending the summit, and they demanded that the paper be withdrawn in order to enable the conference to enter into a serious dialogue. The Egyptian President, however, prevented the holding of any dialogue in search of an acceptable solution. He forced the draft paper to a vote in a manner unprecedented in Arab conferences. This was how the second attempt at an Arab solution to the problem was aborted. The states either voted against, abstained or expressed their reservations; Jordan, the Yemen, Palestine, the Sudan, Libya, Algeria, Mauritania and Tunisia which had boycotted the meeting altogether.

Dear colleague,

This historical and factual presentation makes clear the fact that the issue in question is not merely a dispute over ordinary economic or border matters. We had tolerated such differences or disputes for twenty years, a period during which we were seeking to maintain the best of relations with the former rulers of Kuwait, in spite of their wicked conduct against Iraq. What we are dealing with now is a premeditated conspiracy, in which the former rulers of Kuwait participated wilfully and in accordance with a plan supported by the United States of America, to destabilize the Iraqi economy and undermine its defence capabilities and the potential with which to face the Israeli-Imperialist scheme of aggression and expan sionism against the Arab homeland, the scheme aimed at imposing US hegemony over the region and its oil wealth in partniicular. This was in fact, as described in President Hussein's statement at the Baghdad ARab Summit and in my letter to the Secretary-General of the League of Arab States, a war waged against Iraq.

As regards Iraq's relations with the other states of the region, including Saudi Arabia, none of them offer a case similar in any way to that of Kuwait both from the point of view of history and in terms of the nature of the bilateral relations. We have been keen to establish normal relations with all these states, and have been committed to all our obligations towards them within the framework of our fraternal links. We are keen to maintain these commitments for as long as the states concerned maintain their commitments.

In view of the spurious allegations concerning the so-called Iraqi threats to Saudi Arabia, we have affirmed in every way available to us that there is no Iraqi threat to Saudi Arabia or to any other country in the Gulf. We have made clear our willingness to provide all necessary guarantees that effect, whether on the bilateral level or within the framework of the League of Arab States. We have also stated that we would not object to Saudi Arabia calling in Arab forces for assistance or protection, if the Saudis were afraid, although we still see no basis whatsoever for this fabricated fear.

Another chapter of the problem is to do with the Security Council and the position it has adopted. On the first day of the events, the United States pushed the Security Council into adopting a resolution against Iraq on the ba-

- 14 -

0092

sis of Chapter VII of the UN Charter. I am referring here to resolution 660 of 2 August 1990, which has no precedent of its kind in the whole history of the Security Council. The Council adopted this resolution without even giving Iraq the chance to be heard. It has always been normal practice in the Security Council, while dealing with international crises, to invite the Foreign Ministers of the parties concerned to attend the Council meetings before a resolution is adopted. It was obvious that everything was being conducted under feverish US pressure. On the 6th of August another unprecedented resolution was adopted to impose unjust sanctions against Iraq. Then three other resolutions were adopted for the same purpose. These were resolution 662 (9 August), resolution 664 (18 August) and resolution 665 (25 August, 1990). It was obvious that the United STates had launched a full-scale campaign in which it exercised overtly and covertly, all forms of pressure, intimidation and threats, economic and otherwise, in trying to get member-states to vote for those resolutions proposed by the United States.

On 12th August 1990, President Saddam Hussein announced an initiative in which he called for all outstanding issues in the region to be settled on the basis of the same criteria and principles. He expressed his genuine hope that this intiative would open the door for just and peaceful solutions of all the problems in the region. Western countries, however, rejected this initiative even before inquiring about it or asking for a copy of the text, thus confirming the double-standard they apply to regional and international disputes in comparison to their position towards Israel. These countries have never urged the Security Council to implement against Israel the many resolutions already adopted on the question of Palestine, its people and their rights. This has been their position despite the fact that Israel has been occupying the land of Palestine for several decades and continues to massacre the Palestinian people in all brutality while still occupying the Golan Heights of Syria and Southern Lebanon.

Iraq hereby warns against the dangers of the US scheme to impose hegemony on the Arab nation, plunder its resources and prevent its development and progress. To allow the United States a free hand indealing with regional problems in such a manner arrogant and contemptuous, while implicating other countries along with it, is a matter that constitutes a grave threat to international peace and security, the damages of which will not be confined not only to the interests of the developing third world countries, but will also affect Europe, Japan and all countries seeking to achieve independence in their positions and decisions.

- 15 -

0093

As I address this message to Your Excellency, I trust that the situation shall be studied carefully, taking all facts and factors into consideration. I also hope that the efforts of the international community shall cooperate in their efforts to confront the policy of aggression and adventurism being imposed by the United States of America upon Iraq and the region as a whole; the region that has, for decades bitterly suffered from the US policy of hegemony and blackmail, and the infamous alliance forged between the United States and Israel.

I hope that shall consider dealing seriously with the historic intiative announced by President Saddam Hussein on 12 August 1990, and with the sincere Arab efforts aimed at finding comprehensive Arab solutions to the problems of the region.

I assure you that Iraq, with its faith in peace and justice, shall remain faithfull to its belief in dialogue and in the constructive exchange of views with regard to all bilateral, regional and international issues.

Please accept, Excellency, the assurances of my highest consideration.

(signed)
Tariq Aziz
Deputy Prime Minister and
Minister of Foreign Affairs of
the Republic of Iraq
Baghdad
14 Safar, 1411 H.
4 September, 1990 A.D.

0094

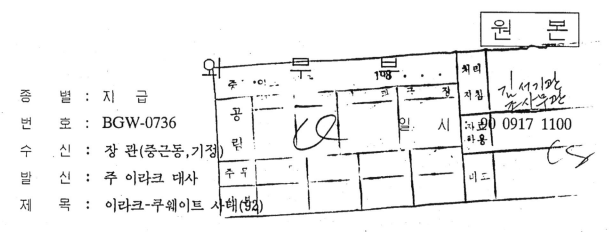

종   별 : 지 급
번   호 : BGW-0736
수   신 : 장 관(중근동,기정)
발   신 : 주 이라크 대사
제   목 : 이라크-쿠웨이트 사태(92)

1. 이라크,식량공급 관련 유엔결의 거부

-주재국 외무성 대변인은 이라크에 대한 식량공급 관련 9.13.자 유엔안보리 결의666호를 거부한다고 발표하면서, 식량의 배급문제는 자유스럽고 정상적인 방법에 의해 이루어져야 하며, 안보리 결의는 국민에 대한 모독이라고 비난함.

-동 대변인은 또한 동 결의안과 관련하여 임명된 AGHA KHAN 특사의 접수를 거부할 것임을 밝힘

2. 부시 미대통령 멧세지에 대한 항의-부시 미대통령이 이라크 국민에게 보내는 T.V 멧세지에 대하여 9.16 이라크 전역에서 항의집회를 가지고 미국과 함께 사우디,이집트를 맹렬히 비난함. 부시 대통령 멧세지에 대하여 INA 통신은 부시는 세계를 미국화 하기를 원하고 있으나 이를 거부하는 나라도 있으며 이라크는 명백히 NO 라고 대답한다고 보도함

3. 훗세인 대통령, 불란서 대통령 성명 반박

-훗세인 대통령은 9.16 미테랑 대통령에게 미국의 편견적인 반이라크 정책을 따르지 말도록 촉구하면서, 이라크군의 주쿠웨이트 불란서 대사관 침입 주장은 악의적이고 조작된것으로 미테랑 대통령의 성명은 사실을 잘알지 못하고 취한 성급한것이라고 비난함

-동 대통령은 불란서의 이라크에 대한 적대적 태도의 강화에 놀라움을 표시하면서 이라크는 미테랑 대통령이 사실 여부를 조사하기를 바란다고 덧붙임. 끝

(대사 최봉름-국장)

중아국	1차보	2차보	미주국	통상국	안기부	대책반

0095

PAGE 1

90.09.17   19:04 BB
외신 1과 통제관

외

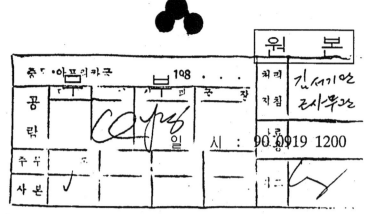

종　별 : 지급
번　호 : BGW-0745
수　신 : 장관(중근동,정일)
발　신 : 주 이라크 대사
제　목 : 이라크-쿠웨이트 사태(93호)

1. 혁명지도위(RCC) 이라크 자산 보호관련 포고발표
- RCC 는 9.18 포고에서 이라크 국내외에 있는 이라크 자산을 동결시킨 외국정부 및 공공기관의 조치는 전적으로 무효이며, 이들 정부및 공공기관은 이라크 자산을 보호할 책임이 있다고 발표함
- 동 포고는 또한 이라크와 계약을 맺은 외국회사들은 모든 장비들을 유지,관리할 법적책임을 가지며, 외국회사들은 그들의 의무태만으로 야기된 모든 손실에 대하여 이라크측은 책임을 지지 않을것이라고 발표함

2. 주재국 국회 유엔안보리 결의 비난
- 이라크 국회는 9.18 성명을 발표, 최근 동 사태와 관련하여 유엔안보리가 채택한 조치 및 결의에 대하여 강력히 비난함. 9.14 자 안보리 결의 667호(주쿠웨이트 외교공관 침입비난)는 사실확인도 없는 성급한것이었으며, 660호도 마찬가지로 공정치못함
- 동 성명은 또한 이라크 정부는 '외교및 영사관계에 관한 비엔나 협정'은 물론 국제헌장 및 규범을 존중하고 있다고 강조함
- 한편 SALEH 주재국 국회의장은 IPU 사무총장에게 보낸 서한에서 외국인의 이라크 억류는 이라크에 대한 외국의 군사위협을 방지하고 전쟁을 피하기 위한 불가피한 조치임을 재강조함

3. 아세안 게임 파견 이라크 선수단발표
9.19.자 당지 B.O 지 보도에 의하면, 이라크 올림픽 위원회는 북경 아세안게임에 12개 종목, 164명의 대표단을 파견하며, 축구대표팀을 8.25.부터 중국에 체류하고있다고 발표 함.끝

(대사 최봉름-국장)

중아국　　1차보　　미주국　　통상국　　정문국　　안기부　　대책반

0096

PAGE 1

90.09.19　　19:38 BB
외신 1과　통제관

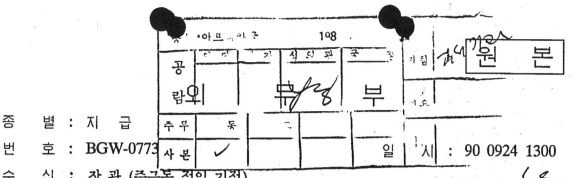

종   별 : 지급

번   호 : BGW-0773

수   신 : 장 관 (중근동,정일,기정)

발   신 : 주 이라크 대사

제   목 : 이라크-쿠웨이트사태 (94호)

1. 주재국의 대미경고 성명발표

-이라크는 9.23 RCC 및 바스당 합동회의후 발표된 성명에서 만약 미국이 군사공격을 감행한다면 걸프지역의 전유전과 이스라엘에 반격, 보복을 할것이라고 발표함.

동성명은 미국은 기습전의 위험을 인식해야하며, 군사공격으로 걸프지역은 수십년동안 빛을 보지 못하게되고 또 걸프지역의 유전지대와 이스라엘은 완전히 달라지게될것이라고 경고함

-성명은 또한 쿠웨이트 합병은 취소할수 없는 최종의 결정임을 강조함

2. 주재국 부시성명 반박

미국은 전쟁을 원치않으며, 걸프만주둔 미군은 방어를 위한것이라는 부시대통령의 성명에 대하여 주재국 정부대변인은 이는 모순되며, 거짓말이라고 반박하면서 선박을 포격하고 공중봉쇄를 준비하면서 어떻게 전쟁을 원치 않는다고 말할수 있느냐고비난함

3. 10개 대사관 무관추방

이라크정부는 9.23 당지 미국, 영국, 프랑스, 서독, 이태리, 스페인, 화란, 그리스, 사우디 및 이집트 대사관의 무관부를 폐쇄하고, 동대사관의 무관및 무관부 직원에 대하여 4-10 일이내에 주재국을 떠나라고 통보하였다고 발표함.

외무성 대변인은 또한 동 10개국 외교관은 바그다드에서 반경 30 KM 이상의 여행을 금지한다고 발표함

4. 쿠웨이트 디나병용 폐지

주재국은 쿠웨이트 디나 소지자에 대하여 9.24-10.6 간 모두 이라크디나로 교환(환율 1:1)하여야하며, 그후 쿠웨이트 디나 사용을 폐지함.끝

(대사 최봉름-국장)

중아국   1차보   2차보   미주국   통상국   정문국   안기부   대책반

0097

PAGE 1

90.09.25   07:43 FC

외신 1과 통제관

IRAQI FOREIGN MINISTER'S TRAVEL TO THE UNGA

-- THE STATE DEPARTMENT HAS REFUSED IRAQ'S REQUEST TO PERMIT
FOREIGN MINISTER TARIQ AZIZ AND HIS PARTY TO TRAVEL TO NEW
YORK FOR THE UN GENERAL ASSEMBLY ABOARD A SPECIAL IRAQI
AIRLINES FLIGHT.

-- THE UNITED STATES SUGGESTED THAT FOREIGN MINISTER
TARIQ AZIZ AND HIS PARTY TRAVEL TO NEW YORK BY COMMERCIAL
MEANS. THE HOST COUNTRY OBLIGATION TO REPRESENTATIVES OF
MEMBERS OF THE UNITED NATIONS IS TO "NOT IMPOSE ANY
IMPEDIMENTS TO TRANSIT TO OR FROM THE HEADQUARTERS
DISTRICT." THERE IS NO OBLIGATION WHATEVER TO AUTHORIZE
ARRIVAL IN THE U.S. BY SPECIAL FLIGHT SO LONG AS OTHER
MEANS OF ACCESS ARE AVAILABLE.

-- ANY NUMBER OF FOREIGN MINISTERS TRAVEL COMMERCIALLY
TO THE UNITED NATIONS GENERAL ASSEMBLY -- THIS YEAR THE
NUMBER IS IN THE NEIGHBORHOOD OF NINETY.

-- IN VIEW OF THE IRAQI GOVERNMENT'S REFUSAL TO ALLOW
FOREIGN NATIONALS TO TRAVEL FREELY FROM IRAQ OR KUWAIT, WE
BELIEVE IT WOULD BE HIGHLY INAPPROPRIATE TO PROVIDE THE
IRAQI FOREIGN MINISTER WITH SPECIAL TREATMENT RELATED TO
TRAVEL TO THE UNITED STATES.

-- WE FIND IT PARTICULARLY IRONIC THAT THE IRAQI
GOVERNMENT SHOULD CITE SECURITY THREATS AS A RATIONALE FOR
SPECIAL TREATMENT SINCE IT IS TERRORIST GROUPS, INCREASINGLY
SPONSORED BY IRAQ, WHICH PRESENT THE GREATEST THREAT TO
INTERNATIONAL AIR TRAVEL.

0098

외 무 부

종 별 :

번 호 : BGW-0774

일 시 : 90 0924 1300

수 신 : 장관(봉일,중근동) 사본:보사부장관

발 신 : 주 이라크대사

제 목 : 주재국 보건장관의 공한내용 보고

주재국 ABDUL SALEM MOHAMMED SAEED 보건장관은 9.11자로 아국 보사부장관 앞으로 대 이라크 경제봉쇄 관련 공한을 당관에 송부하여 온바(9.22 접수), 동공한요지 아래 보고함

1. 미국등 일부 국가의 대이라크 경제봉쇄 조치로 국민의 건강 특히 신생아, 임산부, 노인등의 건강에 큰영향을 미치게되는 식품, 의약품, VACCINE , 유아용 우유및 의료품의 수입이 금지되고 있는바; 이러한 물품은 경제제재의 대상이 되지않으며 또 인도적 견지에서 제외되어야 함.

2. 이러한 비인도적 범죄조치로 치료용 의약품을 구하지 못하여 많은 환자가 고통을 받고 있으며 끝내는 죽음을 초래하게 될것임

3. 미국정부의 식품,의약품 금수조치는 유엔헌장및 국제협약에 위반되는 것으로이라크는 이러한 비합리적 태도에 대한 인도주의적 의무를 요구함

4. 이라크는 귀하에게 귀정부및 국제사회를 통하여 이라크 국민에 대한 불법적 봉쇄 중지를 요구하도록 조치를 취하여 줄것을 호소함. 끝

(대사 최봉름-국장)

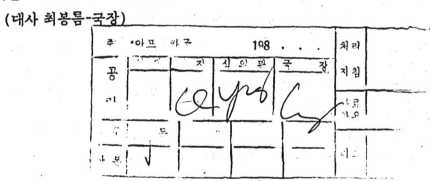

통상국   중아국   보사부

Embassy of
The Republic of Iraq
Seoul

سفارة الجمهورية العراقية
سيئول

NO. 51/90   **Press Release**   28/9/1990

MESSAGE OF PEACE

FROM

SADDAM HUSSEIN

PRESIDENT OF
THE REPUBLIC OF IRAQ

TO
THE PEOPLE OF THE
UNITED STATES OF
AMERICA

BAGHDAD

SEPTEMBER 1990

0100

IN THE NAME OF GOD, THE COMPASSIONATE
THE MERCIFUL

"O Mankind We Have created you Male and
Female and made you into Races and Tribes.
That you may Know One Another. Surely
the Noblest among you in the Sight of God
is the most God fearing of you. God is
all- Knowing, all-Aware."

Saddaq Allahul Adhim
(God's is the word of Truth)

People of the United States of America,

Assalamu Alaikum (peace be upon you),

I say Assalamu Alaikum, rather than "Good
Morning" or "Good Evening", which would have been more
in line with the ways of the West, because when the
Arabs greet other people, they use phrase "Assalamu
Alaikum". Hence you see at the outset that the Arabs

— 1 —

0101

believe in peace even when they greet non-Arabs. They
also commence their address to others by words of good
wishes, optimism and a desire for peace. This is part
of the tradition and heritage of the Arab Nation and
Islam to which we are honoured to belong. I address
you now after President Bush has appeared on our
National television. He expressed to the people of
Iraq his views on the current crisis in our region.
As I address you to express our point of view, within
the space of time available to me, my concern will be
the great majority of the American people, not those
involved in the business of politics. It is the great
majority of the people that constitutes the essence of
any legitimate human issue in accordance with the
concept of democracy. Accordingly, I find it
necessary, to reiterate certain matters already known
to professional politicians through their work.
President Bush has already appeared on Iraqi national
television and presented his views in full after he
voiced his desire to do so on August 30, 1990, along
with his displeasure at the appearance of Saddam
Hussien on US television. Once we had known of
President Bush's desire, and out of respect for
American and Western puplic opinion in general, we
welcomed the idea, through our Minister of
Information. Now that President Bush has expressed
his viewpoint, I should like to present to you some

-2-

0102

important views held by our country and our Nation.
Bush has said to the people of Iraq that the US
administration had no quarrel with them. In proof of
this, he said, the administration had allowed the
Iraqis to purchase some of the goods they needed,
particularly grains, from the US market. He also said
that the US administration had also helped bring about
the ceasefire in the Iraq-Iran war. The US President
did not hit the truth when he said the US
administration had no quarrel with the people of Iraq.
We have evidence that president Bush was himself
involved in the 1986 Iran-Gate or Iran-Contra
conspiracy against Iraq when he was Regan's
Vice-President. This is a well kown fact documented
in the dossier of the case. We received an apology
from President Regan over that affair, which he
described as a mistake not to be repeated. We
accepted the apology which was conveyed to us through
the US Assistant Secretary of State, Mr. Richard
Murphy, on May 11, 1987. Voices had already begun to
be raised in the US and Britain for economic,
technological and scientific sanctions to be imposed
on Iraq, well before the emergence of the current Gulf
crisis. Some of the measures taken against Iraq,
including the embargo on the export of grains and
other commodities, had already been discussed and
adopted by the United States, Britain and other

-3-

0103

Western countries before August 2, 1990, the day on which the Iraqi army extended assistance in the expulsion of the former rulers of Kuwait who had been installed by foreign powers to impose a despotic rule on this severed part of Iraq. Do you know, ladies and gentlemen, why the Bush administration and its ally, Mrs. Thatcher, took those measures to boycott Iraq even before the emergence of what has come to be known as the current Gulf crisis. Why, indeed, have certian voices been raised in the US and Britain promoting the notion that ending the life of Saddam Hussein, by assassinating him, has become a necessity, and encouraging an attack to be perpetrated against vital installations in Iraq? Why did the Iran-Gate conspiracy take place in 1986, involving Mr. Bush himself, an Isareli representative and others?

This had taken place before the deployment of US and British armies to the area. Worse developments may be yet to come. This is because we are Arabs. And since we are genuine in our humanity, we rejected, as we still do, the zionist encroachment upon the land of Palestine, their oppressive practices against the Palestinians and their occupation of Holy Quds (Jerusalem). You are aware, ladies and gentlemen, that we do not stand alone in our rejection of occupation and oppression. We have with us in this

- 4 -

0104

political stand, in addition to the resilient and persevering people of Palestine, the true leaders of the Arab Nation along with its two hundered million people. You are also no doubt aware that there are voices demanding an Israeli withdrawal from the Palestinian land, allowing the people of Palestine to exercise their right to a free life in dignity on their own land, on equal footing with all mankind. These voices have been raised in the American society, even amongst professional politicians, and in the world at large.

Do you know, ladies and gentlemen, how many resolutions have been adopted by the UN Security Council and General-Assembly against the Israeli policies violating the inalienable rights of the Palestinian people and perpetuating Israel's occupation of the lands of Palestine, including Holy Quds, and all the other Arab lands occupied since 1947? More than one hundred sixty resolutions have been adopted by the Security Council alone, along with four hundred more issued by the General Assembly. The United States is known to have vetoed more than 80 Security Council resolutions, the majority of which were resolutions on the Palestinian plight.

Yet, no blockade has ever been imposed against

-5-

Israel as it has been imposed against Iraq, under the pretext of implementing the recent resolutions of the Security Council. Not even a milder course of action has been taken, or armies deployed, against Israel. Such measures were never taken against Israel when it announced its official and final annexation of Arab lands and cities. In the aftermath of the occupation of Lebanon by the Syrian regime which continues to date, no US armies have ever been deployed against that regime; nor have we seen an embargo or a boycott being imposed against the Syrian regime, as we see today against Iraq. None of the resolutions or appeals calling for the withdrawal of foreign armies from Lebanon have been implemented. Why has this been the case. We see now US and Western armies deployed to occupy the land of the Arabian Peninsula, which is sacred to Arabs and Moslems alike, in such a harsh, degrading and arrogant manner as has never been witnessed, except through the story of the attempt made by Abraha the Abbassinian to invade Holy Mecca some 15 centuries ago. The resolutions of the Security Council on the Palestine Question have never been implemented, nor have the resolutions and appeals calling for the withdrawal of the Syrian and Israeli forces from Lebanon. Many other resolutions remain to date unimplemented. Yet we see how the armies of the United States have been deployed against Iraq and how

-6-

0106

the valiant Iraqi people have been denied food and medicine and even their children's milk. This has been imposed through a decision taken exclusively by the United States, contrary to Mr. Bush's claim that those measures were taken by international organisations. The international organisations came indeed later, only to be used as a cover for measures already laid down. The measures taken by the United States and Britain, including their military build-up in the region along with the imposition of the economic embargo and boycott, came well in advance of any official international measures; and then It was the United States and Britain which goaded the international organisations to take those measures. Indeed, the United States and Britain even forced some countries to participate in those measures against their will. Pressure was exerted overtly on Japan, Germany, Italy and other countries. Peasure, in its open form, could be seen every day by the US citizen on television, or heard or read about through the other information media. It is left up to the US citizens to imagine the kind of covert pressure employed in forcing other countries to adopt the policy laid down by the United States in the international organizations.

Do you know, ladies and gentlemen, why

-7-

anything like this has never been done before to
Israel which still occupies the lands of Palestine and
the Arab Nation! Do you know why the same thing has
not been done to the regime of Hafiz Assad which has
been occupying the land of Lebanon since 1976?

The answer is: if such a thing had happened,
it would have given the Arabs a lot of what would set
free their humanity, now fettred by the shackles of
occupation and its impact. If this were never to come
about, it would enable the Arabs to exercise their
proper human role as a nation with an ancient history
behind it, renowned always for its remarkable
contributions to humanity, both culturally and
spiritually in the life of mankind everywhere.

However, nothing of this sort will be allowed
to happen because, Israel, the zionist lobby, arms
dealers and politicians awaiting their election
opportunities in the US and other Western countries,
either do not want it, or indeed cannot voice out
their views. The zionist lobby is capable, through
money, the media and other means, of influencing the
outcome of elections. What has not happened in the
cases of Lebanon, Palestine, Cyprus and other places
in the area and the world at large, is being done only
against Iraq and the Arab Nation. Why has it been

– 8 –

0108

like this?   The reason is that military build-ups and
the aggressive measures related to them, along with
the economic blockade and the even worse measures
which the days ahead may yet unfold, are all factors
undermining the Arab Nation.   The return of Kuwait to
the fold of, its motherland, Iraq, from which it was
long severed and usurped, like an infant separated
from its mother, will further strengthen the Arab
Nation and Iraq in their endeavour to reassert their
role on the human and pan-Arab levels. It will allow
them to show the true example and meaning of Islam, as
dictated by God and conveyed by his Prophet Mohammed,
in a manner free from the kind of distortion and
falsehood that have given Islam a bad name through
infamous rulers in the region including some friends
of the US.   It will also throw light on the necessary
right of humanity to equal rights and duties, on equal
footing with all mankind, regardless of colour, race
and nationality.   This runs counter to the desire of
Israel and the zionist lobby which control the fate of
many politicians in the West,.through the influence
they wield in determining the results of election for
many officials in their countries, as well as in other
matters.

-9-

Ladies and Gentlemen

Although I am deeply unwilling to burden you with details, I find it imperative, in respect of the fact that people should be aware of what is going on around them in life, that I put before you some of the facts which may provide you with the opportunity you need to reach the right judgements, and to distinguish the genuine from the dishonest in the behaviour of professional politicians in your country. Kuwait constitutes the southern part of Iraq, which was severed by the British in 1913, in preparation for the First World War, and in which Britain installed Sir Mubarak al-Sabah to be undisputed Sheikh, as a reward of his services to, and alliance with, the British against the Ottoman Empire which was then in control of the region of Iraq. Thus, the Sheikhdom of Kuwait was turned into a British protectorate. No government in Iraq before us, royal or republican, ever constitutionally recognized this measure.

In order not to burden you with excessive details, I shall cite only three instances out of a long list, every part of which offers an unequivocal confirmation of this fact. In 1938, the Legislative Council in Kuwait decided on two successive occasions that Kuwait should be reunited with Iraq of which it

-10-

0110

was an integral part. The Sheikh of Kuwait, at that time, Ahmed al-Jabir, was forced to dissolve the Legislative Council in an attempt to suppress the voice of the people in Kuwait demanding the return of this part to its motherland, Iraq.

In 1958, Nouri al-Said, the then Prime Minister of Iraq, a close friend of Britain and the West, demanded, at a Baghdad Pact meeting held in Turkey and attended by US Secretary of State John Foster Dulles, that Iraq's severed part of Kuwait be returned.

In 1961, when Britain granted Kuwait independence, Iraq rejected the decision. Prime Minister Abdul Karim Qassim, who was a close friend of the Soviet Union's, took constitutional action to repudiate the British decision. Qassim obtained a constitutional decision to return Kuwait to Iraq appointing the Sheikh of Kuwait Qa'im Maqam (district administrator) of the Qadhaa'(district) of Kuwait, subordinate to the Province of Basrah, which had been the the status of Kuwait prior to its severance from Iraq. Qassim deployed the Iraqi army to put his constitutional decision into effect. He was outmanoeuvred, however, by the British who entered Kuwait with their forces before he could move in.

-11-

This led to complications which prevented Iraq's 1961 constitutional move to restore Kuwait from being realized.

This whole background, notwithstanding, we dealt with the former government of Kuwait in a normal manner. The problem, however, was exacerbated and aggravated when we discovered that the Sheikhs of Kuwait had been involved in a cospiracy to debilitate Iraq economically and politically in order to weaken it militarily and disturb the relationship existing between its people and their leadership. All this came about as a result of our political stand, to which we have made reference, In relation to the right of the Arabs to a free and decent life, along with the right of the people of Palestine to have their freedom, return to their country, achieve their independence and establish their free state on their homeland. We have discovered that the US administration was involved too, in one way or another, in this conspiracy; and so was the king of Saudi Arabia. This fact is partly revealed in a recorded telephone conversation between King Fahad and the ruler of Qatar on 9 July 1990. I am also sending you , along with this message, the tape-recording of that conversation with English subtitles, hoping that the authorities concerned will let you see it. Add to

-12-

0112

this the fact that the former rulers of Kuwait did not
stop at severing Kuwait, when it was still a fledging
town confined to its old wall, but began expanding the
territory of their sheikhdom until · it reached
al-Mitlaa and then expanded their sheikhdom further
by an additional distance of tens of kilometers
between 1963 and 1968. Then the rulers of Kuwait
exploited our preoccupation with the war between us
and Iran to expand further at our expense, by using
our southern oilfields to acquire new oil wells from
which to funnel additional oil for their benefit.

        No warning, however repeatedly stated, could
deter them from that course of action. We have
official documents substantiating all this, which we
place at the disposal of whoever is interested to have
them.

        As President Bush was delivering his statement
with the help of an autocue, he made the calculated
move taking out a piece of paper in which was written
a citation from something I had previously said in
relation to the Syrian regime's occupation of Lebanon.
Granting that the words Mr. Bush cited were literally
mine on that occasion, I suggest, however, that he
should have considered the matter more carefully
before passing his judgement, explicitly or implicitly,

- 13 -

0113

that, having deplored the Syrian interference in, and occupation of, Lebanon, we have fallen into a contradiction through our action in Kuwait.

The case of Lebanon is totally different from that of Kuwait, as I have already pointed out through the facts I have reviewed. Lebanon did not conspire against Syria, while the former Sheikh of Kuwait Jabir al-Ahmed, and his clique did conspire against Iraq. Lebanon committed no aggression against Syria, while the former regime of Kuwait perpetrated aggression against Iraq. In any case, the motives were actively different in the two situations. Although Mr. Bush meant, sought, through quoting my words, to underscore a contradiction between what we say and what we do, in a vain attempt to justify the deployment of his armies, it remains a fact that Mr. Bush had failed to oppose the occupation of Lebanon by Syrian regime. Nor did any of his allies or the traitors involved with him in the conspiracy against the Arab and Islamic Nation, oppose that occupation. Indeed, the US administration had encouraged the Syrian regime at the outset. This may well be supported by the fact that Mr. Bush has been keen recently to reward the Syrian regime for the services it has rendered. He dispatched Secretary of State Baker on an official visit to Damascus on 13-14 September, and gave the

- 14 -

0114

Syrian regime generous financial rewards from the United States and its allies both inside and outside the region.

So what has been regarded by Mr. Bush to be an imputation on us, through the text he quoted from my speech, is in fact a shameful imputation on Bush himself and on all those who adopt double-standards and conflicting criteria in their thinking and behavior and in the solutions they seek to impose on issues, be they those of Lebanon, Palestine or of any others part.

On top of all this , and in order that you may know the extent of the damage caused to an ancient people through that black conspiracy spearheaded by the rulers of Kuwait against Iraq, let me give you just one example in the financial field through which you can make your own judgements. The Iraqi dinar fell to around one twentieth of the Kuwaiti dinar after it had been higher in value than the Kuwaiti currency in 1980. Having seen all doors closed in front of us for a solution that might reassure the Iraqi people about their present and their future, including the failure of the Jeddah negotiations of 31 July 1990, which we conducted with the rulers of Kuwait via a delegation from our side headed by the Vice-Chairman of our

-15-

0115

Revolution Command Council and a delegation from their side headed by the former Prime Minister of Kuwait, we were left with no other alternative but to take the action whih we took on 2 August 1990, in order to halt dange, remove a historical injustice and place Iraq in a position of self-reassurance and of capability to serve its Nation and humanity at large.

Cotrary to what President Bush tells you about Irac having invaded Kuwait without any Kuwaiti provocatio against Iraq, here are some extracts from the warnings which we repeatedly expressed in puplic to the rules of Kuwait but in vain . These are the warnings nich we made in public. There were others which remai unpublished.

Weaddressed the rulers of Kuwait in the presence ol the Arab heads of state during a meeting of the Baqdad Summit Conference on 30 May 1990, by saying:

> War tkes place sometimes through soldiers and amage is inflicted by explosives, killngs or coup attempts. At other times war is launched through economic mean. To those who do not mean to wage war gainst Iraq, I say that this is a kind f war against Iraq.

Then made the following statement on 16 July

- 16 -

0116

1990, in my annual address to the Nation, celebrating the anniversary of Iraq's National Day (the anniversary of the 17-30 July Revolution):

> Because the people of Iraq, who have suffered this deliberate injustice, have enough faith in their right to self-defence and the defence of their rights, they shall never forget the saying: "Rather heads be cut off, than sustenance." If words fail to provide protection, then decisive action must be taken to restore the usurped rights to their owners.

Does not all this constitute warnings made in advance, but in vain?

Was there not a provocation, indeed a flagrant aggression, against Iraq?

Is not all this evidence enough for understanding the measures we took on and after 2 August 1990?

President Bush is aware of all of this and of more facts substantiating the meaning and legitimacy of the measures that we have taken. His administration followed events closely.

The US government and congress were escalating one

-17-

0117

campaign after another against Iraq, and drafting one after another for further measures of boycott and blockade to be imposed against Iraq in the political, economic and other fields. All this had already happened prior to 2 August 1990. The US measures were being taken against us as a reaction to our repeated warnings to the government of Kuwait.

Now after that has taken place and regardless of any agreement or disagreement on the method used, is it practical or logical to call for things to be returned to how they were before 2 August 1990, including the return of the Sheikhs of Kuwait who spent their time hoarding wealth and women to the extent that some of them became unable to recognize their own children in view of their great numbers. Indeed the situation was such that one of them one day expressed his desire to marry a young girl whom he had come across by chance on a previous occasion, only to discover that the girl in question was in fact one of his own daughters, God save us all !!!.....

On 5 August 1990, it was agreed that an Arab Summit Conference would be held amongst Yemen, Jordan, Saudi Arabia, Egypt, and Iraq in order to discuss the new situation and find a solution to the crisis. Instead of convening this conference to which the

- 18 -

0118

parties concerned had all agreed, we were surprised to
see the idea of the conference frozen by the friends
of the United States which had given them instructions
to that effect, with the arrival of the armies in the
Land of Arab and Islamic sanctities in the Arabian
Peninsula, and by the other decisions of the United
States.' This was how we and the international
community lost the opportunity to find an Arab
solution in a calm inter-Arab discussion of the issue.
While this has been the case in the current crisis, we
know that both the United States and its allies had
encouraged an Arab solution to the Lebanese question
for which an Arab committee was formed with the
encouragement of the United States and the blessings
later of the Security Council.

Saudi Arabia was the prime mover in that affair.
You know, ladies and gentlemen, that the people of
Lebanon have made more vital contribution to humanity
than the Sheikhs of Kuwait could ever do. Yet we see
the US administration exerting tireless efforts to
appease the ruler of Syria who occupies Lebanon. The
statements issued in Damascus, at the end of Baker's
visit on 13-14 instant, reveal this fact.

The question is therefore one of politics not of
principles, contrary to what Bush has tried to tell us

- 19 -

in his message to the people of Iraq. Since the issue is a political one not, one of principle in actual US policy, and as long as the question remains a matter of opinion in which each one views matters on the basis of his own judgement and interests, let us then resort to dialogue, rather than to arms, as the road to a common understanding and to acceptable solutions. In such a situation, the Arabs will be better equipped to resolve their problems amongst themselves. If it is desired that the international community should participate in resolving the crises and problems of the region as a whole, then the best course to adopt towards this end will be what we called for in our initiative of 12 August 1990, when we proposed that all the issues of the region, in Palestine, Lebanon and the Gulf should be discussed together and on the same level in the Security Council with a view to arriving at the same principles and criteria to be applied to all issues while taking into consideration the special nature and background of each one of them.

This will be the way that can seriously lead to a comprehensive and lasting solution to all the problems and crises of the region, in the forefront of which is the Palestinian question without whose solution the region can never regain its peace or stability.

- 20 -

0120

Those who view with responsibility the security of the region must address all the factors preceeding the 2nd of August 1990, beginning with the Palestinian question and the occupation of Lebanon by the Syrian army. They should also view the question of Kuwait with realism and in the light of its historical background as an integral part of Iraq . We have proposed that initiative which seeks to resolve all outstanding issues in the region in a manner that ensures the achievement of comprehensive and lasting peace and security. Do you know what has happened, ladies and gentelmen ? Bush rejected our initiative even before seeing its text !! And when we know that the US administration was planning military action against Iraq based in the beginning on the false pretext that Iraq had intended to invade Saudi Arabia, a pretext dismissed by naked facts, it occurred to us that one of the means of giving the US administration a better chance for thinking,while allowing all parties concerned additional time which could be used for dialogue, would be to keep some foreigners, including US citizens as guests in the houses of our staff at some scientific and economic establishments. This was measure, used along with others, in order to prevent the outbreak of a devastating war whose damage would be incalculable to those rushing to it. In any

- 21 -

event, we are only human and we feel the pain of having had to take this measure, inspite of the fact that there are those who keep telling us that the imposition of an economic blockade against Iraq, depriving its people of their food, medicine and even children's milk, is in itself an act of war which allows us, under international law, to detain the subjects of the contries responsible for the blockade. This was what the United States government itself did, during the Second World War, when it detained even its own citizens of Japanese origin. Yet I still say that we are truly pained by this and wish to see the people of Iraq and its National Assembly given any garantees or undertakings from the United States of America pledging its commitments not to launch war or agression against Iraq, a pledge that would enable us immediately to allow all foreigners to leave the country if they so wished. This was what we proposed in our initiative of 19 August 1990, which was again rejected by the US administration immediately and without prior discussion or consideration. I have expressed publicly my desire to enter a TV debate or discussion with Mr. Bush in order to let the world public opinion, including that of the American people, know the facts in detail. But Mr. Bush has turned down this proposal which is why you find me forced now to burden

-22-

you with details. A public TV discussion with Mr. Bush would have generated greater vitality for viewers everywhere and given them a better chance to make their own judgements.

Inspite of this, however, Mr. Bush has complained to you that he could not predict what Saddam Hussein would do or know how Saddam Hussein would think. I ask you, in God's name: how could Mr. Bush know Saddam Hussein or his comrades in the leadership when Mr. Bush refuses to have a direct discussion with Saddam Hussein or enter into direct debate with him on television?

When we invite Mr. Bush to a discussion we do not mean to beg his or any party's acceptance of the idea. We proposed the debate basically out of our respect for world puplic opinion, including the public opinion of the United States. Our objective in such a debate is only to disclose the lies and false allegations that are being made so that people are better informed of the issue in question and hence better equipped to make their own decisions on the basis of what they see as clear and concrete facts.

Should not the opportunity of the debate or the discussion be seized upon by the parties concerned in

-23-

order that opponents may come to know more about each
other? If only Mr. Bush viewed the matter in a
truly responsible and serious manner, free from any
pre-concieved objectives, would he still have refused
to enter into the proposed TV debate. If Mr. Bush had
truth in his side, why should he evade a direct debate
or discussion?

Saddam Hussein's way of thinking is no deep
secret as Mr. Bush seems to suggest. Saddam Hussein's
comrades in the leadership, the people of Iraq and the
Arab Nation as well as good people all over the world,
know him well and can draw their own conclusions about
what he is to say in relation to any forthcoming
measure taken towards public events which call for a
response through words or action. There is nothing
hidden in the policy of Iraq; but Mr. Bush has no
agents planted in our leadership; nor does he have
many spies in our society as indeed some of the US
authorities concerned have publicly complained.

If Mr. Bush and other professional politicians
in the West wanted to know more about the leadership
in Iraq then we say the following: The leadership of
Iraq is a group of God-fearing mortals, sharing the
beliefs of all true worshippers of God aspiring to
please the Almighty, devoted to the service of their

- 24 -

0124

people, refusing to serve tyrants, unenticed by temptation, and unintimidated by the threats of tyrany. We serve our people and Nation deeply and sincerely, and through this service we see ourselves to be serving humanity at large. We are proud to refuse serving tyrants. We protect with our very eyes the rights and the resources of our people. We neither plunder our people's wealth nor keep it to ourselves in banks as is being done by the allies, nay the servants, of the US administration amongst the rulers of the region. We are serious when we address matters of importance, compassionate amongst ourselves and towards all God-fearing and genuine servants of God. Firm in the face of blasphemy, injustice and the exploitation that oppress and starve the poor, we do not bend in the fight for truth, and are fair in determining what we should take or give. We reject the subjugation of people by any force and call for liberty to be granted to all as commanded by God. Whenever called upon, we remain fighters in the service of God and truth, freedom fighters against injustice and its perpetrators, always true to our word. If these signs are sufficient enough for the right conclusions to be made by the US administration or others, then this means that those concerned do not value these qualities, or deem them necessary in those whom they regard to be their freinds amongst the

-25-

0125

rulers of the region. They are not used to seeing any of these attributes in those rulers, a fact for which we bear no guilt. The guilt is theirs and it is they alone who will bear the consequence. The day for which we prepare ourselves is the day of judgement before God, our people and history, when steps, God forbid, go astray.

We respect world public opinion when it is given the chance to be formed only on objective and fair bases. Anything other than this will be something planted by the devils and can only lead to the abyss, yielding no fruit and bringing nothing but vice to its reaper. The impact of God's punishment will be as heavy as the acts of those tempted to go astray.

We, as a people and a Nation, ladies and gentlemen, desire peace as much as do the good amongst you. We want peace but we want it to be comprehensive and durable, rather than just a temporary and superficial arrangement leading to an even more violent explosion at a later stage. We do not want war in which we have had enough experience and whose details are well-known to us. While our difficult circumstances and the war have provided us with the resilience required for the responsiblity and the honour of defending our homland and principles, those

-26-

0126

same circumstances and the war provided us with ample opportunities to consider deeply and patiently any step which we may take, while holding the responsiblity of such a step in honour and firmness. We fear no threats from tyrants and will not fall prey to their temptation.

Mr. Bush, ladies and gentlemen, is sending your sons to war that has no human value or meaning save fatal arrogance fueled by the capabilities of a superpower used to issuing commands which the weak have to obey. All must remember that God is omnipotent. Mr. Bush wants to bring back the sorrows of the United States and humanity by repeating the Vietnam experience, only this time the ordeal will be more violent, demanding greater sacrifices and bigger losses.

Bush tells you, ladies and gentlemen, that he and others are capable of inflicting quick strikes against their targets and end the war that way. You should know, however, (and here I don't mean to issue a threat, for we threaten no one, but only to describe faithfully how we see things and what our decisions are) you should know that if Mr. Bush decided to start a war, it would not be up to him to stop that war. The end of such a war would very much be linked to its

-27-

0127

impact and to the resolve of the people that has
decided to confront tyrany withinyielding strength
for as long as this people an its Nation remain on
the side of truth.

The United States, ladic and gentlemen, will
not lose anything if the devil c aggression and war
were to be removed from Mr. Bsh's eyebrows, and if
the means of war and destructic were to be removed
from the area and the burda of occupation and
degradation of Arab and Moslem snctities were to be
lifted. But the Iraqis and th Arabs, on the other
hand, would loose their humanityand their opportuhity
for a free life in dignity, stuld Mr. Bush have his
way in achieving the desire of Is ill-motivated self.
The Arabs would be in a circustance, void of honour
or meaning, and without a presce to be proud of or a
future ensuring life for tho and their children.
Whenever we have talked in theast and whenever we
find it our duty to remind otlrs of the qualities of
the Iraqi people and its human ole, of the qualities
of the Arab Nation and its hum role, we also remind
of the depth of civilization esablished through their
minds and efforts, of the cultue which they pioneered
to the benefit of humanity asa whole, when we say
that the depth of civilizatiorin Iraq stretches back

- 28 -

0128

to more than 5000 years and that it was Iraq which first taught mankind the form of script and writing more than 5000 years ago. Hammourabi enacted his famous Code around 4500 years ago. The lands of the Arabs have always been, by God's choice, the place of descent for divine messages and the cradle for God's messengers. The Arabs have always been and still are the apostles of the constant faith entrusted with the task of spreading the word of God all over the world.

The guidance and faith that have reached your hearts, ladies and gentlemen, have been conveyed to you by the Arab faithfuls. We have never placed Iraq or the Arab Nation above humanity in any thing we said in the past. Nor do we threaten anybody with the qualities of the people of Iraq and the Arab Nation, although the depth of the qualities must be linked with the depth of civilization; qualities such as endurance, patience, resilience to adversity and readiness to fight in the defence of truth.

As he addressed his message to the people of Iraq, Mr. Bush wanted to voice a threat when he talked about the qualities of the people of the United States by saying: "As Americans, ...there is no Nation on earth with greater resolve or stronger steadiness of purporse." He also placed the American people above

- 29 -

0129

other nations when he gave himself the right to lead mankind and all states in his address to the US Congress on 11 September 1990. In this way, Bush is, in fact, promoting a form of neo-Nazism. God is the One and only. He alone is the One Unchallenged Supreme Leader of mankind and the universe. Any claim deviating from this is a false claim void of truth and bound to be repelled.

Glory is not achieved by aggressive force but through justice, fairness and good example. Humanity would see virtue in the modesty shown by those blessed with power by the Grace of God; the power which God remains capable of taking back, if they fail to show modesty and persist along their path of ignorance.

The glory that comes from power alone can be removed by counter power. It is indeed a glory doomed to oblivion from the moment at which it begins to be built on the basis of aggressive force.

Mr. Bush talked to Congress on 11 September 1990, about the influence of strenghth and vitality as the two elements of leadership. He made no mention of God and did not speak of wisdom. If man loses the bond between his work and God, he loses his spirit. If he loses wisdom, he will, even if he continues to

- 30 -

0130

possess strength and vitality, lose human respect and influence, because he will not be accurate in what he says and does. I do not think that you will disagree with me that whoever loses his soul and the respect of others will lose everything.

Indeed, more important than anything else is the fact that Bush tells you that he brought his armies and the armies of his allies to our region to defend the lifestyle of the American people. Irrespective of the selfish undertones of this statement in which the speaker fails to see the interests of others while pursuing his own, and of the particular danger it carries to humanity as a whole if it were to maintain its generalized dimension, you ought to ask Mr. Bush who is actually threatens the lifestyle of the American people. Have the Arabs or Iraqis ever threatened the lifestyle of the American people? He tells you that he came here to the land of our nation to protect oil and that Iraq should not be allowed to possess 20% of the oil reserves. This makes it incumbent upon you and upon all of us to ask Mr. Bush whether he thinks Iraq intends to sell its oil or to drink it?!..

Iraq sells its oil on the usual market in the West. Iraq sells oil to the United States and the

-31-

West in general. That was the case up to 2 August 1990, when Iraq was selling one third of its oil to the US alone. In any event, if Mr. Bush wanted to issue a new law by which to decide the percentage allowed to any given country of any particular resource or commodity including, the resources of the United States such as grains, then I suggest that Mr. Bush should submit a proposal to that effect to the United Nations. It will then be up to the UN to take a decision which will have to be complied with by all nation and accommodated in the UN Charter.

But if Mr. Bush thinks that he can subjugate humanity and interfere in the details of its life and resources then he is mistaken. This policy on his part is bound to isolate the US from the rest of the world, and make it loathed and despised. It will also cause those who perpetrate this policy to be cursed till the Day of Judgement. I don't wish to burden you with more, but you ought to remember that thousands of children may die of malnutrition due to the lack of children's milk and that the health of many people will detriorate for lack of adequate food and their life will be in danger.

The blockade on the supplies of food, children's milk and medical needs has been a measure

-32-

0132

initiated by the US and the Bush Administration in violation of the UN Charter and of international norms

Preisdent Waldhiem stated, on his visit to Baghdad on 25 August 1990, that such inhuman action cannot be compared in its impact with any other action regardless of the different descriptions given to it.

This action came from a party to which no threat was posed; while Iraq, inspite of the threats posed to its sovereignty and security and to the security of its nation, did not take any measure similar to that action, or matching it in any describtion, motive, form or shape. Those who talk about foreigners being prevented from travel ought to remember that the whole people of Iraq is now prevented from travel and confined to its borders in view of the measures taken against its means of travel, the last of which being the proposal made by certain parties for the imposition of an air blockade against our civil avaition. Have you ever known or heard about measures as boorish, inhuman and unjust as these measures?

When Bush is asked why he opposed the reunification of Iraq and Kuwait while supporting that of Germany and not objecting to the unity in other

- 33 -

0133

parts, he may say to you that he is not against unity but he opposses annexation by force. Without going into details and arguments, you can inform Bush that the Sheikhs of Kuwait were themselves installed by British force. They did not come to rule through democracy or election. Kuwait too had been severed from Iraq by force, and all the attempts for reunification which I have described and which were made through democratic means, including the 1938 attempts of the Legislative Council in Kuwait, were suppressed. Kuwait, Iraq's severed part has been used as a base of conspiracy against Iraq instead of being the part that should support it. There was no other alternative better than what was done, ladies and gentlemen. And we thank God for what has happened.

The claim made by Bush that the majority of the Arabs are with him is inaccurate; I do not want to describe it in other terms. If the desire is there to ascertain the position of the Arab nation, let Mr. Bush agree to the setting up of a working group comprising members of the US Congress to meet with representatives of the people of Iraq from the National Assembly with a view to conducting a joint investigation into, and assesment of, the information and facts relating to the situation.

-34-

0134

Mr. Bush has to promise the UN in advance, however, that he will let you know the true facts as they are, in which case you will have known for certain that the Arab Nation stands entirely with Iraq, and that the people of this nation, along with the Moslems of the world, reject the presence of your armies on the land of Moslem sanctities in the Arabian Peninsula. This nation is on the side of truth not falsehood and no one should be deceived by a bunch of mercenaries, weaklings and traitors trembling within the confines of their hiding-places for fear of the people's anger, especially now that they have been isolated from the course of truth persued by the faithful.

The US adminstration, ladies and gentemen, is placing you in a criticaly embarrassing situation, in addition to the fact that it places you, along with us and the whole of mankind, on the edge of a bottomless abyss. The US adminstration is causing you embarrassment as Americans in that it keeps talking about and bragging over democracy while allying itself to the most backward of governments; governments which are most unrepresentative of their people, most distant from democracy and most distant from God, the One, the Omnipotent, the Almighty.

-35-

The people of Iraq have expressed their view through their demonstrations when they took to the streets in roaring waves protesting what Bush has said in his message to them. They came out immediately after the broadcast of his message in every town and village in Iraq.

I have hereby said my word to you on behalf of the leadership in Iraq; indeed on behalf of all true Arabs and Moslems.

God is the sorce of success
God is great

There are those who on being told "your enemy had mustered great force against you, fear them," grew more tenacious in their faith and replied "Alläh's Help is all Sufficient for Us. He is the best Protector."

Saddaqa Allahuaal Adhim
(God's is the Word of Truth)

- 36 -

0136

외 무 부

종 별 :

번 호 : BGW-0798

일 시 : 90 0929 1300

수 신 : 장관(중근동,정일)

발 신 : 주이라크대사

제 목 : 이라크-팔레스타인연대(95호)

1. 팔레스타인 해방전선지도자 ABU ABBAS 는 주재국 라마단 제1부수상과의 면담에서 만약 미국이 이라크 항공기를 공격한다면 전세계에서 이에 유사한 보복공격을 받게될것이라고 경고함. ABU ABBAS 는 이라크에 대한 육,해,공중의 봉쇄는 침략적인 테러행위라고 말하면서 현재의 싸움은 아랍의 운명을 건 싸움이라고 강조함

2. 한편,9.28 당지 B.O 지에 의하면, 팔레스타인해방 인민전선 지도자 GEORGE HABASH 는 튜니시아 일간지와의 기자회견에서 미국의 아랍장악 음모를 경고하면서,미국의 패권주의를 지원하는 무바락 이집트 대통령과 쏘련의 태도를 비난하였다고보도함

3. 팔레스타인 지도자들은 금번 사태관련 이라크에대한 전폭 지원과 함께 연대감을 표시하고 팔레스타인 독립과 연계하여 공동전선 구축노력을 강화하기로함.끝

(대사 최봉름-국장)

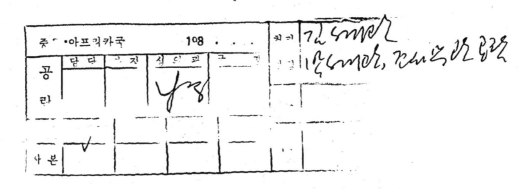

중아국   1차보   정문국   안기부

외 무 부

종 별 :

번 호 : BGW-0819   일 시 : 90 1006 1000

수 신 : 장관(중근동,기정)

발 신 : 주 이라크 대사

제 목 : 쿠웨이트사태관련

1. 10.5 YEVGENY PRIMAKOV 쏘련대통령 고문은 주재국 대통령에게 동국 대통령 친서를 전달하고 쿠웨이트 침공 사태와관련 협의한바, 동 내용은 당지에서 밝혀지지 않았음.(그러나 외신에 의하면 5,000 체류 쏘련인 출국승인을 얻어냈다고함)

2. 10.4 카이후 일본수상은 암만에서 RAMADHAN 주재국 수석부수상과 만나, 쿠웨이트사태의 평화적 수습방안을 논의했으나 주재국은 종래 태도를 고수, 쿠웨이트합병 및 중도사태 일괄타결 주재국 제안(8.12)등을 고집하여 동회담 성과는 없었던것으로 보임

3. HUSSEIN 대통령은 10.3 쿠웨이트합병후 최초로 쿠웨이트시내및 동 전선을 시찰했다고 신문및 TV 등 보도함.

4. 당지 외교단 일부소식봉에 의하면 서방측은 앞으로 1 주일만 더참아보고 주재국의 쿠웨이트철수 반응이 없을경우, 군사행동을 개시할지 모른다는 설이있다고함. 그러나 동 대부분의 무관단은 금년 11 월을 현사태의 결정적인 시기로 보고있다고함. 끝

(대사 최봉름-국장)

예고:90.12.31

중아국   장관   차관   1차보   2차보   청와대   안기부   대적반

구주국   미주국   0138

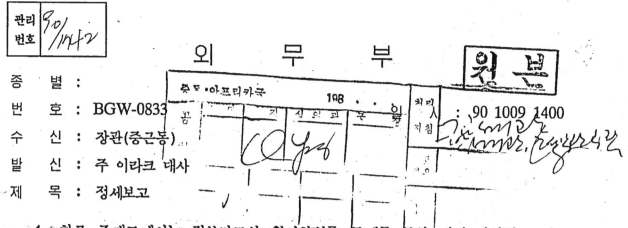

관리
번호 90/1142

외 무 부

종 별 :

번 호 : BGW-0833

수 신 : 장관(중근동)

발 신 : 주 이라크 대사

제 목 : 정세보고

1. 최근 주재국에서는 정부당국의 철저한언론 봉쇄를 통한 대내 심리전 효과로 대부분의 주민들은 사태를 정확히 인식하지 못하고 있으며 사태 장기화로 인한 면역등으로 군사공격 위험성에대한 불안감과 물자부족 상태하에서도 사태 초기에 비해 긴장이 많이 풀린 평소생활 모습을 보이고 있으며, 10.1 이후에는 거리 요소요소에 배치되었던 군인들도 철수하고, 최근에 새로운 상점들이 계속 개점하여 쿠웨이트에서 가져온 다양한 물품들을 판매하기 시작, 사태 이전에는 당지에서 구할수없던 물건들이 터무니없는 고가이기는 하지만 시중에서 판매되고있는 기현상들도 나타나고있음

2. 한편, 주재국은 경제봉쇄 조치에 대응하여 농산물 생산 장려에 총력을 경주 농민들을 징집대상에서 면제시킨데이어 농협을 통해 1 억디나(약 3 억 2,000만불)을 양계, 양어, 축산장려와 밀, 보리, 쌀등 식량 증산및 사료공장 건설, 우물파기및 관개시설등에 집중부자하는한편, 농가에대한 저리 융자혜택등을 주기로했다고 10.9 당지언론에 보도됨.

3.10.9 바그다드 옵서버지는 서울발 로이타 봉신을 인용,"SEOUL POLITICAIAN ON HUNGER STRIKE"제하로 한국의 김대중 야당지도자가 정부의 대소 관계개선및 남북대화등의 성공적 성과 의식, 유권자들의 관심과 지지를 얻기위해 지자제실시, 정치사찰 금지, 내각제 개헌추진 중지등을 요구하며 단식에 들어갔다고 보도했음. 끝

(대사 최봉름-국장)

예고:90.12.31

중아국   차관   •1차보   2차보   정문국   청와대   안기부

PAGE 1

90.10.09 22:23 0139

외신 2과 통제관 CA

관리번호 90/1185

외 무 부

종 별 :

번 호 : BGW-0836

일 시 : 90 1010 1300

수 신 : 장관(중근동)

발 신 : 주 이라크 대사

제 목 : 정세보고

1. 10.9 훗세인대통령은 사정거리가 수백 KM 에 달하고 미국의 공격무기에 대항할수있는 AL-HIJARA(THE STONE) 라는 장거리 미사일을 주재국 기술진이 개발했다고 밝히면서 미국, 이스라엘및 그동맹국들이 아랍점령지로부터 철수하라고 강력히 경고했음

2. 10.9 주재국은 10.7 예루살렘에서 발생한 팔레스타인들에 대한 이스라엘의 학살을 비난하면서 전국적으로 3 일간의 애도 기간을 발표했음

3. 10.9 아지즈 주재국외상은 CNN-TV 와의 회견에서 중동문제에대한 모든 관련 당사자들이 협상을 개시할것을 촉구하면서 이스라엘의 점령지 철수등 아랍전반문제를 동시에 해결할것을 주장한 8.12 자 주재국 기본입장을 되풀이 강조했음

4. 10.9 바그다드 옵서버지는 서울발 AP "RESTRUCTURING ALLIANCES" 제하의 KELLY SMITH TUNNEY 기자 컬럼기사로 2 차대전후 전쟁등 적대관계를 유지해온 한반도및 주변 4 강국이 최근 한.소간 외교관계수립 및 한.중공, 일본,북한간 관계개선 추진등 관계 질서가 재편되는 소용돌이 속에 동북아정치 정세판도의 변화가 일고있다고 한반도 사진과 함께 4 면 주요기사로 크게 보도했음. 끝

(대사 최봉름-국장)

예고:90.12.31

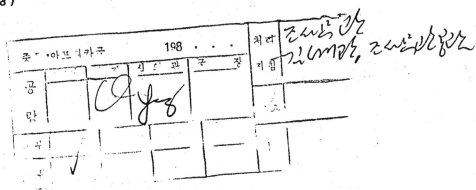

중아국   차관   1차보   2차보   정문국   청와대   안기부

0140

PAGE 1

90.10.10   21:08

외신 2과 통제관 DO

202 걸프 사태 쿠웨이트, 이라크 및 각국 경제 제재

원 본

외 무 부

종 별 :

번 호 : BGW-0866

일 시 : 90 1020 1200

수 신 : 장관(중근동,기정,기재)

발 신 : 주 이라크 대사

제 목 : 외국업체 예금 인출 잠정 동결

연:BGW-767,799

대:WBG-519

1. 최근 주재국은 지난 9.16 자 ACC 결의 377 호 에의한 90 년도 법령 제 57호 (주재국 재산 동결국에대한 대응조치)시행을 위한 각국별, 각업체별 적용 세부실무지침 작업을 계속중이며 동 지침 확정시까지 외국업체들의 예금인출(특히 현찰 인출)을 잠정 중지시키고 있음

2. 이와관련 당지 진출잔류 아국현대, 삼성, 한양, 정우등 4 개업체중 타업체들은 미리 충분한 액수를 미리 인출확보하여 아직 별문제가 없으나 정우의 경우 각종 공과금 납부및 경상비 지출에도 어려움을 겪고 있어 예금인출을위해 은행 관계자들을 계속 접촉중인바, 은행관계자들은 현재까지 한국업체들은 별문제가없는것으로 알고있고 상기 지침 하달시 인출이 가능할것이나, <u>모든 외국업체들에대해 당해국 주재 이라크대사관의 보고내용에따라 동적용 지침이 수시변경될수있다고 언급, 각국 태도를 관찰해가며 선별적 대응 조치를 취할 방침으로 보임</u>

3. 따라서 연호건 해결이 안될경우 당지 아공관 및 진출업체들의 운영에도 애로가 예상되는바, 경제제재와는 별도 차원에서 연호건 기술적 검토처리가 요망됨. 끝

(대사 최봉름-국장)

예고:90.12.31

중아국	차관	1차보	2차보	기획실	정와대	안기부

0141

관리
번호 90/1787

외 무 부

종 별 :

번 호 : BGW-0868

수 신 : 장관(중근동,기정)

발 신 : 주 이라크 대사

제 목 : 정세보고

일 시 : 90 1020 1300

1. 10.19 CHALABI 주재국 석유상은 10.23 부터 전주민들에게 휘발유 배급제실시를 발표하고 앞으로는 쿠폰을 사용해서만 휘발유 주유를 할수있으나 경유, 등유, 액화까스등은 배급대상에서 제외된다고했음

2. 동 조치는 주재국 정유능력의 한계(시설및 화학약품 (155)족등)로 민수용을 억제, 군장비 가동을 위한 군수조달을 원활히하려는데 목적이 있는것으로 보이나, 대부분 주민들이 휘발유를 예비용으로 집에 비축보관함으로서 유사시 큰 위험 요인이 되고있음

3. 10.20 바그다드 옵서버지는 평양발 로이타 통신을 인용,"CHAINA TO VETO SEOUL'S UN APPLICATION, SAY PYONG YANG"제하로 북한 외교부 부부장 강석주가 기자회견을 통해 한국이 단독으로 유엔가입을 신청할 경우, 중공은 거부권을 행사할것으로 자신은 확신하며, 중공은 한국과 외교관계를 수립하지 않을 방침임을 북한측에 확인했다고 언급한것으로 보도했음. 끝

(대사 최봉름-국장)

예고:90.12.31

19901 2 7 에 예고문에
의거 일반문서로 재 분류함.
○

중아국   차관   1차보   2차보   정문국   청와대   안기부

0142

PAGE 1

90.10.20   22:25

외신 2과 통제관 CF

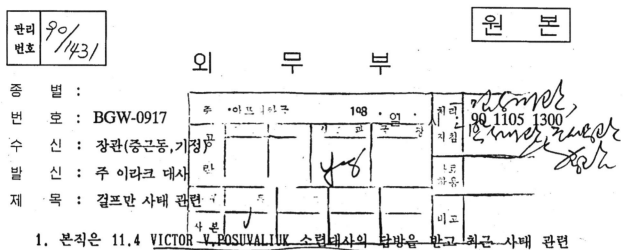

외 무 부

원 본

종 별 :

번 호 : BGW-0917

수 신 : 장관(중근동,기정)

발 신 : 주 이라크 대사

제 목 : 걸프만 사태 관련

90 1105 1300

1. 본직은 11.4 VICTOR V.POSUVALIUK 소련대사의 답방을 받고 최근 사태 관련 의견을 교환한바 동 대사의 언급 내용을 다음 요약 보고함

가. 최근 PRIMAKOV 소련특사의 재차방문시 동 특사는 미국등 관계제국의 진의도를 솔직히 털어놓았으나 HUSSEIN 대통령이 쿠웨이트철수 양보의사를 표한바없어 (그후 동특사는 소위 ARAB SOLUTION 을 위해 SAUDI 에 아랍정상회담 개최를 종용했으나 에집트의 반대에 부딪쳤음), 현재까지 동 방문 성과는 없는형편임

나. 이라크의 쿠웨이트 침공관련, 소련정부는 이라크가 쿠웨이트에서 철수하여야하며(현사태와 기타 아랍제문제는 별개), 쿠웨이트문제를 아랍-이스라엘등제문제와 연계, 일괄 타결 불가능한것으로 보며 그러나 현사태의 군사적 해결을 원치 않는 입장이라고함

다.11.4 현재 3,700 명의 소련인이 이라크에 체류중이며,2 차 PRIMAKOV 방문시 1,000 명 추가 출국허가(1 차방문시 1,500 명)되어 앞으로 3,000 명이 남게될것이라함.

라. 쿠웨이트사태의 군사적해결을 반대한다는 불.소.중.일.독의 보장과 확약이 있으면, 이라크의 모든 인질을 석방할 용의가 있다는 11.3 SALEH 국회의장의 언급과 관련, BAKER 미국무상의 사우디, 바레인 순방과 중공외상 면담등에 대응한 심리전에 불과한것으로 간주한다고함

마.CHALABI 석유상 해임관련, 현재 체포 감금설, 주택연금설등이 회자되고있으며 HUSSEIN KAMIL HASSAN 공업상의 미움을사, 그의 모략에 의해 희생당한것으로 보며(양인간 과거 수차 마찰이 있었고 휘발유 배급제 실시가 희생의 계기였을뿐임.항공기용 고급연료의 주재국 자체 생산은 가능한것이 사실임)어차피 멀지않아 주재국내 휘발유등 부족현상은 필연적으로 닥칠 문제가 아니냐고함

중아국 차관 1차보 2차보 정와대 안기부 대책반

PAGE 1

90.11.05 23:28
외신 2과 통제관 CF 0143

2. 금번 2 차에 걸친 PRIMAKOV 소련특사의 순방외교가 현사태관련, 이라크정부의
태도변화에는 영향을 미치지 못했으나, HUSSEIN 대통령에게 미국등 관련제국의 진의를
파악케하는   계기가되어   서방제국의   인질석방문제를   이용,   미.영을
불.소.중.일.독등에서 분리, 고립시켜, 군사적 공격을 면하려는 시도를 하게되었고
현사태를 아랍자체에서 수습토록 아랍정상회담 개최를 사우디에 종용했으나 에집트의
반대로 동회담 가능성은 희박해졌음
　　그러나 주재국은 8.2 이후 고립된 이라크의 입장을 대변해준 소련에 대해 특별한
느낌과 사후 응분의 고려를 할것으로 사료되며, 불.소 정상회담후 기자회견 내용은
이라크의 쿠웨이트철수에 악영향을 미칠것으로 평가함. 끝
　　(대사 최봉름-국장)
　　예고:90.12.31

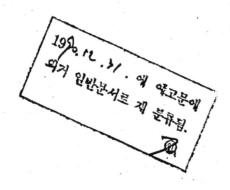

PAGE 2

0144

외 무 부

종 별 :

번 호 : BGW-0930

일 시 : 90 1108 1000

수 신 : 장관(중근동,기정)

발 신 : 주 이라크 대사

제 목 : 정세보고

　　1. 11.7 훗세인주재국 대통령은 당지를 방문중인 빌리 브란트 전 서독수상과의 면담시 동인의 요청에따라 독일인 억류 인질 100 명과 미국.영국, 이태리인 20 명의 인질들에 대한 출국을 허용했음

　　2. 11.7 아지즈 주재국외상은 베이커 미국무장관 사우디 방문시 발표한 작전관할권에 대한 공동성명에 대해 미국주도하에 이라크에대한 군사공격이 감행된다면 사우디가 동 공격에대한 결정에 참여했든 안했든 그책임은 전적으로 사우디가 저야할것이라고 경고했음.

　　3. 11.7 서독 적십자는 주재국 적십자에 약 200 만불 상당의 의약품 및 의료기구들을 기증했음. 끝

　　(대사 최봉름-국장)

예고:90.12.31

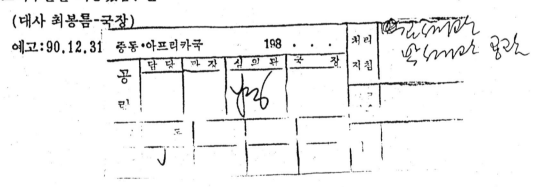

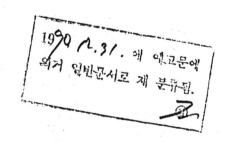

중아국　　차관　　1차보　　정와대　　안기부

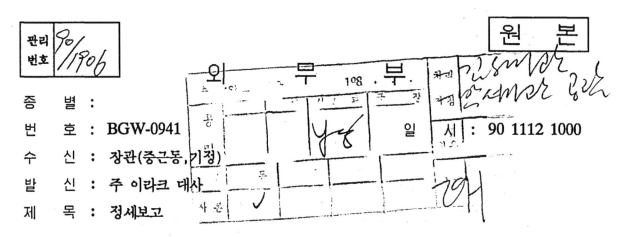

판리번호 90/1906

종 별 :

번 호 : BGW-0941

수 신 : 장관(중근동,기정)

발 신 : 주 이라크 대사

제 목 : 정세보고

일 시 : 90 1112 1000

1. 11.11 훗세인대통령은 당지를 방문중인 JORGENSEN 전 덴마크 총리와의 회담에서 미국이 걸프만 지역에 군사력과 함대를 증강시켜 관련 당사자간 직접 대화 봉로를 차단하고있다고 보도했음

2. 11.11 주재국정부는 훗세인대통령 주재로 RCC 바스당 간부 연석회의를 개최 핫싼 모로코 국왕이 제의한 긴급 아랍정상회의문제를 토의한후 발표한 성명을 봉해 동 정상회의 개최 이전 걸프만 사태 주요 당사자인 이라크측과 관련국간 충분한 사전 협의가 선행되어야할것과, 외국군들의 아랍및 사우디성지에대한 군사 위협이 계속되는한 정사회담은 개최할수 없으며, 훗세인대통령이 동회담에 참가하기 위해서는 회담개최 장소문제등이 고려되어야 한다는등의 조건을 제시했음

3. 11.11 훗세인대통령은 농산물 유봉에 관한 대책회의를 주재, 매점 매석 방지를 위해 주곡농산물 생산자는 반드시 국경 판매회사에 판매해야하며 수매가는 작년대비 20-35 프로 올려주기로하된, 매점매석 행위는 중벌에 처하기로 결정했다고 보도되었음

4. 아동 국제기구 스웨덴 지부에서 모금하고 스웨덴 정부가 대부분 출연한 54 만불 상당의 의약품이 11.11 당지에 도착했다고 11.12 주재국 언론들이 보도했음

5. 최근 주재국 NAZAR ABDUL KARIM 육참총장이 경질되고 후임에 훗세인대통령과 동향(티크리트) 출신으로 이.이전 당시 파우 반도 탈환작전에서 전공을 세운 현 육군작전 참모부장 HUSSEIN RASMEED 중장이 임명되었으며 이는 지난달 유포된 일부 기갑부대 반란 기도설과 관련한 문책 인사라는등의 첩보가 있으나 아직 공식 발표되거나 확인되지 않고있음. 끝

(대사 최봉름-국장)

예고:90.12.31.일반

1990.12.31. 예 예고문에 의처 일반문서로 재 분류됨.

종아국   차관   1차보   2차보   정문국   청와대   안기부   대책반

발 신 전 보

	분류번호	보존기간

WBG-0556   901113 1608 FH

번   호 :

종별 :

수   신 : 주   이라크   대사 . 1층 P형 1차

발   신 : 장 관 (중근동)

제   목 : 걸프 사태전망 (UKW-2104. 중계)

별첨 주영 대사 보고를 타전하니 업무에 참고 바람. 끝.

(대사 - 중동아국장)

19 90 12 31 에 대공문에
의거 일반문서로 재 분류됨.
㊞

		보 안 통 제	기

앙 고 재	90 년 11 월 13 일	중 근 동 과	기안자 성 명		과 장	심의관	국 장		차 관	장 관	

외신과통제 46

0147

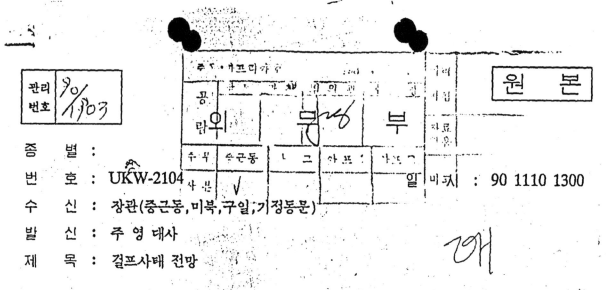

관리번호 : 90/1103

종 별 :

번 호 : UKW-2104

수 신 : 장관(중근동,미북,구일,기정동문)

발 신 : 주 영 대사

제 목 : 걸프사태 전망

일 시 : 90 1110 1300

본직은 11.9(금) 중동지역 전문가인 BRIG. HUNT 전 IISS 부소장을 오찬에 초청, 걸프사태 전망관련 의견 청취하였는 바 동인의 발언요지 아래 보고함.(황준국 2 등서기관 배석)

1. 평화적 타결 가능성 보다 전쟁 가능성이 6 대 4 로 높다고 봄. 왜냐하면 여러가지 가능한 해결방안중에 전쟁이 미국에게 가장 덜 불편한(LEAST UNCOMFORTABLE) 해결책이기 때문임

2. 전쟁없이 이라크군이 쿠웨이트로 부터 철수했을 경우(자진해서 또는 외교적 타협에 의해서) 이라크의 막강한 군사력은 그대로 남게되며 미군등 다국적 군은 걸프로 부터 철수하지 않을 수 없을것임. 그후 이라크는 시간을 두고 핵무기, 화학무기, 장거리 미사일등을 개발 또는 개량하여 사우디.쿠웨이트뿐 아니라 이스라엘을 위협하게 될 것임. 핵무기등으로 무장한 이라크가 예컨대 2 년 후에 무력도발을 감행하거나 또는 그 이전에 안보에 중대한 위협을 느낀 이스라엘이 이라크를 선제 공격하는 상황이 벌어지면 미국으로서는 현재보다 몇배 더 어려운 정치적.군사적 딜레마에 빠지게 될 것임

3. 상기 2 항을 간파하고 있을 이라크로서는 미측의 전쟁준비가 완료되어 전쟁이 임박해지면 세계평화를 내걸고 쿠웨이트로 부터 자진 철수할 가능성이 높음. 이라크군의 철수후에 이라크를 공격하는 것은 정치적으로 불가할 것이므로 결국 미국으로서는 이라크군 철수전에 UN 의 명시적 동의를 구하지 않고 대 이라크 사전 경고없이 전격적인 공중공격을 감행하여 이라크의 공군기지, 미사일기지,화학무기 공장, 테이다 시설, 정유공장, 발전소등을 4-5 일 내에 초토화 시키는 것이 최선의 방책임

4. 동 전격전으로 이라크의 공군을 분쇄하고 봉신.군수 보급선등을 차단하고 나면

중아국 안기부	장관 대적반	차관	1차보	2차보	미주국	구주국	정문국	정와대

90.11.10 23:45 0148

외신 2과 통제관 CW

이라크의 지상군 전력도 현저히 약화되고 승산은 미국쪽에 있음. 그러나전황은 동 전격전 수일동안 이라크가 어떻게 효과적으로 대응하느냐에 달려있음. 최악의 경우 이라크는 화학무기로 인구가 집중되어 있는 이스라엘 도시를 공격할수도 있으며 이결과 이스라엘이 전쟁에 끌려들어 온다면 아랍세계의 동향이 달라지고 전황은 매우 복잡하게 얽힐 것임

5. 이라크가 지금 당장 철수하지 않는것은 미국의 전쟁준비가 아직 끝나지 않았고 가능한 오래 쿠웨이트에 머물면서 미국을 협상에 끌어들여 철수조건을 흥정하려고 하는것임. 흥정 대상은 쿠웨이트이므로 미국, 이스라엘, 쿠웨이트 그리고 강경노선을 견지하고 있는 영국을 제외하고는 세계 모든 나라가 쿠웨이트 이익을 어느정도 희생하는 선에서 전쟁을 회피하는 것이 바람직하다고 생각하고 있는 것으로 보이며 이 사실을 사담 후세인도 알고 이용하려는 것임

6. 미국의 공격 최적시기는 전쟁준비상황, 기후, 국제적 여론등을 종합적으로 고려해 볼때 금년 12 월에서 내년 1-2 월이며 3 월 이후에는 전쟁발발 가능성이 극히 희박하다고 봄.

7. 결론적으로 주어진 조건하에서 소위 평화적 해결은 사담 후세인에게 유리하며 전쟁은 미국에게 장기적 손실을 최소화하는 현실적인 해결 방안임.끝

(대사 오재희-국장)

예고:90.12.31. 까지

외 무 부

종 별 :

번 호 : BGW-0944　　　　　　　　　　일 시 : 90 1113 1000

수 신 : 장관(중근동,기정)

발 신 : 주 이라크 대사

제 목 : 정세보고

　　1. 11.12 후세인대통령은 당지를 방문(11.11-12)중인 전기침 중공외교부장 접견석상에서 오랜 문명국인 이라크 국민들은 어떠한 외부 위협에도 결코 굴복하지 않을것이라고 강조하면서 동 지역의 항고적 평화를 위한 동등하고 상호 존중의원칙에 기초한 진지한 대화의 필요성을 역설했으며, 중공외교부장은 지역및 국제분쟁들의 대화를 통한 평화적 해결을 희망하는 중공정부의 입장을 전달한것으로보도됨

　　2. 한편 11.12 동 중공외교부장은 당지에서 가진 기자회견에서 걸프만 사태의 아랍해결(ARAB SOLUTION)을 지지하며, 중공은 동 지역을 전쟁의 재난에서 구하고 평화적 사태 해결을 위해 노력할것이라고 언급했음

　　3. 11.13 바그다드 옵서버지는 홋세인대통령이 11.10 자 영국 ITN 방송 기자들과의 회견에서 모든 관련당사자들이 역내 모든 분쟁 문제의 포괄적 이고 평화적인 해결을 위해 진지한 대화와 협상 테이블로 나올것을 촉구했는바 상기와같은 일련의 주재국 입장 표명은 당면한 유엔의 대주재국 군사조치행동 결의 가능성을 견제하기위한 평화공세의 일환으로 보임

　　4. 11.13 바그다드 옵서버지는 서울발 AP 통신을 인용, 한국 외무부가 걸프만 사태의 화학전 가능성에대비, 사우디를 포함한 중동지역 한국공관에 방독면을보내기로 결정했다고 보도했음. 끝

(대사 최봉름-국장)

예고:90.12.31

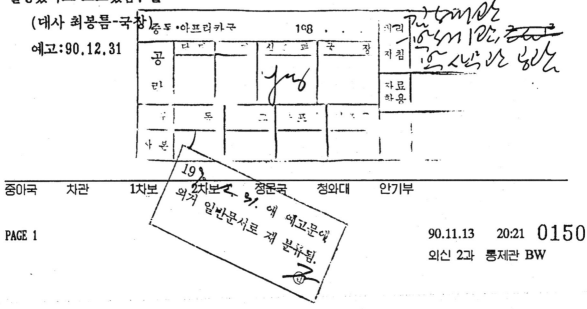

관리 90/
번호 1925

외 무 부

종 별 :

번 호 : BGW-0947   일 시 : 90 1114 1000

수 신 : 장관(중근동,기정)

발 신 : 주 이라크 대사

제 목 : 정세보고

1.11.13 훗세인 대통령은 라마단 제 1 부수상을 모로코에, 하마디 부수상을리비아및 튜니시아에 각각 파견, 각국 지도자들에게 친서를 전달, 모로코가 추진중인 아랍 특별 정사회담 문제에 관한 주재국 입장을 협의했음

2.11.14 바그다드 옵서버지는 걸프만 사태에도 불구하고 주재국은 국제 원자력기구(IAEA)에 대해 자국내 연구용 원자로 시설 핵사찰을 위해 계속 공개할 방침임을 봉보했다고 보도했음

3.11.13 주재국정부는 바스당 자문위원인 AZIA SALEH AL-NOMAN 을쿠웨이트 주지사로 임명했음

4. 주재국을 방문(11.10-13)한 전 이집트 참모총장 SADUDDIN AL SHADHLI 는11.13 당지에서 가진 기자회견에서 걸프만 사태 전망에관해 아래와같이 언급했음

-미국 주도하의 외국군 <u>동맹관계는 전쟁이 안 일어날경우,9-12 개월을 넘기지</u> 못할것임

-시간이 가면 갈수록 파병국들의 반전 여론으로 동 사태는 미 동맹관계의 균열이 발생할것이며 이라크측에 유리해질것임

-전쟁이 안일어날 경우 91 년 상반기 중에는 동 사태가 해결될수 있을것으로 보나, 전쟁이 발생한다면 언제 끝날지 누구도 장담할수 없으며, 향후 10 년간역내 정치 판도에 큰변화가 올것임.끝

(대사 최봉름-국장)

예고:90.12.31

중아국	차관	1차보	2차보	정문국	청와대	안기부	대책반

	분류번호	보존기간

발 신 전 보

WBG-0563   901116 1416 FK   **WBG-0565 (OSP: USW-5100)**

번   호 :   종별 :

수   신 : 주   이라크   대사. ~~총영사~~

발   신 : 장 관 (중근동)

제   목 : 걸프 사태 전망 (USW-5099)

별첨 주 미 대사 보고를 타전하니 업무에 참고 바람. 끝.

(대사 - 중동아국장)

예 고 : 91. 6. 30. 일반

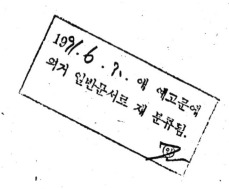

1991. 6. 7. 예 예고문에
의거 일반문서로 재 분류됨.

	보 안 통 제	

앙고재	90년 11월 16일	기안자 성명 강근모과	과 장	국 장	차 관	장 관

외신과통제

0152

외 무 부

종 별 :

번 호 : USW-5099

수 신 : 장관(미북,미안, 중근동)

발 신 : 주 미 대사

제 목 : 걸프 사태 관련 최근 미국내 동향 종합 보고

일 시 : 90 1115 1630

연:USW-5072 (1), 5022 (2), 4931 (3)

당지 언론 분석 및 주재국 각계인사 접촉을 통해 파악한 연호 (2) 부쉬 대통령의 미군 증파 공식발표 이후 관련 동향 및 사태진전 내용을 아래 종합 요약 보고함.

1. 미 행정부의 극한 정책(BRINKMANSHIP) 추진

가. 미 행정부는 10.29. 라성 WORLD AFFAIRS COUNCIL 에서의 베이커 국무장관 연설을 시발로, 부쉬 대통령의 중간 선거 지원을 위한 각종 유세 연설등을 통해 매우 강경한 용어를 사용, 이락의 쿠웨이트 침공을 규탄하고 대이락 무력 사용 가능성을 강력하게 암시함으로써 소위 RHETORIC 상의 변화를 보이기 시작하였음.

나. 특히 중간선거 직후인 11.8. 부쉬 대통령이 OFFENSIVE OPTION 의 확보를 위한 미군 증파를 공식 발표하고, 곧이어 11.9. 체니 국방장관이 사우디 주둔미군의 로테이션 계획을 부인함으로써 여사한 미측의 움직임은 상기 RHETORIC 상의 변화와 함께 미국의 대이락 공격 가능성을 보다 더 분명하게 가시화시켜 주었는바, 11.14. 자 NYT 사설은 이러한 미 행정부의 입장 변화와 관련, DESERT SHIELD 작전이 DESERT SWORD 작전으로 변형 되었다고 표현 함.

다. 한편, 다음과 같은 요인들은 이락측이 쿠웨이트로 부터 자진해서 무조건 철수하지 않는경우, 대규모 증파를 통해 공격 위주로 전환된 사우디 주둔 미군은 실제 전부작전은 내년봄 이전 개시할 가능성을 시사하고 있음.

-사우디 주둔 미군의 로테이션 취소를 기 파견 부대의 작전부입 시점이 임박한 것으로 해석할수있는 점.

-군수 및 보급 차원 뿐만 아니라 40 만에 달하는 대군을 특정지역(특히 외국 군대의 주둔에 민감한 반응을 보여온 사우디)에 장기 주둔 시키는 것은 정치적, 외교적 측면에서도 곤란하다는 점.

| 미주국 | 장관 | 차관 | 1차보 | 미주국 | 중아국 | 정와대 | 안기부 | 대책반 |

-또한 미 국내 정치적 관점에서 볼때, 미국이 이미 천명한 목표를 달성하지못한채 여사한 대규모 병력을 철수하게 되면 이는 부쉬 대통령의 정책적 실수로 인식될 것이라는 점.

-3 월이 되면 "성지 순례"가 시작되고 기온이 상승하기 시작함으로써 군사적으로 작전환경이 불리해지는 점.

-대 이락 경제 봉쇄 전략이 실시된지 3 개월이 경과 했는대도 이락측 이 쿠웨이트로 부터의 철수 움직임을 전혀 보이지 않고 있는점.

라. 그러나 기 보고한바와 같이 현시점에서 미국은 무력사용을 결정한것은 아니며 이러한 극한 정책을 통해 미군사력 배치가 단순한 시위가 아니라 진정한 위협이며, 대 이락 경제 봉쇄 전략으로 부터 대 이락 전면 공격 전략으로의 전환시점이 임박해 있다는점을 이락측에 대해 강력히 암시함으로써, 후세인에 대한압력을 가중, 이락군의 자진 철수를 유도하려는 의도로 보임.

2. 미 의회 반응

가. 행정부의 전기 극한 정책에 대한 미 의회의 반응은 연호 (1) 로 보고한바와 같이, 사우디 주둔 미군 병력 증강 사유에 대한 보다더 상세한 대국민설득이 필요하다는 입장이며, 이러한 토론과정을 통해 행정부의 대 이락 정책이 의회와 국민의 강력한 지지를 받게 되면 이락측이 미군등 다국적군 의 자국 공격 가능성을 보다 더 심각하고, 진지하게 받아들일것이라는 점을 지적하고 있음.

나. 의회의 이러한 움직임은 청문회등 토론 과정을 통해 대 이락 공격에 의해 이룩 하려는 정치적 목적과 전쟁으로인한 인적, 물적 손실과의 보다 구체적인비교 분석을 행하려는 의도로 보이며, 특히 NUNN 의원과 같은 경우는 미국이 보다 더 인내심을 갖고 대 이락 경제 봉쇄 전략의 효과를 주시하여야 할것이라는점을 지적하고 있기도 함.

다. 한편, 연호 (1) 보고와 같이, 11.13. 공화당의 외교통 중진 의원인 LUGAR 상원의원은 사우디 주둔 미군의 대규모 증강으로 인해 미국이 사실상 이락과의 COLLISION COURSE 에 놓이게 되었으므로, 의회 소집을 통해 미국의 군사력 증강 문제등과 관련한 걸프 사태 대응 방안을 공개 논의할것을 제의한바 있으나, 작일 백악관에서 있었던 행정부 및 의회 수뇌부간 회동에서는 의회 특별회기 소집대신 청문회를 포함 현재와 같은 비공식협의를 계속해 나가기로 일단 합의함.

(민주당 지도부는 여사한 특별회기 소집이 결과적으로 민주당도 BUSH 대통령의

PAGE 2

입장을 지원하는 결과가 될지도 모른다는 점에서 반대하고 있음).

　3. 미 언론 및 여론 반응

　가. 전기 의회 반응으로 마찬가지로 , 미 언론 및 언론에 나타난 미국내 여론은 대부분 공개 토론을 통한 미국내 여론 수렴의 필요성을 강조하고 있음.

　특히 "TOO FAR TOO FAST IN THE GULF" 제하의 11.11. 자 NYT 사설은 부쉬 대통령이 의회와 국민에 대해 거의 아무런 사전협의도 없이 새로운 대이락 공격 노선을 택하고 있다고(WHEN MR. BUSH DICTATES A NEW OFFENSIVE POLICY WITH BARELY A NOD TO CONGRESS OR THE BUPLIC. THE SHOWS MORE IMPERIAL IMPATIENCE THAN UNIFIED STRENGTH.) 지적함으로써 상당히 강도 높게 부쉬 대통령의 대 이락 정책을 비판하고, 사우디 내의 미군 공세 전력 강화가 일종의 관성적 반응으로 인해 전쟁으로 치달을 수도 있다는 점을 지적하였음.

　나. 또한 11.12 자 NYT 에 실린 ANTHONY LEWIS 의 " THE LOGIC OF WAR " 제하의 논설도 공개 토론을 통한 미국의 대이락 공격 지지 여론 형성이 후세인의 굴복 유도에 필수적임(PRESIDENT BUSH MUST CONVINCE CONGRESS AND THE PUBLIC THAT THE STAKES ARE WORTH THE RISK OF WAR. ONLY BY DOING SO CAN HE CONVINCESADDAM HUSSEIN THAT HE MUST FEAR MILITARY ACTION.)

　을 지적하고 있음.

　이하 USW-5100 으로 계속

PAGE 3

0155

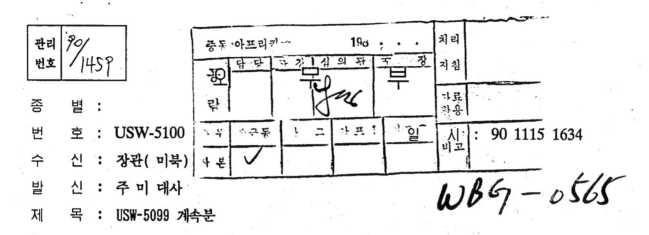

종   별 :

번   호 : USW-5100

수   신 : 장관(미북)

발   신 : 주 미 대사

제   목 : USW-5099 계속분

WBG-0565

한편 , 이락의 군사적 완전 무력화를 주장하는 강경론자인 A.M. ROSENTHAL 및 걸프
사태 발발 초기부터 대이락 무력 공격을 주장해온 HENRY KISSINGER 조차도 의회등을
통한 공개 토론의 필요성에는 모두 공감하고 있는 형편임.

다. 또한 금 11.14. 자 NYT 에 게재된 TOM WICKER 의 " THE WRONG STRATEGY"
제하의 논설은 미국민이 보다 더 인내심을 갖고 대이락 경제 봉쇄 전략의 추이를
지켜볼것("UNTIL IT IS CRYSTAL CLEAR THAT THE EMBARGO AND BLOCKADE ARE FUTILE,
MANY AMERICANS WILL BE HESITANT TO ACCEPT HEAVY CASUALTIES FOR ANYOF THESE
GOALS)을 주장하였음.

4. 관련 국제 동향

가. 한편 베이커 국무장관의 최근 중동 및 구주 순방시 걸프 사태 관련국들은
자국의 이해 득실에 따라 다음과 같이 상이한 반응을 보인것으로 알려짐.

(순방 결과 관련 기자회견 내용은 작일 팩스편 송부한 USW(F)- 3046 참조)

1) 걸프 사태 해결을 위한 관련국간 공동 보조 필요성 및 쿠웨이트 영토 일부
할양등을 통한 동 사태의 부분적 해결 반대등 기본 원칙에 있어서는 견해 일치를
보였으나 다만 대 이락 경제 봉쇄 전략의 효과에 대한 평가 및 동 전략의 적용기간에
관한 견해는 각각 상이함.

2) 사우디, 이집트, 시리아등 소위 전선국가들은 대 이락 무력 공격을 통한이락의
군사적 무력화를 선호하는 반면, 소련, 중공, 프랑스, 터키등은 대이락경제 봉쇄 및
무력 시위를 통한 이락의 쿠웨이트로 부터의 자진 철수 유도 방안을 선호 하고 있음.

3) 쿠웨이트 망명 정부를 제외한 대부분의 관련국들이 향후 2-3 개월은 대 이락
무력공격을 자제함으로써 대 이락 경제 봉쇄의 효과를 좀더 기다려 보자는 입장임.

(다만 이집트, 사우디등 아랍국들은 대이락 공격 결정 이전 이락측에 대해 충분한

미주국   장관   차관   1차보   미주국   중아국   청와대   안기부   대책반

PAGE 1

90.11.16   07:51   0156
외신 2과 통제관 BW

시간적 여유를 주었다는 명분론적 입장에서 여사한 입장을 취하고 있는 반면, 소련, 중공, 프랑스, 터키등은 동 기간중 이락측이 쿠웨이트로 부터의 철수 결정을 내리거나 이락내 반 후세인 세력에 의한 쿠데타 발생등을 기대하고 있음.)

4)아랍권 각국들은 이락측이 상금 사우디 주둔 다국적군을 진정한 군사적 위협으로 받아들이지 않고 있는것으로 봄.

즉, 후세인 대통령은 전쟁이 임박하지 않는 한 쿠웨이트로 부터의 철수를 진지하게 고려할 인물이 아니므로, 미측의 금번 병력 증파 결정에 대해서는 대부분 지지를 표함.

나. 또한 11.11. 모로코의 하싼 왕은 아랍 형제국간의 전쟁을 피하기 위한 긴급 아랍 정상회담 개최를 제의하였는바, 주요 이해 당사국인 사우디가 이락군의 쿠웨이트로 부터의 철수를 회의 참석의 전제조건으로 내세우는 등 상금 회의 자체의 개최 전망이 불투명한 실정임.

5. 결론

가. 걸프 사태와 관련, 현재 부쉬 행정부가 직면하고 있는 가장 큰 어려움은 대이락 압력 가중과 더불어 다국적군 참여국간 결속유지 및 적절한 수준의 대의회, 국민 설명을 통한 범국민적 지지 확보라는 3 가지 서로 다른 차원의 목표를 동시에 추구하여야 하는데에 있음.

즉, 미측이 대이락 위협을 보다더 CREDIBLE 하게 머어 가는 과정이 관련국은 물론 의회와 미 국민들의 눈에는 전쟁임박의 조짐으로 비치고 있으며, 이에 따라 특히 전쟁개시 가부에 관한 미국내의 여론이 비등함으로써 미국의 군사적 위협의 신뢰도를 오히려 저하시키고 있는 역설적 상황이 현재 BUSH 행정부가 처해 있는 딜레마임.

나. 요약컨데, 부쉬 행정부로서는 국내적으로 민주적 방식에 따라, 또 동시에 국제적으로는 관련국간의 CONSENSUS 를 통해 대 이락 공격 여부를 결정해야 하는 어려운 상황인바, 이러한 절차를 통해 미측이 국내 여론을 결집함으로써 소위 애국심을 통한 단결(RALLY-AROUND-THE-FLAG) 의 효과를 거양하는 경우는 이락측에 보다 더 심각한 심리적 압박을 가할수도 있겠으나 , 의회 논의등을 통해서도 행정부 조치에 대한 명백한 지지를 유도치 못하는 경우 이락측은 미국의 군사력을 계속 진정한 위협이 아닌 단순한 무력시위의 차원에서만 인식하게될것임.

즉 엄청난 파괴력을 보유하고있는 초강대국임에도 불구, 미국은 자국의 국내정치 체제에 내재하고 있는 특수성으로 인해 걸프지역에 배치중인 약 40 만의 대군을

군사적 위협수단으로 충분히 활용치 못하고 있는 형편임(이와 관련, 작일기자회견시
베이커 국무장관은 현재와 같은 긴급 상황하에서는 민주주의가 아닌 독재체제
방식으로 정부를 운영하는것이 더 쉬울것이라는 요지의 언급을 함으로써 미 행정부가
현재 체해 있는 어려운 상황을 솔직하게 토로한바 있음.

　　(대사 박동진-차관)

　　91.6.30. 일반

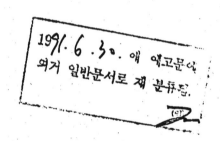

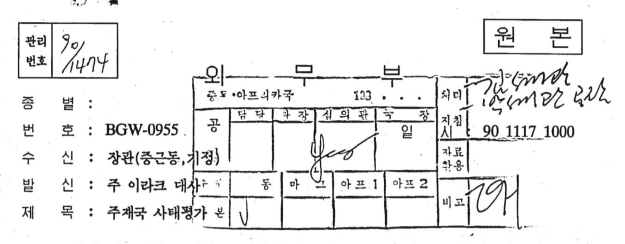

관리
번호 90/1474

외   무   부

종   별 :

번   호 : BGW-0955

수   신 : 장관(중근동, 기정)

발   신 : 주 이라크 대사

제   목 : 주재국 사태평가

1. 당지 외교단및 무관단등 견해와 현지에서 관찰한 주재국사태에 대한 평가를 아래와같이 보고함

2. 사태 발생이후 주재국은 요르단등을 통한 물자반입과 터키, 이란등 주변국경지역에서의 밀무역및 쿠웨이트로부터의 약탈물자등으로 경제제재에 견디어 왔으나 최근 유엔의 봉쇄조치 강화로 물자부족 현상이 점차 심화되어 11월부터는 주민들에 대한 식량 배급을 감량(15-20%)하기 시작했고 쿠웨이트 주둔군들에 대한 식량보급도 제대로 안되어 군사들의 사기도 저하되어 있으나 아직 주민들의일상 식생활에까지 심각한 위협을 받고있는 상태는 아님

3. 한편, 주재국은 미국등 다국적군의 군사공격을 가장 두려워하며, 군사보복 개시의 구실을 제공하지 않기 위해 테러 전략 사용등에는 계속 신중을 기하고있으며, 위장평화공세를 통해 시간을 끌면서 밀, 보리등의 추수가 시작되고 더위가 시작되는 내년 4월까지 버티어 보면 다국적군 동맹관계 및 아랍권의 분열과국제반전 여론등으로 정세가 유리해질것으로 보고 있는것 같으며 이에따라 각개격파식으로 최근 다국적군 동맹관계를 이완시키는데 주력하고 있으나 실제로 다국적군의 군사공격이 임박할경우 쿠웨이트 철수를 기도할 가능성은 있다고 봄.

4. 그러나 주재국이 아무런 피해없이 쿠웨이트로부터 자진 철수하여 미군등다국적군의 철수를 집요하게 요구할 경우 잔류 명분이 없어지게 될것이며, 주재국은 막강한 군사력을 배경으로 역내 정세를 주도 해가면서 쿠웨이트등 주변국에대한 군사 재동원이 하시라도 쉽게 가능하나, 다국적군의 재구성 부입은 현실적으로 매우 어려울것이라는 점에서, 사우디나 쿠웨이트의 실질적 안전보장등 전략상 미국은 차제에 주재국을 무력화시키는 군사조치를 선택할 가능성이 높아가고있는 상황으로 평가됨. 끝

중아국   장관   차관   1차보   2차보   정와대   안기부

(대사 최봉름-국장)
예고:91.6.30

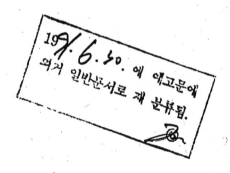

관리
번호 90/1938

외 무 부

종 별 :

번 호 : BGW-0963

일 시 : 90 1119 1000

수 신 : 장관(중근동,기정)

발 신 : 주 이라크 대사

제 목 : 주재국, 억류외국인 단계적출국 허용

1. 11.18 홋세인 대통령 주재로 개최된 주재국 혁명평의회(RCC)회의에서 주재국이 억류중인 외국인들을 평화가 파괴되지 않을경우(UNLESS PEACE WAS DISRUPTED)오는 12.25 크리스마스를 기해 단계적으로 출국을 허용하여 명년 3.15 까지 모두 출국시킬 방침을 결정했다고 11.19 바그다드 옵서버지가 보도했음

2. 이같은 주재국측 결정은 평화 제스처를 통해 당면한 유엔의 대주재국 군사 조치결의 움직임에 제동을 가하면서 명년 봄까지 시간을 끌어가보려는 의도에 기인하는 것으로 보이는바, 관련 동향을 예의주시 특이사항 추보하겠음. 끝

(대사 최봉름-국장)

예고:91.6.30

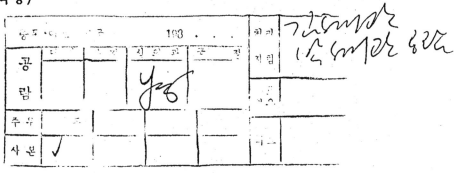

1991. 6. 30. 에 예고문에
의거 일반문서로 재 분류됨.

중아국   1차보   안기부   대책반

관리
번호 90/1351

외 무 부

종 별 :

번 호 : BGW-0970

일 시 : 90 1121 1200

수 신 : 장관(중근동,기정)

발 신 : 주 이라크 대사

제 목 : 정세보고

1. 11.20 주재국의회는 훗세인대통령 요청에따라 주재국내에 억류중인 모든 독일인들의 출국을 허용하기로 결정했으며, 훗세인대통령은 동일 의회에 보낸 상기 출국 허용요청 서한에서 동 조치는 콜 독일총리의 걸프만 사태의 전쟁을 반대하는 입장 표명에대한 감사의 표시라고 밝혔음

2. 최근 당지 일대는 연일 온종일 계속되는 전투기들의 훈련 비행 폭음으로전쟁 긴장감이 고조되고 있으며 11.19 자 주재국 당국의 25 만명 예비병력 쿠웨이트 증파계획 발표와 관련, 징집 대상 연령층및 동가족들이 몇년생까지 이번징집에 행당될지 불안해하며 징집봉고를 대기하는 모습들임

3. 한편 기온인 45 도(섭씨)이상을 오르내리던 혹서기간중에는 일기및 기온보도를 해오던 신문.방송등 주재국언론들이 최근에는 기온이 밤중에는 히터를 가동할정도로 떨어지자 일체 일기보도를 하지않고 있음도 특징임.끝

(대사 최봉름-국장)

예고:90.12.31

1990.12.31. 에 예고문에
의거 일반문서로 재 분류됨.

중아국   차관   1차보   청와대   안기부

관리 번호	90/1773

외 무 부

종 별 :

번 호 : BGW-0985

일 시 : 90 1127 1100

수 신 : 장관(중근동,기정)

발 신 : 주 이라크 대사

제 목 : 정세보고

1. 사담 훗세인대통령은 11.26 바그다드를 방문한 억류 미국인 가족들을 접견한 자리에서 이라크가 핵무기를 개발하고 있다는 11.24 CHENEY 미국방장관의 주장을 부인하고, 미국인 걸프사태 해결을 위한 이라크와의 대화에 응하도록 재차 촉구함

2. 이라크 국회는 11.26 억류 스웨덴인 전원을 석방하기로 결정함.

3. 바그다드 옵서버지는 11.27 일본정부가 이라크에 190 만불 상당의 의약품을 공급키로 허가 했다는 기사를 1 면에 크게 보도함. 일본은 그동안 나카소네전수상을 비롯 3 차에 걸쳐 의원 사절단을 이라크에 파견하고 이라크 집권 바스당 대표단을 12 월중 일본 방문토록 초청하는등 일본인 인질 석방을 위한 외교노력을 활발히 전개하여 왔는바, 금번 의약품 공급 허용결정도 이러한 노력의 일환으로 보임.끝

(대사 최봉름-국장)

예고:90.12.31

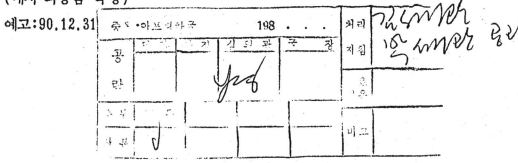

외 무 부

종   별 :
번   호 : BGW-0993   일   시 : 90 1129 1200
수   신 : 장관(중근동,기정)
발   신 : 주 이라크대사
제   목 : 정세보고

1. 바그다드 옵서버지는 11.29 유엔의 대이라크 무력사용 결의안에 중국이 찬성하지 않을것이라는 전기칠 중국외무장관의 발언과 예멘이 동 결의안에 반대키로 했다는 내용을 2면에 크게 보도함

2. 주재국은 당지 독일대사가 전달한 GENSCHER 독일 외무장관의 구두 메시지에 대해 환영의 뜻을 표함. 동 메시지 내용은 걸프 사태 해결를위한 정치적 대화를 독일이 지지한다는 것과 팔레스타인 및 레바논등 역내 기타 문제의 조속해결 필요성을강조한 것으로 알려짐

3. 사담 후세인 대통령은 벨기에 의원단 방문과관련 국회에서 벨기에 인질의 출국허용문제를 토의하도록 요청함. 또한, 주재국은 이태리인 70명이 CAPUCCI 예루살렘 대주교를 따라 11.28 출국하도록 허용함

4. 주재국 외무부 대변인은 이라크가 소련인 출국을 불허하고 있다는 소련 정부의 주장은 근거없다고 부인하고 소련인들은 다만 계약 의무에 따라 남아있을 뿐이이라고 말함

5. 주재국은 12.2-3 간 WORLD PEACE VOICE FROM IRAQ 페스티발을 개최할 예정임.동 페스티발에는 당지에 있는 일본등 서방각국의 평화주의자 242명이 참가할 것이라함.
    끝

(대사 최봉틈-국장)

중아국   1차보   정문국   안기부   2착보   미주국   통상국   대회반

PAGE 1   90.11.30   04:33 DA
                                                  인신 1과 통제관   0164

외 무 부

종   별 :

번   호 : BGW-0996   일   시 : 90 1201 1100

수   신 : 장관(중근동,기정)

발   신 : 주 이라크대사

제   목 : 정세보고

　　1.주재국 정부는 11.30 전일 채택된 대이라크 무력사용 안보리 결의를 거부하는 성명을 발표함. 동 성명에서 주재국정부는 금번 결의가 미국의 압력과 회유(금품제공)에 의해 통과 되었으며 따라서 불법 무효라고 주장함.

　　주재국은 또한 안보리가 팔레스타인 문제관련 다수의 결의를 채택하고도 이의이행에는 성의를 보이지않고 있는 점과 미국의 파나마, 그레나다 침공에 침묵을 지켰던 점등을 들어 금번 이라크에 대한 안보리의 처사가 불공평하다고 말함. 주재국은 만약 침공을 받을 경우에는 전력을 다해 맞설것이며 사우디등 미국을 지원하는난장이들을 궤멸하게 될것이라고 경고함.

　　2.사담훗세인 대통령은 11.30. 49명의 스웨덴인의 출국을 허용함.

　　끝

(대사 최봉름-국장)

중아국   1차보   정문국   안기부   　　　　　　　　　　　　　　　 0165

PAGE 1   90.12.01   18:47 DA

외신 1과 통제관

관리
번호 90-2495

외 무 부

종 별 :

번 호 : BGW-0999   일 시 : 90 1202 1100

수 신 : 장관(중근동,기정)

발 신 : 주 이라크 대사

제 목 : 미국의 외무장관 교환방문 제의에대한 주재국반응

연:BGW-0996

1. 부시 미대통령의 11.29 표제 제의와관련, 사담 후세인대통령은 11.30 혁명평의회 회의를 개최하고, 미국정부가 공식 경로로 동 제의를 해오는 경우 이를 수락할것이라는 요지의 성명을 발표함. 다만, 주재국측은 미국과의 금번 회담에서 걸프사태뿐 아니라 팔레스타인 문제등 역내 다른 문제도 함께 논의해야 한다는 입장을 표명하고 있어, 걸프사태를 유엔결의 테두리안에서 해결하려는 미국측의 입장과는 상당한 차이를 보이고있음

2. 한편, 당지 미국 대사대리에 의하면 동인은 아지즈 외무장관을 방미 초청하는 공식 초청장을 12.1 HAMDOUN 주재국 외무차관에게 전달했다고하며, 아지즈장관의 미국 방문시기는 12.10-17 사이로 제의하였다고함.

3. 주재국은 12.1 벨기에인 인질 전원의 출국을 허용한다고 발표함. 끝

(대사 최봉름-국장)

예고:90.12.31

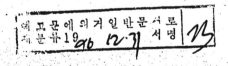

예 고 문 에 의 거 일 반 문 서 로
재 분 류 19 90 12 31 서 명

중아국   1차보   정문국   안기부   미주국 대책반 차관

외 무 부

종 별 :

번 호 : BGW-1010   일 시 : 90 1205 1100

수 신 : 장 관(중근동,기정)

발 신 : 주 이라크 대사

제 목 : 정세보고

1. 주재국은 12.4 모든 소련인의 출국을 허용키로 결정했다고 발표함. 소련인의 출국은 12.5부터 시작되며, 주재국측은 계약상 의무 불이행에 따른 제반문제는 소련정부가 책임을 겨야할것이라고 요구함.

2. 사담 후세인 대통령은 12.4 후세인 요르단국왕, 아라파트 PLO 의장, ALI SALEM AL-BEEDH 예멘 부통령과 당지에서 회담을 개최함. 동회담에서 참석자들은 금번 미.이라크 회담을 환영하고 팔레스타인 문제등 역내 모든 문제의 해결을 위해 공동 노력키로 합의했다고 발표함

3. 세계평화 페스티발(WORLD PEACE FESTIVAL FROM IRAQ)이 예정대로 12.2-4 간 당지에서 개최됨. 동페스티발은 일본 국회의원이며 전 프로레슬러인 MOHAMMED HUSSEIN INOKI 의 주도로 이루어졌으며, 일.미등 각국에서 242명의 평화주의자들이 참가함. 끝

(대사 최봉름-국장)

주▢ •아프리카국			198 . . .	처리 지침	
공람	담당	과장	심의관	국장	
					요
	보				
사 본	✓				

중아국   1차보   정문국   안기부

PAGE 1

0167

90.12.05   21:02 DQ

외신 1과 통제관

걸프사태, 1990-91. 전12권 (V.2 이라크, 1990-91) 229

외 무 부

종 별 :

번 호 : BGW-1013   일   시 : 90 1206 1600

수 신 : 장관(중근동,기정)

발 신 : 주 이라크 대사

제 목 : 정세보고

연:BGW-1010

1. 12.5 당지 미국대사대리에 의하면, AZIZ 주재국 외무장관은 12.17 경 미국을 방문할 예정이라고함

2. 사담 훗세인 대통령은 12.5 유럽의회 의원들을 접견하는 자리에서 이라크가 압력, 위협과 협박에는 결코 굴복하지 않을것 이라고 강조하고, 부시 미대통령이 걸프사태를 다루는데 이중기준을 갖고있다고 비난함. 후세인 대통령은 금번 미.이라크 대화가 협상을 위한것이 아니라 유엔안보리 결의등 상황을 이라크측에 정확히 인식시키기위한 것이라는 미국의 입장을 강력히 비난하고 이라크는 대화를 통한 설득을 원하며 명령을 통보받지는 않을것이라고 말함

3. 12.6 당지 일본대사관에 의하면, 연호 세계평화 페스티발 기간중 INOKI 의원을 따라 당지를 방문한 억류 일본인 가족의 호소가 받아들여져 전략시설에 수용되어있던 일본인 36 명의 출국이 곧 허용될 것이라고함. 또한, 일본인 인질의석방문제 협의를 위해 일본 외무부 영사교민국장이 당지를 방문중이라함. 상기36 명의 석방이 이루어질 경우 당지 억류 일본인은 총 220 여명이 되며 그중 전략시설 수용자는 약 90 명으로 추산됨. 끝

(대사 최봉름-국장)

예고:90.12.31

중아국	차관	1차보	정문국	청와대	안기부

0168

90.12.07 07:16

외신 2과 통제관 BT

외 무 부

종 별 : 지 급

번 호 : BGW-1016
일 시 : 90 1207 1200

수 신 : 장 관 (중근동,기정)

발 신 : 주 이라크 대사

제 목 : 주재국 억류외국인 전원 석방결정

　　1. 사담 후세인대통령은 12.6 억류외국인 전원의 출국을 허용하도록 요청하는 공한을 국회에 송부함. 이에따라 주재국 국회는 금명간 모든 억류외국인의 출국을 허용하는 결정을 내리게 될것으로 예상됨

　　2. 후세인대통령은 이 시점에 억류외국인 전원을 석방키로 결정한 (이유)로서 우선 ① 최근의 미국하원의 대이라크 공격시 의회승인 필요결의 채택과 유럽의회의 AZIZ 외무장관 초청등 미국및 서방여론이 이라크에 유리하게 전개되고 있는 점과, ② 최근 당지에서 정상회담을 가진 후세인 요르단 국왕, AL-BEEDH 예멘 부통령등이 억류외국인 석방을 호소한 점, 그리고 ③ 민병대등 주재국의 병력동원이 완료되어 이제는 외군의 공격에 대한 대비가 갖추어졌다는 점등을 들었음

　　3. 후세인대통령은 그러나 침략군이 아직 아라비아반도의 성지에 주둔하고 있으며 전쟁분위기를 고조시키고 있음을 들어 주재국군및 국민전체가 경계태세를 계속 강화하도록 촉구함.끝

　　(대사 최봉틈-국장)

중 ▪ 아프리카국		198 . . .		처리 지침	
공람	담당	과장	심의관	국장	
					자료 활용
수무 사본	중근동	ㄴ 그	아프1	아프2	비고

중아국　　1차보　　통상국　　정문국　　안기부　　대책반

0169

관리번호 90/1403

외 무 부

종 별 :

번 호 : BGW-1020

일 시 : 90 1208 1200

수 신 : 장관(중근동,기정)

발 신 : 주 이라크 대사

제 목 : 주재국 억류 외국인 전원석방

연:BGW-1016

1. 주재국 국회는 12.7 사담 후세인 대통령의 제의를 압도적 다수로 승인함

2. 이에따라 외국인 출국이 곧 시작될것으로 예상되는바, 다만 당지 일본등몇몇 대사관에 의하면 아직 출국 시간표및 절차등에 대한 주재국측의 통보를 받지 못하였다고 함. 끝

(대사 최봉름-국장)

예고:90.12.31

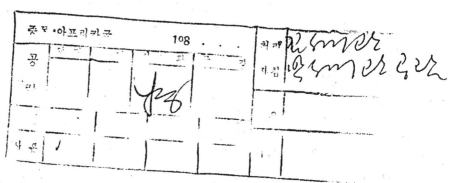

1990. 12. 91. 에 예고문에 의거 일반문서로 재 분류됨.

중아국   차관   1차보   2차보   영교국   청와대   안기부

0170

90.12.08   21:50
외신 2과 통제관 CH

외 무 부

관리
번호 8/0/
2/11

종   별 : 지급

번   호 : BGW-1023   (재수신분)   일   시 : 90 1209 1600

수   신 : 장관(중근동,기정)

발   신 : 주 이라크 대사

제   목 : 정세보고(주재국 억류 외국인 전원 석방동향등)

연:BGW-1013

1. 표제 결정에따라 주재국 당국은 12.8 부터 외국인에 대한 출국비자를 발급하기 시작했다고 하며, 전략시설에 수용되어있던 인질들도 출국준비를 위하여 바그다드로 이동되고있다고함

2. 당지 일본대사관에 의하면, 연호 일본인 36 명이 INOKI 의원을 따라 12.8 출국했다고 하며, 앞으로 12.13 및 12.22 두차례에 걸쳐 특별기를 당지로 보내 억류 일본인 전원을 본국으로 귀환시킬수있도록 주재국측과 교섭중이라고함

3. 주재국외무부는 12.8 당지 미국대사대리에게 AZIZ 외무장관의 부쉬 미국대통령 면담일자를 12.17 로하고, BAKER 미국무장관의 사담후세인 대통령 면담일자를 내년 1.12 로 하도록 제의하였다고 공식확인함. 동 발표에서는 미국측이 당초 다른 일자를 제안해 왔으나 이는 이라크측의 일정상 수락할수없다고 부연하였음. 끝

(대사 최봉름-국장)

예고:90.12.31

1990. 11. 1. 예 예고문에 의거 일반문서로 재 분류됨.

공람 [중동·아프리카국 담당 과장 심의관 국장]

주무 중근동 나그 아표

사본

중아국   차관   1차보   2차보   정문국   안기부

PAGE 1

90.12.10   15:13

외신 2과 통제관 OH171

외 무 부

종 별 :

번 호 : BGW-1027   일 시 : 90 1210 1300

수 신 : 장관(중근동,기정)

발 신 : 주이라크대사

제 목 : 정세보고

   1.관영 INA 통신은 주재국 외무부 소식통을인용, 주재국이 금번 미국과의 대화에서쿠웨이트에 대한 영유권을 고수할것이라고 보도함.

   동보도에의하면 주재국은 12.5 미국측에 금번회담이 진정한 대화희망에 기초해야하며 진지하고 포괄적이며 심층적인 의견교환이 이루어져야 할것이라는 입장을통보했다고함.

   2.바그다드 옵서버지는 주재국이 남부국경지대에 이른바 평화캠프의 설치를 허용키로 했다고 보도함.

   동 평화캠프는 12.14 설치될 예정이며, 우선 영국인 100명이 12.17 동 캠프에 들어오고 이어 미,일등 세계각국에서 참가자들이 입주할것이라고함.

   3.바그다드 옵서버지는 주재국의 억류 외국인 석방 결정에 따라 12.9일단의 이태리,미,영,아일랜드인이 주재국 항공기편으로 당지를 떠났다고 보도함. 끝.

   (대사 최봉름-국장)

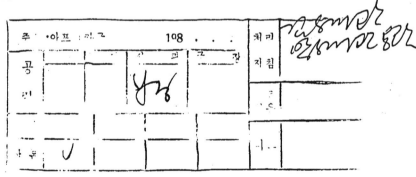

중아국   안기부

                        90.12.11   01:14 CT

                                            외신 1과 통제관

                                                 0172

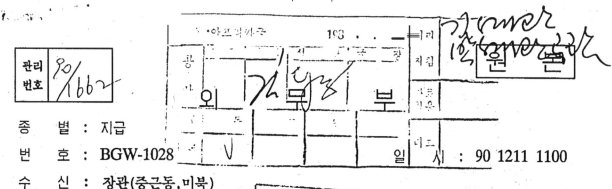

종　　별 : 지급

번　　호 : BGW-1028

수　　신 : 장관(중근동,미북)

발　　신 : 주이라크대사

제　　목 : 주재국 외무차관 브리핑

1991. 6. 20. 에 ...
의거 일반문서로 재 분류함.

1. 본직은 12.10 19:00 H 외무차관이 아시아(중국, 일본제외), 아프리카및 중남미등 30 여개국 주재대사들에게 행한 브리핑에 참석한바, 동주요내용을 다음보고함.

가. 동차관은 참석대사들에게 별전(BGW-1029) 내용의 A-M 를 전교하고 다음과 같이 부언함.

나. 외국인 인질 석방 결정을 함에있어 주재국은 매우 고심했으며 정치적, 재정적인 아무런 조건이 붙지않은 일방적 조치임을 재강조함.

다. 성실한 대화에 주재국은 언제나 응할 용의가 있음을 재천명하고 그러나위협이나 협박에 의한 어떤결정에는 응할수 없으며 위협적 언어사용이 현금 중단되지 않고 있다고 미국정부를 비난함.

라. 식량및 의약품 수입제한에 대해 유엔안보리결의에 의한 봉쇄와는 별개로 인간의 생사, 즉 인권에관한 문제로 취급되어야 한다면서 주재국의 외국인인질석방에 상응하는 식량및 의약품 봉쇄의 해제, 위협적 언어 사용중지와 안보리 재반결의 변경등 적극적 응답이 있어야한다고 호소함.

2. 관찰

가. H 차관은 미.이라크회담의 성공여부를 전망함에있어 "낙관적은 아니나 희망적" 이라는 언급으로 조심하는 태도를 보이면서, 무력충돌은 가능한한 피하려는 주재국입장의 한단면을 처음으로 드러내 보였음.

나. 동차관은 미.이라크 양측이 금번회담에서 각기 자국정부의 입장을 개진하게 될것인데 미측이 동회담에앞서 위협적언동을 계속하고 있는것은 적절치못하다고 함으로써, 주재국이 워싱본회담시 모종의 타협안(아랍-이스라엘문제와의 연계타결등)을 모색하고있음을 암시하고 주재국의 외국인인질 석방조치에

중아국　　차관　　1차보　　2차보　　미주국　　정와대　　안기부

상응하는양보가있어야할것임을 시사, 이라크 체면을 살려줄것을 강력히 요구하고
있는것으로 관찰됨.

　다. 별첨 A-M 에서는 각국이 미국및 안보리에 압력을 행사해주도록
요청하고있으나, 표제브리핑의 전반적분위기와 특히 H 차관이 브리핑중 "각국이
미국에압력을 가해달라는 이야기는 아니며 이는 별개의 문제"라고 언급한점에
비추어아국으로서는 특별한 조치나 주재국에대한 회답은 불필요할것으로 사료됨. 끝.
　예고:91.6.30.

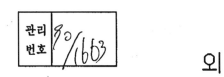

관리
번호 80/1663

원 본

외 무 부

종   별 : 지급

번   호 : BGW-1029   일   시 : 90 1211 1200

수   신 : 지급 장관(중근동, 미북)

발   신 : 주이라크대사

제   목 : 주재국 외무차관 브리핑

연:BGW-1028

연호, 내용을 별첨 보고함.

첨부:상기 전문 끝
(대사 최봉름-차관)

예고:91.6.30

첨부

AIDE-MEMOIRE

1.IRAQ'S DECISION TO ALLOW FOREIGN GUESTS TO LEAVE THE COUNTRY WAS AN IMPORTANT ONE, AND HAS CREATED A GENERAL SENSE OF RELIEF IN THE INTERNATIONAL COMMUNITY ON BOTH THE OFFICIAL AND P(250)PULAR LEVELS. WE, THEREFORE, CALL UPON YOU TO EXERCISE PRESSURE ON THE US ADMINISTRATION AND THE UNITED NATIONS SECURITY COUNCIL IN ORDER TO URGE THEM TO RESPOND IN KIND TO THIS INITIATIVE IN A MANNER THAT WILL SUBSTANTIATE THE VIEW THAT NOBLE AND COURAGEOUS INITIATIVE DO RECEIVE THE APPRECIATION AND POSITIVE RESPONSE THEY DESERVE.

2.WE WISH TO REITERATE TO YOU THE FACT THAT, WHILE IRAQ CANNOT BE GOADED INTO ANY DECISION THROUGH THREAT, INTIMIDATION OR TYRANNICAL DICTATES, IRAQ IS ALWAYS PREPARED TO RESPOND TO, AND INTERACT WITH, NOBLE EFFORTS AND EQUITABLE DIALOGUE CONDUCTED IN GOOD FAITH. IT WAS OUT OF A PARTIAL OPENING IN THE SITUATION THAT IRAQ DECIDED TO GRANT ITS FOREIGN GUESTS THE LIBERTY TO LEAVE OR TO STAY. HAD IRAQ FELT THAT THE SITUATION WAS STILL ONE OF THREAT-MONGERING AND INTIMIDATION, IT WOULD NOT HAVE ACTED AS POSITIVELYAS IT HAS DONE.

3.WE ADDRESS YOU NOW BECAUSE WE ARE CONFIDENT THAT YOU APPRECIATE THE

중아국   차관   1차보   2차보   미주국 정외대 안기부

PAGE 1   90.12.12   08:08
                                          외신 2과 통제관 BW

0175

IMPORTANCE OF DIALOGUE AND NECESSITY OF AVOIDING WAR AND DESTRUCTION. WE CALL UPON YOU TO EXERT YOUR UTMOST EFFORTS TOWARDS CREATING THE PUBLIC OPINION THAT WILL FORCE THE US ADMINISTRATION AND ITS ALLIES TO RESPOND TO IRAQ'S INITIATIVE IN A MANNER COMPATIBLE WITH ITS POSITIVE NATURE, BY LIFTINGALL RESTRICTIONS ON FOOD AND MEDICINE, BY ABANDONING THE LANGUAGE OF THREAT THUS FAR EMPLOYED AND BY CHANGING THE RESOLUTIONS WHICH THE US ADMINISTRATION SUCCEEDED, UNDER CIRCUMSTANCES PAST, IN IMPOSING UPON THE INTERNATIONAL COMMUNITY RESOLUTIONS AS PRECIPITOUS AND PROVOCATIVE AS HAS NEVER BEEN PRECEDENTED IN ANY SIMILAR SITUATION.

10 DECEMBER 1990

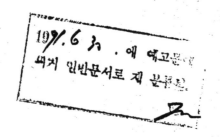

PAGE 2

외 무 부

종 별 :

번 호 : BGW-1032

수 신 : 장관(중근동,기정)

발 신 : 주 이라크 대사

제 목 : 정세보고

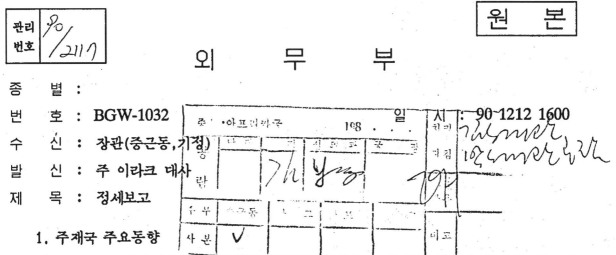

1. 주재국 주요동향

가. JASSIM 공보장관은 12.12 만일 미국이 전쟁을 도발하면 엄청난 희생을 치르게 될것이며 이에대한 전책임은 부쉬 미대통령이 져야할것이라고 경고함. 동장관은 이어 부쉬대통령이 사태발생이래 거짓말을 거듭해왔으며 이른바미국의 전략목표를 간단없이 바꾸어 왔다고 비난함.

나. JASSIM 장관은 12.11 이라크가 쿠웨이트의 일부라도 결코 포기하지 않을것이라고 강조하고, 이라크가 쿠웨이트영토 일부에서의 철수를 전제로한 타협안을모색하고 있다는 최근 언론보도는 헛된 생각에 불과하다고 일축함.

다. SALEH 무역장관은 12.11 미국주도의 대 이라크 경제봉쇄는 이라크국민을아사시키려는 비인도적인 처사라고 말하고 특히 유아용우유및 의약품 금수조치를비난함. 동장관에 의하면 이라크행 유아용 우유가 터키, 불란서, 이집트, 독일,불가리아, 폴란드, 싱가폴등지에 묶여있다고 함.

라. 주재국 외무부대변인은 12.12 미국이 챠드에있던 리비아포로를 강제납치한데 대한 비난성명을 발표함. 이와관련 JASSIM 공보장관은 12.11 이라크와 리비아가 동포로와 교환키위해 당지억류 미국인일부를 리비아로루 옮기는 문제를 협의하고있다는 외신보도를 부인한바 있음.

마. 주재국의 억류외국인 석방방침에 따른 외국인출국이 비교적 순조롭게 이루어지고 있는 가운데 바그다드 옵서버지는 12.11 487 명의외국인이 당지를 출발했다고 금일 보도함.

2. 관찰

가. 주재국은 BAKER 미국무장관의 당지 방문시기를 놓고 미측과 줄다리기를벌이고 있는 가운데 금번 미국과의 대화로 이완될지 모르는 내부결속을 다지기위해 노력하고

중아국   차관   1차보   2차보   영교국   청와대   안기부

있는것으로 보이며, JASSIM 공보장관의 쿠웨이트 불포기 발언이나 대미 경고도
이라크국민을 겨냥한 내부용발언의 의미가 많은것으로 분석됨.

　　나. 주재국은 외국인 인질 석방을통해 미측으로부터 최대한의 양보를 얻어내는
한편 국제여론의 반이라크 성향중화를 도모하고 있으나 미국은 쿠웨이트 완전철수등
요구조건을 누그러뜨리지 않고 있는바, 금번 미.이라크대화의 성패는 미국이 이라크에
대하여 최소한의 체면을 살릴수있는 출구를 허용해줄것인가에 달려있다고 사료됨.
이와관련 AZIZ 장관의 방미시보다는 BAKER 장관의 답방시해결의 실마리가 잡힐
가능성이 많으며, 또한 최근 알제리등의 아랍 해결안 모색 움직임도 변수가
될가능성이 있는것으로 보임.끝.

　　(대사최봉름-국장)
　　예고:90.12.31 일반

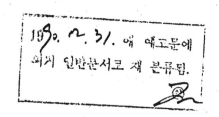

1990. 12. 31. 애 예고문에
에서 일반문서로 재 분류됨.

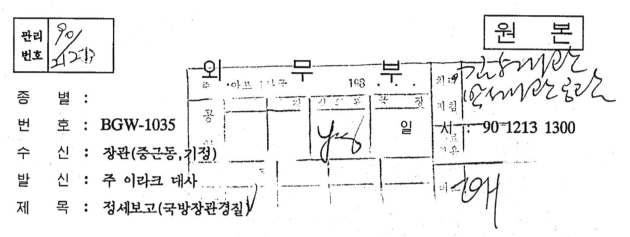

원 본

외 무 부

종 별 :

번 호 : BGW-1035

수 신 : 장관(중근동,기정)

발 신 : 주 이라크 대사

제 목 : 정세보고(국방장관경질)

시 : 90-1213 1300

1.   사담후세인대통령은   12.12   SHANSHEL   국방장관을   해임하고 육군검열단장(INSPECTOR GENERAL)SADI TUMA ABBAS 중장을 신임국방장관으로 임명함.SHANSHEL   전국방장관은   군사문제담당   국무장관으로   임명됨.ABBAS 신임국방장관은 군부내 강경파로서 대이란전시 일선전부사령관으로 많은 활약을 했으며 수도 바그다드의민방위훈련및 방공시설구축을 주도한 인물로 알려짐.

2.   상기와관련 12.13 자 바그다드 옵서버지는 이례적으로 후세인대통령이 SHANSHEL 전국방장관에게 보낸 서한내용을 게제하였는바, 동서한에서 후세인대통령은 2 년여전 SHANSHEL 장군을 국방장관으로 임명할때 동인의 고령과 건강상태를감안 국방장관임기가 2 년을 넘지않도록하겠다고 약속한바있음을 상기하고, 이제 동인의 재직기간이 2 년이넘었으므로 동인이 전에 맡고있던 군사문제담당으로복귀시킨다고 말함.

3.   금번 국방장관경질시 최근 석유장관및 군참모총장 교체시와는달리 교체이유를 발표한것은 군부내 동요등을 우려한 예방조치로 보임.당지에서는 금번교체를 SHANSHEL 전국방장관이   고령(72   세)인점에   비추어   현상황과관련   위기관리능력을높이고 미국에대해 이라크의 임전태세를 과시하는한편,   최근 군참모총장교체와 연계 후세인대통령에대한   군부내불만을   제거하는   일환일   가능성도   없지않은것으로 보고있음. 끝.

(대사 최봉름-국장)

예고:90.12.31 일반

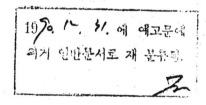

19?0. 12. 31. 에 예고문대
의거 일반문서로 재 분류됨.

중아국   차관   1차보   2차보   정문국   청와대   안기부

외 무 부

종 별 :

번 호 : BGW-1034   일 시 : 90 1213 1200

수 신 : 장관(중근동,기정)

발 신 : 주 이라크 대사

제 목 : 정세보고

1. CHADLI BEN JEDID 알제리대통령이 주재국공식방문차 12.12 당지에도착함. 동 대통령은 사담후세인 대통령과의 회담에서 걸프사태 해결을위한 아랍평화안을 모색할것으로 보임.

2. AZIZ 주재국외무장관은 12.12 최근 유엔안보리의 팔레스타인 문제토의와 관련 미국의 대이스라엘 편향태도를 강력히 비난함. 끝.

(대사최봉름-국장)

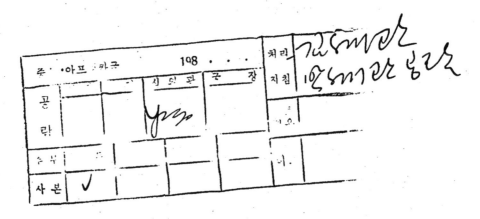

중아국   차관   1차보   2차보   청와대   안기부

PAGE 1

0180

90.12.13   22:01

외신 2과   통제관 BW

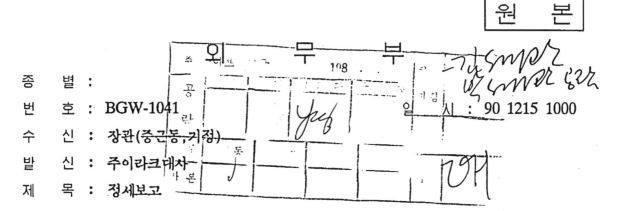

외 무 부

종 별 :

번 호 : BGW-1041

일 시 : 90 1215 1000

수 신 : 장관(중근동,기정)

발 신 : 주이라크대사

제 목 : 정세보고

1. 사담 훗세인 대통령은 12.13 만일 적들이 이라크를 공격한다면 이들을 철저히분쇄할 것이라고 강력한 경고를 발함

2. 주재국 외무부 대변인은 12.13 미국과의 직접대화 일정문제와 관련 대미 비난논평을 발표함. 동 대변인은 베이커장관의 훗세인 대통령 면담일정은 이라크측이 정하는 문제임을 분명히하고 마찬가지로 아지즈장관의 부쉬대통령 면담일정은 미측이 결정할 사항이라고 말함. 동 대변인은 베이커장관의 후세인대통령 면담일자로 미측은 12.20, 21, 22 또는 1.3을제안했으나 이날쩌는 이라크측에 편리하지 않아 대신 (1.12) 를지정한것이라고 말하고, 미측이 아무런 문제가 될수없는 사항을 마치 문제가 있는것처럼 선전하는것으로 미루어 미측이 금번 대화에 성의가 없음이 드러났다고 주장함

3. BEN JEDID 알제리대통령은 12.13 이틀간의 공식방문을 마치고 당지를 출발함. 회담결과는 발표되지 않았으나, 걸프사태와 관련한 모종의 해결방안을 협의한것으로보임

4. 라마단 주채국 제1부수상은 12.14 이라크가 쿠웨이트와 함께 사우디, 바레인, 카탈등을 점령할 계획이었다는 바레인수상의 주장을 부인함. 끝

(대사 최봉름-국장)

중아국   1차보   안기부

0181

PAGE 1

외 무 부

종 별 :

번 호 : BGW-1051
일 시 : 90 1218 1200

수 신 : 장관(중근동,기정)

발 신 : 주이라크대사

제 목 : 정세보고

1. 주재국은 12.17 사담후세인 대봉령 주재하에 혁명지도위(RCC) 및 BAATH 당 지도부 합동회의를 열고 강력한 대미 경고성명을 발표하였는바, 요지는 다음과같음

① -우리는 미국과의 결전준비가 되어있으며, 만약 미국이 공격하면 수많은 사람들이죽고 많은 독재자들이 쫓겨나게 될것임(MANY HEADS WILL ROLLAND MANY THRONUS OF TYRANTE WILL FALL)

② - 반역자들과 시온주의자들의 은신처가 무너져 내릴것이며, 패배한 독재자들의 시체를 독수리가 뜯어 먹게 될것임

③ -쿠웨이트가 이라크의 일부라는 신념에 흔들림이없으며, 이라크의 군.민은 쿠웨이트가 19번째 성이라는 사실을 큰 업적으로 생각하고있음

-걸프사태와 팔레스타인문제와의 연계이유

.걸프사태는 원칙적으로 내부문제로서 제3국이 개입할수 없는 문제임

.국제사회가 걸프사태에 개입할수 있는 명분은 오직 국제법과 유엔헌장 뿐인바, 이와관련 우리는 유엔이 팔레스타인문제에 대해서는 같은 원칙을 적용하고 있지 않음을 강조하고 싶음

.따라서 팔레스타인 문제해결을 위한 도덕적 실질적 전기를 가져오기 위하여 또한 국제법을찾는 자들의 성실성을 묻기 위하여 우리는 역내 모든 현안간의 연계를 주장하는 바임

2. 주재국 국방부는 12.17 모든 57년 출생자들이 12.18부터 3일간 군당국에 신고토록 소집령을 내림. 주재국은 지난달 58년 출생자까지 기소집한바 있음.끝

(대사 최봉름-국장)

중아국   1차보   정문국   안기부

외 무 부

종 별 :

번 호 : BGW-1058

일 시 : 90 1219 1200

수 신 : 장관(중근동,기정)

발 신 : 주이라크대사

제 목 : 정세보고

1. 주재국 외무부대변인은 12.18 AZIZ 외무장관의 미국방문 회담 결렬과 관련 EC외무장관의 AZIZ 장관 면담일정을 취소한 로마 EC 정상회의 결정을 비난하는 논평을 발표함. 동 대변인은 주재국은 아무런 전제조건없이 EC 와 대화할 용의가 있다고 말하고 미.이 라크 대화와 EC. 이라크 대화간에는 전혀 연관이 없다는 주재국 입장을 강조함.또한 동대변인은 EC 가 미국의 영향권을 벗어나 보다 독자적인 대외정책을 추구하기를 바란다고 부언함

2. SAID 주재국 보건장관은 12.18 식량 의약품부족으로 8월이래 5세이하의 아동 2,042명이 사망했다고 발표함.동 장관은 12.3 현재 사망아동이 1,416 명 이라고 발표한바 있었음.끝

(대사 최봉름-국장)

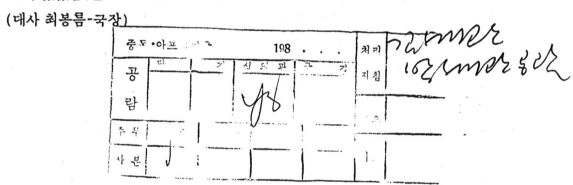

중아국   1차보   정문국   안기부

90.12.20   23:41 DQ

외신 1과 통제관

0183

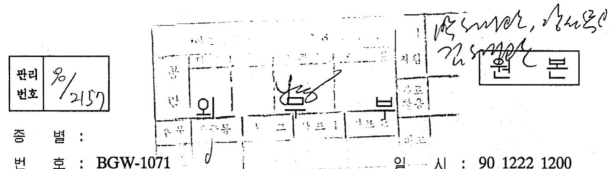

관리
번호 : 90/2157

종 별 :

번 호 : BGW-1071

일 시 : 90 1222 1200

수 신 : 장관(중근동,기정)

발 신 : 주 이라크 대사

제 목 : 정세보고

1. 주재국동향

가. 아지즈 외무장관은 지난 12.17 당지 소련대사를 접견한 자리에서 이라크는 안보리 결의 678 호를 인정하지 않으며 미국과의 회담일자등 문제에서 이라크의 입장이 1 밀리미터도 움직이지 않을것임을 강조했다고 금 12.22 자 바그다드 옵서버지가 보도함. 동 보도에 의하면, 소련대사는 아지즈장관에서 세바르드나제 외무장관의 친서를 전달했다고 하는바, 동서한에서 세바르드나제 장관은 무력충돌 발생가능성에 대한 우려를 표명하고 미.이라크 대화의 필요성을 강조했다고 함.

나. 아지즈 외무장관은 12.21 금번 유엔안보리의 팔레스타인 문제관련 결의내용이 매우 미흡하다고 지적하고, 미국이 국제적으로 최대의 범죄자라고 비난하는 성명을 발표함

다. 주재국은 지난 수일간 국토전역에서 민방위 및 주민소개훈련을 실시하고있는바,12.21 에는 바그다드에서 1 백만명 소개훈련을 실시했다고 발표함. 이와관련, 당지에서는 동일 일부 도로봉쇄 및 차량이동이 목격되기는 했으나 1 백만명 규모의 대규모 이동은 감지되지 않았음을 첨언함

2. 아국관련 동향

아국업체들에 의하면, 주재국 당국은 얼마전부터 대이라크 경제제재 국가에대한 보복조치인 혁명지도위 결정 377 호(90.9.16)를 아국에도 적용키 시작했다고 함. 이에따라 아국업체들은 월 1만디나 한도내에서만 은행예금 인출이 허용되고 있어 운영상 다소의 어려움을 겪고있으며, 일부에서는 공사가 끝난 건설장비의 반출에도 문제점이 발생하고있음. 관련 동향 추보예정임. 끝

(대사 최봉름-국장)

예고:91.6.30 일반

1991. 6. 30 에 예고문에 의거 일반문서로 재 분류됨.

중아국	장관	차관	1차보	2차보	영교국	정와대	안기부

PAGE 1

90.12.22   20:38
외신 2과 통제관 CE

0184

관리번호 90/2168

외 무 부

종 별 :

번 호 : BGW-1075

일 시 : 90 1224 1200

수 신 : 장관(중근동,기정)

발 신 : 주 이라크 대사

제 목 : 외국인 철수등 동향

연:BGW-1057

1. 주재국의 억류 외국인 전원철수 허용결정에 따라 외국인 대다수가 출국, 현재 당지에는 서방국인은 대사관 소속인원외에는 사실상 전혀 없으며(일본경우 민간인 1명, 미.영.불.독등 잔류 민간인 전무), 소련의 경우에는 고위대표단이 방문하여 잔류인원 2 천여명의 출국교섭을 진행하고있으나 주재국측의 계약의무 불이행에 따른 보상각서 서명요구로 교섭이 난항에 빠져있는것으로 파악되고 있음

2. 인도, 방글라데시, 파키스탄등 아시아국가및 수단등은 동국인이 원체 많은데다 철수를 원치 않는인원이 많고또극빈자들이 많아 자국민 철수를 활발히 시행하지 못하고있는 형편이나, 태국은 연호 보고와같이 91.1.10 까지 자국민 전원 철수를 단행할 방침임

3. 당지 주재 각국 대사관은 ① 미.이라크 대화실패및 91.1.15 이 임박할경우 ② 항공로 폐쇄 가능성등이 있음을 우려, 예년보도 많은 인원을 연말휴가등 명목으로 출국시키고 있으며, 이에따라 미대사관은 단 5 명(평소인원 23 명)이 잔류중이며, 일대사관은 18 명중 4 명을 기철수하고 곧 7,8 명을 추가 철수시킬 예정임

4. 한편, 주재국은 91.1 월초부터 주요관공서, 호텔종사원을 지방으로 소개시킬계획을 하달한것으로 확인됨. 끝

(대사 최봉름-국장)

예고:91.6.30

1991. 6.30. 에 예고문에 의처 일반문서로 재 분류됨

중아국   차관   1차보   2차보   정와대   안기부

외　무　부

종　별 :

번　호 : BGW-1079　　　　　　　　　　　일　시 : 90 1226 1300

수　신 : 장 관 (중근동,기정)

발　신 : 주 이라크 대사

제　목 : 정세보고

　　1. 사담훗세인대통령은 12.25 요르단 정당대표들을 접견한 자리에서 중동지역의 평화정착을 위해서는 우선 팔레스타인 해방이 실현되어야하며, 금번사태는 미, 사우디,쿠웨이트의 오랫동안의 반 이라크 음모로 발생한 것이라고 주장함

　　2. JASSIM 주재국 공보장관은 12.24 이라크국민은 미국과 NATO 의 사우디내 군사력 증강에 결코 겁먹지 않을 것이라고 강조함

　　3. 주재국 외무부 대변인은 주재국이 영공침범에 대한 항의공한을 지난 12.17 당지 터키대사관에 전달하였다고 금일 발표함

　　4. 주재국은 미.유엔등 주요 공관장 10명을 소환, 재외공관회의를 개최할 것이라고 알려짐.끝

　　(대사 최봉름-국장)

중아국　　1차보　　정문국　　안기부　　대책반

PAGE 1　　　　　　　　　　　　　　　　　　90.12.27　　02:41 FC

　　　　　　　　　　　　　　　　　　　　외신 1과　통제관

　　　　　　　　　　　　　　　　　　　　　　　　　　　　0186

외 무 부

종 별 :

번 호 : BGW-1086   일 시 : 90 1227 1300

수 신 : 장관(중근동,기정)

발 신 : 주 이라크대사

제 목 : 정세보고

　1.주재국 외무부 대변인은 12.26 최근 일부 공관장 본국소환은 통상적인 협의를 위한 것이며 이들이 협의를 마치는대로 곧 임지로 귀임할것일가 말함으로써 주재국이 사담후세인의 걸프정책에 불만을 가진 재외공관장을 소환했다는 서방언론 보도를 부인함

　2. IGOR BELOUSOV 소련 각료위원회 부위원장이 석유, 개스차관및 외무부 중동국장을 대동, 12.26 당지에서 도착함.

　동 방문목적은 구체적으로 알려지지 않았으나, 주재국 실권자인 KAMEL HASSAN군수산업장과및 WAHAB 내무장관이 공항 영접한 점으로 미루어 주재국측에서는동방문에 상당한 비중을 두는것으로 보임. 바그다드 옵서버지는 12.27 BELOUSOV 부위원장이 무력 사용을 반대하고 중동지역 문제의 평화적 해결을 지지했다고 보도함.

　끝

　(대사 최봉름-국장)

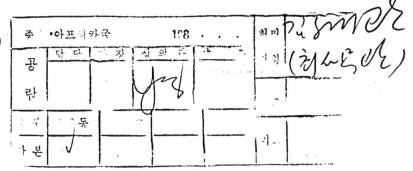

중아국　1차보　정문국　안기부

PAGE 1   90.12.27   22:13 DA

　　　　　　　　　　　　　　　　　외신 1과 통제관

　　　　　　　　　　　　　　　　　　　　　　　0187

외 무 부

종 별 :

번 호 : BGW-1088   일 시 : 90 1229,1200

수 신 : 장관(중근동,기정)

발 신 : 주이라크대사

제 목 : 정세보고

1. 사담후세인 대통령은 12.22 스페인 TV 와의 회견에서 만약 전쟁이 시작되면 우리는 이스라엘이 대이라크 공격에 가담한 것으로 무조건 간주하고 최우선적으로 텔아비브를 공격하겠다고 말함. 후세인 대통령은 동 회견에서 이라크는내년 1.15 를 철수시한으로 정한 안보리 결의를 인정하지 않는다는 입장을 되풀이하고, 또한 소련의 태도가 실망 스럽다고 하면서 세바르드나제 전외무장관이 베이커 미국무장관의 대리 (SURROGATE) 라고 매도하는등 신랄히 비난함

2. 후세인 대통령은 12.24 멕시코 TV 와의 회견에서 전쟁이 발발하면 미군은 정의로운 싸움을 한다는 신념이 없기때문에 반드시 패배할 것이라고 강조하고, 쿠웨이트왕가의 본국 귀환은 일반시민 자격으로만 가능하다고 말함

3. 주재국은 12.26 이라크로 향하던 이른바 아랍평화선 IBN KHALDOON 호가 미.영해 군의 승선 검색을 받고 오만으로 항로를 바꾼 것과관련, 12.27 대대적인 항의 움직임을 보였는바, 주요 동향은 다음과 같음

    -혁명지도위 및 바스당 연석회의 성명발표

    -아지즈 외무장관, 케야르 유엔사무총장앞 항의서한 발송

    -국회 비난성명 발표

    -부녀자 수만명 바그다드 미.영 대사관앞 시위 및 부쉬 미대통령앞 항의서한 전달

4. LONCAR 유고 외무장관이 주재국 방문차 12.28 당지 도착함

5. JASSIM 공보장관은 12.28 일부 서방언론의 미.이라크 비밀접촉설 보도가 사실이 아니라고 부인함

6. 당지 소식통에 의하면 주재국은 휘발유 배급제를 곧 다시 실시할 계획이며, 수도물 정수에 필요한 화학물질 부족으로 각급관서에 수도물을 그냥 먹지 말도록 지시하였다고함.끝

(대사 최봉름-국장)

중아국	장관	차관	1차보	2차보	정문국	안기부	미주국

0188

PAGE 1   90.12.29   20:58 CG

외신 1과 통제관

외 무 부

종 별 :

번 호 : BGW-1095   일 시 : 90 1230 1200

수 신 : 장관(중근동,기정)

발 신 : 주이라크대사

제 목 : 정세보고

사담 후세인 대통령은 12.29 혁명지도위 및 바스당 연석회의를 주재하고
주재국이 내년 1.15이 임박하여 관제 데모를 벌여'이라크 국민은 사담을 원하며
쿠웨이트를 원치 않는다'고 외치게하여 극적으로 쿠웨이트 철수를 단행할지
모른다는 일부 서방언론의 보도가 전혀 근거없다고 부인하고, 이라크는 결코
쿠웨이트를 포기하지 않을것이라고 강하는 성명을 발표함.끝
(대사 최봉름-국장)

중도 • 아프리카국			198 . . .		처리지침	
공람	담당	과장	심의관	국장		
					자료활용	
본	등				비고	
	✓					

종아국   1차보   2차보   정문국   안기부

0189

외　무　부

종　별 :

번　호 : BGW-1098　　　　　　　　　　일　시 : 90 1231 1200

수　신 : 장관(중근동,기정)

발　신 : 주 이라크대사

제　목 : 정세보고

　　1. FADHIL 주재국 종교장관은 세계 회교지도자 회의를 내년 1.9 당지에서 개최한다고 발표함. 동회의에는 요르단, 리비아, 예멘, 시리아, 알제리, 터키,소련,미국, 호주, 유럽국가 등에서 약 350명의 회교지도자, 지식인, 정치인이참석할 예정이라고함

　　2.아랍연맹의 이라크인 관리 12명이 동연맹 본부의 카이로 이전에 항의, 사임했다고함

　　3. LONCAR 유고 외무장관은 12.30 후세인 대봉령과 회담한후, 3일간의 주재국방문을 마치고 동일 출국함.

　　끝

　(대사 최봉름-국장)

중아국　　1차보　　정문국　　안기부

0190

PAGE 1　　　　　　　　　　　　　　　　　90.12.31　　22:01 DA

　　　　　　　　　　　　　　　　　　　외신 1과 통제관

관리 번호	91/1

외 무 부

종 별 :

번 호 : BGW-0010 　　　　　　　　 일 시 : 91 0103 1200

수 신 : 장관(중근동,기정)

발 신 : 주 이라크 대사

제 목 : 정세보고(1.3)

　　1. 사담후세인 대통령은 12.31 남부전선에서 군인들과 송년 만찬을 갖고, 미국, 사우디를 비난하는 연설을 행함. 동 연설에서 후세인 대통령은 18 백만인구를 가진 이라크는 60 개 사단을 동원한 4 억이상의 인구를 가진 국가들은 겨우14 개사단을 동원하였는데 이는 이라크국민이 쿠웨이트가 이라크의 불가분의 영토임을 굳게 믿고 희생을 감수하는 때문이라고 말함. 동 대통령은 또한 FAHD 사우디국왕이 팔레스타인을 위해서는 원조를 아까와 하면서도 미군주둔비용으로는 370억불이나 지출하고 미국여자(여군)의 치마폭에 숨어있다고 비난함

　　2. 후세인대통령은 모든 이라크 군인(계급불문)의 원급을 91.1.1 부터 50 디나씩 인상한다고 1.2 발표함. 동 대통령은 많은 군인들이 장기간 복무를 마친후 다시 소집되었으며 가족생계등 어려움을 겪고 있다고 말하고, 그러나 모든 군인들이 이러한 어려움이 일시적인 것임을 알기때문에 사기는 드높다고 강조함. 주재국은 57 년생 부터 73 년생까지를 전원 군복무 소집한바있으며, 이에따라 당관 현지 고용원 1명(58년생, 9년 6개월 기복무)도 군입대하였음을 첨언함

　　3. KAML HASSAN 주재국 군수산업장관은 1.2 주재국 조기경보기 ADNAN-2 를 자체개발했다고 발표함. 동 경보기의 시험비행은 작년 12.15 성공적으로 수행되었다고함. 주재국은 작년 7 월 최초의 자체개발 조기경보기 ADNAN-1 을 취역시킨바있음

　　4. 주재국은 다국적군에 의해 억류중인 이른바 아랍평화선 IBN KHALDOON 호와 관련, HAMZA 교통체신장관명의로 국제적십자사의 사건 조사를 촉구하고, SALEH 무역장관명의 서한을 케야르 유엔사무총장에게 보내는등 선전활동을 벌임

　　5. 후세인 대통령은 1.2 아라파트 PLO 의장을 접견함.

　　6. AL-SAHAF 외무담당 국무장관이 인도방문차 1.2 출발함. 끝

중아국	장관	차관	1차보	2차보	정문국	정와대	안기부

(대사 최봉름-국장)
예고:91.6.30 일반

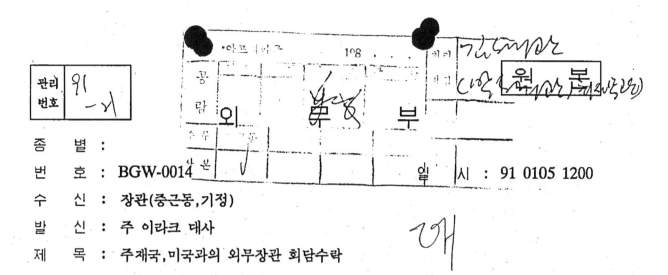

관리
번호 91 -가

종 별 :
번 호 : BGW-0014
수 신 : 장관(중근동,기정)
발 신 : 주 이라크 대사
제 목 : 주재국,미국과의 외무장관 회담수락

일시 : 91 0105 1200

1. 주재국은 미국의 미.이라크 외무장관회담 제의를 수락, AZIZ 외무장관을 1.9 제네바로 파견키로 결정하고, 이를 미측의 회답시한(1.5)보다 하루앞서 1.4 미측에 봉보함

2. AZIZ 외무장관은 상기관련 주재국 국영통신(INA)에 미국과의 대화에 임하는 주재국입장을 발표하였는바, 동 장관은 우선 미측태도가 매우 고압적임을 비난하고, 이라크는 압력을 두려워하지 않으며 위협과 협박에 굴하지 않을것임을 재확인함. 동장관은 금번 이라크가 표제회담을 수락한것은 세계 여론과 국제적으로 인정된 국가간 관계의 원칙을 존중하기 때문이며 결코 미국의 고압적 행태에 굴복한것이 아니라고 강조함. 동 장관은 그동안의 미.이라크 대화 교섭 결과를 상세히 설명하면서 미국의 태도를 비난하고, 금번 BAKER 미국무장관과의 회담에서 주재국은 협박을 단호히 거부하는 확고한 입장을 재천명할것이며, 미측이 공정한 기반위에서 역내 평화및 안보를 위해 노력할 준비가 되어있는지 지켜볼 것이라고 말하고 역내 문제중 팔레스타인 문제가 최우선적으로 다루어져야한다는기존입장을 되풀이함

3. 주재국은 대외적으로는 상기와같이 미측에 양보하지 않겠다는 공식입장을 강조하고있으나, 금번 회담시한까지 평시한 고압적인 미측 제안을 수락한 자체가 굴복이며 주재국이 1.15 이 다가오면서 궁지에 빠져있음을 확인해 준것으로보임. 주재국이 금번 제네바 회담에서 쿠웨이트 전면철수등 극적인 양보를 할것인지는 아직 불투명하나, 당지 외교가에서는 주재국이 금번 회담이 무력충돌을피할수 있는 마지막 기회임을 인식하고 있으며 ①고압적인 미국의 제의를 받아들인점, 미국과의 전쟁에서 전혀 승산이 없음에 따라 ②바그다드시민이 대거 지방 대피 움직임을 보이는등 국내의 동요 가능성이 있는점등에 비추어 EC 측의 선쿠웨이트 철수후 팔레스타인문제 국제회의 개최 방안등 주재국의 최소한 체면을 살리는 타협안을 모색할 가능성이

중아국   장관   차관   1차보   2차보   정문국   청와대   안기부

큰것으로 관측되고 있음. 끝
　　(대사 최봉름-국장)
　　예고:91.6.30

외 무 부

종 별 :

번 호 : BGW-0015

수 신 : 장관(중근동,기정)

발 신 : 주 이라크대사

제 목 : 정세보고(1.5)

일 시 : 91 0105 1200

1. 주재국은 영국정부의 이라크 외교관및 민간인 추방결정을 비난하는 외무부 대변인 논평을 1.4발표함.

2. 주재국은 이라크가 제네바, 비엔나에서의 비밀협상에서 쿠웨이트로부터 철수키로 원칙적으로 동의했다는 붙란서언론 보도를 1.3 부인함

3. 주재국 국회는 1.3 91년도 예산안을 승인함. 예산 총액이나 내역에 대해서는 일체 발표되지 않고 있으며, SADOUN HAMMADI 부수상은 금년도 예산이 이라크 국민의 기본 생활 안정을 위해 기본 소비재및 양곡등 배급품목 조달에 중점을 두었다고만 말함.

끝

(대사 최봉름-국장)

중동ㆍ아프리카국		193 . . .			처리	
공람	단담			곡 장	지침	
무	근동			소		
사 인	✓				니고	

중아국   1차보   정문국   안기부

0195

PAGE 1

91.01.06   08:11 DA
외신 1과   통제관

걸프사태, 1990-91. 전12권 (V.2 이라크, 1990-91)   257

원 본

외 무 부

종   별 : 지 급
번   호 : BGW-0023
수   신 : 장관(중근동,기정)
발   신 : 주 이라크 대사
제   목 : 정세보고

일   시 : 91 0106 1100

1. 본직은 1.6 주재국 국군의날 기념식에 참석한바, 동 행사에 참석한 각국대사들은 작일 부쉬미대통령의 비밀협상불가 연설을 화제로 올리며, 미.이라크 양측의 입장이 팽팽하게 맞서있음을 들어 평화적 해결가능성에 비관적인 견해를 표명함. 동 기념식에는 미, 일, 영, 불등 주요국 대사가 불참, 눈길을 끌었으며, 말레이지아는 이미 공관원 전원이 철수했고 인니는 1.7, 필리핀은 1.9 철수할 예정이라함

2. 주재국 외무부 의전장은 지부티(외교단장), 일본, 인도등 몇몇 대사에게 외무부등 정부관서가 바그다드 서쪽 150KM 에 위치한 RAMADI 시로 소개할 계획이 있음(주재국 공식적으로는 부인)을 시사하며 그경우 외교단도 함께 대피할 의향이 있는지 탐문한것으로 확인됨. 당지 외교단에서는 통신문제, 식료품등 조달문제, RAMADI 시근교의 주요산업 시설및 비행장 소재등 이유로 동 소개제의에 대체로 부정적인 반응을 보이고있음. 끝

(대사 최봉름-국장)
예고:91.12.31

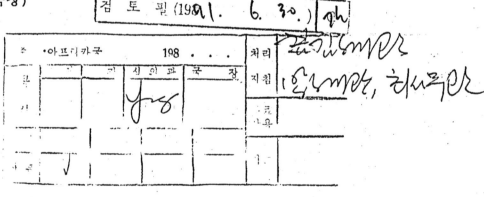

검 토 필 (1991. 6. 30.)

주 •아프리카국		198 . . .	처리 지침	
		시의과	국 장	
	✓			

외 무 부

종 별 :

번 호 : BGW-0025

일 시 : 91 0107 1200

수 신 : 장관(중근동,기정)

발 신 : 주이라크대사

제 목 : 정세보고(1.7)

1.사담 후세인 대통령은 1.6 주재국 국군의날 기념연설에서 이라크의 쿠웨이트 병합은 최종적인것이며 쿠웨이트가 19번째 주라는 강경한 입장을 재확인함.동대통령은 다가오는 댁이 팔레스타인 해방을 위한것이라고 말하고,많은 희생과 오랜 투쟁이 예상되지만 이라크군이 불굴의 소명의식을 갖고 성전에 임할것이라고 강조함

2. JASSIM 공보장관은 1.5 동일 부쉬미대통령의 강경발언이 오만과 헛된 자신감의소산이라고 강력히 비난함

3.바그다드 옵서버지는 주재국이 EC 측의 외무장관 회담 제의를 1.5 거절했다고외신을 인용,사실 보도함

4.쿠바 근로자들은 전쟁위험에도 불구,이라크에 잔류하겠다는 약속을 담은 메시지를 카스트로 대통령앞으로 보냈다고 바그다드 옵서버지가 보도함

4.사담 후세인 대통령이 BBC WORLD SERVICE 청취자에 의해 올해의 인물로 선정되었다고 바그다드 옵서버지가 보도함.끝

(대사 최봉름-국장)

중아국   정문국   안기부   1착번   2착번

0197

PAGE 1

91.01.07   22:56 DP

외신 1과 통제관

걸프사태, 1990-91. 전12권 (V.2 이라크, 1990-91) 259

관리 번호 91 -29

외 무 부

종 별 :

번 호 : BGW-0028

일 시 : 91 0108 1200

수 신 : 장관(중근동,기정)

발 신 : 주 이라크 대사

제 목 : 정세보고

1. 사담 후세인대통령은 1.6 국군의날을 맞아 고위관리및 군관계자를 접견한 자리에서 침략자와의 부쟁은 이라크 영토내뿐아니라 그밖에서도 행해질것이라고 승리가 목전에 있다고 강조함. 동 대통령은 주전장은 이라크가될지 모르나 모든 자유의 부사와 MUJAHIDDIN(성전의 전사)가 침략자를 응징할것이므로 전장은 결국 전세계가 될것이라고 말함

2. 후세인대통령은 1.6 군총사령부회의를 주재한데 이어 1.7 혁명지도위(RCC) 회의와 집권 BAATH 당 고위 군사관계자회의를 잇달아 주재, 내부결속을 다지고 있음

3. 금일 미명 이라크군 병사 일단이 헬기 6 대를 몰고 사우디로 귀순한 사실 및 주재국 JASSIM 공보장관의 동사실 부인 외신보도에 대하여 주재국언론에서는 아직 전혀 발표가없음. 끝

(대사 최봉름-국장)

예고:91.6.30 까지

1991. 6. 30에 예고문에 의거 일반문서로 재분류됨

중아국	장관	차관	1차보	2차보	정문국	청와대	안기부

0198

PAGE 1

91.01.08   22:41

외신 2과   통제관 CF

관리
번호 : 91 37

외 무 부

종 별 : 지급

번 호 : BGW-0035

일 시 : 91 0109 1200

수 신 : 장관(중근동,기정)

발 신 : 주 이라크 대사

제 목 : 정세보고

1. 사담후세인 대통령은 1.7 ARAFAT PLO 의장을 접견하고,1.8 모리타니아 내무장관(대통령 특사)과 당지 소련대사를 접견하였는바, 소련대사는 소련정부 고위층의 친서를 전달했다고 보도됨

2. 바그다드 옵서버지는 후세인대통령의 주요군관계자회의 개최, 건설부장관의 남부 작전구역내 도로망 2,237KM 완공발표, 방공사령관의 HAWK 지대공 미사일 2 개중대 전부배치 완료 발표등을 보도, 주재국 국민의 자신감 및 임전태세 고양을 위한 홍보를 계속하고있음

3. IBRAHIM 혁명지도위 부의장(제2인자)이 HAMMADI 부수상, HAMZA 교통체신장관, AL-SAHAF 외무담당 국무장관을 대동, 이란방문차 1.8 테헤란에 도착함

4. 당지 UAE 대사가 1.9 출국하고, 사우디, 바레인, 카탈대사는 이미 귀국하였으므로 GCC 국가중 오만대사만이 잔류중인것으로 파악됨. 요르단대사는 임기종료후 귀국 아직 후임대사가 도착하지않고 있음. 한편 8.2 이후 연금설이 나돌다 쿠웨이트를 비난하는 성명내고 당지거주하던 전 주이라크 쿠웨이트대사는 1.9주재국 일반여권으로 출국한것이 확인됨. 끝

(대사 최봉름-국장)

예고:91.6.30

중아국　　장관　　차관　　1차보　　2차보　　정문국　　청와대　　안기부

0199

91.01.09 19:25

외신 2과 통제관 BA

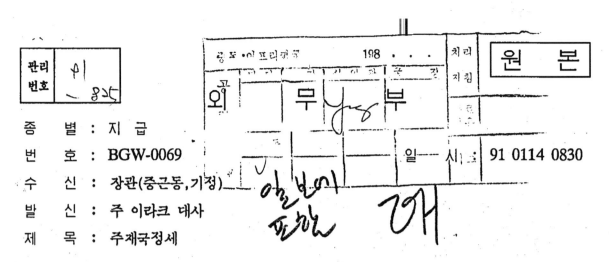

관리
번호 : 외 8

종 별 : 지급
번 호 : BGW-0069
수 신 : 장관(중근동,기정)
발 신 : 주 이라크 대사
제 목 : 주재국정세

1.1.14 주재국언론은 꾸에야르 유엔 사무총장 당지방문관련,1.13 유엔사무총장이 후세인대통령과 회담후 출발했다는 사실만 간략히 사실 보도하고 회담 내용에 관해서는 일체 언급이 없어 회담 성과가 없었던것으로 관측됨

2. 당지 취재 활동중인 아국기자들에 의하면 1.13.22:00 당지공항 출국기자회견에서 꾸에야르사무총장은 아래 요지 언급했다고함

-사태 전망에관해 비관도 낙관도 않지만 희망은 가지고있다

-전쟁발발 가능 여부는 모르겠다

-곧 소집될 유엔안보리에 이번 회담결과를 보고하겠으며 모두가 평화를 원하고있다

3.1.14 현재까지 주재국은 관공서나 주민들을 아직 소개 대피시키지않고 있으며 주재국관리들은 1.15 이후에도 모든 정상적인 일상생활이 유지될것이라고 말하고있음

4.1.14 바그다드 옵서버지는 훗세인대통령이 아사드 시리아대통령에게 이라크와 한편이되어 아랍세계를 위협하는 악마의 세력들과 싸울것을 촉구했다는 내용을 주요 머리기사로 보도했음. 끝

(대사 최봉름-국장)

예고:91.6.30 일반

<table>
<tr><td>중아국</td><td>장관</td><td>차관</td><td>1차보</td><td>2차보</td><td>청와대</td><td>총리실</td><td>안기부</td></tr>
</table>

신무안

外務部 걸프戰 事後對策班

제 목 : 사담 후세인 정권의 장래 문제

91. 3. 12

1. 이라크내 소요 상황

   ○ 2.28 부쉬 미대통령의 정전발표 직후 이라크 제2의 도시인 바스라등 남부
      지역에서 반사담 후세인 시위가 발생한 사실이 처음으로 알려짐.

   ○ 이라크 남부지역의 반사담 후세인 시위는 일반시민과 일부 정부군의
      가담으로 곧 대규모 무장 봉기화 되었으며 이라크 북부지역에 거주하는
      Kurd족도 정부군에 대항, 무장투쟁을 벌이기 시작함.

   ○ 이라크 정부의 외국 특파원 전원 출국조치등 언론통제로 정확한 상황은
      파악키 어려우나, 이란 관영 통신(IRNA)등에 의하면 3.11. 현재 시아파
      반군은 바스라를 수중에 넣고 이라크 남부전역에서 정부군과 치열한
      전투를 벌이고 있으며 북부지역에서는 Kurd족 반군이 유전도시 키르쿡을
      포함 상당한 지역을 장악했다 함. 또한 수도 바그다드에서도 정부군과
      반군간에 바그다드 라디오 방송국을 손에 넣기 위해 교전을 벌이고 있다함.

   ○ 한편, 17개 이라크 반정부 단체는 3.10. 베이루트에서 회합을 갖고
      사담 후세인의 축출과 향후 정부 구성문제 등에 관하여 논의함.

2. 각국의 입장 및 반응

   가. 미국

      ○ 걸프전 기간중부터 사담 후세인의 거세를 사실상의 목표로 추구해온
         미국은 전후 이라크의 배상문제를 이슈화 하는등 사담 후세인의
         국내 정치적 지위 약화를 겨냥한 압력을 가중시켜 왔음.

      ○ 미국은 공식적으로는 이라크 내전에의 불개입을 천명하고 있으나,
         이라크 정부의 반군에 대한 화학무기 사용시 방관하지 않겠다고
         경고(3.10. 베이커 국무장관)하는등 사담 후세인 정권의 퇴진 압력을
         늦추지 않고 있음.

   나. 소련

      ○ 소련은 앞으로 이라크 국민이 지지하는 지도자와 관계를 맺어
         나가야 될 것이라는 입장을 천명(2.28. 베스메르트니크 외무장관),
         소련의 대이라크 정책이 사담후세인과의 운명과는 직접적 관련이
         없음을 분명히 함.

0201

다. 영,불등 서방권

　　ㅇ 사담 후세인이 전후 이라크를 통제하기에 적절치 않은 인물로 보며
　　　(2.27. 허드 영 외무장관), 이라크의 패배로 인해 야기될 각종문제로
　　　사담 후세인 정권이 오래 유지하지 못할 것이라고 논평(2.24. 미테랑
　　　불 대통령) 하는등 사담 후세인의 퇴진을 희망함을 밝힘.

라. 사우디, 이집트 등 반 이라크 진영 아랍권

　　ㅇ 이라크내 사담 후세인 대체세력에 대한 무조건 지지를 약속하고
　　　(2.28. 파드 사우디국왕), 사담 후세인이 신뢰할 수 없는 사람이며
　　　앞으로 그를 상대하지 않겠다고 언명(2.24. 무바락 이집트 대통령)
　　　함으로써 사담 후세인 거세를 바라고 있음을 명백히 함.

　　ㅇ 다만, 동국들은 이라크의 내전이 격화되어 제2의 레바논화 되는 경우
　　　지역 안정에 해롭다는 고려를 하고 있으며 아울러 이란과의 유착
　　　가능성이 큰 시아파의 집권을 내심 바라지 않는 것으로 추측됨.

마. 이란

　　ㅇ 이란은 당초 미국의 사담후세인 정권 전복 주장이 사태를 악화 시킬수
　　　있다고 언급(2.24. 라프산자니 대통령), 현 이라크 정부를 지지하는
　　　듯한 태도를 취했으나, 그후 시아파등의 반정부 무장 투쟁이 본격화
　　　되면서 입장을 바꾸어 사담 후세인의 퇴진을 주장하고 나섬.

　　ㅇ 라프산자니 대통령은 3.8. 사담 후세인이 국민의 뜻에 따라야
　　　할 것이라고 언급, 사담 후세인의 퇴진을 간접 촉구하고, 3.10에는
　　　이라크가 직면한 내전 및 영토 분단 위기에 우려를 표명함.

3. 분석 및 전망

　　ㅇ 사담 후세인 정권은 장기간의 독재정치와 8년간의 이.이전 및 걸프전으로
　　　인한 막대한 인명 피해 및 경제적 손실로 심각한 국민의 저항에 직면하고
　　　있을 뿐 아니라 대외적으로도 미.EC등 서방권과 GCC, 이집트, 시리아,
　　　이란등 주변 국가들이 사담 후세인 거세를 희망하고 있어 동 정권이
　　　장기간 유지되기는 어려울 것으로 보임.

　　ㅇ 그러나, 사담 후세인 이후의 후계정권에 대한 전망은 매우 불투명 한바,
　　　일부에서는 현 정부 핵심세력중 일부와 군부와의 제휴를 통해 사담 후세인을
　　　축출하게 될 가능성이 가장 큰 것으로 예측하고, 만일 새로운 정부의 등장이
　　　조기에 이루어 지지 않을 경우에는 이라크가 제2의 레바논화 될 우려도
　　　있는 것으로 보고 있음.

0202

- 이라크 총인구의 55%를 차지하며 현재 반사담 후세인 세력중 가장
  강력한 시아파는 이란의 영향력 확대를 우려한 사우디등 온건
  아랍국과 미국등 서방권의 반대로 집권이 어려울 것으로 예상되며,
  제2의 세력인 Kurd족은 소수 민족으로서 중앙 정권을 담당할 능력이
  없을 뿐 아니라 이라크와 같이 Kurd 소수 민족 문제를 안고 있는
  터키, 소련등의 견제를 받아 일정 수준 이상의 세력 신장이 불가능할
  것으로 전망

o 이라크 내에 뚜렷한 차기 정권 대안이 떠오르지 않고 있는 점과 이라크의
  내전 격화로 인한 제2의 레바논화가 역내 안정에 도움이 되지 않는다는
  공동인식이 역내외에 넓게 퍼져 있는 점을 고려, 현단계에서 사담 후세인이
  당분간 계속 집권할 가능성도 배제할 수 없으나, 다만 이경우에도 국내외
  제반 여건상 사담 후세인 정권이 앞으로 장기간 유지될 가능성은 별로 없을
  것으로 보임.

o 이라크 정부는 과거 Kurd족 게릴라 탄압으로 이름높은 al-Meguid를
  3.6. 내무장관으로 임명하고 외국 기자 전원의 출국을 명령하는등 반군에
  대한 강력한 무력 진압을 준비하고 있는 것으로 관측되는바, 반군진압에
  화학무기등 지나치게 가혹한 방법을 사용할 경우에는 오히려 주변국의
  대 이라크 무력 개입을 불러 사담 후세인 정권의 조기 붕괴를 가져올
  가능성이 있음.   끝.

0203

外務部 걸프戰 事後 對策班

제 목 : 사담 후세인의 민주화 조치 발표와 정권의 장래   91. 3. 18.

1. 사담 후세인 대통령의 민주화 조치 발표
   ㅇ 사담 후세인 대통령은 3.16 대국민 연설을 통해 민주화 조치를 발표
     하였는바, 이는 ① 새헌법을 마련 국민투표에 회부토록 하며 이에따라
     새국회 구성 ② 다당제 실시 ③ 내각 대폭 개편(집권 Baath당 간부는
     가급적 배제) 및 부흥부 신설을 주요내용으로 하고 있음.
   ㅇ 아울러 동 대통령은 내란 진압 상황에 대하여 남부 시아파의 반란은
     성공적으로 진압되었으며 북부에서는 반란이 아직 계속중이나 곧 진압시킬
     것이라고 말하고, 일부 주변국가들이 그들의 영토를 기지로 삼아 이라크에
     파괴분자를 침투시키고 있다고 비난함.

2. 이라크 내란 동향
   ㅇ 2.28 부쉬 미대통령의 정전발표 직후 남부지역에서 반사담 후세인 시위가
     처음으로 발생함.
   ㅇ 남부지역의 반사담 시위는 일부 정부군의 가담으로 곧 대규모 무장 봉기화
     되었으며 북부지역 거주 Kurd족도 무장투쟁을 개시함.
   ㅇ 이라크 정부의 외국 특파원 전원 출국조치등 언론통제로 정확한 상황은
     파악키 어려우나, 이란 및 반군 소식통에 의하면 북부지역에서는 Kurd족
     반군이 이라크 제3의 도시 모술과 유전도시 키르쿡을 포함 상당한 지역을
     장악하고 있다함. 그러나 한때 제2의 도시 바스라를 장악하는등 큰 세력을
     떨쳤던 남부 시아파 반군은 공화국 수비대등 정부군의 강력한 반격으로
     상당히 약화된 것으로 관측됨.
   ㅇ 한편, 여러 계파를 망라한 23개 이라크 반정부 단체는 3.11-13.간
     베이루트에서 회합을 갖고 사담 후세인의 축출과 과도 연립정부수립을
     결의함.

0204

3. 각국의 입장 및 반응

　　가. 미국

　　　　ㅇ 걸프전 기간중부터 사담 후세인의 거세를 사실상 목표로 추구해온
　　　　　미국은 공식적으로는 이라크 내전 불개입을 천명하고 있으나,
　　　　　반군에 대한 화학무기 사용시 방관하지 않겠다고 경고(3.18. 베이커
　　　　　국무장관)하고 헬기 및 전투기 사용은 정전협정 위반이라고 지적
　　　　　(3.14. 부쉬 대통령)하는등 대이라크 압력을 늦추지 않고 있음.

　　　　ㅇ 부쉬 대통령은 3.13 사담 후세인이 건재하는한 대이라크 관계
　　　　　정상화는 불가능하다고 강조하는 동시 이란의 이라크 영토 침범
　　　　　가능성도 경고하였는바, 이는 사담 후세인의 제거와 이란의 영향력
　　　　　확대 저지라는 일응 상반된 목표를 추구하고 있는 미국의 고민을
　　　　　보여준 것으로 해석됨.

　　나. 소련

　　　　ㅇ 소련은 앞으로 이라크 국민이 지지하는 지도자와 관계를 맺어
　　　　　나가야 될 것이라는 입장을 천명(2.28. 베스메르트니크 외무장관),
　　　　　소련의 대이라크 정책이 사담 후세인 개인의 운명과는 직접적 관련이
　　　　　없음을 분명히 함.

　　다. 영,불등 서방권

　　　　ㅇ 사담 후세인이 전후 이라크를 통제하기에 적절치 않은 인물로 보며
　　　　　(2.27. 허드 영 외무장관), 이라크의 패배로 인해 야기될 각종문제로
　　　　　사담 후세인 정권이 오래 유지하지 못할 것이라고 논평(2.24. 미테랑
　　　　　불 대통령)하는등 사담 후세인의 퇴진을 희망함을 밝힘.

　　라. 사우디, 이집트등 반 이라크 진영 아랍권

　　　　ㅇ 이라크내 사담 후세인 대체세력에 대한 무조건 지지를 약속하고
　　　　　(2.28. 파드 사우디국왕), 사담 후세인이 신뢰할 수 없는 사람이며
　　　　　앞으로 그를 상대하지 않겠다고 언명(2.24. 무바락 이집트 대통령)
　　　　　함으로써 사담 후세인 거세를 바라고 있음을 명백히 함.

　　마. 이란

　　　　ㅇ 이란은 당초 미국의 사담 후세인 정권 전복 주장이 사태를 악화시킬수
　　　　　있다고 언급(2.24. 라프산자니 대통령), 현 이라크 정부의 유지를
　　　　　바라는 듯한 태도를 취했으나, 내란 발생후 시아파 반군에 동조,
　　　　　종래 입장을 바꾸어 사담 후세인의 퇴진을 주장하고 나섬.

o 라프산자니 대통령은 3.8. 사담 후세인이 국민의 뜻에 따라야 할
  것이라고 언급, 사담 후세인의 퇴진을 간접 촉구하고, 3.10에는
  이라크가 직면한 내전 및 영토 분단 위기에 우려를 표명.

o 이란은 이라크내 시아파 반군에 물적 지원을 제공하고 있는 것으로
  추측되며, 이와관련 사담 후세인의 3.16 연설에서도 이란을 겨냥
  주변국의 반군 지원을 비난한 바 있음.

4. 분석 및 전망

o 사담 후세인 정권은 장기간의 독재정치와 8년간의 이.이전 및 걸프전으로
  인한 막대한 인명 피해 및 경제적 손실로 심각한 국민적 저항에 직면하고
  있을 뿐 아니라 대외적으로도 미.EC등 서방권과 GCC, 이집트, 시리아,
  이란등 주변 국가들이 사담 후세인 거세를 희망하고 있어 장기적 관점에서
  동 정권이 안정을 되찾기는 상당히 어려울 것으로 보임.

o 금번 사담 후세인의 민주화 조치 발표는 국민의 불만 무마 및 반정부 세력의
  결속 이완을 노린 정치적 제스츄어로 보이는바, 구체적 시간표가 제시되지
  않은 점과 사담 후세인의 철권통치 전력등으로 보아 동인의 민주화 약속이
  국내외의 신뢰를 얻을 가능성은 별로 없음.

o 사담 후세인 이후의 후계정권에 대한 전망은 매우 불투명 한바, 일부에서는
  현 정부 핵심세력중 일부와 군부와의 제휴를 통해 사담 후세인을 축출하게
  될 가능성이 가장 큰 것으로 예측하고, 만일 새로운 정부의 등장이 조기에
  이루어 지지 않을 경우에는 이라크가 제2의 레바논화 되어 지역안정을 해칠
  가능성에 대해 아랍과 서방이 모두 우려하고 있음.

o 이라크 총인구의 55%를 차지하며 현재 반사담 후세인 세력중 가장 강력한
  잠재력을 가진 시아파는 이란의 영향력 확대를 우려한 사우디등 온건
  아랍국과 미국등 서방권의 반대로 집권이 어려운 것으로 예상되며,
  제2의 세력인 Kurd족은 소수 민족으로서 중앙정부를 담당할 능력이 없을 뿐
  아니라 이라크와 같이 Kurd 소수 민족 문제를 안고 있는 터키, 소련등의
  견제를 받아 일정 수준 이상의 세력 신장이 불가능할 것으로 전망됨.

o 이라크 내에 뚜렷한 차기 정권 대안이 떠오르지 않고 있는 점과 이라크의
  내전 격화로 인한 제2의 레바논화에 대한 우려를 고려할 때, 현단계에서
  사담 후세인이 당분간 계속 집권할 가능성도 있으나 이경우에도 국내외
  제반 여건상 사담 후세인 정권이 앞으로 장기간 유지될 가능성은 크지
  않을 것으로 보임.   끝.

0206

외 무 부

원 본

종 별 :

번 호 : KUW-0054   일 시 : 91 0324 1600

수 신 : 장 관(중동일,기정)

발 신 : 주 쿠웨이트대사

제 목 : 이라크 개각에 대한 쿠웨이트측 논평

     3.24. 외교단 브리핑에서 AL-SHAHEEN 외부차관은 이라크 개각과 관련, 사담 후세인이 항상 수상직을 겸임해 왔던것이 관례인데, 이번 개각에서는 이를 겸임치 않는것이주목된다면서, 이는 이라크 내부에서 사담의 전권적인 위치에 이상이 생기고 있음을보여주는 징후로 보인다고 논평했음. 끝.

     (대사-국장)

중아국   안기부

0207

PAGE 1   91.03.24   23:01 CT

                           외신 1과 통제관

관 리 번호 91/180

외 무 부

종 별 : 지급

번 호 : JAW-1715

일 시 : 91 0324 1720

수 신 : 장관(중동일, 아일(사본:주일대사)

발 신 : 주 일 대사대리(일정)

제 목 : 이라크 내각 개편

"대책반" 보고되각됨
(언론+공관 보고 종합)

이라크 국영 라디오 방송은 3.23. 후세인 대통령이 내각을 대폭 개편, 회교 시아파인 하마디 전 부수상을 수상으로 하는 신 내각을 발족시켰다고 발표한바, 동 내용과 배경을 아래 보고함.(언론 종합)

1. 신 내각 내용과 성격

0 후세인 대통령은 아직까지 겸임하고 있는 수상직을 3 인의 부수상의 1 인이었던 하마디에게 양도 하였으나, 여전히 혁명평의회 회장, 군 최고사령관, 바트당 서기장직을 보유함.

0 부수상겸 외상이었던 아지즈는 부수상에, 신 외상에는 아하마드 후세인 호다이르 대통령실 수석이 임명됨.

0 후세인 대통령의 심복인 내상, 공업.군사상, 국방상, 국방담당 국무상등 약 반수의 각료가 유임되어 후세인 정권의 골격은 그대로 유지되고 있음.

0 신 내각에는 3 인의 쿠르드족 각료가 포함됨.

2. 배경

0 이같은 신 내각 발족은 후세인 대통령이 지난 3.16. 연설에서 밝힌 이라크 재건을 위한 정치개혁의 일환이나, 지금까지의 일인독재 체제만으로는 시아파, 쿠르드족등에 의한 반정부 폭동을 평정할수 없다는 판단에 따라 정부내의 비주류인 회교 시아파인 하마디 부수상을 수상으로 내세워 반란세력을 회유하고자 하는 시도로 보여짐.

3. 반응

0 일 외무성 당국자는 3.23. 이라크 내각개편과 관련, " 후세인 대통령이 국제사회로 부터의 비판을 돌리려는 시도로서 일종의 정권 연명책" 이라고 논평함. 또한 하마디 수상기용에 관하여는 그가 이란과 밀접한 관계가 있는 시아파에 속하고

중아국 안기부	장관	차관	1차보	2차보	아주국	아주국	정문국	청와대

PAGE 1

0208

91.03.24 18:03

외신 2과 통제관 DO

있고, 미국에도 거부감이 없는 인물이기 때문에 이들 국가로 부터의 압력을 유화시키려는 방편이며, 하마디는 후세인 정권내에서 비교적 권력의 비중이 낮았던 인물로서 대통령이 실권을 장악하고 있는 구도에는 변함이 없다고 논평함.

0 이라크 반정부 세력인 이슬람 혁명 최고평의회 및 쿠르드 민주당은 이번 내각 개편에 강하게 반발, 후세인이 퇴진하지 않는 한 계속 부쟁하겠다는 성명을 각각 발표함.

0 부쉬 미대통령도 동 개편과 관련, 후세인이 권좌에 남아 있는한 이라크와의 관계개선은 있을수 없다고 후세인 대통령을 비난함. 끝.

(대사대리 남홍우-국장)

예고: 원본접수처: 91.6.30 일반

사본접수처: 91.6.30. 파기

외 무 부

종 별 :

번 호 : AVW-0345   일 시 : 91 0325 1930

수 신 : 장 관(중동일,구이,청와대외교,기정)

발 신 : 주오스트리아대사

제 목 : 사담의 생존 전략

3.25자 DIE PRESSE는 SADDAMS LETZTES AUFGEBOT 제하 다음과같은 논평을 게재하였음.

1.권력유지를 위한 사담의 전략은 마치 그에게 예외적인 일(AUSSERGEWOEHNLICHES)이 전혀없었던 것처럼 또한 이란과 쿠웨이트에서의 모험후에 국토가 불바다가된일이 없었던 것처럼 구태의연하게 진행되고있음. 사담의 전략은 쉽게 간파될수있음. 북으로 부터는 쿠르드족과 남으로부터는 시아파에 의해 압박을 받고있는 그는 우선 한쪽을 평정시키고 그다음에 나머지 한쪽으로 진압하겠다는 전략을 구사하고있음.

2.사담의 근위부대에게 패배를 안겨줄수있는 군사적으로 보다 강한 적은 쿠르드족임. 따라서 사담은 시아파를 일단 자기쪽으로 끌어 들이려고노력하고있음. 지난 금요일 사담은 백발이 성성한 시아파의 아야틀라 KHOIE를 대동하고 TV에 나타났음. 바그다드정부는 KHOIE가 성지 NAJAF의 친안 회복을 위해 노력해준데 대해 사담에게 감사를 표명했다고 공식발표했음.

3.그러고나서 사담은 신임 수상에 시아파인 HAMMADI임명하는등 내각개편을 단행했음.내각개편으로 쿠르드족 출신의 부통령은 해임되었고 AZIZ외상도 그동안 지켜왔던외상직을 잃게되었으나 사담의 측근들은 보직을 그대로 유지하거나 또는 보다 높은직위를얻게 되었음. 이러한 개각은 정치적 화장술(POLITISCHE KOSMETIC)이라 불리고있음.

4.금번 개각을 볼때 사담의 추종세력이 더이상 확대될수없음이 나타났음. 따라서구시대인물들로 채워진 사담의 신정부는 그의 마지막 정부가될것임. 또한 저항세력을 분열시킴으로서 이를 약화시키려는 사담의 계산은 성공하지못할것임. 시아파인들이 사담의 망상으로 인해 앞으로 얼마만한 시련과 비애를 견뎌야 할것인지는알수없음. 한가지 확실한 것은 시아파인들이사담의 이러한 책략에

중아국   1차보   2차보   구주국   정문국   청와대   안기부

넘어가지는 않을것이라는사실임.

(대사 이장춘)

外務部 걸프戰 事後 對策班

題 目 : 이라크 內閣 改編

91. 3. 25.
中 東 1 課

1. 內閣 改編 內容

   o 사담후세인 大統領은 3.23. 自身이 兼任해오던 首相職에 Saadoun Hammadi
     副首相(革命評議會 委員中 唯一한 시아派)을 任命하고 Khodeir 大統領
     秘書室長을 새 外務長官으로 任命하는등 內閣 改編을 斷行함. 同 大統領
     側近인 內務, 國防, 軍需産業長官등 主要 部處 長官들은 留任되었고,
     Tariq Aziz 前 副首相兼 外務長官은 副首相職만을 繼續 維持하게 됨.

   o 이에 앞서 후세인 大統領은 3.22. Kurd족 出身인 Marouf 副統領을 解任하고
     Ramadan 第1副首相을 새 副統領으로 任命함.

   o 상기 외에도 금번 內閣 改編에서 약 半數의 閣僚가 更迭되었고 新內閣에
     3인의 Kurd족 閣僚가 包含 되었다고 하는 一部 言論 報道가 있음.
     (新內閣 全體 名單은 未詳)

2. 分析 및 評價

   o 금번 內閣 改編에서 사담후세인은 79년 執權以來 兼任해온 首相職을 내어
     놓았으나 아직도 最高 意思決定 機構인 革命評議會(RCC) 議長과 軍 最高
     司令官, 執權 Baath당 書記長職을 保有 하고 있어 內閣 改編으로 同人의
     絶對 權力者로서의 地位에 어떠한 變化가 있다고 보기는 어려움. 단,
     쿠웨이트 外務次官은 3.24. 外交團 브리핑에서 사담후세인의 首相職 抛棄에
     注目하고 同人의 絶對的인 位置에 異常이 생기고 있는 徵候라고 論評함.

   o 금번 內閣 改編에 대하여 日本 外務部 當局者는 후세인 大統領의 政權
     延命策이라고 論評하였으며, 부쉬 美大統領도 사담후세인이 權座에 남아있는
     한 이라크와의 關係 改善은 있을수 없음을 다시한번 분명히 함. 아울러,
     이라크 回敎 革命 最高 評議會(SAIRI), Kurd 민주당등 反政府 勢力들도
     이번 內閣 改編에 意味를 附與하지 않고 후세인이 退陣하지 않는한 繼續
     鬪爭하겠다는 立場을 表明함.

0212

o 사담후세인 大統領이 首相職을 내어놓고 유일한 시아파 閣僚이며 그동안
이란과의 協商 窓口를 맡아온 Hammadi 副首相을 새 首相으로 起用한 것은
국내 시아파와 그 背後 支援國인 이란을 懷柔하는 동시에 1人 獨裁體制에
變化가 있음을 보여주어 自身에 대한 國內外의 退陣 壓力을 多少라도 緩和해
보려는 苦肉之策으로 分析되나, 동인이 實權을 繼續 掌握하고 있는한 이러한
試圖가 成果를 거둘 可能性은 稀薄함.

o Aziz 外務長官 更迭에 대해서는 걸프事態 期間中 아랍권의 支持 確保 失敗등에
따른 問責性 人事로 보는 見解도 있으나, 同人이 副首相職을 繼續 保有하고
있고 또 걸프戰 期間中 蘇聯을 2回 訪問, 平和案을 이끌어 내는등 外務長官
으로서의 職務 遂行에 큰 失手가 없었음을 勘案할때, 걸프戰 敗戰後 새로운
人物을 外交 一線에 내세워야할 必要性에 따른 循環人事로 보는 것이 보다
妥當할 것으로 보임.

o 한편, Marouf 副統領의 更迭은 동 職責이 儀禮的인 자리임에 비추어
實質的으로 큰 意味는 없겠으나 다만 同人이 Kurd족에 대한 配慮로 副統領職에
있었다고 보았을때 報道대로 今番 改閣에서 Kurd족 3명이 閣僚에 새로 任命
되었다면 Kurd족에 대한 配慮는 繼續되고 있다고 보아야 할것임.

o 今番 改閣은 3.16. 사담후세인이 對國民 談話를 통해 民主化 改革 措置를 發表
하면서(3.18.자 대책반 보고서 "사담후세인의 민주화 조치 발표와 정권의 장래"
참조), 大規模 內閣 改編을 約束한데 따른 것으로 보며, 一部 言論에는 쿠데타
說도 있었으나 사담후세인의 政府內 權力基盤이 弱化된 結果로는 보지 않는것이
一般的인 觀察임.

| 參 考 | Saadoun Hammadi 新任 首相 略歷 |

- 生年月日 : 1930. 6.22.   (이라크 南部 回敎聖都 Kerbala 出生)
- 學 歷 : 베이루트 American大 卒 (農業學 博士)
  美 Wisconsin大 修學 (經濟學)
- 主要經歷 : Al-Jumhoriya紙 編輯長
  바그다드大 經濟學 敎授
  農業改革長官 (1963)
  石油·鑛物長官 (1968-74)
  外務長官 (1974-80)
  國會議長 (1980-89)
  副首相(1989·現在) ※ 對外問題擔當 國務長官 兼任   끝.

외 무 부

종 별 :

번 호 : JOW-0830   일   시 : 91 1119 1200

수 신 : 장관(중동일) 사본:주이라크대사

발 신 : 주 요르단대사

제 목 : 이라크현황

　　1. 바그다드 소재 삼성종합건설(주) 송영환차장이 11.18 당관에 알려온바 아래와같음

　　가. 최근 후세인대통령은 공식집회에 참석하지 않고 있다하며,11.4 주무리알다리 준공식에도 부수상이 참석하였다함.(후세인대통령은 준공식 2 일전 밤에 불시 동 다리를 방문하였다함)

　　나. 시중의 물건등은 전과 변함이 없으나 위조지폐가 많이 나돌고 있고, 일부 가게에서는 위조지폐판독기를 준비 위조여부 확인후 물건을 팔고있으며, 현재일부식품은 터어키로부터 유입되고 있다함

　　다. 최근 이라크에서 요르단비자를 신청할경우 약 10 일 정도 소요된다고하며, 제 3 국에서 이라크 비자를 신청할경우에도 주재국 관련기관을 통한 외무성의 비자케이블이 없으면 비자를 발급 받지 못하는 실정임

　　2. 삼성전자 두바이직원 1 명이 현재 이라크 방문중에 있으며, 요르단주재 (주)대우직원 1 명이 11.19, 럭키금성직원 2 명이 11.22, 미수금및 상품상담차 입국예정이며 또한 정우개발직원 1 명이 비자발급 신청중에 있음.

　　3. 현대건설직원에 의하면 11 월말경 이라크 남부도시 바스라 현장업무를 위해 15 명이 입국예정이며, 동 업무가 끝나면 일부직원은 귀국할것이라고함

　　4. 삼성종합건설(주)송영환차장이 11.19 본사로 귀임함에 따라 현재 이라크체재 아국인 총인원은 15 명임.끝

　　(대사 이한춘-국장)

중아국　　차관　　2차보　　분석관　　청와대　　안기부　　중계

기록물종류	일반공문서철	등록번호	2020120213	등록일자	2020-12-28
분류번호	772	국가코드	XF	보존기간	영구
명 칭	걸프사태, 1990-91. 전12권				
생 산 과	북미1과/중동1과	생산년도	1990~1991	담당그룹	
권 차 명	V.3 각국의 경제제재 I , 1990.8.2-10				
내용목차					

0001

외 무 부

종 별 : 초긴급

번 호 : JAW-4764

일 시 : 90 0802 1522

수 신 : 장 관(중근동,아일,정일)

발 신 : 주 일 대사(일정)

제 목 : 이락의 쿠웨이트 침공

연: JAW(F)-2323

당지 NHK 15:00 뉴스는 이락의 전격적인 쿠웨이트 침공으로 쿠웨이트 주요 정부기관 및 군사거점이 점령됨으로써, 사실상 쿠웨이트 수도는 이라크에 완전 제압된것으로 보인다고 보도하고, 한편 미국은 금번 이락의 군사행동을 '침략'이라고 규정하면서 긴급 안보리 소집을 요구한 것으로 보도하였음. 끝

(대사 이원경-국장)

駐 日 大 使 舘   (Page 2 - 1)

2323

JAW(F) :   日時: "지급"

受   信:長   官 (중근동, 경일, 아일

発   信:駐日大使 (일정   )   '90 8--2 14:57   刊)

題   目 이락, 쿠웨이트 침공

표제관련, 당지 공동통신의   별첨 기사를
지급 참고하시기 바랍니다.

첨부: 상기 1 매

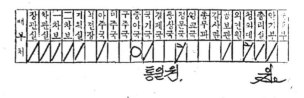

0003

KyodoNews キヨウドウ ... カンコクタイシカン セイムブ ☎03 582 8706 '90 08/02 14:38 ☑001/001

共 X 1 T 3 5 2 外信 7 3 S
◎ ク ラ ⑨ シ ④ 2 号

▽クウェート打倒と発表
【バクダッド⑨ド二日AP＝共同】
イラク革命評議会は二日、クウェート政府が打倒されたと発表した。

（丁）④（5）90 8 2 14 8

← 0004

駐 日 大 使 舘

2325

J A W (F) :　　　　　　　　　　日時：

受　　　信：長　官 (차관실, 중근동, 아일)

發　　　信：駐日大使 (　일정　　　　　　)

題　　　目　　이락크의 쿠웨이트 침공　　　'90 8 --2 {8 :33　　　　　　刊)

"긴급"

　　　별첨과 같이 일정측의 성명문 Text를
첨부합니다.

外務大臣臨時代理談話　　　　平成二年八月二日

イラク軍のクウェイト領侵攻について

一、現地時間二日未明、イラク軍がクウェイトとの国境を越え、クウェイト領内に侵攻したとの情報に接しており、極めて遺憾である。

二、わが国としては、事態の推移を深く憂慮しており、イラク、クウェイト両国間に存在する諸問題が、武力によることなく、話し合いにより平和的に解決されることを強く希望する。

0006

記者会見における内閣官房長官発言要領

平成二年八月二日

（午後四時）

イラク軍のクウェイト侵攻について

一、本二日未明、イラク軍がクウェイト領内に侵攻したとの情報に接しており、極めて遺憾である。

二、わが国としては、かかる事態の悪化を深く憂慮しており、直ちにイラク軍の撤退を要請するとともに、イラク、クウェイト両国間に存在する諸問題が、武力によることなく、話し合いにより解決されることを強く希望する。

0007

외 무 부

종 별 : 긴 급

번 호 : UKW-1432

일 시 : 90 0802 1230

수 신 : 장관(중동,구일)

발 신 : 주 영 대사

제 목 : 쿠웨이트 사태에 관한 주재국 반응

1. 이라크의 쿠웨이트 침공관련, 외무성 W. WALDEGRAVE 국무상은 금 8.2(목) 아침 성명을 발표, 이라크의 무력 침략을 비난하고 군사행동 중지및 즉각 철군을 요구함. 또한 아랍제국들이 협력하여 사태의 평화적 해결을 모색토록 촉구함.

2. 금후 전망에 관한 8.2. 오전 당지 TV 보도요지는 아래와 같음.

가. 걸프 아랍제국이 이라크의 침략행위에 대해 대처할 능력이 극히 제한된 상황에서 미국의 힘에 의존하는 수밖에 없으나 미국으로서도 군사적 개입으로 대응하기는 정치적으로 어려움이 크므로 외교적, 경제적 방안에 주력할 것임.

나. 소련은 동 사태에 대처하는데 있어 미국과 긴밀하게 협조할 여건이 있는 것으로 보며, 대 이라크 군사물자 지원이 중단되기를 기대함.

다. 이라크의 쿠웨이트 점령은 국제여론을 무시해온 후세인의 과거 행태로 보아 장기화될 가능성이 있으며, 쿠웨이트내에 자국이 선호하는 정권이 수립되어 이라크의 요구사항이 충족될때까지 철수하지 않을 가능성이 있음.

라. 유엔안보리 긴급회의나 아랍연맹등을 통하여는 적절한 해결방안이 강구되기 어려울것으로 봄.

3. 한편, 외무성 중동과 P.CLARKE 이라크 담당관에 의하면, 이라크의 장기목표를 알수는 없으나 금번 군사행동은 쿠웨이트 완전병합 기도에 가까운 매우 심각한 것으로 보이며 영국은 UN 안보리 및 구주공동체(EC) 국가들과 긴밀히 협의하며 대책을 강구중이라고함. 끝.

(대사 오재희-국장)

중아국	장관	차관	1차보	2차보	구주국	정문국	정와대	안기부

0008

90.08.02   21:22
외신 2과   통제관 CN

외 무 부

종 별 : 긴 급

번 호 : CNW-1148   일 시 : 90 0802 1030

수 신 : 장 관(중근동,미북,국연,정일)

발 신 : 주 카 나 다 대사

제 목 : 이락의 쿠웨이트 침공(자료응신 제 39 호)

대 : WCN-0782

1. 주재국 CLARK 외상은 8.2.(목) 오전 발표된 성명에서 이락의 쿠웨이트에 대한 군사행동은 "전적으로 수락할수 없는 침략(A TOTALLY UNACCEPTABLE AGGRESSION)" 이라고 강력히 규탄하면서, 전부의 즉각적인 중지와 쿠웨이트로부터의 이락 병력의 즉각적이고 전면적인 철수를 촉구함.(동 성명전문 별첨 FAX 참조)

2. 카나다는 비상임 이사국으로서 8.2. 유엔 안보리에서 채택된 이락 침공규탄결의안을 공동 제안한바 있으며, 주 유엔 카나다 대사는 안보리 발언에서 이락의 침공은 유엔 헌장과 국제법의 극악한 위반행위라고 규정하고 국제사회가 이락에 대해 단호하게 대처할 것을 촉구함.

3. 주재국 외무부측은 금일 오전중 동 사태에 따른 대처 방안에 관해 협의중에 있는바, 카측 입장이 구체화 되는대로 추보 위계임.끝

(대사 - 국장)

첨부 : CNW(F)-0074

예고문 : 90.12.31. 까지

중아국 　장관 　차관 　1차보 　2차보 　미주국 　국기국 　정문국 　정와대
안기부

PAGE 1   90.08.03   00:40 0009

외신 2과 통제관 CN

외 무 부

종 별 : 긴 급

번 호 : FRW-1406　　　　　　　　　　일 시 : 90 0802 1800

수 신 : 장관(중근동,구일,정일)

발 신 : 주 불 대사

제 목 : 이라크,쿠웨이트 침공

대:WFR-1472

1. 표제관련, 주재국 외무성 REGNAULD-FABRE 담당관 확인에 의하면, 주재국 정부는 금 8.2. 오후 하기 요지 성명을 발표하였음.

- 이락측의 쿠웨이트 침공을 강력히 비난

- 이락군의 즉각적인 철수 요구

- 유엔 안보리의 긴급 소집 요청

2. 동 담당관을 통해 확인한 기타 표제 사태 상화 아래 보고함.

- 이락군은 금일 04:30(파리시간) 쿠웨이트를 침공 4-5 시간만(   )에 쿠웨이트 전역을 점령함.

- 쿠웨이트 AL-SABAH 국왕은 금일 오전 헬기로 탈출, 현재 사우디내에 은신중이며, 쿠웨이트 행정은 이락군 통제하에 있음.

- 현재 쿠웨이트내 교전상황은 없으며, 쿠웨이트 거주 외국인등에 대한 신변상의 위협도 없는 것으로 알고있음.

- 현재 주재국도 쿠웨이트 주재 불대사관과의 교신이 불통상태임.

3. 본건 진전사항, 수시 추보하겠음. 끝.

(대사 노영찬-국장)

예고:90.12.31. 까지

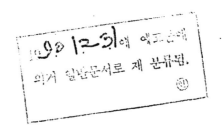

외 무 부

종 별 :

번 호 : YGW-0362

일 시 : 90 0802 1700

수 신 : 장관(근동,중동,동구이,정일)

발 신 : 주 유고 대사

제 목 : 이락의 쿠웨이트 침공에 대한 LONCAR 외상 성명

LONCAR 외상의 8.2자 표제 규탄 성명(전문)을 아래 타전함.

STATEMENTTHE OFFICIAL CIRCLES AND THEYUGOSLAV PUBLIC ARE SHOCKED AND DEEPLYCONCERNED AT THE NEWSOF THE ARMED INTERVENTION BY IRAQ IN THE TERRITORY OFKUWAIT. CONDEMNING THE USE OF FORCE AS AN INADMISSIBLEMETHOD OF SETTLING DISPUTES, ESPECIALLY BETWEEN NON-ALIGNEDCOUNTRIES, YUGOSLAVIA CALLS FOR AN IMMEDIATE WITHDRAWAL OFIRAQI TROOPS FROM KUWAIT AND FOR THE PEACEFUL SETTLEMENT OFTHE DISPUTETHROUGH NEGOTIATIONS. PROCEEDING FROM THEPRINCIPLES OF THE UNITED NATIONS CHARTER AND OF THE POLICYOF NON-ALIGNMENT, AS WELL AS ITS OWN RESPONSIBILITY AS THECURRENT CHAIRMAN OF THE NON-ALIGNED MOVEMENT, THE YUGOSLAVGOVERNMENT PARTICULARLY EMPHASIZES THAT THE WORLD AND IN THENON-ALIGNED MOVEMENT ARE DIRECTED AT FINDING WAYS OFRESOLVING INTERNATIONAL PROBLEMS THROUGH DIALOGUE ANDCOOPERATION. THERE IS A FIRM CONVICTION IN YUGOSLAVIA THATWHOEVER RESORTS TO FORCE AND AGGRESSION ASSUMES A GRAVERESPOSIBILITY. ALSO, THAT THERE IS NO DISPUTE BETWEENSTATES, ESPECIALLY NEIGHBOURING STATES, THAT CANNOT BERESOLVED THROUGH DIALOGUE AND NEGOTIATIONS. AS CHAIRMAN OFTHE NON-ALIGNED MOVEMENT, YUGOSLAVIA WILL TAKE ALL MEASURESSO THAT THE NON-ALIGNED COUNTRIES TOGETHER AT RESTORINGPEACE, ASSURING THE RESPECT OF THE TERRITORIAL INTEGRITY ANDSOVEREIGNTY OF THE STATE OF KUWAIT AND AT SETTLING THISDISPUTE SOLELY THROUGH PEACEFUL MEANS. IN THE INTEREST OFINTERNATIONAL PEACE AND SECURITY, AND IN ACCORDANCE WITHINTERNATIONAL LAW, THE ATTAINMENT OF THAT GOAL ALSO IMPLIESTHAT ALL OTHER INTERNATIONAL FACTORS REFRAIN FROM DIRECTINTEREFERENCE WHICH COULD RESULT IN WIDER

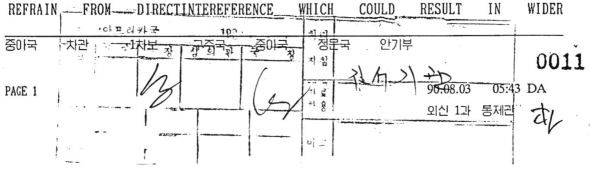

ADVERSEDEVELOPMENTS.

끝

외 무 부

종 별 :

번 호 : CNW-1151　　　　　　　　　　　　일 시 : 90 0802 1800

수 신 : 장 관(중근동,미북,국연,정일)

발 신 : 주 카 나 다 대사

제 목 : 이락의 쿠웨이트 침공(2) (자료응신, 제 80 호)

　　　연 : CNW-1148

　　　대 : WCN-0782

　　　연호 이락의 쿠웨이트 침공사태 관련 8.2. 당지 언론들의 평가 특기사항 아래 보고함.

　　1. 금번 이락의 쿠웨이트 침공은 유엔 헌장 및 국제법을 정면으로 위반하는침략행위임. 유엔을 비롯 전세계 언론이 이를 규탄하고 즉각적인 이락군의 철수 및 쿠웨이트 정부의 원상회복을 촉구하고 있어 이락은 완전 고립상태임.

　　2. 동 사태 수습을 위해 현 단계에서 미국 및 이집트, 사우디등 아랍 인접관계국들의 군사개입 가능성은 없으나 외교적.경제적인 제재조치를 통한 대이락 압력행사 노력이 적극 전개 될것으로 봄.

　　3. 아울러 8.2. 유엔 안보리 결의에 대한 이락의 반응여하에 따라 유엔을 통한 헌장 제 7 장 규정에 따른 집단적 제재조치도 강구될수 있을것으로 봄.

　　4. 이락의 후세인 대통령이 중동정세에 있어 새로운 문제아로 등장했으며, 특히 이락의 화학무기, 신예 미사일, 이이전쟁을 통한 훈련된 대규모 군사력등은중동 평화에 심각한 위협이 되고 있음.

　　5. 국제사회의 대이락 압력 가중에 따라 이락내 반 후세인 쿠테타의 가능성도 배제할수 없다는 관측도 있음. 끝

　　(대사 - 국장)

　　예고문 : 90.12.31. 까지

중아국 안기부	장관	차관	1차보	2차보	미주국	국기국	정문국	청와대

0013

PAGE 1　　　　　　　　　　　　　　　　　　　90.08.03　　07:50

　　　　　　　　　　　　　　　　　　　　　외신 2과　통제관 FE

외 무 부

종 별 : 긴 급

번 호 : CNW-1152   일 시 : 90 0802 1800

수 신 : 장 관(중근동,미북,국연,정일)

발 신 : 주 카 나 다 대사

제 목 : 이락의 쿠웨이트 침공(3)

연 : CNW-1148,1151

대 : WCN-0782

1. 표제 관련 주재국 외무부 SVOBODA 유엔 과장에 의하면, 실무자선에서 미국의 경제 제재조치(자산동결, 식료품 이외 품목 수출입 금지등)와 유사한 대이락 경제제재 조치를 주재국에서 취할것을 건의했는바, CLARK 외상이 최종적인 결정을 할 것이며, 동 결정전에 유엔 안보리 동향, 여타국가의 조치도 참작하게 될것이라고 함.

2. 동 과장은 8.2.(목) 저녁 안보리 상임 이사국간의 협의에 이어 전 이사국 협의가 있을 예정이라고 하고 이락측이 수일내 쿠웨이트에서 철군하지 않을 경우 효과적인 제재조치를 취하도록 안보리에서 결정할 가능성이 높다고 함.

3. 다만 아랍 리그와 시리아측이 제의한 아랍 정상회의가 소극적(TIMID)인 입장을 취할 경우에는 유엔 안보리 및 여타 국가의 제재조치에 대하여 부정적인 영향을 미치게 될 것이라 함. 끝

(대사 - 국장)

예고문 : 90.12.31. 까지

중아국 안기부	장관	차관	1차보	2차보	미주국	국기국	정문국	총리실

0014

외 무 부

종 별 : 지급

번 호 : MOW-0305   일 시 : 90 0802 2200

수 신 : 장관(마그,중동)

발 신 : 주 모로코 대사

제 목 : 이락 쿠웨이트 무력침공

주재국 외무성 외무담당국무상은 금 8.2. 18:30 당지 주재 외교단을 3 개 지역으로 구분 외무성에 긴급 초치, 이락에 의한 쿠웨이트 무력 침공 점령사태에관해 주재국 입장을 다음과 같이 설명 통보하고, 아랍 형제국간의 불행한 분쟁이 조속히 해결되도록 모든 우방국의 협력을 요망하였음.

-다음-

주재국 국왕은 금 8.2. 오전 긴급 각료회의를 소집, 이락의 쿠웨이트 무력 침공사태를 토의하고 다음 조치를 취하였음.

1. 이락의 군사 개입은 모든 관계 국제법규에 위반하며, 모로코는 이를 강력히 규탄하며, 이락군의 즉각 철수를 요구함.

2. 모로코 정부는 침공 당시 쿠웨이트 정부만을 합법정부로 간주하며 그외 어떤 쿠웨이트 기관과도 일체 관계를 갖지 않을 것임.

3. 이사태에 관해 카이로에서 긴급회의중인 아랍연맹 각료회의가 취하는 모든 조치를 전폭 지지 단행할 것임.

동국무상은 모로코의 모든 평화애호 우방국들이 이락의 무력침략을 강력히 규탄하고 즉각 철군을 요구하여 이 불행한 사태가 하루속히 해결되도록 적극 협력을 요망하고, 각국 본국 정부가 이사태와 관련하여 취한 조치를 주재국에 통보하여 줄 것을 요망함.

본사태와 관련 아국 정부 입장 표명 여부 및 그 내용 회시 바람.

(대사 이종업-국장)

예고:90.12.31 일반.

중아국	장관	차관	1차보	2차보	중아국	정문국	청와대	안기부

0015

PAGE 1   90.08.03   08:39
                                              외신 2과 통제관 FE

협 조 문 용 지

분류기호 문서번호	국연 2031- **223**	(	)		결 재	담당	과장	국장
시행일자	1990. 8. 3.							

수　신 　 각.실국장, 외고안보연구원장 　 발　신 　 국제기구조약국장 　 (서명)

제　목 　 이락의 쿠웨이트 침공에 관한 안보리 결의안 송부

　　　　이락의 쿠웨이트 침공에 대하여 쿠웨이트 및 미국의 요청에

따라 8.2. 오전 긴급 안보리가 소집되었는 바, 동 안보리에서 만장

일치로 채택한 결의(660호)을 별첨 송부하오니 업무에 참고하시기

바랍니다.

　　첨　부 : 표제결의안 1부.　　끝.

0016

1505 - 8 일 (1)　　"내가아낀 종이 한장 늘어나는 나라살림"　　190㎜×268㎜(인쇄용지 2 급 60g / ㎡)
85. 9. 9 승인　　　　　　　　　　　　　　　　　　　　　　　　가 40-41 1990. 3. 15

안보리 결의(660호) 전문

o 공동제안국 : 미.영.불.카나다.콜롬비아.코트디브와르.이디오피아
            핀랜드.말레이지아 (9개국)

o 결의내용 :

The Security Council,

Alarmed by the invasion of Kuwait on 2 August 1990 by the military forces of Iraq, determining that there exists a breach of international peace and security as regards the Iraqi invasion of Kuwait,

Acting under articles 39 and 40 of the Charter of the United Nations.

1. Condemns the Iraqi invasion of Kuwait

2. Demands that Iraq withdraw immediately and unconditionally all its forces to the positions in which they were located on August 1, 1990

3. Calls upon Iraq and Kuwait to begin immediately intensive negotiations for the resolution of their differences and supports all efforts in this regard, and especially those of the Arab League

4. Decides to meet again as necessary to consider further steps to ensure compliance with this resolution

0017

M.T.T. [MEDIA TAPES AND TRANSCRIPTS] LTD.

40 QUEEN STREET • SUITE 800 • OTTAWA K1P 5Y7 — (613) 234-4868 — FAX (613) 236-3370

PROGRAM: EMISSION:	SCRUM	DATE: DATE: AUGUST 3, 1990
NETWORK / STATION: RESEAU / STATION:	-----	TIME: HEURE: 16:30

JOE CLARK RE IRAQ INVASION OF KUWAIT

CLARK: When you're ready...okay. I have issued statements beginning early yesterday morning regarding the invasion of Kuwait by Iraq, but I understood that some of you wanted to speak to me personally about it so I wanted to accommodate that. We have condemned this action by Iraq.

Nous avons convoqué l'ambassadeur irakien ici plusieurs fois pour communiquer la position canadienne et aussi poser des questions et indiquer que nous en sommes pas satisfaits par la réponse de l'Irak. Nous avons supporté la résolution du Conseil de Sécurité; nous avons été pleinement impliqués dans l'élaboration de cette résolution.

We are now in the process of working with other countries who are members of the Security Council, looking at further actions that might be taken multilaterally by the United Nations, by the Security Council to give force to the resolution that was passed yesterday. We will also be prepared to consider other actions by Canada perhaps regardless of, depending upon what the United Nations does, perhaps regardless of the UN action. I'd be pleased to try to reply to any specific questions you might have.

0018

- 2 -

Q: Mr. Clark, what can you tell us about the safety of
       Canadians working in Iraq, and specifically the Canadian
oilfield worker who was detained by the Iraqis?

CLARK: I can't give you a specific answer on that specific
           question, regarding the one individual, except that we
believe that others are safe, to our knowledge, and we naturally expect
that person to be treated with...to be freed. To be allowed to come out
of the territory if he chooses, and if not, to have his rights respected.
There are clear duties that apply to occupying powers, in this case Iraq,
in regards the safety of individuals who are affected. And among the
messages we'll be communicating to the Iraqis is that we expect those
responsibilities they have as an occupying power to be respected in the
case of this Canadian.

Q: M. Clark, qu'est-ce que vous pouvez nous dire des
       actifs du Koweit, de l'Irak ici au Canada et est-ce que
c'est possible de geler ces actifs-là?

CLARK: C'est possible de les geler ici. Nous n'avons pas les
           mêmes lois ici qui existent en Angleterre ou aux
États-Unis, mais nous avons fait un arrangement avec les institutions
financières canadiennes pour effectuer, en effet, une situation où on
peut geler les actifs koweitiens dans les institutions financières
canadiennes ici, au Canada, ou ailleurs dans le monde. Nous avons un
plus grand pouvoir s'il y a une déclaration... des mesures économiques

0019

- 3 -

adoptées par les Nations-Unies. Mais nous sommes confiants que la
situation, que l'arrangement que nous avons maintenant avec les
institutions financières canadiennes peut avoir comme résultat de geler
les actifs du Koweit.

Q: Maintenant, en pratique, est-ce qu'il faut une réunion
du Cabinet, une décision du Cabinet, ou ça peut se faire
facilement?

CLARK: Ca peut se faire facilement après que nous avons eu
les communications par la voie du ministère des Finances
canadien avec l'Association des banquiers canadiens pour avoir un
arrangement, et nous sommes confiants que ça va marcher.

Q: Is it possible we're making unexpected wheat sales
in the last few weeks to Iraq (inaudible) Washington
where an agriculture official says that Iraq has been going to Canada and
Australia and others to buy grain, probably in anticipation of
conservative(?) action by the U.S.

CLARK: I can't comment on an unconfirmed report, an
anonymous agriculture official in Washington. There
would naturally be a distinction between sales that might have been made
in anticipation of something happening, that on the one hand; and on the
other hand an action to backfill(?), to move in behind the sanction
(inaudible). It is the policy of this country not to backfill, not to
move in behind sanctions, not to take advantage of measures that have

0020

- 4 -

been taken by other countries for Canadian sales. So, just to be clear on this particular point, I haven't seen that report. I would expect that given past practice and the understanding of the Canadian Wheat Board and Canadian policy, that there would not have been any action that would be of a nature of backfilling.

Q: Excuse me, Mr. Clark---

Q: Could you tell us whether one of these other actions
            that Canada may take on its own is to stop grain sales to
Iraq?

CLARK: The question of the involvement of food in sanctions,
            that might be contemplated by the United Nations. It is
a matter that is under consideration now. It has not been the practice
of most nations to use food as a weapon. And so if there are sanctions
approved by the Security Council of the United Nations, past practice
would suggest that food would not be among those sanctions. Whatever the
measures adopted by the United Nations, Canada will support them. And we
are of course involved in the discussion of what those might be.

Q: (inaudible) freezing Kuwaiti assets?

CLARK: We have taken some actions to freeze Kuwaiti assets
            in Canadian financial institutions. We do not have the
same legal basis as exists in the United Kingdom or the United States to
freeze them in the way they do. So what we have done is entered into an

0021

arrangement with the Canadian Bankers Association that we are confident
will be effective, by which there will be a de facto freezing of Kuwaiti
assets in Canadian institutions, whether those institutions are in Canada
or elsewhere. The question of Iraqi assets does not particularly arise
because there are not significant amounts of Iraqi assets in Canadian
financial institutions.

Q: Does that mean that Kuwaiti money could not be taken
            out of Canada? What essentially is the effect of this?

CLARK: In effect it means that Kuwaiti money cannot be taken
            out of Canada on the basis of an arrangement reached
between the government of Canada and the Canadian Bankers Association.
There is an additional power that can be triggered under Canadian law to
give effect to a resolution of the United Nations relating to specific
economic measures. The United Nations has not yet taken such an action,
so our law is not yet triggered. But in the interim we have a way that
we believe will work to freeze assets of Kuwaitis in Canadian financial
institutions in Canada or elsewhere.

Q: What is the figure (inaudible)?

CLARK: I can't estimate that, but it is significant.

Q: Mr. Clark, if the UN went ahead with embargoing ship-
            ments of grain to Iraq, would Canadian farmers be
subsidized? Sales to Iraq were quite high...

- 6 -

CLARK: Those are hypothetical questions at the moment. I'm sorry, I don't have the answers to that. They've not been considered. As I said in answer to an earlier question, the practice has been to exempt food from those kinds of actions, and that's a matter that's under discussion now. As we try to seek consensus in the United Nations for a series of measures that will work, everyone knows that sanctions are a most imperfect instrument. It's not something anyone likes to resort to, but this is an extraordinary circumstance. If they are to work, they have to be broadly subscribed to. They're more likely to be broadly subscribed to if the package is broad enough to recommend itself to a wide range of countries.

One of the other issues of course here, speaking of the question of the involvement of a large number of countries, is that Canada thinks it is very important that among other Arab states (they) make very clear their condemnation of this violation of sovereignty and this disruption of international order and international law. We've communicated that view to the ambassadors of various Arab states here. We understand the complexity of the situation they are facing, but this is an extraordinary situation, perhaps one of the most dangerous developments in the Middle East in the last 20 years. The first time in nearly 20 years in which there has been this act of deliberate use of military power, and that we would hope, expect that they should, the region itself, would also act to ensure that the sovereignty of Kuwait is restored and respected, and that ordinary international practice prevails.

0023

- 7 -

Q: --some of the options of Canada when you talk about
            the joint (inaudible) of action, but what might Canada do
which might have an effect (inaudible)?

CLARK: I don't really want to get into that at this stage.
            I think that our principal focus, the best thing that we
could do at this stage, is be part of the actions of the United Nations.
But we are looking at a range of other matters that relate to export
practices, other things that are within the power of Canada alone.

Q: Is force contemplated?

CLARK: No. Certainly not by Canada.

Q: What is the status of the Canadian oilfield worker?
            Are you saying you still don't know exactly where it
stands---?

CLARK: I don't know where he is, but there are duties that
            apply to an occupying power with respect to persons in
the situation like this individual. We expect those responsibilities to
be fully exercised by Iraq.

Q: Was he working with other Americans, who seem to be
            detained as well?

CLARK: We've been in touch with a wide range of countries

~ 8 ~

on all aspects of this matter, and certainly it would be our normal practice to be working with other countries who have people whose whereabouts are not guaranteed. At the moment I don't have an answer. I don't have an answer. My officials may to your precise question about co-operation with Americans, and my officials have been in touch with a number of other countries. I spoke this morning to Douglas Hurd who is on his way to a meeting of the European Community foreign ministers, which of course is an important meeting in terms of trying to shape a consensus that could be reflected in any further action by the UN Security Council.

Q: Do you have an estimate, Mr. Clark, of how much is being frozen in Canada?

CLARK: No, I don't.

*****

걸프사태, 1990-91. 전12권 (V.3 각국의 경제제재 I, 1990.8.2-10) 301

주 이 씨 대 표 부

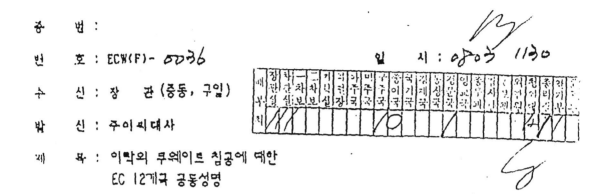

종 별 :

번 호 : ECW(F)- 0036

수 신 : 장 관 (중동, 구일)

발 신 : 주이씨대사

제 목 : 이락의 무웨이트 침공에 대한
EC 12개국 공동성명

        "The Community and its Member States have followed with apprehension during
the last weeks the increase in tension in the dispute between Iraq and some Arab
countries. They have welcomed the diplomatic efforts that Arab countries and the Arab
League itself were deploying and refrained from any stance and initiative in order to
preserve such initiatives from any interference. Following the break down of talks
held in Jeddah under Arab auspices, the Community and its Member States are now
gravely concerned at the latest developments in the dispute and in particular at the
military aggression carried out by Iraq against Kuwait, not only a hostile action to a
neighbour country, but also a dangerous threat to peace and stability in the region.
The Community and its Member States strongly condemn the use of force by a member
State of the UN against the territorial integrity of another State; this constitutes a
breach of the UN Charter and an unacceptable means to solve international differences.
They therefore fully support the resolution adopted today by the Security Council.
The Community and its Member States call upon all governments to condemn this
unjustified use of force and to work for an early re-establishment of the conditions
for the immediate resumption of peaceful negotiations. In this light, they ask for an
immediate withdrawal of Iraqi forces from Kuwaiti territory. The Community and its
Member States maintain the matter under review and are ready to take under
consideration further initiatives".

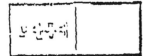

(총 / 매)

0026

외 무 부

종 별 :

번 호 : HKW-2063   일 시 : 90 0803 1400

수 신 : 장관(중근동,아이,정일,기정)

발 신 : 주 홍콩 총영사

제 목 : 이라크의 쿠에이트 침공에 대한 중국반응

1. 중국은 이라크 군대의 쿠웨이트 침공사태를 크게 우려 8.2 아래 요지의 외교부 대변인 성명을 발표함.

' 중국정부는 제3세계 국가들간에 근본적인 이익에 관해 갈등이 없으며, 어느 국가도 분쟁해결을 위해 무력사용을 수단으로 이용해서는 않된다고 항상 믿어왔음. 이라크와 쿠웨이트는 공히 중국의 친구들인바, 중국은 군사활동의 즉각적인 중지와 평화적 협상에 의한 분쟁해결을 호소함.'

2. 중국은 89.12 양상곤의 쿠웨이트 방문및 90.3 전기침의 이라크 방문을 봉해 동 국가들과의 교역증진에 주력하는 동시에 관계강화를 기해 왔으므로 어느 일방을 지지하기가 곤란할것으로 보이며, 동 사태의 악화가 중국의 대중동 외교추진에 불리한영향을 초래할것을 우려 조기수습을 위한 외교적 노력을 강화할것으로 보임.끝.

(총영사 정민길-국장)

동아국   1차보   이주국   정문국   안기부

0027

PAGE 1   90.08.04   08:36 DN
                                                    외신 1과 통제관

외 무 부

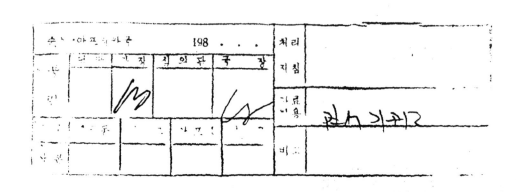

원 본

종 별 :

번 호 : USW-3583

일 시 : 90 0803 1922

수 신 : 장 관(중동,미북,동구일)

발 신 : 주 미 대사

제 목 : 미소 공동 성명

연: USW-3571

1. BAKER 장관은 (8.3(금)) 모스크바에서 쉐바르드나제 소련 외무장관과 이락군의 쿠웨이트로부터의 무조건 철수를 촉구하는 공동 성명을 발표하였음.

2. 동 성명에서는 소련이 이미 대 이락 무기 수출금지 조치를 취하고 미국이 이락의 자산 동결조치를 취한점을 거론하면서 국제 사회가 이락에 대한 무기 공급을 중단할것을 촉구하고 특히 ARAB LEAGUE 등 인근국들이 유엔 안보리결의가 효과적으로 수행되도록 가능한 모든 조치를취할것으로 촉구하였음.

3. 동 성명 내용 별첨 FAX 송부함.

첨부: USW(F)-1699

(대사 박 동진--국장)

중아국 　 1차보 　 미주국 　 구주국 　 정문국 　 안기부

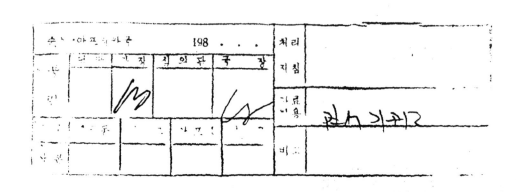

EXCERPT OF JOINT US-USSR STATEMENT
DEMANDING IRAQI WITHDRAWAL FROM KUWAIT
AS READ BY
SECRETARY OF STATE JAMES BAKER, III

FRIDAY, AUGUST 3, 1990

.STX

SEC. BAKER: In response to this blatant transgression of the
basic norms of civilized conduct, the United States and the Soviet
Union have each taken a number of actions, including the Soviet
suspension of arms deliveries and the American freezing of assets.
The Soviet Union and the United States reiterate our call for
unconditional Iraqi withdrawal from Kuwait. The sovereignty,
national independence, legitimate authorities, and territorial
integrity of the state of Kuwait must be completely restored and
safeguarded.

The United States and the Soviet Union believe the
international community must not only condemn this action, but also
take practical steps in response to it. Today, we take the unusual
step of jointly calling upon the rest of the international community
to join with us in an international cutoff of all arms supplies to
Iraq. In addition, the Soviet Union and the United States call on
regional organizations, especially the League of Arab States, all
Arab governments, as well as the nonaligned movement and the Islamic
Conference, to take all possible steps to ensure that the United
Nations Security Council resolution is carried out.

Governments that engage in blatant aggression must know that
the international community cannot and will not acquiesce in -- Bend
of available feed) --

.ETX

END

0029

외 무 부

종 별 :

번 호 : CNW-1165   일 시 : 90 0803 2100

수 신 : 장 관(중근동,미북,국연,정일)

발 신 : 주 카나다 대사

제 목 : 이락의 쿠웨이트 침공(4)(자료응신 제 81 호)

연 : CNW-1148,1151,1152

이락의 쿠웨이트 침공사태 관련 8.3. 오후 외무부 MICKLEBURG 중동 담당관으로 부터 파악한 카나다 정부 조치상황개요를 아래 보고함.

1. 금일 2 차로 주카나다 이락 대사를 외무성으로 초치, 카측의 규탄 입장과 쿠웨이트 체류 카나다인의 안전보장을 위한 이락정부의 필요조치를 촉구하는 카측 입장 전달하였으며 아울러 주 이락 카나다 대사대리로 하여금 이락 외무성에 상기 입장 전달토록 조치했다함.

2. 유엔의 집단적 제재조치가 강구돼야 한다는 입장에서 유엔 안보리 이사국과 긴밀한 협의 진행중(금일저녁 안보리 이사국간의 비공식 협의 참가예정이며 내주초까진 안보리에서의 결의 채택이 있을것으로 전망)

3. 클라크 외무장관은 작일 규탄 성명발표에 이어 8.3. 오후 기자회견을 갖고 금번 사태를 최근 20 년간 가장 위험한 중동정세 발전으로 평가, 쿠웨이트의 주권회복을 촉구하고 아울러 카나다 금융기관 보유 쿠웨이트 재산 동결을 위한 조치를 취했음을 밝힘.

(동 기자회견 전문 별첨 FAX 참조)

4. 아울러 카 정부는 당분간 신임 주이락대사(현재 공석중) 임명절차를 보류키로 했다함.

5. 상기 여타 대이락 쌍무관계 차원에서의 제재조치는 상금 제반 OPTION 을 검토중에 있으나 일단 유엔 안보리의 집단적 제재조치 토의경과를 지켜본후 최종 결정케 될것임. 현재로선 쌍무적 제재조치 보다는 유엔을 통한 집단적 제재조치 강구에 중점을 두고 있음.

6. 현재로선 쿠웨이트 소재 카나다인의 철수계획은 없다함. 쿠웨이트 소재

중아국 안기부	장관	차관	1차보	2차보	미주국	국기국	정문국	정와대

외신 2과 통제관 FE

카나다인은 442 명으로 등록되어 있으며(이중 다수는 휴가등으로 타국 여행중) 현재까지 181 명과 전화 연락등을 통해 사태 안정시까지 외출 삼가토록 권고함.

7. 일부 카나다인들이 육로로 사우디로 피신하고 있는바 주 사우디 카나다 공관직원 2 명을 쿠웨이트. 사우디 국경지역 KHAFTY 에 파견하여 동 카나다인들에 대한 편의제공등 지원 활동중임.

8. 현재 카나다내 쿠웨이트 자산은 약 30 억불로 추정되고 있으며 이락의 자산은 극히 미미한 것으로 알려짐. 또한 89 년 카나다의 대 이락 수입은 2,300 만불(주요품목: 석유, 카페트), 수출은 2 억 5800 만불(주요품목 : 곡물, 고무 및 기계부품)이며, 카 수출개발 공사는 그간 대이락 수출업자에 수출신용 금융을제공해 왔으나 90.3 월부터 이락측의 저조한 채무상환 실적을 고려 수출금융 제공에 신중을 기해오고 있었다함을 참고로 첨언함.

첨부 : 클라크 장관 기자회견 전문 (CNW(F)-0077). 끝

(대사 - 국장)

예고문 : 90.12.31. 까지

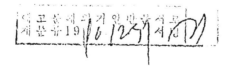

CNW(A)-0C7 900803 2000 (8매)
(전부록)

M.T.T. (MEDIA TAPES AND TRANSCRIPTS) LTD.

80 QUEEN STREET • SUITE 500 • OTTAWA K1P 5Y7 — (613) 236-8088 — FAX (613) 236-3370

PROGRAM: EMISSION: SCRUM	DATE: DATE: AUGUST 3, 1990
NETWORK / STATION: RESEAU / STATION: -----	TIME: HEURE: 16:30

JOE CLARK RE IRAQ INVASION OF KUWAIT

CLARK: When you're ready...okay. I have issued statements
beginning early yesterday morning regarding the invasion
of Kuwait by Iraq, but I understood that some of you wanted to speak to
me personally about it so I wanted to accommodate that. We have condemned
this action by Iraq.

Nous avons convoqué l'ambassadeur irakien ici plusieurs
fois pour communiquer la position canadienne et aussi poser des questions
et indiquer que nous en sommes pas satisfaits par la réponse de l'Irak.
Nous avons supporté la résolution du Conseil de Sécurité; nous avons été
pleinement impliqués dans l'élaboration de cette résolution.

We are now in the process of working with other countries
who are members of the Security Council, looking at further actions that
might be taken multilaterally by the United Nations, by the Security
Council to give force to the resolution that was passed yesterday. We
will also be prepared to consider other actions by Canada perhaps
regardless of, depending upon what the United Nations does, perhaps
regardless of the UN action. I'd be pleased to try to reply to any
specific questions you might have.

FOR INTERNAL USE ONLY / POUR USAGE INTERNE

0032

- 2 -

Q: Mr. Clark, what can you tell us about the safety of
            Canadians working in Iraq, and specifically the Canadian
oilfield worker who was detained by the Iraqis?

CLARK: I can't give you a specific answer on that specific
            question, regarding the one individual, except that we
believe that others are safe, to our knowledge, and we naturally expect
that person to be treated with...to be freed. To be allowed to come out
of the territory if he chooses, and if not, to have his rights respected.
There are clear duties that apply to occupying powers, in this case Iraq,
in regards the safety of individuals who are affected. And among the
messages we'll be communicating to the Iraqis is that we expect those
responsibilities they have as an occupying power to be respected in the
case of this Canadian.

Q: M. Clark, qu'est-ce que vous pouvez nous dire des
            actifs du Koweit, de l'Irak ici au Canada et est-ce que
c'est possible de geler ces actifs-là?

CLARK: C'est possible de les geler ici. Nous n'avons pas les
            mêmes lois ici qui existent en Angleterre ou aux
États-Unis, mais nous avons fait un arrangement avec les institutions
financières canadiennes pour effectuer, en effet, une situation où on
peut geler les actifs koweitiens dans les institutions financières
canadiennes ici, au Canada, ou ailleurs dans le monde. Nous avons un
plus grand pouvoir s'il y a une déclaration... des mesures économiques

0033

- 3 -

adoptées par les Nations-Unies. Mais nous sommes confiants que la
situation, que l'arrangement que nous avons maintenant avec les
institutions financières canadiennes peut avoir comme résultat de geler
les actifs du Koweit.

Q: Maintenant, en pratique, est-ce qu'il faut une réunion
            du Cabinet, une décision du Cabinet, ou ça peut se faire
facilement?

CLARK: Ça peut se faire facilement après que nous avons eu
            les communications par la voie du ministère des Finances
canadien avec l'Association des banquiers canadiens pour avoir un
arrangement, et nous sommes confiants que ça va marcher.

Q: Is it possible we're making unexpected wheat sales
            in the last few weeks to Iraq (inaudible) Washington
where an agriculture official says that Iraq has been going to Canada and
Australia and others to buy grain, probably in anticipation of
conservative(?) action by the U.S.

CLARK: I can't comment on an unconfirmed report, an
            anonymous agriculture official in Washington. There
would naturally be a distinction between sales that might have been made
in anticipation of something happening, that on the one hand; and on the
other hand an action to backfill(?), to move in behind the sanction
(inaudible). It is the policy of this country not to backfill, not to
move in behind sanctions, not to take advantage of measures that have

0034

been taken by other countries for Canadian sales. So, just to be clear
on this particular point, I haven't seen that report. I would expect
that given past practice and the understanding of the Canadian Wheat
Board and Canadian policy, that there would not have been any action that
would be of a nature of backfilling.

Q: Excuse me, Mr. Clark---

Q: Could you tell us whether one of these other actions
            that Canada may take on its own is to stop grain sales to
Iraq?

CLARK: The question of the involvement of food in sanctions,
            that might be contemplated by the United Nations. It is
a matter that is under consideration now. It has not been the practice
of most nations to use food as a weapon. And so if there are sanctions
approved by the Security Council of the United Nations, past practice
would suggest that food would not be among those sanctions. Whatever the
measures adopted by the United Nations, Canada will support them. And we
are of course involved in the discussion of what those might be.

Q: (inaudible) freezing Kuwaiti assets?

CLARK: We have taken some actions to freeze Kuwaiti assets
            in Canadian financial institutions. We do not have the
same legal basis as exists in the United Kingdom or the United States to
freeze them in the way they do. So what we have done is entered into an

- 5 -

arrangement with the Canadian Bankers Association that we are confident
will be effective, by which there will be a de facto freezing of Kuwaiti
assets in Canadian institutions, whether those institutions are in Canada
or elsewhere. The question of Iraqi assets does not particularly arise
because there are not significant amounts of Iraqi assets in Canadian
financial institutions.

Q: Does that mean that Kuwaiti money could not be taken
            out of Canada? What essentially is the effect of this?

CLARK: In effect it means that Kuwaiti money cannot be taken
            out of Canada on the basis of an arrangement reached
between the government of Canada and the Canadian Bankers Association.
There is an additional power that can be triggered under Canadian law to
give effect to a resolution of the United Nations relating to specific
economic measures. The United Nations has not yet taken such an action,
so our law is not yet triggered. But in the interim we have a way that
we believe will work to freeze assets of Kuwaitis in Canadian financial
institutions in Canada or elsewhere.

Q: What is the figure (inaudible)?

CLARK: I can't estimate that, but it is significant.

Q: Mr. Clark, if the UN went ahead with embargoing ship-
            ments of grain to Iraq, would Canadian farmers be
subsidized? Sales to Iraq were quite high...

0086

- 6 -

CLARK;   Those are hypothetical questions at the moment. I'm

sorry, I don't have the answers to that. They've not

been considered. As I said in answer to an earlier question, the

practice has been to exempt food from those kinds of actions, and that's

a matter that's under discussion now. As we try to seek consensus in the

United Nations for a series of measures that will work, everyone knows

that sanctions are a most imperfect instrument. It's not something

anyone likes to resort to, but this is an extraordinary circumstance. If

they are to work, they have to be broadly subscribed to. They're more

likely to be broadly subscribed to if the package is broad enough to

recommend itself to a wide range of countries.

One of the other issues of course here, speaking of the

question of the involvement of a large number of countries, is that

Canada thinks it is very important that among other Arab states [they]

make very clear their condemnation of this violation of sovereignty and

this disruption of international order and international law. We've

communicated that view to the ambassadors of various Arab states here. We

understand the complexity of the situation they are facing, but this is

an extraordinary situation, perhaps one of the most dangerous

developments in the Middle East in the last 20 years. The first time in

nearly 20 years in which there has been this act of deliberate use of

military power, and that we would hope, expect that they should, the

region itself, would also act to ensure that the sovereignty of Kuwait is

restored and respected, and that ordinary international practice

prevails.

0037

- 7 -

Q: ---some of the options of Canada when you talk about
              the joint (inaudible) of action, but what might Canada do
which might have an effect (inaudible)?

CLARK: I don't really want to get into that at this stage.
              I think that our principal focus, the best thing that we
could do at this stage, is be part of the options of the United Nations.
But we are looking at a range of other matters that relate to export
practices, other things that are within the power of Canada alone.

Q: Is force contemplated?

CLARK: No. Certainly not by Canada.

Q: What is the status of the Canadian oilfield worker?
              Are you saying you still don't know exactly where it
stands---?

CLARK: I don't know where he is, but there are duties that
              apply to an occupying power with respect to persons in
the situation like this individual. We expect those responsibilities to
be fully exercised by Iraq.

Q: Was he working with other Americans, who seem to be
              detained as well?

CLARK: We've been in touch with a wide range of countries

0038

- 8 -

on all aspects of this matter, and certainly it would be our normal practice to be working with other countries who have people whose whereabouts are not guaranteed. At the moment I don't have an answer. I don't have an answer. My officials may to your precise question about co-operation with Americans, and my officials have been in touch with a number of other countries. I spoke this morning to Douglas Hurd who is on his way to a meeting of the European Community foreign ministers, which of course is an important meeting in terms of trying to shape a consensus that could be reflected in any further action by the UN Security Council.

Q: Do you have an estimate, Mr. Clark, of how much is being frozen in Canada?

CLARK: No, I don't.

                    *****

0039

외　무　부

종　별 : 지　급

번　호 : CNW-1166　　　　　　　　　　일　시 : 90 0805 1700

수　신 : 장 관(중근동,미북,국연,정일)

발　신 : 주 카 나 다 대사

제　목 : 이락의 쿠웨이트 침공(5) (자료응신 제 82 호)

　　　연 : CNW-1165

　　　1. 이락의 쿠웨이트 침공관련 주재국 정부는 연호 쿠웨이트 자산 동결 조치에 이어
8.4. 아래 추가 제재조치를 발표하였음.

　　　가. 이락 및 쿠웨이트산 원유 수입금지

　　　나. 대 이락 수출통제를 위해 이락을 수출통제 대상지역 리스트에 포함.

　　　다. 카. 이락간 무역, 경제, 기술 협력 협정 효력 중단 및 최혜국 대우 폐지

　　　라. 카 정부의 대 이락수출 관련 지원활동 중단, 카 기업의 대이락. 쿠웨이트 신규
사업에 대한 수출개발 공사(EDC)의 금융지원 중단

　　　마. 카. 이락간 학술, 문화, 스포츠 교류 양해각서 효력 중단

　　　2. 상기관련 외무부 발표전문 별첨 FAX 송부함.

　　　3. 한편, 8.2. 사태 발발 직후부터 쿠에이트에서 행방불명 된것으로 알려진
카나다인 석유공장 근로자 1 명 (GRAHAM PIERCE)이 24 명의 서구인 (미국인 11명
포함) 과 함께 이락측에 의해 바그다드로 이송되어 호텔에 억류중인 것으로
판명되었으며 카 외무부는 현재 동인의 석방 및 안전 귀국을 위해 이락측과 협상중에
있다함.

　　　(대사 - 국장)

　　　첨부 : CNW(F)-0078

　　　예고 : 90.12.31. 까지

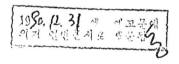

News Release   Communiqué

Secretary of
State for
External Affairs

Secrétaire
d'État aux
Affaires
extérieures

CNW(A)-0018

90 0805 1500

NO. 166   (전부분)   (2페이지)   August 4, 1990

CANADA ANNOUNCES FURTHER MEASURES AGAINST IRAQ

The Secretary of State for External Affairs, the Right Honourable Joe Clark, today commented on developments related to the Iraqi invasion of Kuwait.

"The Government of Canada has continued to pursue consultations with its friends and allies on the situation in the Middle East," Mr. Clark noted. In the course of those consultations, Prime Minister Mulroney had a lengthy discussion with President George Bush of the United States to review efforts to bring collective international pressure on Iraq to end its occupation of Kuwait. Both the Prime Minister and Mr. Clark will be speaking to other of their colleagues in the international community in the coming days. As well, negotiations continue in the UN Security Council on the adoption of a package of comprehensive collective sanctions against Iraq.

Mr. Clark also noted that the Government had earlier today decided on further steps to reinforce Canada's condemnation of Iraq's invasion and occupation of Kuwait. These included:

- an embargo on imports of Iraqi and Kuwaiti origin oil;

- placing Iraq on the Area Control List under the Export and Import Permits Act which will allow Canadian exports to Iraq to be controlled;

- suspension of the Canada-Iraq Agreement on Trade, Economic and Technical Cooperation and termination of Most Favoured Nation Treatment. This action will mean that Iraqi imports to Canada, other than oil which is being totally embargoed, will face higher tariffs;

.../2

1/2

004

P.3/3

— 2 —

   — the suspension of all trade and business promotion activity by the Government of Canada on behalf of Canadian exports to Iraq. In addition the Export Development Corporation (EDC) will be instructed to cease providing any financial coverage on new business activities of Canadian companies in Iraq and Kuwait;

   — suspension of the Canada-Iraq Memorandum of Understanding on Academic, Cultural and Sports relations.

    Canada has already taken action to freeze Kuwaiti assets in Canada.

— 30 —

For further information, media representatives may contact:

Media Relations Office
External Affairs and International Trade Canada
(613) 995-1874

CN(F)78 - 2/2

0042

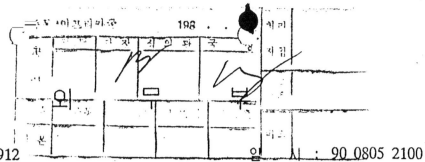

종   별 :

번   호 : ITW-0912   일   시 : 90 0805 2100

수   신 : 장관(구일,중근동,기정,국방부)

발   신 : 주이태리대사

제   목 : 걸프전쟁 주재국 반응

1. 쿠웨이트 침공사태관련 긴급 소집된 EC 정무총구장회의(로마)는 8.4.오전 3시간반동안 회의를 가진후 대이락 경제제재 조치가 포함된 하기내용의 공동성명을 발표하였음.

　　　-이락의 쿠웨이트 침공 규탄 및 무조건 즉각 철수 재천명

　　　-침공자가 수립한 쿠웨이트내 정부당국 승인거부

　　　-UN 안보리 결의 660호 지지 및 이락의 동 결의 준수 촉구

　　　-쿠웨이트의 재산보호 노력

　　　-6개 경제제재조치 채택

　　　0 이락 및 쿠웨이트로부터 석유 수입금지

　　　0 EC 각국내 이락재산 동결조치 채택

　　　0 대이락 무기 및 기타 군사장비 판매금지

　　　0 대이락 군사분야협력 전면중지

　　　0 이락과 과학기술 협력중지

　　　0 이락상품 GSP 수혜중지

　　　-국가간 분쟁문제 평화적 해결노력 및 분쟁지 긴장해소 노력

　　　-쿠웨이트 합법정부 회복등 분쟁문제 해결 위해 아랍국가와 접촉강화

2. 상기 공동선언문합의에 따라 주재국 각의는 금 8.5(일) 회의에서 대이락 경제제재 시행조치를 채택할 예정이라함.

　　　(대사 김석규-국장).

구주국　　중아국　　안기부　　국방부　　1차보　　김현구

0043

PAGE 1   90.08.06   08:05 CG

　　　　　　　　　　　　　　　　　　　　　　　외신 1과　통제관

외 무 부

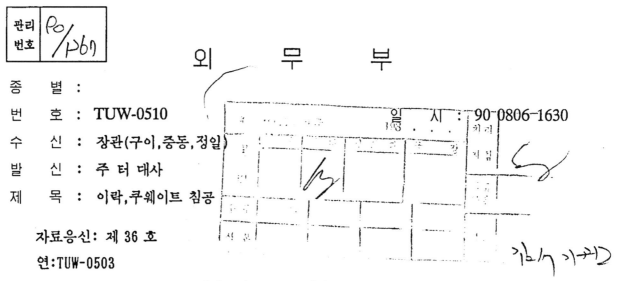

종 별 :

번 호 : TUW-0510

수 신 : 장관(구이,중동,정일)

발 신 : 주 터 대사

제 목 : 이락,쿠웨이트 침공

일 시 : 90-0806-1630

자료응신: 제 36 호

연:TUW-0503

1.TAHA YASSIN RAMAZN 이락 제 1 부수상은 HUSSEYIN 이락 대통령의 멧세지를 휴대하고 8.5 주재국 OZAL 대통령을 면담, 쿠웨이트 신정권의 승인, 터키를 경유 수출하는 이락 2 개 송유관의 폐쇄와 미국이 요청하는 대이락 경제제재 조치에 터키가 가담하지 말고 엄정한 중립을 지켜줄것을 요청하였으나, 터키는 쿠웨이트의 주권과 영토의 보전이 조속 회복되기를 바라며 이락군대의 쿠웨이트로부터의 무조건 철수를 요청한것으로 알려짐.

2. 또한 미국 BUSH 대통령은 OZAL 대통령과 통화, 터키가 2 개 송유관의 폐쇄등 대이락 경제제재 조치에 가담하여줄것을 요청하였으나 터키는 일단 중동분쟁에 중립을 지킬것임을 봉보한것으로 알려짐.

3. 이락은 KIRKUR 유전으로부터 2 개의 송유관을 이용, 터키의 YUMURTALIK 항구를 봉하여 1 일 150 만 바렐의 석유를 수출하고 있으며, 약 100 만 바렐은 사우디아라비아를 통하여 수출하고 있어 터키를 경유하는 2 개 송유관이 폐쇄될 경우 이락은 경제적으로 심한 타격을 받을것으로 전망됨.

4. 이란, 이락 전쟁의 엄정한 중립을 지켜온 터키는 유엔안보리의 대이락 경제제재 조치가 채택되고 이에대한 각국의 반응을 본후, 대이락 경제제재 조치여부를 검토할것으로 관측되고 있음.

(대사대리 민병규-국장)

예고:90.12.31. 까지

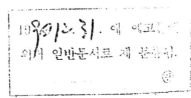

구주국	장관	차관	1차보	2차보	중아국	정문국	정와대	안기부

0044

90.08.07   00:11

외신 2과 통제관 CW

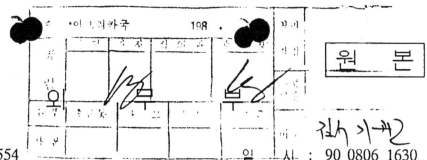

종   별 :

번   호 : ECW-0554   일   시 : 90 0806 1630

수   신 : 장 관 (중근동,구일,기협,통이,동자부,재무부,상공부)

발   신 : 주 EC 대사대리

제   목 : 이락의 쿠웨이트 침공 (자료응신 제 67호)

    연: ECW-0552

    1. EC 12 개국은 이태리 요청으로 8.4. 로마에서 긴급소집된 EPC 정무총국장
회의에서 이락의 쿠웨이트 침공에대한 제재조치로서 하기사항을 결정하고, 이락에
의해설립된 쿠웨이트 임시정부를 불승인하는 입장을 밟힘 (관련성명내용 별도 FAX
송부)

    - 이락및 쿠웨이트로부터의 석유 금수
    - EC 회원국내 이락 자산동결
    - 이락에 대한 무기및 기타 군사장비 판매금지
    - 군사분야에 있어 이락과의 여하한 협력중지
    - 이락과의 과학기술협력 중지
    - 이락에 대한 GSP 공여 중지

    2. EC 집행위측은 EC 12 개국의 쿠웨이트및 이락으로부터의 원유수입이 EC
전체원유수입의 약 10.9 프로에 달하는 것으로 추산하고 하기사항을 고려할때 금번
석유금수 조치가 EC 회원국의 원유조달에 심각한 지장을 초래하지 않을 것으로 분석함

    - EC 회원국들의 현 원유비축량은 130백만본으로서 105 일분의 소비에 상당

    - 1970년대 원유파동시 서구국가간에 구축된 상호지원및 결속 메카니즘이 계속
유효하며 석유공급위기시 IEA 및 EC 차원에서 재가동 가능성

    3. 당지 언론및 석유전문가들은 금번사태로 최근유가가 북해산 BRENT 유 기준,
배럴당 24불이상으로 상승하였으며, 이러한 강세기조는 서방측의 제재조치 확산으로
당분간 지속될 것으로 전망 (일부에서는 배럴당 30불까지 상승전망) 하고 있으나,
동사태가 어떤 형식으로든 진정되면 유가는 다시 배럴당 21-22불수준으로 안정될
것으로 예상하고 있음

중아국	1차보	구주국	경제국	통상국	정문국	안기부	재무부	상공부
동자부	2차보							

4. 이러한 전망의 근거는

1) 이락경제가 서방측의 제재조치에 장기간 버틸수 있을 만큼 좋지 못하기 때문에 금번사태가 장기간 지속될 것으로는 보지 않으며,

2) 금번 사태 이전에는 일산 2백만배럴정도 원유공급 초과현상을 시현하였으며,

3) 현재 OECD 국가들은 약 100일 정도의 석유를 비축하고 있기 때문임

5. 다만 당지 전문가들은 앞으로 비 OPEC회원국들의 신규 유전개발 가능성이 적기때문에 이번 사건을 계기로 OPEC회원국들이 재결속시 1990년대중 제3의 원유위기 도래 가능성을 우려하고 있음. 끝

(대사대리 신장범-국장)

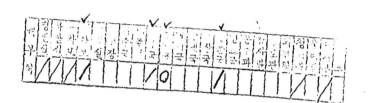

주 이 씨 대 표 부

종   별 :

번   호 : ECW(F)- 00의   일   시 : 0806 1630

수   신 : 장 관 (중근동, 구일)

발   신 : 주이씨대사

제   목 : 이라크의 쿠웨이트 침공에 대한 EC 공동성명

		198 . . .	처 리 지 침	
		과 국 장		
			참 고 활 용	
부 분			비 고	

문서 기간

(총 2 매)

0047

EUROPEAN POLITICAL COOPERATION

PRESS RELEASE

P. 56/90   Brussels, 4 August 1990

STATEMENT ON IRAQ'S INVASION OF KUWAIT

The Community and its member States reiterate their unreserved condemnation of the brutal Iraqi invasion of Kuwait and their demand for an immediate and unconditional withdrawal of Iraqi forces from the territory of Kuwait, already expressed in their statement of August 2.

They consider groundless and unacceptable the reasons provided by the Iraqi Government to justify the military aggression against Kuwait, and they will refrain from any act which may be considered as implicit recognition of authorities imposed in Kuwait by the invaders.

In order to safeguard the interests of the legitimate Government of Kuwait they have decided to take steps to protect all assets belonging directly or indirectly to the State of Kuwait.

The Community and its member States confirm their full support for UN Security Council Resolution n. 660 and call on Iraq to comply with the provisions of that resolution. If the Iraqi authorities fail so to comply, the Community and its member States will work for, support and implement a Security Council resolution to introduce mandatory and comprehensive sanctions.

As of now, they have decided to adopt the following:

- an embargo on oil imports from Iraq and Kuwait;

- appropriate measures aimed at freezing Iraqi assets in the territory of member States;

- an embargo on sales of arms and other military equipment to Iraq;

0048

- the suspension of any cooperation in the military sphere with Iraq;

- the suspension of technical and scientific cooperation with Iraq;

- the suspension of the application to Iraq of the System of Generalized Preferences.

The Community and its member States reiterate their firm conviction that disputes between States should be settled by peaceful means, and are prepared to participate in any effort to defuse the tension in the area.

They are in close contact with the Governments of several Arab countries and follow with utmost attention the discussion within the Arab League and the Gulf Cooperation Council. They hope that Arab initiatives will contribute to the restoration of international legality and of the legitimate Government of Kuwait. The Community and its member States are ready to lend their full support to such initiatives and to efforts to resolve by negotiations the differences between the States concerned.

The Community and its member States are carefully monitoring the situation of EC nationals in Iraq and in Kuwait; they maintain strict coordination in order to guarantee their safety.

0049

외 무 부

종 별 : 지 급

번 호 : UNW-1465   일 시 : 90 0806 1730

수 신 : 장 관(국연,중동,봉이,경협이,기정)

발 신 : 주 유엔대사

제 목 : 안보리(이락-쿠웨트 분쟁)

1. 금 8.6 14:00-16:00 표제건 토의를 위한 안보리가 속개됨. 이라크에 대한 포괄적인 경제제재 조치를 주내용으로 한 결의안이 찬 13-반0-기권2(큐바, 예멘)로 채택됨2. 카나다, 콜롬비아, 코트디브와르, 이디오피아, 핀랜드, 미, 영, 불 말레이지아, 쟈이데등10개국이 공동제안한 동 결의안의 주요내용은 아래와 같음 (가) 이라크가 결의안 660호를 이행하지 않았음.

(나) 이라크. 또는 쿠웨이트 상품의 수입전면금지

(다) 이라크 또는 쿠웨이트 상품의 수출 촉진활동 또는 환적 금지. 동 목적의 대이라크, 쿠웨이트자금 이동 금지

(라) 무기등 군사장비를 포함한 모든 상품의 대이라크, 쿠웨이트 판대 또는 공급및 동 촉진활동 금지

(마) 모든 국가에 의한 이라크 또는 쿠웨이트 '내상업적, 산업적 또는 공공 사업기관에 대한 어떠한 자금이나 재정적, 경제적 자원 제공금지.

(바) 유엔 비회원국을 포함한 모든 국가가 동 결의안 이전의 계약이나 허가에도불문하고 동결의안의 재규정을 엄격히 준수할것을 촉구

(사) 동 결의안 규정에도 불구하고 쿠웨트의 정당한정부에 대한 지원을 금지하는것은 아님.

(아) 모든국가들이 점령국에 의하여 수립된 어떠한 정권도 승인치 않을것과 쿠웨트의 정당한정부의 자산을 보호 하기 위해 적절한 조치를 취할것을 촉구함.

3. 안보리 회원국 발언 요지

0 쿠이이트

이라크에 대한 제제조치 촉구

0 이라크

국기국	장관	차관	1차보	2차보	중아국	경제국	통상국	안기부

PAGE 1

90.08.07 08:50 WH

외신 1과 통제관 0050

이라크군의 철수가 개시되었음. 동 결의안은 분쟁해결에 도움이 되지 않음.

0 미국 이라크는 결의안 660호를 계속 이행치 않고 있으며 점령군을 철수하기보다는 장기체류 준비를하고있음. 헌장 7장 에의한 강제조치가 필요함.

0 핀란드

유엔헌장상의 기본원칙 준수 필요

0 말레이지아

동결의안 채택이 역외국가에 의한 무력 사용의전조가 되어서는 안됨.

0 자이레

비동맹운동의 원칙에 따라 이라크에 의한 결의안 660호 이행을 촉구함. 자이레의 금번결의안 지지는 미래 무력사용국에 대한 하나의경고임.

0 큐바

이라크가 결의안 660호에 따른 철수의사를 밝혔음. 금번 결의안은 분쟁해결에 기여하기보다는 미국에 의한 중동지역 지배 목적에 기여하는것임.

0 예멘

예멘이 동 분쟁 해결을 위해 적극 중재에 나서고있음. 중동지역 내부문제에 외세가 개입해서는 안됨.

0 영,불,중,소등 여타국:

유엔헌장상 원칙 준수촉구

4. 관찰 및 평가

0 유엔 안보리가 결의안 661호 같은 포괄적인 경제제재 조치를 채택한것은 1965로데지아에 대한 제제조치 이래 두번째임.

0 유엔 안보리 5개 상임이사국이 동 조치에 모두찬성 표결함으로써 이들 강대국이 지역분쟁의 평화적 해결 원칙 준수 촉구 및 국가간 분쟁해결 목적의 무력 불사용원칙 위반국에 대한 강력한 제제조치 결의를 공동 표명한바, 이는 국제평화와 안전의유지를 위한 최근 점증하는 안보리의 역할을 재확인하고 금후 지역분쟁 처리의 본보기로 작용할 것으로 판단됨.

0 일부 안보리 국가는 금번 제제조치 결의안 채택이 금후 미국등에 의한 군사적제제조치의 전단계조치 또는 군사조치의 발판으로 이용될 가능성에 대해 우려를 표명하였음.

0 금번 결의안은 모든 유엔 비회원국에 의한 동일한 제제조치의 이행을

PAGE 2

0051

촉구하고있는바, 아국이 취해야할 사항에 대한 검보가 필요한 것으로 사료됨. 금번 결의안에따라 안보리내에 설치될 위원회에 아국이 취한 조치를 통보해야할 필요성에도 대비하여야 할 것으로 사료됨.

　　　첨부:동결의안 전문 UNW(F)-120
　　끝
　　(대사 현홍주-국장)

UNITED NATIONS

SECURITY
COUNCIL

PROVISIONAL

S/21441
6 August 1990

ORIGINAL: ENGLISH

<u>Canada, Colombia, Côte d'Ivoire, Ethiopia, Finland,
France, Malaysia, United Kingdom of Great Britain
and Northern Ireland, United States of America
and Zaire: draft resolution</u>

The Security Council,

<u>Reaffirming</u> its resolution 660 (1990),

<u>Deeply concerned</u> that this resolution has not been implemented and that the invasion by Iraq of Kuwait continues with further loss of human life and material destruction,

<u>Determined</u> to bring the invasion and occupation of Kuwait by Iraq to an end and to restore the sovereignty, independence and territorial integrity of Kuwait,

<u>Noting</u> that the legitimate Government of Kuwait has expressed its readiness to comply with resolution 660 (1990),

<u>Mindful</u> of its responsibilities under the Charter for the maintenance of international peace and security,

<u>Affirming</u> the inherent right of individual or collective self-defence, in response to the armed attack by Iraq against Kuwait, in accordance with Article 51 of the Charter,

<u>Acting</u> under Chapter VII of the Charter of the United Nations,

1. <u>Determines</u> that Iraq so far has failed to comply with operative paragraph 2 of resolution 660 (1990) and has usurped the authority of the legitimate Government of Kuwait;

2. <u>Decides</u>, as a consequence, to take the following measures to secure compliance of Iraq with operative paragraph 2 and to restore the authority of the legitimate Government of Kuwait;

1484E

3-1

0053

3. Decides that all States shall prevent:

- (a) The import into their territories of all commodities and products originating in Iraq or Kuwait exported therefrom after the date of this resolution;

- (b) Any activities by their nationals or in their territories which would promote or are calculated to promote the export or transshipment of any commodities or products from Iraq or Kuwait; and any dealings by their nationals or their flag vessels or in their territories in any commodities or products originating in Iraq or Kuwait and exported therefrom after the date of this resolution, including in particular any transfer of funds to Iraq or Kuwait for the purposes of such activities or dealings;

- (c) The sale or supply by their nationals or from their territories or using their flag vessels of any commodities or products, including weapons or any other military equipment, whether or not originating in their territories but not including supplies intended strictly for medical purposes, and, in humanitarian circumstances, foodstuffs, to any person or body in Iraq or Kuwait or to any person or body for the purposes of any business carried on in or operated from Iraq or Kuwait, and any activities by their nationals or in their territories which promote or are calculated to promote such sale or supply of such commodities or products;

4. Decides that all States shall not make available to the Government of Iraq or to any commercial, industrial or public utility undertaking in Iraq or Kuwait, any funds or any other financial or economic resources and shall prevent their nationals and any persons within their territories from removing from their territories or otherwise making available to that Government or to any such undertaking any such funds or resources and from remitting any other funds to persons or bodies within Iraq or Kuwait, except payments exclusively for strictly medical or humanitarian purposes and, in special humanitarian circumstances, foodstuffs;

5. Calls upon all States, including States non-members of the United Nations, to act strictly in accordance with the provisions of this resolution notwithstanding any contract entered into or licence granted before the date of this resolution;

6. Decides to establish, in accordance with rule 28 of the provisional rules of procedure of the Security Council, a Committee of the Security Council consisting of all the members of the Council, to undertake the following tasks and to report on its work to the Council with its observations and recommendations:

- (a) To examine the reports on the progress of the implementation of this resolution which will be submitted by the Secretary-General;

2

0054

- (b). To seek from all States further information regarding the action taken by them concerning the effective implementation of the provisions laid down in this resolution;

7. Calls upon all States to co-operate fully with the Committee in the fulfilment of its task, including supplying such information as may be sought by the Committee in pursuance of this resolution;

8. Requests the Secretary-General to provide all necessary assistance to the Committee and to make the necessary arrangements in the Secretariat for the purpose;

9. Decides that, notwithstanding paragraphs 4 through 8, nothing in this resolution shall prohibit assistance to the legitimate Government of Kuwait, and calls upon all States:

- (a) To take appropriate measures to protect assets of the legitimate Government of Kuwait and its agencies; and

- (b) Not to recognize any régime set up by the occupying power;

10. Requests the Secretary-General to report to the Council on the progress of the implementation of this resolution, the first report to be submitted within thirty days;

11. Decides to keep this item on its agenda and to continue its efforts to put an early end to the invasion by Iraq.

3

외 무 부

종 별 :

번 호 : TUW-0518

일 시 : 90 0807 1642

수 신 : 장관(구이,중동,정이)사본:국방부장관

발 신 : 주 터 대사

제 목 : 이락, 쿠웨이트 침공

자료응신:제 37 호

연:TUW-0510

1. 8.6 이락은 터키를 경유 수출하는 2 개의 석유관중 1 개를 폐쇄하고 잔여 1 개의 석유관도 75 프로 감량조치하였음.

2. BAKER 미 국무장관은 8.8 터키를 방문, 중동사태에서 터키의 대이락 경제제재 조치 합류및 군사개입 가능성에 대비한 터키기지 이용문제등을 협의할 것으로 보임. 이에대하여 터키는 향후 아랍국가와의 관계등을 고려하여 대이락 경제제재 조치에도 가능한한 늦게 합류하고 터키기지를 이용한 군사개입은 반대하는 신중한 입장을 보일것이 예상됨.

3. 터키는 전체 석유수입의 64 프로를 이락에 의존하고 있으며 현재 6 만명의 터키 근로자가 이락에 근무하고 있고 터키를 경유하는 송유관 수입이 연간 4 억불에 달하고 있어 대이락 경제제재 조치에 가담할 경우 연간 약 20 억불의 손해를 보게될것이라함.

4. 또한 터키는 그간 미 상원의 아르메니아인 법안, 미, 그리스 방위협정 서명에 따른 터.미관계 불편등과 EC 가입신청에 대하여 EC 제국으로부터 냉대를 받아왔으나 금번 중동사태로 지정학적인 중요성이 재인식된 부수적인 효과를 거두게 되어 금번 기회를 외교적으로 최대한 이용할것으로 관측됨.

(대사대리 민병규-국장)

예고:90.12.31. 일반

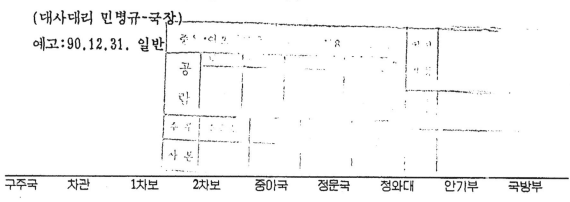

구주국	차관	1차보	2차보	중아국	정문국	정와대	안기부	국방부

외 무 부

종 별 :

번 호 : CNW-1175

일 시 : 90 0807 1810

수 신 : 장 관(중근동, 미북, 정일)

발 신 : 주 카 나 다 대사

제 목 : 이락의 쿠웨이트 침공(6)

연 : CNW-1166

1. 멀루니 수상은 8.6. 미국을 방문 부쉬 대통령과 만찬을 갖고 이락의 쿠웨이트 침공에 따른 중동지역 정세와 대 이락 국제압력 행사를 위한 공동 대처 방안에 관해 협의 하였다 함.

2. 카 정부는 연호 대 이락 제재조치 발표외에도 유엔 안보리 채택 대 이락공동제재 조치 결의안의 공동 제안국이 된바 있으며 금번 사태 해결을 위한 대이락 국제압력 행사에 미국등 관련국과 긴밀히 협력하고 있다함. 주재국 수상실의 관련 발표문 별첨 FAX 송부함. 끝

첨부 : CNW(F)-0080

(대사 - 국장)

예고문 : 90.12.31. 까지

중아국	차관	1차보	2차보	미주국	정문국	청와대	안기부

Office of the
Prime Minister

Cabinet du
Premier ministre

CANADA

Release

Date: August 6, 1990

For release: Immediate

SITUATION IN THE PERSIAN GULF

President Bush has invited the Prime Minister to the White House tonight to review the current situation. The dinner meeting is part of the ongoing series of consultations which the President is holding with concerned parties.

The Prime Minister and the President have spoken several times during the last few days concerning the serious situation in the Persian Gulf and to review efforts to bring collective international pressure on Iraq to end its occupation of Kuwait. In this context, the Prime Minister held a lengthy discussion with President Ozal of Turkey yesterday. Both the Prime Minister and the Secretary of State for External Affairs have consulted with their colleagues extensively on this question.

Canada, in addition to the significant bilateral measures recently announced by Mr. Clark, has co-sponsored a resolution in the Security Council proposing comprehensive collective sanctions against Iraq.

0058

외 무 부

종   별 :

번   호 : BRW-0466   일   시 : 90 0807 2000

수   신 : 장 관(중근동,기협,미남,정일,국방,기정동문)

발   신 : 주 브라질 대사

제   목 : 이라크-쿠웨이트 사태(자료응신 90-37호)

연: BRW-0457

대: WBR-0350

1. 주재국 정부는 무기 수출국으로서의 이라크의 중요성및 대이락 원유의존도로 인해 제재조치가 어려울것이라는 예상에도 불구하고 90.8.6. 외무, 경제, 기간산업부등 관계부처 회의를 열고 유엔안보리의 대이라크 봉상제재 결의를 존중, 이라크 및 쿠웨이트와 봉상관계를 단절하기로 결정하였음. 이와관련 주재국 외무부 대변인은 주재국 정부가 유엔안보리 결의를 즉각적이고 완전하게 준수할것이라고 발표하였으며, 최근까지도 주재국이 대이락 무기수출을 계속하고 있다는일부 외국 언론보도를 부인하였음.

2. 주재국 정부는 대이라크및 쿠웨이트 봉상금지조치를 위한 대통령령을 조만간 공포할 예정이며, 이미 8.6. 부터 양국가 교역을 금지하고 있다함.

3. 브라질은 이라크-쿠웨이트 양국으로부터 일일 원유도입량 55 만배럴의 35프로에 해당하는 19 만배럴(이라크 16 만 배럴(89 년도 25.2 만 배럴), 쿠웨이트 3 만배럴)을 수입하고 있는바, 대 이라크및 쿠웨이트 봉상금지 결정에 따라브라질 석유공사가 원유수입 협정이 체결된 10 개국과 원유추가 도입 교섭을 개시할것이라 하며, 주재국의 일일 원유도입 현황은 다음과 같음.

- 이라크 : 16 만 배럴
- 쿠웨이트: 3 만 배럴
- 사우디 : 14 만 배럴
- 이란: 10 만 배럴
- 현물시장: 6 만 배럴
- 기타국가: 6 만 배럴

중아국   차관   1차보   2차보   미주국   경제국   정문국   청와대   안기부 **0059**
국방부

PAGE 1

계: 55 만 배럴
끝

(대사 김기수-국장)

외 무 부

번   호 : JAW-4887

수   신 : 장관(통이, 경일, 기협, 아일, 중근동)

발   신 : 주 일 대사(경제)

제   목 : 일 정부의 대 이라크 제재조치

암호수신

일 시 : 90 0808 0952

통일

연 : JAW-4829

8.6. 일정부가 취한 대이라크 경제제재 조치가 일본 경제에 미치는 영향 및동 제재조치 장기화에 대비한 일정부의 대책등을 언론보도 중심으로 아래 종합보고함.

1. 전반적 영향 평가 및 전망

0 금번 이라크에 대한 경제제재 조치가 석유수급 핍박 및 석유가 인상에 따른 물가상승을 통해 경제전반에 어떤 영향을 미칠것인가에 일정부 당국, 업계 및전문가들은 당분간은 44 개월동안 지속되어온 대형경기를 감속시키는 일은 거의 없을것으로 전망

- 수급면에서는 현재는 석유 비수요기이고 석유 비축량이 142 일분(1 차 오일쇼크시는 58 일분)에 달해, 당분간은 수입 감소분을 비축량 방출로 보충가능하는 점

- 또한 1,2 차 오일쇼크후 에너지 절약대책 및 기술혁신 진전으로 원유 수입가격이 물가에 미치는 영향은 20% 정도로 2 차 오일쇼크에 비해 매우 적게 되었다는 점

0 다만, 최근 국내물가가 상승기조에 있어 원유가 상승이 이러한 물가상승기를 부채질할 우려가 있다는 관측이 대두되고 있는바, 대장성은 공정금리 인상을 고려할 상황은 아니라고 하면서도 물가동향에 대해 경계심을 표시하고, 석유업계의 편승 인상행위를 감시할 방침을 밝히고 있음.

- 석유가에 대해서는 부기적 매입이 활발해져 당분간은 상승이 불가피한 것으로 보는 견해가 유력하나, 상승폭에 대해서는 견해가 다양

- OPEC 세계 석유 전문가들은 중장기적 관점에서 배럴당 25 달러 이상이 되면 에너지 절약화 및 석탄등 대체 에너지에의 전환으로 석유수요가 감퇴되므로, 25달러 수준이 한계라고 전망

통상국   차관   2차보   아주국   중아국   경제국   경제국

PAGE 1

90.08.08   13:24   0061

외신 2과 통제관 BN

O 한편, 금번 사태가 장기화되면 원유가 상승 및 석유수급 핍박을 통해 적지않은 영향이 있을것으로 전망

- 대쿠웨이트 석유제품 수입 의존도가 약 14% 정도로, 공급면에서의 영향이 서서히 나타날것으로 예측

- 대 쿠웨이트 및 이라크 원유 수입 의존도가 12% 정도인바, 과거 원유수입량의 3.4%가 감소한 정도로 제 1,2 차 오일쇼크가 발생했던 점으로 미루어 낙관 불허

2. 제재조치에 대한 업계의 반응 및 영향 평가

O 일본 산업계는 전반적으로 정부의 제재조치를 불가피한 조치로 받아들이고 있으나, 동 조치의 장기화에는 경계감을 표시하고 있는바, 특히 석유업계 및 플랜트 수출업계는 적지않은 영향을 받게될 것으로 우려

O 석유업계는 금년 상반기 쿠웨이트 및 이라크 양국으로부터의 원유 수입량이 일일 평균 40 만 베럴에 달하고 있어 정부의 원유 수입금지 조치에 대한 심각한 반응

O 이란, 이라크 전후 부흥계획 참여를 대이라크 무역 및 경제교류를 확대해온 상사 및 메이커등 수출업체는 대형 프로젝트 추진에 큰 타격이 있을것으로 우려하고, 대이라크 채권회수가 동국의 석유수입 감소로 어려워질 것으로 전망

- 89 년 대형 종합상사의 대이라크 계약건수는 총 7 건 430 억엥, 미쯔이 물산등에 의한 대쿠웨이트 담수화 플랜트는 1 건 50 억엥에 달하고, 그외에 대이라크 엥차관 제공을 겨냥한 민간업계간 대형 상담이 추진중

- 일본기업 약 100 개사의 대이라크 채권은 현재 7,000 억엥으로 이중 통산성 소관 무역보험 대상은 4,300 억엥 정도인바, 이라크는 88 년 말부터 대일 석유 수출대금의 약 25%, 90.2 부터는 45%가 주로 이자분으로 지불해 왔으나, 원금은 거의 그대로인 상태

O 여타 업계는 제재조치도 직접적 영향은 거의 없다고 평가

- TV, 비디오등 전기기계 부문의 대이라크 수출은 89 년도 100 억엥(수출구성비 1%)에 불과

- 철강의 대이라크 수출량은 90.1-5 간 4.4 만톤으로 전체수출의 0.7%

- 89 년 자동차의 수출은 이라크에 2,183 대, 쿠웨이트에 22,897 대에 불과

3. 일정부 및 업계의 제재조치 장기화 대비책

가. 일정부의 대책

O 대 업계 석유수입선 다변화등 요청

- 8.6. 봉산성은 석유업계에 대해 원유, 가솔린등 석유제품, 액화석유가스(LPG)의 수입선을 여타국으로 다변화하도록 요청하여, 각 석유회사는 여타 산유국에 대해 대일 공급 계약량의 증량교섭에 착수

　　O 원유의 대 쿠웨이트 및 이라크 수입의존도 12%

　　. 석유제품의 대쿠웨이트 수입의존도 14%

　　. LPG 의 대쿠웨이트 수입의존도 12.7%

- 이와 더불어 석유업계가 고가의 원유를 구입치 않도록 지도하고, 석유가의 편승인상을 자숙하도록 요청(주유소등 판매업자에 대한 가격조사 강화방침)

　　O 석유 비축분(현재 142 일분) 방출

- 8.6. 봉산성은 석유판매 회사등에 대한 민간 비축의무를 경감하여 민간 비축분을 방출할수 있도록 결정한데 이어, 석유 수요기인 9 월부터 국가 비축분을 방출한다는 방침하에 방출가격 산출등 구체방안 검토 착수

- 여타 산유국의 증량에는 어느정도 한계가 있을것으로 보고 원유 수입감소분의 보충을 봉해 가격인상을 억제하는 것이 목적

　　O 원유처리 한도량증대

- 8.6. 봉산성은 가솔린등 석유제품을 생산하는 원유의 처리한도량을 증대하는 방침을 결정, 관련 업계에 전달

- 89 년 대쿠웨이트 석유제품 수입 비중이 전체의 14%에 달하고 있어 제재조치 장기화시 제품수급에 악영향이 발생할것에 대비, 석유제품 수입 감소분을 국내생산으로 보충하는 것이 목적

　　O 업계 지원

V- 일정부는 제재기간이 장기하될 경우, 민간기업의 보험청구 증가로 봉산성의 무역보험 지붙이 급증할 것어 대비, 무역보험 특별회계의 운용자금 확보조치 강구

　　. 현재 민간기업의 무역보험 채권은 이락크관련 채권 4,300 억엥, 쿠웨이트관련 채권 900 억엥 정도로 90 년도내 지붙기한을 맞는 무역보험 채권은 약 800억엥 정도로 추산

- 한편, 봉산성은 대쿠웨이트 및 이라크 수출 의존도가 높은 중소기업을 대상으로 금수조치가 기업경영에 미치는 영향을 조사, 피해가 광범할 경우 자금을 대부하는 긴급융자 제도 검토 착수

　　O 종합적 에너지 절약 대책 검토

PAGE 3

0063

- 자원에너지청은 <u>1,2 차 오일쇼크와 같은 위기적 상황이 아니라고 보고, 석유</u> <u>사용량 규제등 강경대책은 당분간 취할 생각이 없다고</u> 하면서도 제재조치가 장기화할 것에 대비, 사우디등에 증산을 요청함과 동시에 석유 수요, 공급면에 대책 수립검토 예정

- 73 년, 79 년의 오일쇼크때는 석유사용절감, 주유소 영업시간 단축, 네온싸인 및 냉난방 사용억제등의 종합에너지 절약대책을 작성, 실시한바 있음.

나. 민간업계 반응

0 이라크 및 쿠웨이트 진출업체들은 현지사원의 안전확보에 전력을 기울이고 있으며, 일부에서는 제재조치 장기화에 대비, 현지 인원 감소 또는 폐쇄등 대책 검토

0 특히 대형 종합상사들은 정부의 제재조치가 장기화될 경우, 원유가격 및 상사활동등에 영향이 클것으로 보고, 현지사원 안전대책, 석유정세 및 금후 사업전망등을 분석, 대응책 강구. 끝

(공사 이한춘-국장)

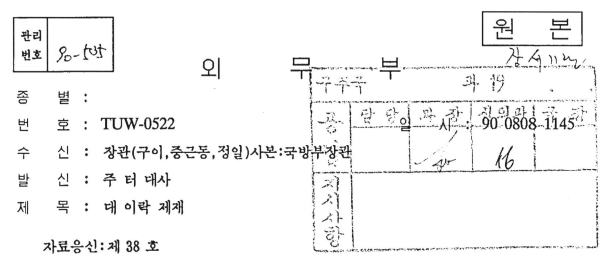

관리
번호 : 8p-ᅵ냐

외　　무　　부

종　　별 :

번　　호 : TUW-0522

수　　신 : 장관(구이,중근동,정일)사본:국방부장관

발　　신 : 주 터 대사

제　　목 : 대 이락 제재

자료응신 : 제 38 호

1. 8.7. 주재국정부는 터키를 경유 수출해온 YUMURTALIK 항구에서의 이락 원유수출을 금지하고, 터키내 쿠웨이트, 이락 재산동결, 터키를 통한 이락의 수출입을 금지하는등 유엔의 대이락 경제제재 조치를 준수하는 조치를 발표 하였음.

2. 야당 및 언론은 주재국잊이란, 이락 전쟁시 중립을 지켰음을 상기하고 성급한 주재국 정부의 대 이락 제재 조치에 비판적이나, OZAL 정부는 NATO 및 서 방국과의 결속등을 고려, 예상보다 빨리 제재 조치를 취한것으로 보임.

3. 주재국 NCIRLIK 기지에는 F-111 기 14 대가 새로 배치된 것으로 알려지고 있으며, 금 8.8. BAKER 미 국무장관의 방터시 주재국 군사기지의 이용문제가 논의될 것으로 관측됨.

(대사대리 민병규-국장)

예고:90.12.31. 까지

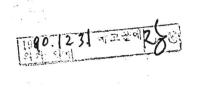

구주국　　차관　　1차보　　중아국　　정문국　　청와대　　안기부　　국방부

PAGE 1

90.08.09　　03:09　**0065**

외신 2과　통제관 DH

외 무 부

종 별 : 긴 급

번 호 : USW-3634   일 시 : 90 0808 1115

수 신 : 장관(미북, 중근동, 기협, 청와대)

발 신 : 주 미 대사

제 목 : 부쉬 대통령 연설

대:WUS-2630

연:USW(F)-1743

대호, 금 8.8. 09:00 실시한 BUSH 대통령 연설 주요 내용 요지를 하기 보고함 (연설문 전문은 연호 팩스 송부)

1. 연설 주요 내용

가. 금번 미군 병력의 사우디 파견은 CAUSE OF PEACE 를 위한 결정인바, 이에 대한 지지를 호소함 (체니 국방장관의 사우디, 이집트, 모로코 측과의 성공적 협의 강조)

나. 동 미군 병력은 사우디 내에서 방어적 태세를 견지할것이라는 점을 강조함.

(쿠웨이트를 탈환하기 위한 것이 아님을 분명히 천명)

다. 여사한 파병결정 이전, 미국으로서는 전례없이 긴밀하게 관련국간 협의 과정을 거쳤으며, 군사력 동원이외의 가능한 모든 수단을 동원하여 사태를 해결코자 노력하였음.

라. 이락은 쿠웨이트 공격개시 직전까지도 여사한 공격은 없을 것이라고 장담하고서도 아무런 이유 없이 미사일등을 동원 쿠웨이트를 전격 침공하바 이락에 의한 쿠웨이트 괴뢰정권 수립 및 영토적 획득은 미국으로서는 결코 용납할수 없음. 어떠한 침략도 격퇴하려는 미국의 결심을 과소 평가해서는 안될것임. 마. 미국은 금번 사태 해결을 위한 다음의 4 대원칙을 천명함.

-쿠웨이트로 부터 이라크 군의 즉각적이고 , 무조건적인 전면 철수

-쿠웨이트 합법 정부 (왕정) 의 복구

-중동지역의 안정과 안전 유지

-동지역내 미국민의 안전확보

바. 이락 후세인 대통령의 쿠웨이트 불침공 약속 및 쿠웨이트로 부터의 조속 철군

미주국 안기부	장관	차관	1차보	2차보	중아국	경제국	정문국	청와대

PAGE 1   90.08.09   04:20   0066

외신 2과 통제관 DH

약속등은 식언으로 끝났는바, 1939 년 히틀러에 대해 취했던 유화 정책과 같은 방식으로는 금번사태를 해결할수 없을것임.

즉, 이락이 사우디를 침공하지 않을 것이라고 가정하는 것은 현명치도 않고 비현실적인 가정임.

이락은 현재 추가적 증원없이도 사우디를 공격할수 있을 만한 병력을 사우디 국경에 배치하고 있음.

사. 금번 쿠웨이트 침공사태로 야기된 위기는 미국만의 문제가 아니라 세계전체의 문제임. 따라서 유엔 안보리의 규탄 및 의무적 제재조치 결정을 환영하며, 일본, 영국도 적극 참여하고있음. 쏘련, 중공도 대 이락 무기 공급을 중단하기로 결정하였음. 미국은 유엔 안보리의 제재조치가 실효를 거둘수 있도록 계속 자신의 역할을 수행할것임.

아. 사우디의 주권과 독립은 미국의 VITAL INTEREST 인바, 미국은 방어적인 자세를 견지하면서 우방국인 사우디를 지켜 나갈것임. 미국도 많은 원유를 중동에 의존하지만 여타 우방국은 더욱 취약한 상황임. 미국은 이지역에서 의 평화 유지 의무가 있음.

자. 또한 금번 사태관련, 산유국의 원유 생산량 증가, 미국등 서방동맹국들의 전략비축 원유 사용, 석유소비 절약 운동 전개 및 정유회사의 가격조작, 부당이윤 행위등의 자제등을 촉구함.

2. 당관 평가

가. 금일 연설을 통해, BUSH 대통령은 미국의 파병 결정이 국제적인 협조하에 이루어 졌다는 점을 강조하고, 또 이락의 후세인 대통령을 히틀러에 비유함으로써 , 이락의 호전성을 중점 부각하고 미국의 단호한 입장을 천명 하였는바,사우디 파병 결정에 대한 국내외의 지지를 확보키 위한것임.

(특히 , NUNN , DODD 상원의원등 및 ASPIN 하원의원 등 민주당계 중진의원들이 부쉬 대통령의 파병 결정에 전폭적인 지지를 표한점등을 감안할때, 금일 연설은 국가위기 사태시 애국심의 고취를 통해 국민적 단결력을 고양시키는 " RALLY- AROUND- THE- FLAG" 의 효과를 거두는데 도움이 될것으로 보이며 , 실제로 국민 여론도 부쉬 대통령을 크게 지지하고 있음)

나. 또한 , BUSH 대통령은 금일 연설시 미측의 파병 성격이 "방어적" 임을 두 차례에 걸쳐 강조하고 사우디의 안전이 미국의 사활적 이익 이라는점을 지적하였는바, 이는 현단계에서 미국의 목적인 대이라크 전면전을 통한 전쟁 발발 이전 상태로의

PAGE 2

회복에 있다기 보다는 , 이락의 사우디 침공은 곧 대미 선전포고에해당한다는 점을 이락으로 하여금 인식 시킴으로써, 현상태에서 이락의 군사행 동 확대를 우선 중지시키고 이락이 국제원유가를 좌지우지 하게되는 결과를 방지코자 하려는 것으로 분석됨. 또한 미국은 계속 아랍제국의 지지 확보를 통해 주 사우디 병력을 다국군화 하도록 시도할것으로 보임.

(당지 전문가에 따르면, 미측이 이락과의 전면전 수행을 위해서는 2 개 중무장 보병 사단과 약 700-800 대의 전폭기 동원이 필요 하다함)

한편, 당지 일부 언론은 HUSSEIN 의 실각을 위한 대안도 검토하고 있다고 보도한바 있음.

(대사 박동진- 국장)

예고:90.12.31. 까지

외 무 부

종   별 :

번   호 : SZW-0484   일   시 : 90 0808 1700

수   신 : 장 관(중근동,정일)

발   신 : 주 스위스 대사

제   목 : 경제제재 조치(자료응신 제 29호)

연: SZW-0481

1. 연호 이락의 쿠웨이트 침공 비난 성명에 이어, 8.7. 주재국 연방각의는 대이락,쿠웨이트에 대한 하기 요지의 경제제재 조치를 공포함.

  - 이락및 쿠웨이트에 대한 수출입및 통과금지 (단, 의약품, 인도적인 목적의물품수출, 통과는 허용)

  - 이락및 쿠웨이트 회사및 개인에 대한 지불, 대부금지

  - 상기 위반시 거래액의 10배에 해당하는 벌금징구

2. 중립정책을 추구하는 주재국으로서 상기와 같이 종래에 볼수 없었던 강력한경제제재 조치를 취하게된 배경으로는 이락의 침공이 명백하며, 이에 대한 유엔의제재결의등 국제사회의 분위기를 감안, 금번사태의 경우만은 주재국으로서도 중립정책을 국익에 맞게 해석한 것으로 보임.

3. 다만, FELBER 외상은 금번조치가 주재국 외교정책상 기본적인 전환을 의미하는것은 아니라고 해석, 향후 여타 사태시 UN 등 제재결의에 주재국이 동조해야할의무는 지지 않겠다는 뜻을 밝힌것으로 평가됨. 끝

  (대사 이원호-국장)

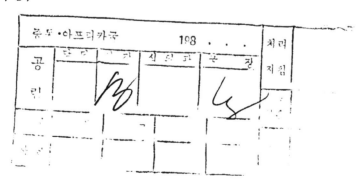

중아국   1차보   2차보   구주국   정문국   안기부

PAGE 1   90.08.09   04:51 DA

외신 1과 통제관 0069

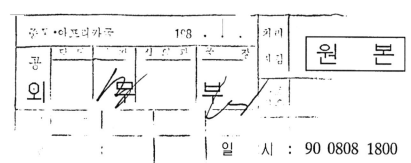

종 별 :

번 호 : SDW-0753

일 시 : 90 0808 1800

수 신 : 장관(중근동,구이,국방부)

발 신 : 주 스웨덴 대사

제 목 : 대이락제재 조치

　1.주재국 정부는 유엔 안보리 결의에 따라 8.7 아래와같이 이락및 피점령쿠웨이트에 대한 무역전면 금지및 경제제재 조치를 결정, 즉시 시행하였음

　가.수출입의 전면금지 (일부 의약품, 의료기기및 식품류는 예외 조치가능)

　나.경제관계 증진조치 전면중지

　다.지불정지및 동지역 관련 거래에 있어서의 신용 제공금지

　라.동지역 목적지의 모든 교봉운송의 스웨덴 봉과금지

　2.상기 조치 위반자에 대해 벌금이나 징역형에 처할수 있으며, 이로인해 발생한 손해에 대해서 정부가 개인이나 상사에 대해 보상할 필요가 없음

　3.참고사항

　가. 재 스웨덴 이락재산: 121 백만크라운 (21백만불)

　이락의 대스웨덴 부채: 90배만크라운 (16백만불)

　나. 재스웨덴 쿠웨이트재산: 438백크라운 (78백만불)

　쿠웨이트의 대스웨덴부채: 88백크라운 (15.7백만불)

　다. 대이락 무역액: 수출 558백만크라운 (1억불), 수입 236백만크라운 (42백만불)

　라. 대쿠웨이트 무역액(89년도),: 수출 343백만크라운 (61백만불), 수입72백만크라운 (13백만불)

　마.스웨덴 상사는 이락및 쿠웨이트에 각각 9개사 진출중

　바.스웨덴은 수입원유중 약 2퍼센트를 이락으로부터 수입. 끝

　(대사 최동진-국장)

중아국 　　1차보 　　2차보 　　구주국 　　정문국 　　안기부 　　국방부

PAGE 1

90.08.09 　05:15 DA

외신 1과 통제관

0070

외 무 부

종 별 :

번 호 : ITW-0930   일 시 : 90 0808 1600

수 신 : 장관(구일,경일,경이,중근동,기협,기정,국방부)

발 신 : 주 이태리대사

제 목 : 이락, 쿠에이트사태

　　1.이락의 쿠에이트 침공에 대한 EC 및 UN 의대이락 경제 제재조치 (군수물자 금수, 무역금지 조치등)에 따라 이태리는 이락과 현재 진행중인 하기 주요사업 (군수물자 공급 및 건설공사 계약)의 불이행으로 많은 벌과금 부담등이 예상된다고함.

　　가.군수물자

　　O FINCANTIERI 사 군함 11대(프리컷함 4, 코르벳함 6, 보조함 1) 및 헬기 10대 공급 계약 3.5조 리라 (약 30억불)

　　O SELENIC-ELSAG 사 미사일(전자), OTOMELARA-FINBREDA (함포), FIAT 항공, ELMER, WHITEHEAD, SNIA 사등

　　나.공사계약

　　O GIE 사(DANRA, MOSUL DAM, BAYI, EL ANBAR, ELMUSSAIB, SHEMAL 지역 발전시설)

　　O IMPREGILO, ITALSTRADE 사의 공동수주 댐공사

　　O SNAMPROGETTI, SAIPEM 사 송유관(IPSA 지역)및 윤활유 플랜드(BASSORA 지역)

　　O SAIPEM, NUOVO PIGNONE 사 석유시추(KIRKUK 및RUNAILA 지역)

　　O TPL 사 화학, 정유시설

　　O DANIELI 사 전기, 철강시설

　　O FOCHI 사 비료 및 액체관련 플랜트

　　2.상기 공급 및 공사계약 불이행시 일부사업은 이태리 수출보험공사 (SACE) 에의거 80 프로가 보상되나 국영기업인 FINTANTIERI 사의 군함 및 헬기공급은 계약액 과다로 SACE 에 의해 10프로 정도밖에 보상되지 않고 있어 추가부담은 정부에 의존할 것이라 함.

　　(대사 김석규-국장)

구주국 국방부	1차보	2차보	중아국	경제국	경제국	경제국	정문국	안기부

PAGE 1

외신 1과 통제관 0071

걸프사태, 1990-91. 전12권 (V.3 각국의 경제제재 I, 1990.8.2-10)　347

외 무 부

종 별 :

번 호 : NRW-0504　　　　　　　　　　일 시 : 90 0808 1420

수 신 : 장관(중근동,구이,기정동문)

발 신 : 주 노르웨이대사

제 목 : 이락의 쿠웨이트 침공

　　주재국 BONDEVIK 외무장관은 8.7. 기자회견을 통해 대이락 제재조치를 지지하는 주재국의 입장을 밝혔음. 동장관은 주재국이 유엔의 모든 결의를 따를것이며,쿠웨이트 신정권은 이락에 의해 강제로 수립 되었기 때문에 이를 승인하지 않을것임을 아울러 밝혔음. 주재국 정부는 동일자로 쿠웨이트 채권이 이락의 손에 들어가지 않도록 동결하기로 결정 하였음. 끝

　　(대사 김정훈-국장)

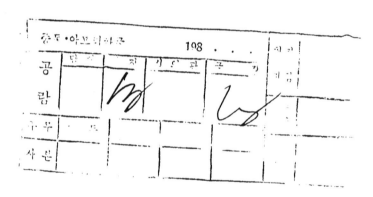

중아국	차관	1차보	2차보	구주국	정문국	안기부	장관

PAGE 1　　　　　　　　　　　　　　　　　　　90.08.08　22:13 DA

　　　　　　　　　　　　　　　　　　　　외신 1과 통재관　0072

외 무 부

종 별 :

번 호 : CNW-1180   일 시 : 90 0808 1730

수 신 : 장 관(미북,통일,국연,중근동)

발 신 : 주 카 나 다 대사

제 목 : 중동사태

조공사는 8.8. 외무부 FRASER 정보국장을 면담하고, SVOBODA 유엔 과장을 오찬에 초청 중동 사태에 관해 의견을 교환했는바, 양인의 언급 내용중 참고사항은 다음과 같음.

1. 페르샤만과 홍해에서의 BLOCKADE 가 어렵지 않으므로 이락 및 쿠웨이트산 원유 금수조치는 그 시행이 용이할 것으로 보이며 이락과 쿠웨이트에 대한 무역 봉제도 주변국(터키, 이란, 시리아등)에서 육로 이용등 방법으로 이락을 특별히 도와줄것같지 않으므로 큰 문제가 되지 않을 것으로 봄. 다만, 윤단에서 자국항구와 육로를 이락이 이용하도록 도와줄 가능성은 없지 않으나 미국, 카나다,EC 제국, 일본, 스위스등의 적극적인 참여에 비추어 안보리의 집단 경제제재 조치는 실효를 거둘수 있을 것으로 봄.

2. 이란과의 전쟁 종결후 얼마 않되어 다시 예비군을 재소집하는데 대해 이락 국민간에 붊만이 있다는 대사관 보고가 있었고, 또 앞으로 경제 제재조치에 따른 생필품의 부족현상에 대해 국민의 붊만이 있을 것으로 예상되나 이락의 무자비하고 유능한 보안군이 이러한 대중의 붊만을 철저하게 봉제할 것이므로 훗세인 대통령에 대한 이락내 붊만세력의 규합은 어려울 것으로 보임.

단, 훗세인대통령이 눈에뷔는 실수를 할 경우 군부등 이락 지배층의 반란 가능성은 배제할수 없음.

3. 쿠웨이트에서의 단기간내에 이락이 철수할 가능성은 적으며 점령 상태가장기화 될것으로 보임. 아랍권내에는 강력한 아랍 지도자의 출현을 바라는 경향이 있고 쿠웨이트 왕족의 치부에 대해 붊만스럽게 생각하는 사람도 많으므로 아랍권의 훗세인 대통령의 평가와 지지도는 미국측의 평가와는 크게 다르다는 점을 참작할 필요가 있음.

미주국 정와대	장관 안기부	차관	1차보	2차보	중아국	국기국	통상국	정문국

PAGE 1   90.08.09   08:12 0073
                                                               외신 2과 통제관 CW

4. 이락측은 쿠웨이트에 있는 외국인을 바그다드로 이송, 그곳에서 출국하게 하는것으로 보이는바, 앞으로 이락측이 미국인, 영국인을 볼모로 잡아들 가능성은 없지 않으나 여타 외국인은 모두 출국시킬것으로 보이므로 카나다는 이 문제에 관해 크게 우려하지 않고 있음. 끝

(대사 - 국장)

예고문 : 90.12.31. 까지

PAGE 2

0074

외 무 부

관리
번호 PO-1500

종   별 :

번   호 : CNW-1183

일   시 : 90 0808 2000

수   신 : 장 관(중근동,미북,정일)

발   신 : 주 카나다 대사

제   목 : 이락의 쿠웨이트 침공(7) (자료응신 제 83 호)

연 : CNW-1175,1166

1. 멀루니 수상은 8.8. 기자회견을 갖고 이락측의 사실상 쿠웨이트 병합에 따른 금번 사태의 심각성을 지적. 카나다로서는 기 발표한 대 이락제재조치와 유엔 안보리 결의안(661 호)을 철저히 이행할 것임을 강조하면서 다만, 미군의 사우디 파견과 관련한 카나다 군대의 다국적군 참여 문제는 현재로선 관계국으로부터의 요청이 없었다고 밝히고 8.10. 브랏셀 개최 예정인 NATO 외상회의 경과를 보아 필요성 여부를 검토하겠다고 하였음.

2. 또한 멀루니 수상은 금번 대 이락 교역중단 제재조치에 따른 카나다 곡물 수출업계의 피해(89 년 대이락 수출 2 억 5800 만불중 약 95 프로가 곡물 수출)에 관하여는 카 정부가 적절한 보상 조치를 취할 것임을 밝혔으며, 아울러 금번 사태에 따른 국제 원유가 인상이 카나다에 미칠 영향에 관하여는 카나다의 원유시장이 대부분 자체 생산 공급과 여타지역으로 부터의 일부 수입으로 충분하고이락. 쿠웨이트등 중동 지역에의 의존도가 미미하기 때문에 카 국내시장에 별다른 타격이 없을 것이라고 전망하였음.

3. 한편, 카 정부는 미군의 사우디 파견등 정세 악화 전망에 따라 사우디 동부 쿠웨이트 국경 인접지역 소재 카나다 인들은 필수 인력을 제외하고는 동 지역에서 철수토록 권고조치 하였다 함. 현재 사우디엔 약 4,000 명의 카나다인이 거주하고 이중 약 1,000 여명이 사우디 동부 국경 인접 지역에 소재하고 있는 것으로 알려짐.끝

(대사 - 국장)

예고문 : 90.12.31. 까지

중아국	장관	차관	1차보	2차보	미주국	정문국	청와대	안기부

0075

PAGE 1

90.08.09   10:15

외신 2과 통제관 CW

외 무 부

종 별 : 긴 급

번 호 : USW-3648 (통일)

일 시 : 90 0808 1841

수 신 : 장관(미북,중근동,기협,기정) 사본:대통령 비서실장

발 신 : 주 미 대사

제 목 : 국무부 정례 브리핑(대 이락 경제 제재 참여 문제)

금 8.8 국무부 정례 브리핑시 대이락 경제 제재 조치에의 아국 참여 문제 관련 질문에 대해 BOUCHER 부대변인은 현재로서는 아는바 없으나, 추후 알아 보겠다는 요지로 답변하였는바, 동 질의 응답 전문은 다음과같음.

Q ARE YOU AWARE OF ANY COUNTRIES THAT HAVE INDICATED THAT THEY WILL NOT COMPLY WITH THE UNITED NATIONS RESOLUTION ON SANCTIONS ?. I'M THINKING OF TWO MAJOR OIL PURCHASERS OF IRAQI AND KUWAITI OIL, NAMELY SOUTH KOREA, WHICH IS NOT A MEMBER OF THE UN, AND INDIA.

MR. BOUCHER I HADN'T -- I DON'T HAVE ANY INFORMATION ON THAT. I'LL CHECK AND SEE IF THERE'S SOMETHING.

Q I UNDERSTAND THAT ASSISTANT SECRETARY SOLOMON WAS IN SOUTH KOREA--,,MR.BOUCHER HE IS IN SOUTH KOREA, I BELIEVE TODAY AND TOMORROW.

Q -- AND HAD DISCUSSIONS THERE, AND THE INDICATIONS ARE THAT HE DID NOT RECEIVE ANY COMMITMENT FROM THE SOUTH KOREAN GOVERNMENT TO RESPECT THOSESANCTIONS.

MR.BOUCHER WELL, I THINK WE'LL PROBABLY WANT TO SEE WHAT THE RESULTS OF HIS DISCUSSIONS ARE AND WHAT THEY SAY AND WHAT WE'RE PREPARED TO SAY ABOUT IT, BUT I WILL KEEP IT IN MIND AND LOOK INTO IT.

(대사 박동진-장관)

예고:90.12.31 까지

미주국	장관	차관	1차보	2차보	중아국	경제국	정문국	청와대
안기부								

외 무 부

종 별 : 긴 급

번 호 : USW-3649   일 시 : 90 0808 1841

수 신 : 장관(중동,미북,국연,봉일,경이,기정) 사본:주사우디대사-중계필

발 신 : 주 미 대사

제 목 : 미국의 대이락-사우디 조치(국무부 동맹국 브리핑)

연 USW-3627,3634,3638

대 WUS-2634

1. 국무부는 8.8 오전 지난 8.1-2 이르쿠츠크에서 있었던 미소 외무장관 회담 결과를 NATO, 일본, 아국, 호주등 동맹국측에 브리핑하는 기회에 미 행정부의대이락 조치의 배경과 현황을 설명하고, 동맹국들의 이해와 지지를 요청하였음(중동 문제에 대한 브리핑시에는 사우디, 쿠웨이트 대사관측도 참석하였음)

2. 금일 브리핑시 KIMMIT 정무차관과 JACK COLBY 중근동 서남아 담당 부차관보가 실시하였으며, 당관에서도 이승곤공사(김영목서기관 배석)가 참석하였는바 미측 브리핑 요지 다음임.

가. 금번 사우디 파병 조치의 취지

-금번 사우디 파병 조치는 이락의 침략 확산을 방지하는데 목적이 있으며, 동 조치는 사우디, 쿠웨이트 정부의 요청에 따른 것임.

-현재 베이커 장관등 미 행정부측의 주요 외교 노력은 유엔 안보리의 대이락 금수 결의를 효과적으로 시행하는것과 사우디 파병을 다국군화 하는데에 집중되고 있음.

나. 이락의 원유 수출 봉쇄

-현재 이락의 터키 관통 송유관은 이미 효과적으로 차단되었으며, 사우디를통한 송유도 중단되고 있음.

다. 지상군 대치 동향

-현재 쿠웨이트내의 이락군은 증강되고 있으며 , 이락으로부터 신규 부대가부입되고 있음(국방부측은 이락군의 지대지 미사일 반입, 화학무기 반입 가능성 우려)

-이락군은 현재 사우디에 대한 공격이 가능한 포진을 하고 있음.

중아국	장관	차관	1차보	2차보	미주국	국기국	경제국	통상국
정문국	정와대	안기부						

0077

PAGE 1   90.08.09   09:56
                                          외신 2과 통제관 CW

-사우디내 도착한 미군은 현재로서는 취약한 방어 태세에 있는바, 참호 구축및 병참 장비 부입등을 통해 방어 태세를 취하고 있음.

라. 다국적군 구성을 위한 미국의 노력

-미행정부는 이락의 사우디 침공을 저지하기 위한 다국적군 구성을 낙관하는바, 이미 사우디-이락 국경 인전지역에 GCC 연합군(5 개 연대)이 배치되어 있고, 이집트와 모로코도 다국적 참여 가능성을 배제하고 있지 않고 있음(미국은 이집트, 모로코가 궁극적으로 다국군에 참여할것으로 기대)

-금일 영국 정부는 사우디 정부의 요청에 따라 영국 해.공군 지원을 발표하였음.

-MUBARAK 이집트 대통령은 범 아랍군이 구성되지 않는 경우, 사우디 방어 다국군에 참여치 않을것이라고 언명하였으나, 동 대통령이 긴급 아랍 정상회의를소집한것은 범 아랍군 구성을 제안하려는것으로 미측은 이해하고 있음.

- 미국이 구상하고 있는 다국적군의 지휘 계통은 사우디 및 각 외국군의 지휘를 유엔의 우산아래 두고, 서방 동맹국군과 범 아랍군이 2 원적으로 작전 통제체제를 갖는것임.

-소련은 상금 다국군 참여에 동의하지는 않았으나, 최소한 서방측과 협의 채널은 OPEN 하고 있는 상태이며, 참여도 불가능하지 않을것으로봄.

마. 외국인 소개 문제

-현재 미국은 연호 보고(USW-3627)와 적십자를 통한 서방국 공동 소개를 추진하고 있음. 이락 및 쿠웨이트내 외국인의 현황과 동신변에 대한 이락측의 보장문제는 각 채널별로 일치하지 않는바, 미측으로서는 외국인 문제 대한 정보 교환을 환영할것임(미국은 주 이락 공관원의 감축을 추진하고 있으나 상금 이락측은 공관원의 출국을 금지)

-미측이 어제(8.6) 발표한 걸프만 지역에 대한 여행 지침은 신규 여행의 금지와 동 지역 체류자의 자발적인 철수를 권고하고 있는바, 동 지침 작성에는 사우디 원유 증산 필요성을 고려, 미국 기업의 급격한 철수를 방지해야한다는데 주안점이 주어졌음.

-한편, 소련측도 이락내 소련인 신변 문제에 지대한 관심을 보이고 있음(약8,000 정도 체제 추산)

바. 이락의 쿠웨이트 합병 가능성

-현재 이락측은 이락-쿠웨이트 연맹(UNION)을 거론하고 있는바, 동 UNION 이 구체적으로 어떠한 형태가 될지는 현재로서는 알수 없음.

-다만, 이락측은 쿠웨이트가 식민세력에 의해 이락으로부터 불법적으로 분리되었으므로 이락과 쿠웨이트는 통합되어야한다는 주장을 해온점에 유의하고 있음.

3. 관찰

-미 행정부는 현재로서는 미군 파병및 다국군 구성을 통한 이락의 사우디 침공 방지와 국제적 금수 조치를 통한 이락군의 쿠웨이트 철수라는 이원적 전략을 추진하고 있는것으로 보이며, 특히 이락과의 교역 금지를 위한 유엔 안보리 결의가 구속적(MANDATORY)이라는점을 강조, 실질적인 대이락 경제 봉쇄가 가능토록 하는데 주력해 나갈것으로 보임(다만 인도적 차원에서의 식량 교역 문제는 터키등 관련국의 입장과 유엔 결의 내용을 고려, 다소 신축적 입장을 보이고 있으나, 미국으로서는 모든 물자, 용역의 교역 일체를 금지하였음)

-미측의 다국군 구성(이집트, 모르코 동참등)에 대한 기대는 매우 낙관적이나 일부 관측통들은 요르단의 이락 동조등으로 범 아랍군 구성등은 상당히 어려울것으로 보고 있음. 현재 베이커 장관이 명 8.9 터키측과 협의를 마치고 8.10 NATO 외상들과 협의를 갖을 예정인바, 다국군 구성을 위한 동맹국들의 참여 방식은 동 일련의 협의가 종료된후 보다 분명해질것으로 예상됨.

-원유의 전략 비축분 사용 문제와 관련, 미 행정부는 상금 주요 선진국들에대해 구체적 제안을 하고 있지는 않은것으로 관찰되는바, 동 비축분의 구체적 사용 방법과 관련, 일본등 일부 국가들은 국제 에너지 기구 또는 OECD 에서의 토의를 선호할 가능성도 있음.

-현재 미 행정부 인사들은 아국의 대이락 경제제재 조치 참여 여부를 문의해오고 있는바, 이에 대한 아국 정부의 입장 지급 회시 바람.

(대사 박동진-장관)

예고:90.12.31 일반

韓國、이라크제재 同參

政府는 9일 이라크의 쿠웨이트 침공과 관련하여 유엔안보리 결의안에 따라 이라크에 대한 경제제재조치를 취하기로 결정했다.

이에따라 정부는 이날 오후 정부측무회의가 끝난뒤 노태우대통령주재로 전관계장관회의를 열어 경제협력한 이라크에 대한 구체적인 제재조치를 위한 유엔안보리 결의안 66호를 지지한다고 밝히고 『우리는 유엔외 회원국은 아니지만 이 결의안에 ...

외 무 부

종 별 : 지 급

번 호 : JAW-4934   일 시 : 90 0809 1513

수 신 : 장관(기협,경일,봉일,중근동,동자부)

발 신 : 주 일 대사(경제)

제 목 : 이라크.쿠웨이트 사태

대 : WJA-3334

연 : JAW-4887

대호관련 일본 봉산성 국제자원과 관계관등 접촉 및 전문가의 언론인터뷰 내용을 중심으로 아래 종합 보고함.

1. 금번 사태에 대한 전망

0 봉산성 관계자는 금번 사태의 장기화 및 확산여부에 대해서는 이라크, 미국, 사우디의 태도가 주요 변수가 될것이라는 것 이외에 자신있는 전망을 할수 없어, 석유수급대책에 고심하고 있는바, 현재로서는 장기화될것을 상정, 정세변화에 따른 단계적 수급대책을 검토하고 있다고함.

0 한편 중동 경제연구소 관계자는 미국의 사우디 파병 및 사우디의 동 파병수용 결정 관련 이러한 상황전개가 분쟁을 확대시켜 해결이 장기화될 것으로 관측하고 있는바, 이는 교섭에 의한 해결을 시도할 경우 이라크의 교섭 대상국이될수 있었던 사우디를 대이라크 포위망에 참여시킴으로써 교섭을 어렵게 하고 이라크를 힘으로 굴복시키는 길밖에 남지 않게 될 것이기 때문이라고 설명하고 있음.

0 경제 기획청은 대이라크 경제조치가 일본의 경기 및 물가에 미치는 영향을 분석하기 위해, 동청내 관계부서간 연락회의를 설치키로 하였는바, 이는 미국의 사우디 파병으로 분쟁이 장기화될 가능성이 커졌다는 인식에 따른것으로 관측됨.

2. 국제 석유수급 및 유가 전망

가. 국제수급전망(봉산성 관계자 발언요지)

0 이라크는 세계 석유소비량의 3.5%, 쿠웨이트는 2.2%를 생산하고 있어서 양국의 생산이 세계 석유수급에 미치는 영향을 무시할수 없는바, 금번 사태가 장기화되면 국제적 석유수급 핍박으로 인한 큰 영향이 있을것임.

| 경제국 | 장관 | 차관 | 1차보 | 2차보 | 중아국 | 경제국 | 통상국 | 청와대 |
| 안기부 | 동자부 | | | | | | | |

0081

PAGE 1

O 다만 OECD 가맹국의 비축량이 현재 4 억 6,800 만톤으로서 81 년 이래 최고수준에 달하고 있고, 여타 산유국에 생산능력이 있으며, 현재는 석유 비수요기임을 감안할때, 단기적으로는 국제수급에의 영향이 적을것으로 봄.

O 사우디로 사태가 확산되어 사우디로부터의 공급이 단절될 경우에는, 국제석유수급에 미칠 영향은 심대할 것인바, IEA(국제에너지기관) 주관하에 석유 비축량 방출 등 국제수급 대책이 검토.협의될 것으로 봄.

- 현재 IEA 가입국의 석유 비축의무는 90 일분임.

O 국제 석유수급 전망을 위해서는 산유국의 생산동향 및 소비국의 수요동향을 지켜볼 필요가 있는바, 8.9. 개최될 IEA 긴급회의에서 정세판단, 대처 및 각국간 대책조정등이 협의될 것임.

- 석유수급핍밥 정도는 수요의 억제 및 산유국의 공급증가에 달려 있는바, 현재 OPEC 국의 증산 움직임은 보이지 않고 있는 실정임.

　나. 국제 유가 전망

O 봉산성 관계자는 쿠웨이트 및 이라크산 석유 수입금지가 석유가를 앙등시킬 우려가 있으나, 상승폭에 대해서는 예측하기 힘들며, 유가상승이 단기적으로 진정되지 않으면 IEA 에서 대책을 강구하게 될 것으로 본다고 말함.

O 석유 및 종합상사등 업계에서는 국제 석유가는 IEA 각국 협조에 의한 비축 방출 및 사우디등의 증산에 의해 영향을 받을 것인바, 가령 사우디가 증산을 결정할 경우 8.8. 현재 두바이산 원유의 현물가격 24.15($/1B)보다 2-3 달러 하락할 것이라는 견해가 강하며, 사태가 사우디로 확산될 경우는 배럴당 30 달러까지 앙등할 것이라는 견해도 있음.

- 석유업계는 증산 여력이 있는 산유국은 14 개국 정도로 증산에 기대를 걸수있는 산유국은 사우디(일일 증산여력 200 만 배럴) 베네주엘라(동 100 만배럴), UAW(동 80 만 배럴)등 3 개국이라고 보고있음.

- 한편 최근 사우디의 증산 결정 보도에 대해 사실여부 확인은 석유회사 및 상사의 공급희망량 제시에 대해 사우디측이 공급량을 봉보해 올 8 월 중순경이 될 것으로 보고있음.

O 한편 석유전문가들은 연호 1 항과 같이 중장기적 관점에서는 배럴당 25 달러가 석유가의 한계라고 보고 있음.

　3. 일정부 대책

PAGE 2

0082

0 봉산성 관계관에 의하면 일 정부는 금번 사태가 사우디로 확산될 것에 대비하는 대책은 아직 검토하고 있지 않다고 함.

0 현재로서는 석유공급선 대체, 석유소비량 감축, 석유비축방출을 기본으로하여 연호 3 항과 같은 대책을 검토하고 있으며, 대 이라크 경제조치의 효과 및 중동사태 추이에 따라 단계적으로 실시할 예정인바, 우선은 수요면에서의 억제에 중점을 두고 실시할 것이라함.

0 한편 금번 사태에 의한 영향은 일 정부뿐만 아니라 모든 소비국이 함께 받는 것이므로, 일본만이 두드러진 대 산유국 공급증가 교섭을 비난의 대상이 될 우려도 있으므로 IEA, OECD 등과의 협조를 긴밀히 하고자 한다고 말함. 끝

(공사 이한춘-국장)

예고:90.12.31.일반

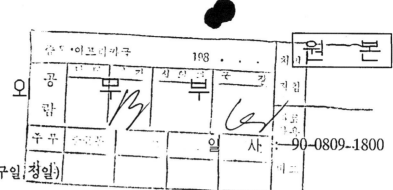

종 별 : 지 급
번 호 : HOW-0338
수 신 : 장관(중근동,구일청일)
발 신 : 주 화란 대사
제 목 : 대 이락 제재 (자료응신 제 71호)

연: WHO-0333

1. 주재국 정부는 8.8 성명을 통해 걸프지역에대한 이락의 예상되는 침략을 억제하기 위해 미국 정부로부터 군사적 지원 요청이 있었음을 확인하는 한편, 이락에 대해 자행된 침략이 용납될 수 없음을 명백히 하기 위해 국제적 역량이 결집되어야 할것이라고 발표함.

2. 주재국 정부는 걸프만 사태가 서구제국의 중대한 이해에 치명적인 위협이 되고 있는 만큼 미국과 공동책임을 부담해야 한다는 인식을 갖고 미측의 요청에 대해 적극적인 입장을 취할 것으로 예상되나, 최종입장은 EC 및 NATO 외상회의 결과를 보아가며 결정할 것으로 보여짐.

3. 주재국 의회나 언론도 군사적 지원 (해상봉쇄를 위한 해군 함정 파견 예상) 에 공정적인 반응을 보여주고 있는바, 의회 다수는 주재국의 군사적 지원은 UN 또는 NATO 의기치하에 참가하게 되기를 희망하고 있음.

4. 한편, 주재국 정부는 사우디 동부 쿠웨이트 접경지역 체류 주재국 국민의 철수 계획에 착수한 것으로 알려짐.

(대사 최상섭-국장)

중아국   1차보   구주국   정문국   안기부

외 무 부   통일

종 별 :

번 호 : CNW-1188   일 시 : 90 0809 1800

수 신 : 장관(중근동,미북,정일)

발 신 : 주 카나다 대사

제 목 : 이락의 쿠웨이트 침공(8)(자료응신 제 84 호)

연 : CNW-1183

1. 표제 관련 클라크 외무장관은 8.8. 유엔 안보리 결의 661 호의 이행을 카 정부가 제정한 시행규칙을 발표한바, 동 시행규칙은 주재국의 유엔법(UNITED NATIONS ACT)에 의거, 대이락 및 쿠웨이트 수입의 전면 금지(8.6. 자), 대이락 및 쿠웨이트 수출의 전면금지(8.7. 자), 대이락 및 쿠웨이트 수출금융지원 중단, 대이락 또는 쿠웨이트 자금 이전 불허 및 이락 또는 쿠웨이트 정부 및 그 산하기관 자산의 동결등의 조치를 발효시키고 있음.

2. 상기관련 발표문및 시행규칙 전문 별첨 송부함.

첨부 : CNW(F) -0081 끝

(대사 -차관)

예고:90.12.31까지

| 중아국 | 장관 | 차관 | 1차보 | 2차보 | 미주국 | 정문국 | 정와대 | 안기부 |

통상국

90.08.10   07:55   0085
외신 2과   통제관 CW

News Release   Communiqué

Secretary of
State for
External Affairs

Secrétaire
d'État aux
Affaires
extérieures

CNW(弁)-0081
(첨부물)

NO. 170

900809 1150

August 8, 1990

CNW-1188의 첨부

MR. CLARK ANNOUNCES REGULATIONS
ON SANCTIONS AGAINST IRAQ

The Secretary of State for External Affairs, the Right Honourable Joe Clark, today announced that the Government has put regulations in place to give effect to the United Nations sanctions against Iraq.

"The seriousness of the situation required that we act immediately to ensure that Canada demonstrate its commitment to collective international action to bring an end to the Iraqi occupation of Kuwait," stated Mr. Clark. "It is important that other countries also act expeditiously to enforce the United Nations sanctions."

The following measures have been put into force under the authority of the United Nations Act:

Imports:

- all Iraqi and Kuwaiti imports to Canada are prohibited as of August 6 (the date of the United Nations Resolution). Goods in transit prior to that date will be permitted entry.

Exports:

- all exports from Canada to Iraq and Kuwait are prohibited, effective August 7.

Credits:

- all unused export credits will cease and the Government will not issue further export credits for Iraq and Kuwait.

...../2

1/8

0086

P.2/9

Funds and Assets:

- effective immediately, no funds can be transferred to Iraq or Kuwait and any assets or securities of the Iraqi and Kuwaiti governments or their agencies are frozen.

- 30 -

For more information, media representatives may contact:

Media Relations Office
External Affairs and International Trade Canada
(613) 995-1874

2/6

0087

CANADA

PRIVY COUNCIL • CONSEIL PRIVÉ

P.C. 1990-1676
7 August, 1990

HIS EXCELLENCY THE GOVERNOR GENERAL IN COUNCIL, on the recommendation of the Secretary of State for External Affairs, pursuant to section 2 of the United Nations Act, is pleased hereby to make the annexed Regulations giving effect to a resolution of the Security Council of the United Nations concerning Iraq.

CERTIFIED TO BE A TRUE COPY - COPIE CERTIFIÉE CONFORME

3/6

0088

CLERK OF THE PRIVY COUNCIL - LE GREFFIER DU CONSEIL PRIVÉ
AUG 08 '90 19:44 EXT AFF ISEC 613 992 6346

90-725-01
(SOR/DORS)

REGULATIONS GIVING EFFECT
TO A RESOLUTION OF THE
SECURITY COUNCIL OF THE UNITED NATIONS
CONCERNING IRAQ

Short Title

1. These Regulations may be cited as the United Nations Iraq Regulations.

Interpretation

2. In these Regulations,

"Canadian" means a person who is a citizen within the meaning of the Citizenship Act or a body corporate incorporated by or under the laws of Canada or a province; (Canadien)

"Canadian ship" has the same meaning as in the Canada Shipping Act; (navire canadien)

"credit" includes loans, overdrafts, letters of credit, guarantees, bankers' acceptances, credit insurance, and performance or payment bonds; (crédit)

"goods" includes commodities, articles or products of any kind but does not include medical supplies or food intended solely for humanitarian purposes; (biens)

"property" means any real or personal property; (propriété)

"security" means any share of a body corporate or any bond, debenture, note or other evidence of indebtedness. (titre)

Her Majesty

3. These Regulations are binding on Her Majesty in right of Canada or a province.

Prohibitions

4. (1) No person in Canada shall knowingly import into Canada any goods originating in Iraq or Kuwait that are exported therefrom after August 6, 1990.

4/6

0089

(2) No person in Canada and no Canadian outside Canada shall knowingly sell, supply, tranship or otherwise deal in, or attempt to sell, supply, tranship or otherwise deal in, any goods originating in Iraq or Kuwait that are exported therefrom after August 6, 1990.

(3) No person in Canada and no Canadian outside Canada shall knowingly do anything that causes, assists or promotes, or is intended to cause, assist or promote, any act or thing prohibited by subsections (1) and (2).

5. (1) No person in Canada shall knowingly export any goods to any person in Iraq or Kuwait.

(2) No person in Canada and no Canadian outside Canada shall knowingly sell or supply or attempt to sell or supply any goods that are outside Iraq or Kuwait to any person in Iraq or Kuwait.

(3) No person in Canada and no Canadian outside Canada shall knowingly do anything that causes, assists or promotes, or is intended to cause, assist or promote, any act or thing prohibited by subsections (1) and (2).

6. (1) No person in Canada and no Canadian outside Canada shall knowingly send, pay, transfer or remit, directly or indirectly, any money, cheques, bank deposits or other financial resources, or cause any money, cheques, bank deposits or other financial resources to be sent, paid, transferred or remitted, directly or indirectly, to any person in Iraq or Kuwait or to any other person on the direction or order of any person in Iraq or Kuwait.

(2) No person in Canada and no Canadian outside Canada shall knowingly send, transfer, remit or assign any money, cheques, bank deposits or other financial resources held by, on behalf of or on account of the Government of Iraq or Kuwait or any agencies of or bodies controlled by Iraq or Kuwait.

(3) No person in Canada and no Canadian outside Canada shall knowingly make available to or permit the use by the Government of Iraq or any commercial, industrial or public utility undertaking in Iraq or Kuwait of any funds, monetary resources, credit, extension of credit or deposit facilities.

(4) No person shall knowingly transfer, sell, assign, dispose of, export, endorse or guarantee the signature on any security held by, on behalf of or in the name of the Government of Iraq or Kuwait or any agencies of or bodies controlled by Iraq or Kuwait.

(5) No person shall knowingly transfer, pay for, export, dispose of or otherwise deal with any property or any interest in property held by the Government of Iraq or Kuwait or any agencies of or bodies controlled by Iraq or Kuwait.

7. No owner or master of a Canadian ship shall knowingly carry, or cause or permit to be carried, any goods

(a) originating in Iraq or Kuwait and exported therefrom after August 6, 1990; or

(b) destined for Iraq or Kuwait.

Offences

8. (1) Every person who contravenes any provision of these Regulations is guilty of an offence and liable

(a) on summary conviction, to a fine not exceeding two hundred dollars or to imprisonment for a term not exceeding three months, or to both; or

(b) on conviction on indictment, to a fine not exceeding five thousand dollars or to imprisonment for a term not exceeding five years, or to both.

(2) Where an offence has been committed under these Regulations by a corporation, every officer, director or agent of the corporation who directed, authorized, assented to, acquiesced in or participated in the commission of the offence is a party to and guilty of the offence and is liable on conviction to the punishment provided for the offence, whether or not the corporation has been prosecuted or convicted.

9. Notwithstanding sections 4 to 7, no person commits an offence under these Regulations by doing any act or thing prohibited by these Regulations if, before that person does that act or thing, the Secretary of State for External Affairs certifies in writing that, in the opinion of the Secretary of State for External Affairs,

(a) United Nations Security Council Resolution 661 (1990) of August 6, 1990 does not intend that such acts or things be prohibited; or

(b) such acts or things are for the purpose of assisting the legitimate Government of Kuwait.

6/8

0091

1600

P.7/9

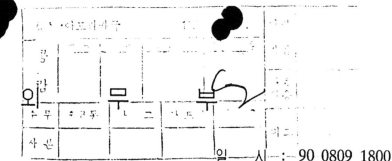

관리
번호 PO/84P

종 별 :

번 호 : UNW-1490

수 신 : 장관(국연,구이,중근동,기정)

발 신 : 주 유엔 대사

제 목 : 주유엔 스위스 대표부 관계자 접촉

일 시 : 90 0809 1800

금 8.9 훈서기관이 주 유엔 스위스 대표부 SCHAETTI 1 등서기관과 오찬시, 동인의 언급내용중 특기사항을 아래 보고함.

1. 리헤텐 스타인의 유엔가입 신청 동향

가. 최근 리헤텐스타인의 외교담당 대사가 도착, 유엔각 지역그룹과 협의를가진바 있으며, 금주말 또는 내주초 가입신청서를 제출할 예정으로 알고있음.

나. 스위스로서는 리히텐스타인의 가입에 전혀 이의가 없으며, 7 월초경 서구그룹회의시 그룹전체로서는 동 가입을 지지하기로 결정한바 있음.

다. (스위스와 리히텐스타인의 관계에 따른 리히텐스타인과의 관계는 양국간 조약에 근거하여, 경제적으로는 리히텐스타인이 단일 통화(스위스 프랑), 세관등 스위스에 제반 INFRASTRUCTURE 등을 사용하고 있고, 외교적으로는 대외교섭사항에 대하여는 사안별로 (CASE BY CASE BASIS) 리히텐스타인의 요청이 있을때에만 이를 대행하고있음. 즉 이러한 업무대행은 전적으로 리히텐스타인의 의사에따라 이루어지는 것이며 스위스로서는 리히텐스타인을 스위스와 동등한 주권국가로 취급하고있음.

라. 금번 유엔가입신청은 리히텐스타인의 이러한 주권적 권리에 입각, 동국정부가 직접 신청하는것이며, 스위스가 유엔회원국이 아니므로 대행할수도 없음.

2. 스위스의 대이락 제재 유엔결의안 참여

가. 스위스는 유엔 옵서버 국가로서 과거 남아프리카 및 로디지아에 대한 유엔의 경제제재시는 "COURANT NORMAL"(기존관계만 최소한 유지함)정책에 입각, 소극적인 참여에 그렸으나, 금번 이락의 쿠웨이트 침략의 경우 안보리 결의안 이행에 전적으로 참여키로 했음.

나. 따라서 이락 및 쿠웨이트의 스위스 은행내 예금등 자산동결 조치를 취한바 있으며, 안보리 결의안 채택 직후 주 스위스 이락 대사가 1.3 백만 스위스 프랑을

국기국   구주국   중아국   정문국   정와대   안기부

0092

인출코자 하였으나 거부당한 사례가 있음.

　다. 다만 스위스로서는 이락의 쿠웨이트 침공직후 유엔의 경제제재 결의안 채택전에 이미 독자적으로 국내적인 조치를 취한바 있으므로 스위스의 제재조치는 대내외적 측면을 모두 반영한다고 하겠음.(쿠웨이트의 경우 신정권의 합법성 문제등 실제적 이유가 은행자산 동결의 한 요인이라고함)

　라. 이러한 조치는 최근 스위스가 나미비아 독립전 의료요원 파견, UNTSO (유엔 팔레스타인 휴전감시기구)에 옵서버 참가등 유엔활동의 참여 강화 경향과 맥을 같이 하는것임.

　3. 유엔 옵서버국의 ECOSOC 및 동 관련기구 결의안 참여 문제

　가.(윤서기관이 ECOSOC 의사규칙 72 조에 따라 유엔 비회원국이 ECOSOC 결의안에 참여하는 문제에 관해 스위스의 견해를 문의한데 대해)유엔의 여타 기구와 달리 ECOSOC 및 동 산하 기구의 경우 유엔 비회원국의 경우에도 일단 초청이 될경우 투표권은 없어도 해당결의안의 공동 제안국으로에 참여할수 있음.

　나. 스위스로서는 89.7 ECOSOC 제 2 차 회기시 "OPERATIONAL ACTIVITIES" 에 관한 결의안에 공동제안국으로 참여한바 있으나, 동 결의안안 채택되지 못함.금번 90.7 ECOSOC 제 2 차 회기에서 채택된 "체르노빌 원자력 발전소 사고 지원문제 결의안"에 쏘련등과 함께 공동제안국으로 참여 하였음. 동 결의안은 스위스가 ECOSOC 공동 제안국으로 참여해서 성공한 최초의 사례임.

　다. 산하위원회로서는 인권위원회 (COMMISSION HUMAN RIGTHS) 45 차 회기 (89.1-3) 시 "종교 및 신념을 근거로한 모든 차별 철폐 선언이행" 결의안 (ECOSOC 89/44)에 공동제안국으로 참여한바 있음.

　라. 스위스로서는 향후 유엔활동에 적극 참여한다는 입장에서 ECOSOC 및 산하기구 결의안중 특히 인도적 사안의 경우 공동제안국 가담을 보다 적극화할것으로 예상함. 끝

(대사 현홍주-국장)

예고:90.12.31 일반

외 무 부

종 별 : 지급

번 호 : USW-3666

일 시 : 90 0809 1610

수 신 : 장관(봉일)

발 신 : 주 미 대사

제 목 : 대 이라크 교역 금지 조치

대 WUS-2622

대호 미국의 대 이라크 교역 금지 조치에 대해 아래 보고함.

1. 법령 제정여부

0 미 대통령은 INTERNATIONAL EMERGENCY ECONOMIC POWERS ACT(77.9.28. 50 U.S.C. 1701)에 의해 외국에서 발생한 사태로 인해 미국의 국가 안보, 외교 정책 및 경제가 심각한 위협을 받게 되고, 동 위협에 따라 국가 비상 사태를 선포했을경우, 해당 외국과의 금융및 상업적 거래를 광범위하게 규율할수 있는 권한을 갖고 있음.

0 따라서 미국의 경우 외국과의 교역 금지를 위한 별도의 법률 제정 절차는필요없으며, 대통령의 행정 명령(EXECUTIVE ORDER)공포로 가능함.

0 8.2 부쉬 미 대통령은 상기 IEEPA 법에 따라 미국내 이락 자산 동결 및 이락과의 교역 금지를 위한 EXECUTIVE ORDER 12722 및 미국내 쿠에이트 자산 동결을 위한 EXECUTIVE ORDER 12723 을 공포하였음(별첨 1,2 참조)

2. 일반 상품 교역 금지의 시행 방법 및 내용

가. 시행 시기 8.2 EXECUTIVE ORDER 공포와 동시에 발효

나. 금지 내용

0 이락산 상품 및 서비스의 미국 수입(출판물등 정보 자료 제외)

0 미국산 상품, 기술 및 서비스의 대이락 수출(출판물등 정보 자료 및 인도적 구호 목적의 기증품 제외)

0 미국인에 의한 대이락 수송관련 거래 이락인이나 이락에 등록된 선박및 항공기에 의한 대미국 수송

0 미국인의 이락 수출품(목적지 불문)구입

0 미국인의 이락내 공업, 상업 및 정부 프로젝트 관련 계약 이행

통상국	차관	1차보	2차보	미주국	중아국	정문국	청와대	안기부

0 미국인의 이락 정부 및 기관에 대한 차관및 대출 제공

0 미국인에 의한 미국인의 이락 여행관련 거래 및 이락내 미국인과의 거래(이락내 체류자의 이락 출발 및 언론 활동을 위한 여행 제외)

0 상기 금지 내용을 위반하거나 위반할 목적을 가진 미국인의 거래

0 상기 미국인에는 미국 국적인, 미국 영주권 소유자, 미국 법인 및 미국내체류자 포함.

다. 시행 방법

0 행정 명령 공포와 동시에 각 행정기관은 교역 금지를 위한 기관별 구체적 조치를 강구, 시행함(예를 들어 재무부 소속 OFFICE OF FOREIGN ASSETS CONTROL 은 즉시 연방 준비 은행과 민간 투자 회사에 미국내 이락 자산을 동결을 지시하며, 세관은 대이락 수출품 및 수입품의 봉관 보류 및 압류등의 조치를 취함)

0 금번 교역 금지 조치와 관련 미 재무부가 8.9 현재까지 취한 추가 조치는아래와같음(별첨 3,4,5 참조)

- 8.2 이전 계약이 체결되어 이미 미국으로 수송중인 원유와 관련, 동 원유가8.2 0501 시 이전에 적재되었고 10.1 1159 까지 미국에 도착되며, B/L 이 8.2 이전에 발급되었을 경우 수입은 허가되나 해당 원유 대금은 미국내의 동결 구좌(BLOCKED ACCOUNT)에 예치됨(8.3 자)

-기타 쿠웨이트 관련 기업의 미국내 영업 계속 및 쿠웨이트 관련 증권의 미국내 거래 규제등 자산 동결 관련 조치

0 미 재무부는 과거 이란, 리비아, 니카라구아, 남아공, 파나마에 대한 자산 동결 또는 교역 금지 행정 명령 공포후 2-3 주내에 동 행정명령 실시를 위한 자산 동결 또는 교역 금지의 구체적인 내용, 잠정 조치, 용어정의, 벌칙등을 포함한 시행령을 제정, 공포하였는바, 금번에도 향후 2-3 주내에 이와 유사한 시행령을 제정할 예정임(과거 시행령중 리비아 관련 시행 별첨 6 참조)

0 한편 미국은 자산 동결 또는 교역 금지 조치로 인한 민간 업체의 피해 발생에 대해서는 보상 조치를 해주지 않는다함.

첨부: 관련 자료 USW(F)-1759

(대사 박동진-국장)

예고:90.12.31 일반

PAGE 2

보안 통제	외

주 미 대 사 관

번 호 : USW(F) - 1759
수 신 : 장 관 (통일)
발 신 : 주미대사
제 목 : 첨부 (3411H) 표지제외

0096

THE WHITE HOUSE

Office of the Press Secretary

For Immediate Release   August 2, 1990

EXECUTIVE ORDER

- - - - - - -

BLOCKING IRAQI GOVERNMENT PROPERTY
AND PROHIBITING TRANSACTIONS WITH IRAQ

By the authority vested in me as President by the
Constitution and laws of the United States of America, including
the International Emergency Economic Powers Act (50 U.S.C. 1701
et seq.), the National Emergencies Act (50 U.S.C. 1601 et seq.),
and section 301 of title 3 of the United States Code.

I, George Bush, President of the United States of America,
find that the policies and actions of the Government of Iraq
constitute an unusual and extraordinary threat to the national
security and foreign policy of the United States and hereby
declare a national emergency to deal with that threat.

I hereby order:

Section 1. All property and interests in property of the
Government of Iraq, its agencies, instrumentalities and
controlled entities and the Central Bank of Iraq that are in the
United States, that hereafter come within the United States or
that are or hereafter come within the possession or control of
United States persons, including their overseas branches, are
hereby blocked.

Section 2. The following are prohibited, except to the
extent provided in regulations which may hereafter be issued
pursuant to this Order:

(a) The import into the United States of any goods or
services of Iraqi origin, other than publications and other
informational materials;

(b) The export to Iraq of any goods, technology (including
technical data or other information controlled for export
pursuant to Section 5 of the Export Administration Act (50 U.S.C.
App. 2404) or services from the United States, except
publications and other informational materials, and donations of
articles intended to relieve human suffering, such as food,
clothing, medicine and medical supplies intended strictly for
medical purposes;

1759 - 1

0097

    (c) Any transaction by a United States person relating to
transportation to or from Iraq; the provision of transportation to
or from the United States by any Iraqi person or any vessel or
aircraft of Iraqi registration; or the sale in the United States
by any person holding authority under the Federal Aviation Act of
1958, as amended (49 U.S.C. 1514), of any transportation by air
which includes any stop in Iraq;

    (d) The purchase by any United States person of goods for
export from Iraq to any country;

    (e) The performance by any United States person of any
contract in support of an industrial or other commercial or
governmental project in Iraq;

                                              (OVER)

                        - more -

                    1759 - 2

                                                        0098

(f) The grant or extension of credits or loans by any United States person to the Government of Iraq, its instrumentalities and controlled entities;

(g) Any transaction by a United States person relating to travel by any United States citizen or permanent resident alien to Iraq, or to activities by any such person within Iraq, after the date of this Order, other than transactions necessary to effect such person's departure from Iraq, or travel for journalistic activity by persons regularly employed in such capacity by a newsgathering organization; and

(h) Any transaction by any United States person which evades or avoids, or has the purpose of evading or avoiding, any of the prohibitions set forth in this Order.

For purposes of this Order, the term "United States person" means any United States citizen, permanent resident alien, juridical person organized under the laws of the United States, or any person in the United States.

Section 3. This order is effective immediately.

Section 4. The Secretary of the Treasury, in consultation with the Secretary of State, is hereby authorized to take such actions, including the promulgation of rules and regulations, as may be necessary to carry out the purposes of this Order. Such actions may include prohibiting or regulating payments or transfers of any property or any transactions involving the transfer of anything of economic value by any United States person to the Government of Iraq, its instrumentalities and controlled entities, or to any Iraqi national or entity owned or controlled, directly or indirectly, by Iraq or Iraqi nationals. The Secretary may redelegate any of these functions to other officers and agencies of the Federal government. All agencies of the United States government are directed to take all appropriate measures within their authority to carry out the provisions of this Order, including the suspension or termination of licenses or other authorizations in effect as of the date of this Order.

This Order shall be transmitted to the Congress and published in the Federal Register.

/s/ George Bush

The White House,
August 2, 1990.

# # #

1759 - 3

0099

칙부 2)

THE WHITE HOUSE

Office of the Press Secretary

For Immediate Release   August 2, 1990

EXECUTIVE ORDER

- - - - - - -

BLOCKING KUWAITI GOVERNMENT PROPERTY

By the authority vested in me as President by the Constitution and laws of the United States of America, including the International Emergency Economic Powers Act (50 U.S.C. 1701 et seq.), the National Emergencies Act (50 U.S.C. 1601 et seq.), and 3 U.S.C. 301.

I, George Bush, President of the United States, find that the situation caused by the invasion of Kuwait by Iraq constitutes an unusual and extraordinary threat to the national security, foreign policy and economy of the United States and have declared a national emergency to deal with that threat.

I hereby order <u>blocked all property and interests in property of the Government of Kuwait or any entity purporting to be the Government of Kuwait, its agencies, instrumentalities and controlled entities and the Central Bank of Kuwait</u> that are in the United States, that hereafter come within the United States or that are or hereafter come within the possession or control of United States persons, including their overseas branches.

For purposes of this Order, the term "United States person" means any United States citizen, permanent resident alien, juridical person organized under the laws of the United States or any person in the United States.

The Secretary of the Treasury is authorized to employ all powers granted to me by the International Emergency Economic Powers Act to carry out the provisions of this Order.

This Order is effective immediately and shall be transmitted to the Congress and published in the <u>Federal Register</u>.

/s/ George Bush

The White House,
August 2, 1990.

1759 -4
# # #

TREASURY NEWS

Department of the Treasury ● Washington, D.C. ● Telephone 566-2

첨부3)

FOR IMMEDIATE RELEASE   Contact: Barbara Clay, 566-2041
August 3, 1990   Cheryl Crispen, 566-5252

THE TREASURY DEPARTMENT TODAY ANNOUNCED THE FOLLOWING ACTIONS:

1. OIL CONTRACTS ENTERED INTO PRIOR TO AUGUST 2, 1990, AND
    ENROUTE TO THE UNITED STATES

Importation of Iraqi and Kuwaiti oil will be permitted where
(1) the oil was loaded prior to the effective date (5:01 a.m.
Eastern Daylight Time (EDT), August 2, 1990), was intended for
ultimate delivery to the United States, and was imported into the
United States before 11:59 p.m. EDT, October 1, 1990; (2) the
Bill of Lading was issued prior to the effective date; (3) any
balance not yet paid to Iraq or Kuwait for the shipment must be
paid into a blocked account in the United States; and (4) such
transaction is reported to the Blocked Assets Section, Office of
Foreign Assets Control.

2. TRANSACTIONS OF KUWAITI-CONTROLLED U.S. FIRMS

A general license will be issued authorizing U.S. financial
institutions to accept deposits and clear checks written on the
blocked accounts of Kuwaiti-controlled firms in the United
States, and in general to operate such firms' blocked bank
accounts, provided that no benefit to the Government of Iraq
arises from transactions in the blocked accounts. In order to
utilize the general license, Kuwaiti-controlled firms will be
required to register with the Office of Foreign Assets Control's
Blocked Assets Section. Financial institutions holding such
firms' accounts will be required to verify that registration had
occurred. This will facilitate the normal day-to-day financial
functions of Kuwaiti firms in the United States and permit
payment of employees and creditors and the purchase of goods and
services in the ordinary course of the firms' business.

1759 - 5

0101

- 2 -

3. REINVESTMENT AUTHORITY

In the management of portfolio investments and securities blocked pursuant to Executive Order 12723 representing interests of the Government of Kuwait, bank and investment companies will be authorized to manage such blocked property and to reinvest the proceeds of such property in assets subject to the jurisdiction in the United States, provided that no investment results in an otherwise prohibited transfer of financial or economic benefit to the Government of Iraq. Prior to engaging in any transaction pursuant to this general license, the U.S. person must register with the Blocked Assets Section, Office of Foreign Assets Control, and provide regular reports as directed concerning such transactions.

4. COMPLETION OF FOREIGN EXCHANGE CONTRACTS

Foreign exchange contracts entered into for the account of the Government of Kuwait prior to 5:00 a.m. EDT, August 2, 1990, may be completed, provided: (1) all exchange transactions are completed prior to August 16, 1990; (2) funds are received in the U.S. prior to payment; and (3) all payments received for the account of the Government of Kuwait go into a blocked account.

The Treasury Department expects to issue regulations shortly.

1759-6

0102

DEPARTMENT OF THE TREASURY
WASHINGTON
OFFICE OF FOREIGN ASSETS CONTROL
KUWAIT ASSETS CONTROL REGULATIONS
GENERAL LICENSE NO. 1

재무(4)

Completion of Certain Securities Transactions.

(a) Commercial banking or investment banking institutions within the United States are hereby authorized to complete, on or before August 16, 1990, irrespective of their stated completion date, transactions entered into prior to 5:00 a.m. Eastern Daylight Time, August 2, 1990, involving securities purchased, sold, lent, or borrowed for the account of the Government of Kuwait, its agencies, instrumentalities, and controlled entities, and the Central Bank of Kuwait (the "Government of Kuwait"), provided the following terms and conditions are complied with, respectively:

(1) The proceeds of such sale by, or return of funds to, the Government of Kuwait are credited to a blocked account in a commercial banking or investment banking institution within the United States in the name of the person for whose account such sale or return was made; and

(2) The securities so purchased by, or lent or returned to, the Government of Kuwait are held in a blocked account in a commercial banking or investment banking institution within the United States in the name of the person for whose account the purchase, borrowing, or loan was made.

(b) This section does not authorize the crediting of the proceeds of, or funds received with respect to, Government of Kuwait securities held in a blocked account or a sub-account,

1759—1

0103

- 2 -

or securities returned with respect to funds held in a blocked
account or sub-account, to a blocked account or sub-account
under any name or designation which differs from the name or
designation of the specific blocked account or sub-account in
which such funds or securities were held.

Issued: August 2, 1990

R. Richard Newcomb

Director

Office of Foreign Assets Control

1759 -8

0104

DEPARTMENT OF THE TREASURY
WASHINGTON

AUG 0 5 1990

Dear Mr. Patrikis:

You have asked about the status of various banks under
Executive Order No. 12723 signed by President Bush on
August 2, 1990, blocking all property in which the Government
of Kuwait has an interest. We have had only a brief time to
consider this question and, based on the information
available to us within this period and consultation with the
Government of Kuwait, we have determined that the banks
listed below in Category I should be considered blocked
entities owned by the Government of Kuwait.

Category II contains the names of banks that should not be
considered blocked entities, based on the information
available to us at this time. However, we will need further
information from these banks by August 18, concerning their
ownership and control, if they are to continue to be included
in Category II.

Category III contains the names of banks in which the
Government of Kuwait and the government of another country
subject to sanctions under the International Emergency
Economic Powers Act each have a substantial ownership
interest. We are reviewing with these institutions relevant
issues pertaining to ownership and control. We anticipate
making a final determination regarding their status by
August 18, 1990. In the meantime, we are licensing
transactions between those banks and persons subject to the
jurisdiction of the United States. The range of such
licensed transactions will be the same as the range of
permitted transaction between persons subject to the
jurisdiction of the United States and banks listed in
Category II. No such transactions may result in the transfer
of funds to the Government of Kuwait or the Government of
Iraq.

Finally, Category IV banks are those in which we have learned
the Government of Kuwait has such a significant financial
stake by virtue of loans and guarentees as to be considered
in de facto control and, thus, these banks are also blocked.
The limitation applicable to transactions by persons subject
to U.S. jurisdiction with Category I banks will also be
applicable to transactions by such persons with Category IV
banks.

17°59-9

0105

CATEGORY I

Bank of Kuwait & Middle East
Burgan Bank
Central Bank of Kuwait
Credit de Bergues
Kuwait Finance House
Savings and Credit Bank

CATEGORY II

Bahrain Middle East Bank
Banco Atlantico
Dao Heng Bank
Gulf International Bank B.S.C.
Kuwait and Bahrain Bank
Kuwait French Bank
Kuwait Real Estate Bank
National Bank of Kuwait
Swiss Kuwaiti Bank
UBAF Arab American Bank
United Bank of Kuwait

CATEGORY III

Arab African International Bank
Arab Banking Corp
Arab Hellenic Bank
Arab Turkish Bank
Banco Arabe Espanol

CATEGORY IV

Al-Ahlie Bank of Kuwait
Commercial Bank of Kuwait
Industrial Bank of Kuwait
The Gulf Bank

Sincerely,

R. Richard Newcomb
Director
Office of Foreign Assets Control

Ernest T. Patrikis
General Counsel and
  Executive Vice President
Federal Reserve Bank of New York
33 Liberty Street
New York, New York 10045

1759-10

0106

er, or furskins, classifiable under Schedule 1, Part 5, "Hide, Skins, and Leather; Furskins" (including TSUS numbers 120.11 through 120.50, 121.10 through 121.65, 123.00 through 123.50, and 124.10 through 124.80), of animals that are taken from the wild in South Africa, and that are not cultivated, ranched, or otherwise the product of animal husbandry, the following signed certificate shall be filed with the U.S. Customs Service upon making an entry of such goods from South Africa:

These _____ [hides, skins, leather, or furskins], classifiable under TSUS number(s) _____ [from Schedule 1, Part 5, "Hide, Skins, and Leather; Furskins" (including TSUS numbers 120.11 through 120.50, 121.10 through 121.65, 123.00 through 123.50, and 124.10 through 124.80)], are from _____ [type of animal] that were taken from the wild in South Africa, and that were not cultivated, ranched, or otherwise the product of animal husbandry. The requirements of Title 50 of the Code of Federal Regulations (Wildlife and Fisheries), including those relating to endangered species, have been fully complied with in removing these articles from South Africa, and all applicable import certificates required pursuant to Title 50 are presented with this entry.

[52 FR 7855, Mar. 13, 1987]

Subpart I—Miscellaneous

§ 545.901 Paperwork Reduction Act notice.

The information collection requirements in §§ 545.503, 545.504, 545.601, and 545.602 have been approved by the Office of Management and Budget (OMB) and have been assigned control number 1505-0091. The information collection requirements of § 545.807 have been approved by OMB and assigned control number 1505-0097. The information collection requirements of §§ 545.603 and 545.604 have been approved by OMB and assigned control number 1505-0098.

[52 FR 7274, Mar. 10, 1987]

PART 550—LIBYAN SANCTIONS REGULATIONS

1759-11

0107

AUTHORITY: 50 U.S.C. 1701 et seq.; E.O. 12543, 51 FR 875, Jan. 9, 1986; E.O. 12544, 51 FR 1235, Jan. 10, 1986.

SOURCE: 51 FR 1354, Jan. 10, 1986, unless otherwise noted.

Subpart A—Relation of this Part to Other Laws and Regulations

§ 550.101 Relation of this part to other laws and regulations.

(a) This part is independent of Parts 500, 505, 515, 520, 535, 540, and 545 of this chapter. Those parts do not relate

1759—12   519

to Libya. No license or authorization contained in or issued pursuant to those other parts authorizes any transaction prohibited by this part. In addition, licenses or authorizations contained in or issued pursuant to any other provision of law or regulations do not authorize any transaction prohibited by this part.

(b) No license or authorization contained in or issued pursuant to this part relieves the involved parties from complying with any other applicable laws or regulations. In particular, no license or authorization contained in or issued pursuant to this part authorizes the importation of petroleum products which would be banned by Presidential Proclamation 5141 of December 22, 1983 or Executive Order 12538 of November 15, 1985.

Subpart B—Prohibitions

§ 550.201 Prohibited imports of goods or services from Libya.

Except as authorized, no goods or services of Libyan origin, other than publications and materials imported for news publication or news broadcast dissemination, may be imported into the United States.

§ 550.202 Prohibited exports of goods, technology or services to Libya.

Except as authorized, no goods, technology (including technical data or other information) or services may be exported to Libya from the United States, except publications and donated articles intended to relieve human suffering, such as food, clothing, medicine and medical supplies intended strictly for medical purposes.

§ 550.203 Prohibited transportation-related transactions.

Except as authorized, the following are prohibited:

(a) Any transaction by a United States person relating to transportation to or from Libya;

(b) The provision of transportation to or from the United States by any Libyan person or any vessel or aircraft of Libyan registration; or

(c) The sale in the United States by any person holding authority under the Federal Aviation Act of any transportation by air which includes any stop in Libya.

§ 550.204 Prohibited purchases of goods from Libya.

Except as authorized, no U.S. person may purchase goods for export from Libya to any other country.

§ 550.205 Prohibited engagement in contracts.

Except as authorized, no U.S. person may perform any contract in support of an industrial or other commercial or governmental project in Libya.

§ 550.206 Prohibited grants or extensions of credits or loans.

Except as authorized, no U.S. person may grant or extend credits or loans to the Government of Libya.

§ 550.207 Prohibited transactions relating to travel to Libya or to activities within Libya.

Except as authorized, no U.S. person may engage in any transaction relating to travel by any U.S. citizen or permanent resident alien to Libya, or to activities by any U.S. citizen or permanent resident alien within Libya, after the effective date, other than transactions:

(a) Necessary to effect the departure of a U.S. citizen or permanent resident alien from Libya;

(b) Relating to travel to, from, or within Libya prior to February 1, 1986 to perform acts prohibited by §§ 550.201, 550.202, 550.203, 550.204, or 550.205 after that date; or

(c) Relating to journalistic activity by persons regularly employed in such capacity by a newsgathering organization.

This section prohibits the unauthorized payment by a U.S. person of his own travel or living expenses to or within Libya.

§ 550.208 Evasions.

Any transaction for the purpose of, or which has the effect of, evading or avoiding any of the prohibitions set forth in this subpart is hereby prohibited.

1759 —13

520

0109

§ 550.209 Prohibited transactions involving property in which the Government of Libya has an interest; transactions with respect to securities.

(a) Except as authorized by regulations, rulings, instructions, licenses, or otherwise, no property or interests in property of the Government of Libya that are in the United States that hereafter come within the United States or that are or hearafter come within the possession or control of U.S. persons, including their overseas branches, may be transferred, paid, exported, withdrawn or otherwise dealt in.

(b) Unless authorized by a license expressly referring to this section, the acquisition, transfer (including the transfer on the books of any issuer or agent thereof), disposition, transportation, importation, exportation, or withdrawal of, or the endorsement or guaranty of signatures on or otherwise dealing in any security (or evidence thereof) registered or inscribed in the name of the Government of Libya is prohibited irrespective of the fact that at any time (either prior to, on, or subsequent to 4:10 p.m. e.s.t., January 8, 1986) the registered or inscribed owner thereof may have, or appears to have, assigned, transferred or otherwise disposed of any such security.

[51 FR 2462, Jan. 16, 1986]

§ 550.210 Effect of transfers violating the provisions of this part.

(a) Any transfer after 4:10 p.m. e.s.t., January 8, 1986, which is in violation of any provision of this part or of any regulation, ruling, instruction, license, or other direction or authorization thereunder and involves any property in which the Government of Libya has or has had an interest since such date is null and void and shall not be the basis for the assertion or recognition of any interest in or right, remedy, power or privilege with respect to such property.

(b) No transfer before 4:10 p.m. e.s.t., January 8, 1986, shall be the basis for the assertion or recognition of any right, remedy, power, or privilege with respect to, or interest in, any property in which the Government of Libya has or has had an interest since such date,

unless the person with whom such property is held or maintained had written notice of the transfer or by any written evidence had recognized such transfer prior to such date.

(c) Unless otherwise provided, an appropriate license or other authorization issued by or pursuant to the direction or authorization of the Secretary of the Treasury before, during or after a transfer shall validate such transfer or render it enforceable to the same extent as it would be valid or enforceable but for the provisions of the International Emergency Economic Powers Act and this part and any ruling, order, regulation, direction or instruction issued hereunder.

(d) Transfers of property which otherwise would be null and void or unenforceable, by virtue of the provisions of this section, shall not be deemed to be null and void or unenforceable pursuant to such provisions, as to any person with whom such property was held or maintained (and as to such person only) in cases in which such person is able to establish each of the following:

(1) Such transfer did not represent a willfull violation of the provisions of this part by the person with whom such property was held or maintained:

(2) The person with whom such property was held or maintained did not have reasonable cause to know or suspect, in view of all the facts and circumstances known or available to such person, that such transfer required a license or authorization by or pursuant to this part and was not so licensed or authorized, or if a license or authorization did purport to cover the transfer, that such license or authorization had been obtained by misrepresentation or the withholding of material facts or was otherwise fraudulently obtained; and

(3) Promptly upon discovery that: (i) Such transfer was in violation of the provisions of this part or any regulation, ruling, instruction, license or other direction or authorization thereunder, or (ii) such transfer was not licensed or authorized by the Secretary of the Treasury, or (iii) if a license did purport to cover the transfer, such license had been obtained by misrepresentation or the withholding of mate-

rial facts or was otherwise fraudulently obtained; the person with whom such property was held or maintained filed with the Treasury Department, Washington, D.C., a report in triplicate setting forth in full the circumstances relating to such transfer. The filing of a report in accordance with the provisions of this paragraph shall not be deemed to be compliance or evidence of compliance with paragraphs (d)(1) and (2) of this section.

(e) Unless licensed or authorized pursuant to this part, any attachment, judgment, decree, lien, execution, garnishment or other judicial process is null and void with respect to any property in which on or since 4:10 p.m. e.s.t., January 8, 1986, there existed an interest of the Government of Libya.

[51 FR 2462, Jan. 16, 1986]

Subpart C—Definitions

§ 550.301 Effective date.

The "effective date" means:

(a) 12:01 a.m. Eastern Standard Time (e.s.t.), February 1, 1986, with respect to the transactions prohibited by §§ 550.201, 550.202, 550.203, 550.204, and 550.205;

(b) 8:06 p.m. Eastern Standard Time (e.s.t.), January 7, 1986, with respect to transactions prohibited by §§ 550.206 and 550.207; and

(c) 4:10 p.m. Eastern Standard Time (e.s.t.), January 8, 1986, with respect to transactions prohibited by § 550.209.

[51 FR 2463, Jan. 16, 1986]

§ 550.302 Libya; Libyan.

The term "Libya" means the country of Libya and any Libyan territory, dependency, colony, protectorate, mandate, dominion, possession, or place subject to the jurisdiction thereof. The term "Libyan" means pertaining to Libya as defined in this section.

§ 550.303 Libyan origin.

The term "goods or services of Libyan origin" includes:

(a) Goods produced, manufactured, grown, or processed within Libya;

(b) Goods which have entered into Libyan commerce;

(c) Services performed in Libya or by a Libyan national who is acting as an agent, employee, or contractor of the Government of Libya, or of a business entity located in Libya. Services of Libyan origin are not imported into the United States when such services are provided in the United States by a Libyan national who, during indefinite residency in the United States, works as, for example, a teacher, athlete, restaurant or domestic worker, or a person employed in any other regular occupation.

§ 550.304 Government of Libya.

(a) The "Government of Libya" includes:

(1) The state and the Government of Libya, as well as any political subdivision, agency, or instrumentality thereof, including the Central Bank of Libya;

(2) Any partnership, association, corporation, or other organization substantially owned or controlled by the foregoing;

(3) Any person to the extent that such person is, or has been, or to the extent that there is reasonable cause to believe that such person is, or has been, since the effective date, acting or purporting to act directly or indirectly on behalf of any of the foregoing;

(4) Any other person or organization determined by the Secretary of the Treasury to be included within paragraph (a) of this section.

(b) A person specified in paragraph (a)(2) of this section shall not be deemed to fall within the definition of Government of Libya solely by reason of being located in, organized under the laws of, or having its principal place of business in, Libya.

[51 FR 2463, Jan. 16, 1986, as amended at 53 FR 5571, Feb. 25, 1988]

§ 550.305 Libyan person.

The term "Libyan person" means any Libyan citizen, any juridical person organized under the laws of Libya, or any juridical person owned or controlled, directly or indirectly, by a Libyan citizen or the Government of Libya.

§ 550.306 Person.

The term "person" means an individual, partnership, association, corporation, or other organization.

§ 550.307 United States.

The term "United States" means the United States and all areas under the jurisdiction or authority thereof.

§ 550.308 United States person.

The term "United States person" or, as abbreviated, "U.S. person," means any United States citizen, permanent resident alien, juridical person organized under the laws of the United States, or any person in the United States.

§ 550.309 License.

Except as otherwise specified, the term "license" shall mean any license or authorization contained in or issued pursuant to this part.

§ 550.310 General license.

A general license is any license or authorization the terms of which are set forth in this part.

§ 550.311 Specific license.

A specific license is any license or authorization issued pursuant to this part but not set forth in this part.

§ 550.312 Credits or loans.

The term "credits" or "loans" means any transfer or extension of funds or credit on the basis of an obligation to repay, or any assumption or guarantee of the obligation of another to repay an extension of funds or credit. The term "credits" or "loans" includes, but is not limited to: overdrafts; currency swaps; purchases of debt securities issued by the Government of Libya after January 7, 1986; purchases of a loan made by another person; sales of financial assets subject to an agreement to repurchase; renewals or refinancings whereby funds or credits are transferred to or extended to the Government of Libya; and draw-downs on existing lines of credit.

§ 550.313 Transfer.

The term "transfer" shall mean any actual or purported act or transaction, whether or not evidenced by writing, and whether or not done or performed within the United States, the purpose, intent or effect of which is to create, surrender, release, transfer, or alter, directly or indirectly, any right, remedy, power, privilege, or interest with respect to any property and, without limitation upon the foregoing, shall include the making, execution, or delivery of any assignment, power, conveyance, check, declaration, deed, deed of trust, power of attorney, power of appointment, bill of sale, mortgage, receipt, agreement, contract, certificate, gift, sale, affidavit, or statement; the appointment of any agent, trustee, or fiduciary; the creation or transfer of any lien; the issuance, docketing, filing, or the levy of or under any judgment, decree, attachment, injunction, execution, or other judicial or administrative process or order, or the service of any garnishment; the acquisition of any interest of any nature whatsoever by reason of a judgment or decree of any foreign country; the fulfillment of any condition, or the exercise of any power of appointment, power of attorney, or other power.

[51 FR 2463, Jan. 16, 1986]

§ 550.314 Property; property interests.

The terms "property" and "property interest" or "property interests" shall include, but not by way of limitation, money, checks, drafts, bullion, bank deposits, savings accounts, debts, indebtedness, obligations, notes, debentures, stocks, bonds, coupons, any other financial securities, bankers' acceptances, mortgages, pledges, liens or other rights in the nature of security, warehouse receipts, bills of lading, trust receipts, bills of sale, any other evidences of title, ownership or indebtedness, letters of credit and any documents relating to any rights or obligations thereunder, powers of attorney, goods, wares, merchandise, chattels, stocks on hand, ships, goods on ships, real estate mortgages, deeds of trust, vendors' sales agreements, land contracts, real estate and any interest therein, leaseholds, ground rents, options, negotiable instruments, trade acceptances, royalties, book accounts,

accounts payable, judgments, patents, trademarks or copyrights, insurance policies, safe deposit boxes and their contents, annuities, pooling agreements, contracts of any nature whatsoever, and any other property, real, personal, or mixed, tangible or intangible, or interest or interests therein, present, future or contingent.

[51 FR 2463, Jan. 16, 1986]

§ 550.315　Interest.

Except as otherwise provided in this part, the term "interest" when used with respect to property shall mean an interest of any nature whatsoever, direct or indirect.

[51 FR 2464, Jan. 16, 1986]

§ 550.316　Blocked account; blocked property.

The terms "blocked account" and "blocked property" shall mean any account or property in which the Government of Libya has an interest, with respect to which payments, transfers or withdrawals or other dealings may not be made or effected except pursuant to an authorization or license authorizing such action.

[51 FR 2464, Jan. 16, 1986]

§ 550.317　Domestic bank.

(a) The term "domestic bank" shall mean any branch or office within the United States of any of the following which is not a Libyan entity: Any bank or trust company incorporated under the banking laws of the United States or of any state, territory, or district of the United States, or any private bank or banker subject to supervision and examination under the banking laws of the United States or of any state, territory or district of the United States. The Secretary of the Treasury may also authorize any other banking institution to be treated as a "domestic bank" for the purpose of this definition or for the purpose of any or all sections of this part.

(b) The term "domestic bank" includes any branch or office within the United States of a foreign bank that is not a Libyan entity.

[51 FR 2464, Jan. 16, 1986]

§ 550.318　Entity.

The term "entity" includes a corporation, partnership, association, or other organization.

[51 FR 2464, Jan. 16, 1986]

§ 550.319　Entity of the Government of Libya; Libyan entity.

The terms "entity of the Government of Libya" and "Libyan entity" include:

(a) Any corporation, partnership, association, or other entity in which the Government of Libya owns a majority or controlling interest, any entity substantially managed or funded by that government, and any entity which is otherwise controlled by that government;

(b) Any agency or instrumentality of the Government of Libya, including the Central Bank of Libya.

[51 FR 2464, Jan. 16, 1986]

§ 550.320　Banking institution.

The term "banking institution" shall include any person engaged primarily or incidentally in the business of banking, of granting or transferring credits, or of purchasing or selling foreign exchange or procuring purchasers and sellers thereof, as principal or agent, or any person holding credits for others as a direct or incidental part of its business, or any broker; and each principal, agent, home office, branch or correspondent of any person so engaged shall be regarded as a separate "banking institution."

[51 FR 2464, Jan. 16, 1986]

Subpart D—Interpretations

§ 550.401　Reference to amended sections.

Reference to any section of this part or to any regulation, ruling, order, instruction, direction or license issued pursuant to this part shall be deemed to refer to the same as currently amended unless otherwise so specified.

§ 550.402　Effect of amendment of sections of this part or of other orders, etc.

Any amendment, modification, or revocation of any section of this part or of any order, regulation, ruling, instruction, or license issued by or under the direction of the Secretary of the Treasury pursuant to section 203 of the International Emergency Economic Powers Act shall not, unless otherwise specifically provided, be deemed to affect any act done or omitted to be done, or any suit or proceeding had or commenced in any civil or criminal case prior to such amendment, modification, or revocation, and all penalties, forfeitures, and liabilities under any such order, regulation, ruling, instruction or license shall continue and may be enforced as if such amendment, modification, or revocation had not been made.

§550.403 Extensions of credits or loans to Libya.

(a) The prohibition in §550.205 applies to the unlicensed renewal of credits or loans in existence on the effective date.

(b) The prohibition in §550.205 applies to credits or loans extended in any currency.

§550.404 Import and export of goods in transit before the effective date.

(a) Section 550.201 does not apply to goods:

(1) If imported by vessel, where the vessel arrives within the limits of a port in the United States prior to the effective date with the intent to unlade such goods; or

(2) If imported other than by vessel, where the goods arrive within the Customs territory of the United States before the effective date.

(b) Section 550.202 does not apply to goods:

(1) If exported by vessel or airline, where the goods are laden on board before the effective date; or

(2) If exported other than by vessel or airplane, where the goods have left the United States before the effective date.

[51 FR 1354, Jan. 10, 1986, as amended at 51 FR 2484, Jan. 16, 1986]

§550.405 Payments in connection with certain authorized transactions.

Payments are authorized in connection with transactions authorized under Subpart E.

§550.406 Offshore transactions.

(a) The provisions contained in §§550.209 and 550.210 apply to transactions by U.S. persons in locations outside the United States with respect to property in which the U.S. person knows, or has reason to know, that the Government of Libya has or has had any interest since 4:10 p.m. EST, January 8, 1986, including:

(1) Importation into such locations of, or

(2) Dealings within such locations in, goods or services of Libyan origin.

(b) Example. A U.S. person may not, within the United States or abroad, purchase, sell, finance, insure, transport, act as a broker for the sale or transport of, or otherwise deal in, Libyan crude oil or petroleum products refined in Libya.

(c) Note. Exports or reexports of goods and technical data, or of the direct products of technical data (regardless of U.S. content), not prohibited by this part may require authorization from the U.S. Department of Commerce pursuant to the Export Administration Act of 1979, as amended, 50 U.S.C. App. 2401 et seq., and the Export Administration Regulations implementing that Act, 15 CFR Parts 368-399.

[53 FR 5572, Feb. 25, 1988]

§550.407 Transshipment through the United States prohibited.

(a) The prohibitions in §550.202 apply to the import into the United States, for transshipment or transit, of goods which are intended or destined for Libya.

(b) The prohibitions in §550.201 apply to the import into the United States, for transshipment or transit, of goods of Libyan origin which are intended or destined for third countries.

§550.408 Imports from third countries; transshipments.

(a) Imports into the United States from third countries of goods containing raw materials or components of Libyan origin are not prohibited if those raw materials or components have been incorporated into manufactured products or otherwise substantially transformed in a third country.

(b) Imports into the United States of goods of Libyan origin which have been transshipped through a third country without being incorporated into manufactured products or otherwise substantially transformed in a third country are prohibited.

§ 550.409 Exports to third countries; transshipment.

(a) Exports of goods or technology (including technical data and other information) from the United States to third countries are prohibited if the exporter knows, or has reason to know, that:

(1) The goods or technology are intended for transshipment to Libya (including passage through, or storage in, intermediate destinations) without coming to rest in a third country and without being substantially transformed or incorporated into manufactured products in a third country, or

(2) The exported goods are intended specifically for substantial transformation or incorporation in a third country into products to be used in Libya in the petroleum or petrochemical industry, or

(3) The exported technology is intended specifically for use in a third country in the manufacture of, or for incorporation into, products to be used in Libya in the petroleum or petrochemical industry.

(b) For the purposes of paragraph (a) of this section:

(1) The scope of activities encompassed by the petroleum and petrochemical industries shall include, but not be limited to, the following activities: Oil, natural gas, natural gas liquids, or other hydrocarbon exploration (including geophysical and geological assessment activity), extraction, production, refining, distillation, cracking, coking, blending, manufacturing, and transportation; petrochemical production, processing, manufacturing, and transportation;

(2) Exports subject to the prohibition in paragraph (a) of this section, include not only goods and technology for use in third-country products uniquely suited for use in the petroleum or petrochemical industry, such as oilfield services equipment, but also goods and technology for use in prod-

ucts, such as computers, office equipment, construction equipment, or building materials, which are suitable for use in other industries, but which are intended specifically for use in the petroleum or petrochemical industry; and

(3) Goods and technology are intended specifically for a third-country product to be used in Libya if the particular product is being specifically manufactured to fill a Libyan order or if the manufacturer's sales of the particular product are predominantly to Libya.

(c) Specific licenses may be issued to authorize exports to third countries otherwise prohibited by paragraph (a)(2) of this section in appropriate cases, such as those involving extreme hardship or where the resulting third-country products will have insubstantial U.S. content.

(d) Exports of goods or technology from the United States to third countries are not prohibited where the exporter has reasonable cause to believe that:

(1) Except as otherwise provided in paragraph (a) of this section, the goods will be substantially transformed or incorporated into manufactured products before export to Libya, or

(2) The goods will come to rest in a third country for purposes other than reexport to Libya, e.g., for purposes of restocking the inventory of a distributor whose sales of the particular goods are not predominantly to Libya, or

(3) The technology will come to rest in a third country for purposes other than reexport to Libya.

(e) Note: Exports or reexports of goods and technical data, or of the direct products of technical data (regardless of U.S. content), not prohibited by this part may require authorization from the U.S. Department of Commerce pursuant to the Export Administration Act of 1979, as amended, 50 U.S.C. App. 2401 et seq., and the Export Administration Regulations Implementing that Act, 15 CFR Parts 368 through 399.

[51 FR 22803, June 23, 1986; 51 FR 25635, July 15, 1986]

1759-19

§550.410 Release from bonded warehouse or foreign trade zone.

Section 550.201 does not prohibit the release from a bonded warehouse or a foreign trade zone of goods of Libyan origin imported into a bonded warehouse or a foreign trade zone prior to the effective date.

§550.411 Publications.

For purposes of this part, publications include books, newspapers, magazines, films, phonograph records, tape recordings, photographs, microfilm, microfiche, and posters, including items described in the following:

(a) 15 CFR 399.1, Control List, Group 5, CL No. 75991: microfilm that reproduces the content of certain publications, and similar materials.

(b) 15 CFR 399.1, Control List, Group 9, CL No. 79991: certain publications and related materials.

§550.412 Termination and acquisition of an interest of the Government of Libya.

(a) Whenever a transaction licensed or authorized by or pursuant to this part results in the transfer of property (including any property interest) away from the Government of Libya, such property shall no longer be deemed to be property in which the Government of Libya has or has had an interest unless there exists in the property another such interest the transfer of which has not been effected pursuant to license or other authorization.

(b) Unless otherwise specifically provided in a license or authorization issued pursuant to this part, if property (including any property interest) is transferred to the Government of Libya, such property shall be deemed to be property in which there exists an interest of the Government of Libya.

[51 FR 2464, Jan. 16, 1986]

§550.413 Payments to Libya prohibited.

The prohibition of transfers of property or interests in property to the Government of Libya in §550.209 applies to payments and transfers of any kind whatsoever, including payment of debt obligations, fees, taxes, and royalties owed to the Government of Libya, and also including payment or transfer of dividend checks, interest payments, and other periodic payments. Such payments may be made into blocked accounts as provided in §550.511.

[51 FR 2464, Jan. 16, 1986]

§550.414 Exports of Libyan-titled goods.

(a) The prohibitions contained in §550.209 shall apply to any goods in the possession or control of a U.S. person if the Government of Libya had title to such property as of 4:10 p.m. e.s.t., on January 8, 1986, or acquired title after such time.

(b) Section 550.209 does not prohibit the export to Libya of the goods described in paragraph (a) of this section if such export is either not prohibited by §550.202 or permitted by an authorization or license issued pursuant to this part.

(c) If the goods described in paragraph (a) of this section are not exported as described in paragraph (b) of this section, the property shall remain blocked and no change in title or other transaction regarding such property is permitted, except pursuant to an authorization or license issued pursuant to this part.

[51 FR 2464, Jan. 16, 1986]

§550.415 Advance payments.

The prohibitions contained in §550.209 do not apply to goods manufactured, consigned, or destined for export to Libya, if the Government of Libya did not have title to such goods on or at any time after 4:10 p.m. e.s.t., January 8, 1986. However, if such goods are not exported to Libya prior to 12:01 p.m. e.s.t., February 1, 1986, then any advance payment received in connection with such property is subject to the prohibitions contained in §550.209.

[51 FR 2464, Jan. 16, 1986]

§550.416 Imports of Libyan goods and purchases of goods from Libya.

The prohibitions contained in §550.209 shall not apply to the goods described in §§550.201 and 550.204 if the importation or purchase of such goods is either not prohibited by §§550.201 and 550.204 or permitted by

§ 550.417

an authorization or license issued pursuant to this part. However, any payments in connection with such imports or purchases are subject to the prohibitions contained in § 550.209.

[51 FR 2464, Jan. 16, 1986]

§ 550.417 Letters of credit.

(a) Q. Prior to 4:10 p.m. e.s.t., January 8, 1986, a bank that is a U.S. person has issued or confirmed a documentary letter of credit for the Government of Libya as account party in favor of a U.S. person. The bank does not hold funds for the Government of Libya out of which it could reimburse itself for payment under the letter of credit. The U.S. person presents documentary drafts for exports to Libya made after 4:10 p.m. e.s.t., January 8, 1986. May the bank pay the U.S. exporter against the drafts?

A. No. Such a payment is prohibited by §§ 550.206 and 550.209, as an extension of credit to the Government of Libya and a transfer of property in which there is an interest of the Government of Libya.

(b) Q. On the same facts as in paragraph (a), the bank holds deposits for the Government of Libya. May it pay on the letter of credit and debit the blocked funds for reimbursement?

A. No. A debit to a blocked account is prohibited by § 550.209 except as licensed.

(c) Q. On the same facts as in paragraph (a), the Government of Libya, after 4:10 p.m. e.s.t., January 8, 1986, transfers funds to the bank to collateralize the letter of credit for purposes of honoring the obligation to the U.S. exporter. Is the transfer authorized and may the bank pay against the draft?

A. Yes. In accordance with § 550.515, the transfer by the Government of Libya to the bank is licensed. The funds are not blocked and the bank is authorized to pay under the letter of credit and reimburse itself from the funds.

(d) Q. Prior to 4:10 p.m. e.s.t., January 8, 1986, a foreign bank confirms a documentary letter of credit issued by its U.S. agency or branch for a non-Libyan account party in favor of a Libyan entity. Can the U.S. agency or branch of the foreign bank transfer

funds to that foreign bank in connection with that foreign bank's payment under the letter of credit?

A. No, the payment of the U.S. agency or branch is blocked, unless the foreign bank made payment to the Libyan entity prior to 4:10 p.m. e.s.t., January 8, 1986.

[51 FR 2465, Jan. 16, 1986]

§ 550.418 Payments from blocked accounts for U.S. exporters and other obligations prohibited.

No debits may be made to a blocked account to pay obligations to U.S. persons or other persons, including payment for goods, technology or services exported prior to 12:01 a.m. e.s.t., February 1, 1986, except as authorized pursuant to this part.

[51 FR 2465, Jan. 16, 1986]

§ 550.419 Acquisition of instruments, including bankers' acceptances.

Section 550.209 prohibits the acquisition by any U.S. person of any obligation, including bankers' acceptances, in which the documents evidencing the obligation indicate, or the U.S. person has actual knowledge, that the transaction being financed covers property in which, on or after 4:10 p.m. e.s.t., January 8, 1986, the Government of Libya has an interest of any nature whatsoever.

[51 FR 2465, Jan. 16, 1986]

§ 550.420 Indirect payments to the Government of Libya.

The prohibition in § 550.209 on payments or transfers to the Government of Libya applies to indirect payments (including reimbursement of a non-U.S. person for payment, as, for example, on a guarantee) made after 4:10 p.m. e.s.t., January 8, 1986.

[51 FR 2465, Jan. 16, 1986]

§ 550.421 Setoffs prohibited.

A setoff against a blocked account, whether by a bank or other U.S. person, is a prohibited transfer under § 550.209 if effected after 4:10 p.m. e.s.t., January 8, 1986.

[51 FR 2465, Jan. 16, 1986]

528

0117

Subpart E—Licenses, Authorizations, and Statements of Licensing Policy

§ 550.501 Effect of license or authorization.

(a) No license or other authorization contained in this part, or otherwise issued by or under the direction of the Secretary of the Treasury pursuant to section 203 of the International Emergency Economic Powers Act, shall be deemed to authorize or validate any transaction effected prior to the issuance of the license, unless such license or other authorization specifically so provides.

(b) No regulation, ruling, instruction, or license authorizes a transaction prohibited under this part unless the regulation, ruling, instruction, or license is issued by the Treasury Department and specifically refers to this part. No regulation, ruling, instruction, or license referring to this part shall be deemed to authorize any transactions prohibited by any provision of Parts 500, 505, 515, 520, 535, 540, or 545 of this chapter unless the regulation, ruling, instruction or license specifically refers to such provision.

(c) Any regulation, ruling, instruction, or license authorizing a transaction otherwise prohibited under this part has the effect of removing a prohibition or prohibitions in Subpart B from the transaction, but only to the extent specifically stated by its terms. Unless the regulation, ruling, instruction, or license otherwise specifies, such an authorization does not create any right, duty, obligation, claim, or interest in, or with respect to, any property which would not otherwise exist under ordinary principles of law.

§ 550.502 Exclusion from licenses and authorizations.

The Secretary of the Treasury reserves the right to exclude any person or property from the operation of any license or to restrict the applicability thereof to any person or property. Such action shall be binding upon all persons receiving actual or constructive notice thereof.

§ 550.503 Imports pursuant to Executive Order 12538.

Petroleum products loaded aboard maritime vessels at any time prior to November 17, 1985 may be imported into the United States if such importation would be permitted pursuant to Executive Order 12538 of November 15, 1985 (50 FR 47527).

§ 550.504 Certain exports authorized.

All transactions ordinarily incident to the exportation of any item, commodity, or product from the United States to or destined for Libya are authorized if such exports are authorized under one or more of the following regulations administered by the Department of Commerce:

(a) 15 CFR 371.6, General license BAGGAGE; accompanied and unaccompanied baggage;

(b) 15 CFR 371.13, General license GUS: shipments to personnel and agencies of the U.S. Government;

(c) 15 CFR 371.18, General license GIFT: shipments of gift parcels;

(d) 15 CFR 379.3, General license GTDA: technical data available to all destinations.

§ 550.505 Certain imports for diplomatic or official personnel authorized.

All transactions ordinarily incident to the importation of any goods or services into the United States from Libya are authorized if such imports are destined for official or personal use by personnel employed by Libyan missions to international organizations located in the United States, and such imports are not for resale.

§ 550.506 Certain services relating to participation in various events authorized.

The importation of services of Libyan origin into the United States is authorized where a Libyan national enters the United States on a visa issued by the State Department for the purpose of participating in a public conference, performance, exhibition or similar event.

1759-22   529

0118

§ 550.507 Import of public ████ns authorized.

The importation into the United States is authorized of all Libyan publications as defined in § 550.411.

§ 550.508 Import of certain gifts authorized.

The importation into the United States is authorized for goods of Libyan origin sent as gifts to persons in the United States where the value of the gift is not more than $100.

§ 550.509 Import of accompanied baggage authorized.

Persons entering the United States directly or indirectly from Libya are authorized to import into the United States personal accompanied baggage normally incident to travel.

§ 550.510 Telecommunications and mail transactions authorized.

All transactions of common carriers incident to the receipt or transmission of telecommunications and mail between the United States and Libya are authorized.

§ 550.511 Payments to blocked accounts in domestic banks.

(a) Any payment or transfer of credit, including any payment or transfer by any U.S. person outside the United States, to a blocked account in a domestic bank in the name of the Government of Libya is hereby authorized, provided that such payment or transfer shall not be made from any blocked account if such payment or transfer represents, directly or indirectly, a transfer of any interest of the Government of Libya to any other country or person.

(b) This section does not authorize any transfer from a blocked account within the United States to an account held by any bank outside the United States. This section only authorizes payment into a blocked account held by a domestic bank as defined in § 550.317.

(c) This section does not authorize:

(1) Any payment or transfer to any blocked account held in a name other than that of the Government of Libya where such government is the ulti-mate beneficiary o █ uch payment or transfer; or

(2) Any foreign exchange transaction in the United States including, but not by way of limitation, any transfer of credit, or payment of an obligation, expressed in terms of the currency of any foreign country.

(d) This section does not authorize any payment or transfer of credit comprising an integral part of a transaction which cannot be effected without the subsequent issuance of a further license.

(e) This section does not authorize the crediting of the proceeds of the sale of securities held in a blocked account or a sub-account thereof, or the income derived from such securities to a blocked account or sub-account under any name or designation which differs from the name or designation of the specific blocked account or sub-account in which such securities were held.

(f) This section does not authorize any payment or transfer from a blocked account in a domestic bank to a blocked account held under any name or designation which differs from the name or designation of the specified blocked account or sub-account from which the payment or transfer is made.

(g) The authorization in paragraph (a) of this section is subject to the condition that written notification from the domestic bank receiving an authorized payment or transfer is furnished by the transferor to the Office of Foreign Assets Control confirming that the payment or transfer has been deposited in a blocked account under the regulations in this part and providing the account number, the name and address of the Libyan entity in whose name the account is held, and the name and address of the domestic bank.

(h) This section authorizes transfer of a blocked demand deposit account to a blocked interest-bearing account in the name of the same person at the instruction of the depositor at any time. If such transfer is to a blocked account in a different domestic bank, such bank must furnish notification as described in paragraph (g) of this section.

1759—23

0119

[51 FR 2465, Jan. 16, 1986]

§ 550.512 Payment of certain checks and drafts and documentary letters of credit.

(a) A bank which is a U.S. person is hereby authorized to make payments from blocked accounts within such bank of checks and drafts drawn or issued prior to 4:10 p.m. e.s.t., January 8, 1986, provided that:

(1) The amount involved in any one payment, acceptance, or debit does not exceed $5,000; or

(2) The check or draft was in process of collection by a bank which is a U.S. person on or prior to such date and does not exceed $50,000; or

(3) The check or draft is in payment for goods furnished or services rendered by a non-Libyan entity prior to 4:10 p.m. e.s.t., January 8, 1986.

(4) The authorization contained in paragraph (a) of this section, shall expire at 12:01 a.m., February 17, 1986.

(b) Payments are authorized from blocked accounts of documentary drafts drawn under irrevocable letters of credit issued or confirmed in favor of a non-Libyan entity by a bank which is a U.S. person prior to 4:10 p.m. e.s.t., January 8, 1986, provided that (1) the goods that are the subject of the payment under the letter of credit have been exported prior to 4:10 p.m. e.s.t., January 8, 1986; and (2) payment under the letter of credit is made by 12:01 a.m. e.s.t., February 17, 1986.

(c) Paragraphs (a) and (b) of this section, do not authorize any payment to a Libyan entity except payments into a blocked account in a domestic bank in accordance with § 550.511.

[51 FR 2465, Jan. 16, 1986]

§ 550.513 Completion of certain securities transactions.

(a) Banking institutions within the United States are hereby authorized to complete, on or before January 21, 1986, purchases and sales made prior to 4:10 p.m. e.s.t., January 8, 1986, of securities purchased or sold for the account of the Government of Libya provided the following terms and conditions are complied with, respectively:

(1) The proceeds of such sale are credited to a blocked account in a banking institution within the United States in the name of the person for whose account the sale was made; and

(2) The securities so purchased are held in a blocked account in a banking institution within the United States in the name of the person for whose account the purchase was made.

(b) This section does not authorize the crediting of the proceeds of the sale of securities held in a blocked account or a sub-account thereof, to a blocked account or sub-account under any name or designation which differs from the name or designation of the specific blocked account or sub-account in which such securities were held.

[51 FR 2466, Jan. 16, 1986]

§ 550.514 Transfers between accounts located in the United States for credit to Government of Libya.

Transfers are authorized by order of a foreign bank which is not a Libyan entity from its account in a domestic bank (directly or through a foreign branch or subsidiary of a domestic bank) to an account held by a domestic bank (directly or through a foreign branch or subsidiary) for a second foreign bank which is not a Libyan entity and which in turn credits an account held by it abroad for the Government of Libya. For purposes of this section, "foreign bank" includes a foreign subsidiary, but not a foreign branch, of a domestic bank.

[51 FR 2466, Jan. 16, 1986]

§ 550.515 Payment by the Government of Libya of obligations to persons within the United States.

(a) The transfer of funds after 4:10 p.m. e.s.t., January 8, 1986, by, through, or to any banking institution or other person within the United States solely for purposes of payment of obligations owed by the Government of Libya to persons within the United States is authorized, provided that there is no debit to a blocked account. Property is not blocked by virtue of being transferred or received pursuant to this section.

(b) A person receiving payment under this section may distribute all

1759-24 531

or part of that payment to anyone, provided that any such payment to the Government of Libya must be to a blocked account in a domestic bank.

[51 FR 2466, Jan. 16, 1986]

§ 550.516 Unblocking of foreign currency deposits held by U.S. persons overseas.

Deposits in currencies other than U.S. dollars held abroad by U.S. persons are unblocked, provided, however, that conversions of blocked dollar deposits into foreign currencies are not authorized.

[51 FR 2466, Jan. 16, 1986]

§ 550.560 Transactions related to travel to, and residence within, Libya by immediate family members of Libyan nationals.

(a) *General License.* Subject to compliance with the registration requirements set forth in paragraph (d) of this section, the following transactions are authorized in connection with travel to, from and within Libya and residence within Libya by U.S. citizens and permanent resident aliens who are immediate family members of Libyan nationals:

(1) All transportation-related transactions ordinarily incident to travel to, from and within Libya.

(2) All transactions ordinarily incident to residence within Libya, including payment of living expenses and the acquisition in Libya of goods for personal use or consumption there.

(3) All transactions incident to the processing and payment of checks, drafts, traveler's checks, and similar instruments negotiated in Libya by any person licensed under this section.

(4) The purchase within Libya and importation as accompanied baggage of items for noncommercial use, provided that the aggregate value of such purchases imported into the United States conforms to limitations established by the United States Customs Service.

(b) *Definition.* For purposes of this section, the term "immediate family member" means a spouse, child, parent, mother-in-law, father-in-law, son-in-law or daughter-in-law.

(c) *Specific Licenses.* Specific licenses authorizing the transactions set

forth in paragraph (b) of this section may be issued in appropriate cases to persons similarly situated to the persons described in paragraph (b) of this section where such specific licenses are necessary to preserve the integrity of established family units.

(d) *Registration.* (1) The general license set forth in this section is available only to those U.S. citizens and permanent resident aliens who register their eligibility in writing with either of the following:

Embassy of Belgium, Ali Obeydah St., Ibn El Jarah No. 1, Immeuble Chirlando, Tripoli, Libya, Telephone: 37797

or

Licensing Section, Office of Foreign Assets Control, Department of the Treasury, Washington, DC 20220, Telephone: (202) 376-0236.

Registration under this paragraph is deemed complete upon receipt at one of the above addresses of a letter, signed by or on behalf of each eligible U.S. citizen or permanent resident alien being registered, containing the following information:

(i) The name and the date and place of birth of the U.S. citizen(s) or permanent resident alien(s) registering (the "registrant"), including the name on which the registrant's most recent U.S. passport or Alien Registration Receipt Card was issued, if different;

(ii) If applicable, the place and date of the registrant's naturalization as a U.S. citizen, and the number of the registrant's naturalization certificate, or, for permanent resident aliens, the Alien Registration Number of the registrant's Alien Registration Receipt Card;

(iii) The name, relationship, and address of the Libyan national with whom the registrant resides as an immediate family member and whose relationship forms the basis for the registrants's eligibility under this general license; and

(iv) The number and issue date of the registrant's current U.S. passport, and the most recent date on which the passport was validated by the U.S. Department of State for travel to Libya; or, if the registrant does not hold a current U.S. passport, the country, issue date, and number of the regis-

1759—25

trant's current passport or other travel document, if any.

(2) The lack of validation of a registrant's U.S. passport for travel to Libya does not affect eligibility for the benefits of the general license set forth in this section for persons who otherwise qualify. Current information on travel document status as requested in paragraph (d)(1) of this section must, however, be furnished to register a registrant's eligibility for this license.

(e) *Other Requirements.* The general license set forth in this section shall not operate to relieve any person licensed hereunder from compliance with any other U.S. legal requirements applicable to the transactions authorized pursuant to paragraph (a) of this section.

[51 FR 19752, June 2, 1986]

§550.568 Certain standby letters of credit and performance bonds.

(a) Notwithstanding any other provision of law, payment into a blocked account in a domestic bank by an issuing or confirming bank under a standby letter of credit in favor of a Libyan entity is prohibited by §550.209 and not authorized, notwithstanding the provisions of §550.511, if either (1) a specific license has been issued pursuant to the provisions of paragraph (b) of this section or (2) ten business days have not expired after notice to the account party pursuant to paragraph (b) of this section.

(b) Whenever an issuing or confirming bank shall receive such demand for payment under such a standby letter of credit, it shall promptly notify the account party. The account party may then apply within five business days for a specific license authorizing the account party to establish a blocked account on its books in the name of the Libyan entity in the amount payable under the credit. In lieu of payment by the issuing or confirming bank into a blocked account and reimbursement therefor by the account party. Nothing in this section relieves any such bank or such account party from giving any notice of defense against payment or reimbursement that is required by applicable law.

(c) Where there is outstanding a demand for payment under a standby letter of credit, and the issuing or confirming bank has been enjoined from making payment, upon removal of the injunction, the account party may apply for a specific license for the same purpose and in the same manner as that set forth in paragraph (b) of this section. The issuing or confirming bank shall not make payment under the standby letter of credit unless (1) ten business days have expired since the bank has received notice of the removal of the injunction and (2) a specific license issued to the account party pursuant to the provisions of this paragraph has not been presented to the bank.

(d) If necessary to assure the availability of the funds blocked, the Secretary may at any time require the payment of the amounts due under any letter of credit described in paragraph (a) of this section into a blocked account in a domestic bank or the supplying of any form of security deemed necessary.

(e) Nothing in this section precludes the account party on any standby letter of credit or any other person from at any time contesting the legality of the demand from Libyan entity or from raising any other legal defense to payment under the standby letter of credit.

(f) This section does not affect the obligation of the various parties of the instruments covered by this section if the instruments and payments thereunder are subsequently unblocked.

(g) For the purposes of this section, (1) the term "standby letter of credit" shall mean a letter of credit securing performance of, or repayment of any advance payments or deposits under, a contract with the Government of Libya, or any similar obligation in the nature of a performance bond; and (2) the term "account party" shall mean the person for whose account the standby letter of credit is opened.

(h) The regulations do not authorize any U.S. person to reimburse a non-U.S. bank for payment to the Government of Libya under a standby letter of credit, except by payments into a blocked account in accordance with

1759-26 ---

0122

§ 550.511 or paragraph (b) or (c) of this section.

(i) A person receiving a specific license under paragraph (b) or (c) of this section shall certify to the Office of Foreign Assets Control within five business days after receipt of that license that it has established the blocked account on its books as provided for in those paragraphs. However, in appropriate cases, this time period may be extended upon application to the Office of Foreign Assets Control when the account party has filed a petition with an appropriate court seeking a judicial order barring payment by the issuing or confirming bank.

(j) The extension or renewal of a standby letter of credit is authorized.

[51 FR 2466, Jan. 16, 1986]

Subpart F—Reports

§ 550.601   Required records.

Every person engaging in any transaction subject to this part shall keep a full and accurate record of each transaction in which he engages, including any transaction effected pursuant to license or otherwise, and such records shall be available for examination for at least two years after the date of such transaction.

§ 550.602   Reports to be furnished on demand.

Every person is required to furnish under oath, in the form of reports or otherwise, at any time as may be required, complete information relative to any transaction subject to this part, regardless of whether such transaction is effected pursuant to license or otherwise. Such reports may be required to include the production of any books of account, contracts, letters, and other papers connected with any transaction in the custody or control of the persons required to make such reports. Reports with respect to transactions may be required either before or after such transactions are completed. The Secretary of the Treasury may, through any person or agency, conduct investigations, hold hearings, administer oaths, examine witnesses, receive evidence, take depositions, and require by subpoena the attendance and testimony of witnesses and the production of all books, papers, and documents relating to any matter under investigation.

[51 FR 1854, Jan. 10, 1986, as amended at 51 FR 2467, Jan. 16, 1986]

§ 550.605   Reports of U.S. persons with foreign affiliates that engage in Libyan transactions.

(a) *Requirement for reports.* Reports are required to be filed on or before August 15, 1986, in the manner prescribed in this section, with respect to all foreign affiliates that engaged in Libyan transactions at any time between July 1, 1985 and June 30, 1986.

(b) *Who must report.* A report must be filed by each U.S. person owning or controlling any foreign affiliate that engaged in Libyan transactions at any time between July 1, 1985 and June 30, 1986. A single U.S. person within a consolidated or affiliated group may be designated to report on each foreign affiliate of the U.S. members of the group. Such centralized reporting may be done by the U.S. person who owns or controls, or has been delegated authority to file on behalf of, the remaining U.S. persons in the group.

(1) *Reporting exemption.* A U.S. person is exempt from the filing requirements of this section if the Libyan transactions of all foreign affiliates of such person, and of such person's consolidated or affiliated group, for the period from July 1, 1985, through June 30, 1986, had an aggregate value not exceeding $50,000.

(2) *U.S. branches of foreign entities.* The Libyan transactions of an entity organized or located outside the United States, and which is not owned or controlled by U.S. persons, are not subject to the reporting requirements of this section merely because such foreign entity has a U.S. branch, office, or agency that constitutes a U.S. person pursuant to § 550.308.

(c) *Contents of report.* The following information shall be provided concerning each foreign affiliate that engaged in Libyan transactions during the Reporting Period (with responses numbered to correspond with the numbers used below):

1759-27   534

0123

(1) Identification of reporting U.S. person.

(i) Name;

(ii) Address (indicate both street and mailing address, if different);

(iii) Name and telephone number of individual to contact (indicate title or position, if applicable);

(iv) Relationship to foreign affiliate and percentage of direct and/or indirect ownership.

(2) Identification of foreign affiliate.

(i) Full entity name;

(ii) Address (street and mailing addresses);

(iii) Country in which organized or incorporated, and entity type (corporation, partnership, limited liability company, etc.).

(3) Information on Libyan transactions of each foreign affiliate. (Data provided in response to paragraphs (c)(3) (i), (ii), (iii), and (iv) of this section shall be separately stated for Periods I and II, as defined in paragraph (e)(3) of this section, with aggregate data in response to paragraphs (c)(3) (i), (iii), and (v) of this section further segregated between sales and purchase transactions.)

(i) Brief but complete description of the nature of goods or technology sold or purchased, or of services rendered or purchased, by the foreign affiliate in Libyan transactions during the Reporting Period, and, for each type of transaction, identification of the Libyan end-user(s) or vendor(s) of the goods, technology, or services;

(ii) Number of employees involved in Libyan transactions to the extent of at least 25% of their time during Period I or Period II, categorized by nationality and location (example: Five [nationality] employees in Libya);

(iii) Approximate amount (in U.S. dollars) of revenue from, or expense for, Libyan transactions of the foreign affiliate during the Reporting Period;

(iv) Approximate amount (in U.S. dollars) of (A) taxes, (B) rents, and (C) royalties (state each separately) paid to the Government of Libya or Libyan entities (as defined in §§ 550.304 and 550.319) during the Reporting Period;

(v) Anticipated revenue from, or expense for, Libyan transactions of the foreign affiliate (in U.S. dollars) for the period from July 1, 1986 through June 30, 1987;

(vi) Anticipated number of employees involved in Libyan transactions to the extent of at least 25% of their time for the period from July 1, 1986 through June 30, 1987.

(d) *Where to report.* Reports should be prepared in triplicate, two copies of which are to be filed with the Census Section, Unit 605, Office of Foreign Assets Control, Department of the Treasury, Washington, DC 20220. The third copy shall be retained for the reporter's business records.

(e) *Definitions.* For the purposes of this section, the following terms have the meanings indicated below:

(1) "Foreign affiliate" means an entity (other than a U.S. person as defined in § 550.308) which is organized or located outside the United States, and which is owned or controlled by a U.S. person or persons.

(2) "Libyan transactions" means (i) sales of goods or technology, or the provision of services (including brokerage and financial services), to, or for the benefit of, the Government of Libya, persons within Libya, or Libyan entities wherever located, or (ii) purchases of goods, technology, or services from the Government of Libya, persons within Libya, or Libyan entities wherever located.

(3) "Reporting Period" means the 12-month period from July 1, 1985, through June 30, 1986. The Reporting Period is divided into two six-month periods: "Period I" consists of the six-month period ended December 31, 1985; "Period II" consists of the six-month period ending June 30, 1986.

[51 FR 25634, July 15, 1986; 51 FR 26687, July 25, 1986]

§ 550.630 Reports on Form TFR-630 (TDF 90-22.32).

(a) *Requirement for reports.* Reports on Form TFR-630 (TDF 90-22.32) are hereby required to be filed on or before November 20, 1987, in the manner prescribed herein, with respect to all property held by any United States person at any time between 4:10 p.m. e.s.t., January 8, 1986, and June 30, 1987, in which property the Government of Libya or any

1059-28

Libyan entity has or has had any interest.

(b) *Who must report.* Reports on Form TFR-630 (TDF 90-22.32) must be filed by each of the following:

(1) Any U.S. person, or his successor, who at 4:10 p.m. e.s.t., January 8, 1986, or any subsequent date up to and including June 30, 1987, had in his custody, possession or control, directly or indirectly, in trust or otherwise, property in which there was, within such period, any direct or indirect interest of the Government of Libya or any Libyan entity, whether or not such property continued to be held by that person on June 30, 1987; and

(2) Any business or non-business entity in the United States in which the Government of Libya or any Libyan entity held any financial interest on January 8, 1986, or any subsequent date up to and including June 30, 1987.

(c) *Property not required to be reported.* A report on Form TFR-630 (TDF 90-22.32) is not required with respect to:

(1) Property of a private Libyan national; and

(2) Patents, copyrights, trademarks and inventions, but this exemption shall not constitute a waiver of any reporting requirement with respect to royalties due and unpaid.

(d) *Filing Form TFR-630 (TDF 90-22.32).* Reports on Form TFR-630 (TDF 90-22.32) shall be prepared in triplicate. On or before November 20, 1987, two copies shall be sent in a set to Unit 630, Office of Foreign Assets Control, Department of the Treasury, Washington, DC 20220. The third copy must be retained with the reporter's records.

(e) *Certification.* Every report on Form TFR-630 (TDF 90-22.32) shall contain the certification required in Part E of the form. Failure to complete the certification shall render the report ineffective, and the submission of such a report shall not constitute compliance with this section.

(f) *Confidentiality of reports.* Reports on Form TFR-630 (TDF 90-22.32) are regarded as privileged and confidential.

(Approved by the Office of Management and Budget under control number 1505-0102)

[52 FR 35548, Sept. 22, 1987]

§ 550.635 Reports on Form TFR-635 (TDF 90-22.33).

(a) *Requirement for reports.* Reports on Form TFR-635 (TDF 90-22.33) are hereby required to be filed on or before November 20, 1987, in the manner prescribed herein, with respect to claims for losses due to expropriation, nationalization, or other taking of property or businesses in Libya, including any special measures such as Libyan exchange controls directed against such property or businesses; claims for debt defaults, for damages for breach of contract or similar damages; and personal claims for salaries or for injury to person or property.

(b) *Who must report.* Reports on Form TFR-635 (TDF 90-22.33) must be filed by every U.S. person who had a claim outstanding against the Government of Libya or any Libyan entity which arose before June 30, 1987. No report is to be submitted by a U.S. branch of a foreign firm not owned or controlled by a U.S. person.

(c) *Filing Form TFR-635 (TDF 90-22.33).* Reports on Form TFR-635 (TDF 90-22.33) shall be prepared in triplicate. On or before November 20, 1987, two copies shall be sent in a set to Unit 635, Office of Foreign Assets Control, Department of the Treasury, Washington, DC 20220. The third copy must be retained with the reporter's record.

(d) *Certification.* Every report on Form TFR-635 (TDF 90-22.33) shall contain the certification required on Part C of the form. Failure to complete the certification shall render the report ineffective, and the submission of such a report shall not constitute compliance with this section.

(e) *Confidentiality of reports.* Reports on Form TFR-635 (TDF 90-22.33) are regarded as privileged and confidential.

(Approved by the Office of Management and Budget under control number 1505-0103)

[52 FR 35549, Sept. 22, 1987]

(1759 -29)

0125

Subpart G—Penalties

§ 550.701 Penalties.

(a) Attention is directed to section 206 of the International Emergency Economic Powers Act, 50 U.S.C. 1705, which provides in part:

A civil penalty of not to exceed $10,000 may be imposed on any person who violates any license, order, or regulation issued under this title.

Whoever willfully violates any license, order, or regulation issued under this title shall, upon conviction, be fined not more than $50,000, or, if a natural person, may be imprisoned for not more than ten years, or both; and any officer, director, or agent of any corporation who knowingly participates in such violation may be punished by a like fine, imprisonment, or both.

This section of the International Emergency Economic Powers Act is applicable to violations of any provision of this part and to violations of the provisions of any license, ruling, regulation, order, direction, or instruction issued by or pursuant to the direction or authorization of the Secretary of the Treasury pursuant to this part or otherwise under the International Emergency Economic Powers Act.

(b) Attention is also directed to 18 U.S.C. 1001, which provides:

Whoever, in any matter within the jurisdiction of any department or agency of the United States knowingly and willfully falsifies, conceals or covers up by any trick, scheme, or device a material fact, or makes any false, fictitious or fraudulent statements or representation or makes or uses any false writing or document knowing the same to contain any false, fictitious or fraudulent statement or entry, shall be fined not more than $10,000 or imprisoned not more than five years, or both.

(c) Violations of this part may also be subject to relevant provisions of the Customs laws and other applicable laws.

§ 550.702 Detention of shipments.

Import shipments into the United States of goods of Libyan origin in violation of § 550.201 and export shipments from the United States of goods destined for Libya in violation of § 550.202 shall be detained. No such import or export shall be permitted to proceed, except as specifically authorized by the Secretary of the Treasury. Such shipments shall be subject to licensing, penalties or forfeiture action under the Customs laws or other applicable provision of law, depending on the circumstances.

§ 550.703 Prepenalty notice.

(a) *When required.* If the Director of the Office of Foreign Assets Control (hereinafter "Director) has reasonable cause to believe that there has occurred a violation of any provision of this part or a violation of the provisions of any license, ruling, regulation, order, direction or instruction issued by or pursuant to the direction or authorization of the Secretary of the Treasury pursuant to this part or otherwise under the International Emergency Economic Powers Act, and the Director determines that further proceedings are warranted, he shall issue to the person concerned a notice of his intent to impose a monetary penalty. The prepenalty notice shall be issued whether or not another agency has taken any action with respect to this matter.

(b) *Contents—(1) Facts of violation.* The prepenalty notice shall:

(i) Describe the violation.

(ii) Specify the laws and regulations allegedly violated.

(iii) State the amount of the proposed monetary penalty.

(2) *Right to make presentations.* The prepenalty notice also shall inform the person of his right to make a written presentation within thirty (30) days of mailing of the notice as to why a monetary penalty should not be imposed, or, if imposed, why it should be in a lesser amount than proposed.

[53 FR 7357, Mar. 8, 1968]

§ 550.704 Presentation responding to prepenalty notice.

(a) *Time within which to respond.* The named person shall have 30 days from the date of mailing of the prepenalty notice to make a written presentation to the Director.

(b) *Form and contents of written presentation.* The written presentation need not be in any particular form, but shall contain information sufficient to indicate that it is in response to the prepenalty notice. It should contain responses to the allegations in the prepenalty notice and set forth the reasons why the person believes the penalty should not be imposed or, if imposed, why it should be in a lesser amount than proposed.

[53 FR 7357, Mar. 8, 1988]

§ 550.705 Penalty notice.

(a) *No violation.* If, after considering any presentations made in response to the prepenalty notice, the Director determines that there was no violation by the person named in the prepenalty notice, he promptly shall notify the person in writing of that determination and that no monetary penalty will be imposed.

(b) *Violation.* If, after considering any presentations made in response to the prepenalty notice, the Director determines that there was a violation by the person named in the prepenalty notice, he promptly shall issue a written notice of the imposition of the monetary penalty to that person.

[53 FR 7358, Mar. 8, 1988]

§ 550.706 Referral to United States Department of Justice.

In the event that the person named does not pay the penalty imposed pursuant to this subpart or make payment arrangements acceptable to the Director within thirty days of the mailing of the written notice of the imposition of the penalty, the matter shall be referred to the United States Department of Justice for appropriate action to recover the penalty in a civil suit in a Federal district court.

[53 FR 7358, Mar. 8, 1988]

Subpart H—Procedures

§ 550.801 Licensing.

(a) *General licenses.* General licenses have been issued authorizing under appropriate terms and conditions certain types of transactions which are subject to the prohibitions contained in Subpart B of this part. All such licenses are set forth in Subpart E of this part. It is the policy of the Office of Foreign Assets Control not to grant applications for specific licenses authorizing transactions to which the

provisions of an outstanding general license are applicable. Persons availing themselves of certain general licenses may be required to file reports and statements in accordance with the instructions specified in those licenses.

(b) *Specific licenses*—(1) *General course of procedure.* Transactions subject to the prohibitions contained in Subpart B of this part which are not authorized by general license may be effected only under specific licenses. The specific licensing activities of the Office of Foreign Assets Control are performed by its Washington office and by the Foreign Assets Control Division of the Federal Reserve Bank of New York.

(2) *Applications for specific licenses.* Applications for specific licenses to engage in any transaction prohibited under this part are to be filed in duplicate with the Federal Reserve Bank of New York, Foreign Assets Control Division, 33 Liberty Street, New York, NY 10045. Any person having an interest in a transaction or proposed transaction may file an application for a license authorizing such transaction, and there is no requirement that any other person having an interest in such transaction shall or should join in making or filing such application.

(3) *Information to be supplied.* The applicant must supply all information specified by the respective forms and instructions. Such documents as may be relevant shall be attached to each application except that documents previously filed with the Office of Foreign Assets Control may, where appropriate, be incorporated by reference. Applicants may be required to furnish such further information as is deemed necessary to a proper determination by the Office of Foreign Assets Control. Failure to furnish necessary information will not be excused because of any provision of Libyan law. If an applicant or other party in interest desires to present additional information or discuss or argue the application, he may do so at any time before or after decision. Arrangements for oral presentation should be made with the Office of Foreign Assets Control.

(4) *Effect of denial.* The denial of a license does not preclude the reopening of an application or the filing of a

further application. The applicant or any other party in interest may at any time request explanation of the reasons for a denial by correspondence or personal interview.

(5) *Reports under specific licenses.* As a condition of the issuance of any license, the licensee may be required to file reports with respect to the transaction covered by the license, in such form and at such times and places as may be prescribed in the license or otherwise.

(6) *Issuance of license.* Licenses will be issued by the Office of Foreign Assets Control acting on behalf of the Secretary of the Treasury or by the Federal Reserve Bank of New York, acting in accordance with such regulations, rulings, and instructions as the Secretary of the Treasury or the Office of Foreign Assets Control may from time to time prescribe, or licenses may be issued by the Secretary of the Treasury acting directly or through a designated person, agency, or instrumentality.

§ 550.802 Decisions.

The Office of Foreign Assets Control or the Federal Reserve Bank of New York will advise each applicant of the decision respecting filed applications. The decision of the Office of Foreign Assets Control with respect to an application shall constitute a final agency action.

§ 550.803 Amendment, modification, or revocation.

The provisions of this part and any rulings, licenses, authorizations, instructions, orders or forms issued hereunder may be amended, modified, or revoked at any time.

§ 550.804 Rulemaking.

(a) All rules and other public documents are issued by the Secretary of the Treasury upon recommendation of the Director of the Office of Foreign Assets Control. Except to the extent that there is involved any military, naval, or foreign affairs function of the United States or any matter relating to agency management or personnel or to public property, loans, grants, benefits, or contracts, and except when interpretive rules, gener-

al statements of policy, or rules of agency organization, practice, or procedure are involved, or when notice and public procedure are impracticable, unnecessary, or contrary to the public interest, interested persons will be afforded an opportunity to participate in rulemaking through the submission of written data, views, or arguments, with oral presentation at the discretion of the Director. In general, rulemaking by the Office of Foreign Assets Control involves foreign affairs functions of the United States. Wherever possible, however, it is the practice to hold informal consultations with interested groups or persons before the issuance of any rule or other public document.

(b) Any interested person may petition the Director of the Office of Foreign Assets Control in writing for the issuance, amendment or revocation of any rule.

§ 550.805 Delegation by the Secretary of the Treasury.

Any action which the Secretary of the Treasury is authorized to take pursuant to Executive Order 12543 may be taken by the Director of the Office of Foreign Assets Control, or by any other person to whom the Secretary of the Treasury has delegated authority so to act.

§ 550.806 Rules governing availability of information.

(a) The records of the Office of Foreign Assets Control which are required by 5 U.S.C. 552 to be made available to the public shall be made available in accordance with the definitions, procedures, payment of fees, and other provisions of the regulations on the disclosure of records of the Office of the Secretary and of other bureaus and offices of the Department issued under 5 U.S.C. 552 and published as Part 1 of this Title 31 of the Code of Federal Regulations.

(b) Any form issued for use in connection with this part may be obtained in person from or by writing to the Office of Foreign Assets Control, Treasury Department, Washington, DC 20220, or the Foreign Assets Control Division, Federal Reserve Bank of

New York, 33 Liberty Street, New York, NY 10045.

§ 550.807 Customs procedures: Merchandise specified in § 550.201.

(a) With respect to merchandise specified in § 550, 201, appropriate Customs officers shall not accept or allow any:

(1) Entry for consumption or warehousing (including any appraisement entry, any entry of goods imported in the mails, regardless of value, and any informal entry);

(2) Entry for immediate exportation;

(3) Entry for transportation and exportation;

(4) Entry for immediate transportation;

(5) Withdrawal from warehouse;

(6) Entry, transfer or withdrawal from a foreign trade zone; or

(7) Manipulation or manufacture in a warehouse or in a foreign trade zone, unless:

(i) The merchandise was imported prior to 12:01 a.m., Eastern Standard Time, February 1, 1986, or

(ii) A specific license pursuant to this part is presented, or

(iii) Instructions from the Office of Foreign Assets Control, either directly or through the Federal Reserve Bank of New York, authorizing the transactions are received.

(b) Whenever a specific license is presented to an appropriate Customs officer in accordance with this section, one additional legible copy of the entry, withdrawal or other appropriate document with respect to the merchandise involved shall be filed with the appropriate Customs officers at the port where the transaction is to take place. Each copy of any such entry, withdrawal or other appropriate document, including the additional copy, shall bear plainly on its face the number of the license pursuant to which it is filed. The original copy of the specific license shall be presented to the appropriate Customs officers in respect of each such transactions and shall bear a notation in ink by the licensee or person presenting the license showing the description, quantity and value of the merchandise to be entered, withdrawn or otherwise dealt with. This notation shall be so placed

and so written that there will exist no possibility of confusing it with anything placed on the license at the time of its issuance. If the license in fact authorizes the entry, withdrawal or other transactions with regard to the merchandise, the appropriate Customs officer, or other authorized Customs employee, shall verify the notation by signing or initialing it after first assuring himself that it accurately describes the merchandise it purports to represent. The license shall thereafter be returned to the person presenting it and the additional copy of the entry, withdrawal or other appropriate document shall be forwarded by the appropriate Customs officer to the Office of Foreign Assets Control.

(c) If it is unclear whether an entry, withdrawal or other action affected by this section requires a specific Foreign Assets Control license, the appropriate Customs officer shall withhold action thereon and shall advise such person to communicate directly with the Federal Reserve Bank of New York, Foreign Assets Control Division, 33 Liberty Street, New York, New York 10045 to request that instructions be sent to the Customs officer to authorize him to take action with regard thereto.

Subpart I—Miscellaneous

§ 550.901 Paperwork Reduction Act notice.

The information collection requirements in §§ 550.210(d), 550.511 (g) and (h), 550.568 (b), (c), and (l), 550.601, 550.602, and 550.801(b) (2), (3), and (5) have been approved by the Office of Management and Budget and assigned control number 1505-0092. The information collection requirements in §§ 550.560 (c) and (d) and 550.605 have been approved by the Office of Management and Budget and assigned control number 1505-0093.

[51 FR 28933, Aug. 13, 1986]

1759–33

540

0129

hereunder may be amended, modified, or revoked at any time.

§ 555.804 Rulemaking.

(a) All rules and other public documents are issued by the Secretary of the Treasury upon recommendation of the Director of the Office of Foreign Assets Control. Except to the extent that there is involved any military, naval, or foreign affairs function of the United States or any matter relating to agency management or personnel or to public property, loans, grants, benefits, or contracts, and except when interpretive rules, general statements of policy, or rules of agency organization, practice, or procedure are involved, or when notice and public procedure are impracticable, unnecessary, or contrary to the public interest, interested persons will be afforded an opportunity to participate in rulemaking through the submission of written data, views, or arguments, with oral presentation in the discretion of the Director. In general, rulemaking by the Office of Foreign Assets Control involves foreign affairs functions of the United States. Wherever possible, however, it is the practice to hold informal consultations with interested groups or persons before the issuance of any rule or other public document.

(b) Any interested person may petition the Director of the Office of Foreign Assets Control in writing for the issuance, amendment or revocation of any rule.

§ 555.805 Delegation by the Secretary of the Treasury.

Any action that the Secretary of the Treasury is authorized to take with respect to the subject matter of this part may be taken by the Director of the Office of Foreign Assets Control, or by any other person to whom the Secretary of the Treasury has delegated authority so to act.

§ 555.806 Rules governing availability of information.

(a) The records of the Office of Foreign Assets Control that are required by 5 U.S.C. 552 to be made available to the public shall be made available in accordance with the definitions, proce-dures, payment of fees, and other provisions of the regulations on the disclosure of records of the Office of the Secretary and of other bureaus and offices of the Department issued under 5 U.S.C. 552 and published as Part 1 of this Title 31 of the Code of Federal Regulations.

(b) Any form issued for use in connection with this part may be obtained in person from or by writing to the Office of Foreign Assets Control, Treasury Department, Washington, D.C. 20220, or the Foreign Assets Control Division, Federal Reserve Bank of New York, 33 Liberty Street, New York, NY 10045.

PART 560—IRANIAN TRANSACTIONS REGULATIONS

Subpart A—Relation of this Part to Other Laws and Regulations

Sec.

0130

관리 번호	90-475

외 무 부

종 별 : 지 급

번 호 : JAW-4958   일 시 : 90 0810 1451

수 신 : 장관(통일,통이,기협,경일,중근동,상공부)

발 신 : 주 일 대사(경제)

제 목 : 대 이라크 교역금지조치

대 : WJA-3351

연 : JAW-4856

대호관련, 주재국 통산성 관계관 접촉등을 통해 탐문한 결과를 아래 보고함.

1. 별도 법령 제정등 조치 여부

O 8.5 대 이라크 제재조치를 결정한 주재국 관계 각료회의시, 제재조치 결정에 가장 큰 문제점으로 근거법령이 없다는 점이 지적되었으나, 국제적 필요성을 우선하여 먼저 제재방침을 정하고 구체내용에 관해서는 법령적 뒷받침을 마련, 실시키로 했던 것으로 보임.

O 이에따라 통산성은 쿠웨이트 및 이라크로 부터의 수입금지와 관련, 90.9.9자 통산산업성 고시 310 호를 발표하였는바, 동 고시는 수입무역 관리령 (1949년) 에 입각하여 제정된 통산성고시 170 호 (1966 년) 를 일부개정한 것으로서, 수입승인 대상지역 및 대상품목으로 이라크, 쿠웨이트 원산 또는 선적의 모든 화물을 추가하는 형식을 취하고 있음.

 - 동 고시 310 호 발표와 함께 통산성은 하기 2 항의 내용을 관계기관 및 업계에 통보하였음.

O 또한 통산성 관계자에 의하면, 대쿠웨이트 및 이라크 수출제재 조치에 관해서도 수입금지 조치와 유사한 방법으로 금주 또는 내주초에 공표할 예정이라고함.

2. 구체 시행시기, 방버, 내용등(통산성의 대업계 및 관계기관 통보내용)

O 통산성 고시 310 호에 의해 이라크 및 쿠웨이트를 원산지 또는 선적지로하는 모든 화물의 수입은 90.8.9. 이후부터 승인제로 이행함.

O 이에따라 8.9 이후 상기 화물을 수입하는 경우는 통산대신의 승인을 받아야 하는바, 동 화물이 90.8.8 이전에 선적된 경우를 제외하고는 수입승인을 하지

통상국 안기부	장관 상공부	차관	2차보	중아국	경제국	경제국	통상국	청와대

않을것임.

　　0 수입승인을 하는 경우에 있어서도 수입 무역관리령 규정 (제 11 조 1 항) 에
의해 조건 부여가 가능함. 끝

　　(공사 이한춘-국장)

　　예고 : 90.12.31. 일반

외 무 부

종 별 :

번 호 : AUW-0605   일 시 : 90 0810 1730

수 신 : 장관(중근동,아동,봉일,기정,사본:국방부장관)

발 신 : 주 호주 대사

제 목 : 대 이라크 제재

연:AUW-0588,0599

대:AM-0145

1. 연호 주재국은 대이라크 해상봉쇄에 참여키 위해 군함 2 척 (GUIDED MISSILE FRIGATES) 와 원유보급선 1 척 (OIL REPLENISHMENT TANKER) 을 중동지역에 파견키로 결정함.

2. HAWKE 주재국 수상은 금 7.10 기자회견을 갖고 금번 해군함 파견은 대 이라크, 쿠웨이트 해상봉쇄, 여타 중동 산유국을 위한 원유수송로 확보, 이라크의 더이상의 침공 저지를 목적으로 취해진 결정이며, 현재 시드니에 정박중인 상기 3척은 8.13(월)출항, 중동지역으로 출동할 예정이라고 밝힘. 상기 군함 2 척에는 각각 함대공 미사일, 함대함 미사일, 전자식 반격장치, SEA HAWK 헬기등이 장착될것으로 알려짐.

3. 금번 결정은 미국의 요청에 대해 호주가 호응한것으로서, 현재 이라크, 쿠웨이트 및 주변 중동국가에 호주인이 잔류하고 있음에도 불구, 대이라크 국제제재조치에 적극 참여하겠다는 호주의 의지를 표명한것이라고 해석되고 있음.끝.

(대사 이창수-국장)

예고:90.12.31. 일반.

중아국   차관   1차보   아주국   통상국   정문국   청와대   안기부   국방부

	분류번호	보존기간

발 신 전 보

번   호 : ~~WECM0020~~ 900810 1745 AO   종별 :
WECM-20

수   신 : 주   EC 회원국   대사 ■■■사

발   신 : 장 관   (통일)

제   목 : 대이라크 제재

연 : AM-0145

1. 이라크의 쿠웨이트 침공관련, EC 12개국은 8.4 로마개최 EPC 정무총국장
   회의에서 이라크 및 쿠웨이트로부터의 석유금수, EC 회원국내 이라크 자산
   동결, GSP 수혜정지등을 내용으로 하는 대이라크제재 공동성명을 발표하였는바,
   동 공동성명을 구체화하기 위하여 주재국이 취한 시행조치 내용을 가급적
   상세히 파악 보고바람.

2. 또한 UN 안보리가 8.6 상품교역 및 재정·경제적 자원 제공까지를 금지하는
   포괄적 대이라크 제재결의안을 채택한것과 관련하여, 주재국이 동 결의안을
   반영, 추가로 취한 조치에 관해서도 보고바람.

3. 아울러 실제로 대이라크 제재조치를 시행하는 경우, 각국이 입게되는 불이익
   내지 영향관련, 아래사항 보고바람.
   가. 대이라크 및 쿠웨이트 교역량(전체대비비중 포함)
   나. 대이라크 및 쿠웨이트 투자 현황
   다. 이라크 및 쿠웨이트의 대주재국 채무 내역
   라. 이라크 및 쿠웨이트내 체류국민현황
   마. 기타 참고사항.   끝.

통상국장 김 삼 훈
(이·쿠사태 대책반장 한병현)

예고 : 90.12.31 일반

중동아프리카국장:

	보 안	
	통 제	

앙 고 재	90 년 8 월 10 일	통 상 I 과	기안자 성명 최종현		과 장		통상국장		차 관	장 관		외신과통제

0134

외 무 부

종 별 :

번 호 : CHW-1272
일 시 : 90 0810 1400

수 신 : 장관(아이,중근동,기정)

발 신 : 주 중대사

제 목 : 이락, 쿠웨이트 침공

연: CHW-1265

연호 주재국은 전일 유보적인 태도를 변경, 이락의 침략행위를 아래와같이 비난함.

가. 이등휘 총통

-중화민국은 국제정의, 평화수호 입장에서 UN안보리의 대이락 제재 결의안을 찬성하고 부시 미대통령의 성명을 지지함.

나. 학백촌 행정원장

-미국은 침략자에게 제재를 함으로써 중동및 세계평화와 안정을 유지하여 주기희망함.

다. 외교부 성명

-이락의 쿠웨이트 합병및 중동지역의 평화와 안전을 위태롭게하는 행위를 비난하며, UN 안보리의 대이락 제재 결의안을 찬성하며 지지함.

-전반적 정세를 고려후 적절한 조치 예정임. 끝

(대사 한철수-국장)

아주국   1차보   중아국   정문국   안기부

PAGE 1
90.08.10   20:18 DA

외신 1과   통제관

0135

걸프사태, 1990-91. 전12권 (V.3 각국의 경제제재Ⅰ, 1990.8.2-10) 411

외 무 부

종 별 : 지 급

번 호 : UKW-1493

일 시 : 90 0810 1400

수 신 : 장 관 (중근동,구일,미안)

발 신 : 주 영 대사

제 목 : 걸프사태

걸프사태에 관한 주재국 관련동향을 당지언론보도를 종합, 아래와 같이 보고함.

1. TOM KING 국방상은 8.9(목) 각의를 마친후 영국의 걸프지역 파병규모에 관해서 약 1,000여명의 병력을 포함하는 하기내용을 발표함.

가. 12대의 TORNADO F3 으로 구성된 1개 전부비행중대 (사이프러스에서 사우디로파견), RAPIER 지대공 미사일 분대와 VC10 급유기 및 C130 HERCULES 수송기

나. JAGUAR 전부가 12대와 NIMROD 해상정찰기및 3개 기뢰 탐지기로 구성된 1개 (YORK구축함과 JUPITER 및 BATTELAXE 호위함, ORANGELEAF 보급선으로 구성된 해상병력은 이미 현지 파견)전부비행 중대

2. 영국의 파병내역은 미국및 사우디측과의 긴밀한 협의하에 결정되었고, 신속배치가 가능한 장비로 구성되어 있음.

3. TOM KING 국방상은 현재로서는 항공모함은 파견되지 않을 것이라고 밝히고 영국의 지원이 전적으로 방어적 성격임을 강조함. 동 국방상은 또한 이락의 화학무기사용 가능성에 대해 경고하였으나 미국이나 영국이 화학무기에 대응하여 핵무기를 사용할 가능성에 관해서는 과거관례대로 언급하기를 거부함.

4. 대처수상은 8.9(목) 부쉬 대통령과 전화회담을 가지고 영국의 파병내역에 관해 통보했으며, 이태리수상과도 전화협의를 통해 협력을 요망함.

5. 이락측이 8.9(목) 국경폐쇄로 외국인의 출국을 금지함에 따라 이락내 2,000 명, 쿠웨이트내 3,000명에 달하는 영국인의 안위가 문제로 되고있으며, TOM KING 국방상은 이들이 이락측의 인질로 이용된다면 이를 용인할수 없을 것이라고 말함.

6. 나토 및 EC 외상들은 금 8.10(금) 브럿셀에서 회동하고 공동대처 방안을 협의함.끝.

(대사 오재희-국장)

중아국	1차보	미주국	구주국	정문국	안기부	홍상극	차관	장관

90.08.11   00:09 FC

외신 1과 통제관   0136

주 영 대 사 관

총 **5** 매
(5-)

번 호 : UKW(F)- **0233**   DATE: **90. 8. 10 /700**

수 신 : 장 관 (중근동,구일,미안,(통일))

제 목 : 걸프사태 (외무성대변인 정제정명)

(90. 8. 10 (금) EC   외상회담 성명 포함

배부처	장관실	차관실	一차보	二차보	기획실	기관장	아주국	미주국	구주국	중아국	국기국	경제국	통상국	정문국	영교국	총무과	감사관	정보관	외연원	청와대	총리실	안기부	기타
	/	/		/		/			/		/		/		/		/					/	

0137

(5-2)

FCO SPOKESMAN: FRIDAY 10 AUGUST 1990

DECLARATION ON THE SITUATION IN THE GULF

Spokesmen drew attention to the declaration made by the Twelve on the Gulf in Brussels on 10 August:

"The invasion of Kuwait by Iraqi forces has already provoked an unreserved condemnation by the Community and its member states, which have not only called for the immediate and unconditional withdrawal of Iraqi forces from the territory of Kuwait, but also clearly stated the unacceptability of the situation created by Iraqi military aggression against Kuwait.

Accordingly they reject the announced annexation of Kuwait which is contrary to international law and therefore null and void, as stated in UN Security Council Resolution 662. The same applies to the announced removal of Diplomatic Missions from Kuwait and to any attempt by the Iraqi authorities to exert powers of government within the territory of Kuwait.

They have noted with appreciation the wide international solidarity which developed following the aggression and led to effective action by the UN Security Council. They welcome the role played by the United Nations and they will strive to maintain and further enhance such international solidarity.

The Community and its member states immediately after the Iraqi invasion adopted a set of measures against Iraq and subsequently have swiftly introduced legislation to implement UN Security Council Resolution 661, which they consider a fundamental instrument to restore international legality.

0138

(5-3)

The Community and its member states have already expressed their
grave concern for the situation of foreigners in Iraq and Kuwait. No
effort or initiative will be spared to ensure that EC citizens be
allowed full and unconditional freedom of movement within and out of
those countries. Precise requests to this end have already been
addressed to the Iraqi authorities, whom they hold fully accountable
for the safety of their citizens. The Presidency will continue to
ensure the appropriate coordination aimed at guaranteeing the safety
of EC citizens in Iraq and Kuwait.

The Community and its member states, having also in mind the vital
European interests in the stability, territorial integrity and
sovereignty of the states of the area, are ready to take further
intitiatives in the framework of United Nations Charter that will
prove necessary to contain the conflict. They note that certain
member states have already taken useful steps also to this end. They
are strongly determined to engage in broad efforts to afford the
necessary international solidarity with other states in the area
threatened by the same aggressor in their efforts to comply with UN
Security Council Resolution 661, and to force Iraq to restore Kuwait
sovereignty in compliance with UN Security Council Resolution 662.

They have decided to maintain close contact with Arab governments
and to offer their assistance to Arab efforts aimed at defusing
tensions and restoring international legality, within the framework
of UN Security Council Resolutions 660, 661, and 662. They hope that
the Summit of Arab Heads of State and Government convened today in
Cairo may take concrete measures to this end. The Presidency will
discuss with the Arab side the possibility of cooperation aimed at
achieving this common purpose."

IRAQ/KUWAIT

British Community Numbers
Spokesman said that since the crisis had begun we had been trying to
establish more accurate figures for the numbers in the British
communities in Iraq, Kuwait and Saudi Arabia. We had now
established current working estimates. These could not be regarded
as absolutely accurate but were the best guide we had.   The
numbers in Iraq and Kuwait added up to close to 5,000, as in our
previous estimates, but there were clearly more people in Kuwait
than we had originally estimated. The numbers for the British
communities, all approximate, were as follows:

IRAQ : 500 resident
       46 visiting
       90 evacuees from Kuwait

KUWAIT : 3,000 resident
         1,000 visiting

SAUDI ARABIA :   Eastern province : 1,500-2,000
                 Riyadh   : 5,000
                 Jedda   : 6,000

0139

Situation report

(5-4)

Iraq

Spokesman said that the morale of the British Community remained good under the circumstances. There were no reports of harrassment of British subjects. Our Embassy had regular consular access including to members of the British Liaison Team and evacuees from Kuwait. There had been some movement of the latter around different hotels in Baghdad and the Embassy was seeking to establish specific locations. But we had no reports of any being in difficulty.

The Iraqi Ministry of Foreign Affairs had told Embassies that Iraqi frontiers were now closed to everyone except diplomats, who must wait seven days for travel permission. There was no indication of when the borders would open.

In response to questions Spokesman said that our Embassy in Baghdad had told us that some of those in the reported convoy which had been turned back from the Kuwait/Saudi border had now shown up in Baghdad. We did not yet have full details or numbers.

Kuwait

Spokesman said that the Iraqi authorities had told diplomats in Kuwait that Western European, Canadian, Australian and American citizens would not be able to leave Kuwait.

The Iraqi authorities had also announced that Diplomatic Missions in Kuwait should close and move their activities to Baghdad by 24 August. We and our partners and allies were pressing the Iraqi authorities on their specific intentions. Our aim would be to keep diplomatic staff in Kuwait for as long as possible to provide consular protection. In answer to further questions, Spokesman said that our position on the request to close Embassies in Kuwait was quite clear. We did not recognise the annexation of Kuwait. SCR 662 quite clearly stated the position of the international community. The annexation was an illegal act. We did not propose to close the Embassy.

Spokesman said that our Embassy's ability to communicate with the British Community continued to be limited by the absence of telephones. They were however in touch through our system of wardens. The morale of the British Community was good and we believed all members of the Community were well. So far as we knew, no serious incidents involving British subjects had taken place.

In response to questions about the situation in Kuwait, Spokesman said that more Iraqi troops had deployed along the coast. There were increasing reports of low morale among Iraqi soldiers. There were reports of increased looting. Electricity and water still functioned. Food supplies were adequate. The airport remained closed, although the runways were serviceable. Flight BA 149 was still on the tarmac as were Egypt Air, Royal Moroccan and MEA planes.

0140

(5-5)

Saudi Arabia

Spokesman said that the Embassy was watching the situation closely.
At the moment our consular advice was that the Community should
continue their normal business. However, we had issued advice that,
as a precautionary measure, companies and individuals in the Eastern
province should make arrangements for dependents and non-essential
members of staff to leave.

0141

외 무 부

종 별 : 지급

번 호 : UKW-1494

수 신 : 장관 (통일 중근동) 사본: 상공부

발 신 : 주영대사

제 목 : 걸프사태 (경제제재)

일 시 : 90 0810 1700

대: AM-0145

유엔 안보리결의 661호를 집행하기 위하여 90.8.9(목) 0시를 기해 주재국
국내법으로 발효한 '유엔 이락 및 쿠웨이트 (유엔제재)령 1990' 과 동 해설자료를 금
8.10(금) FAX (UKW (F)-0232) 편 송부함.끝.

(대사 오재희-국장)

통상국	1차보	중아국	정문국	안기부	상공부	장관	차관	2차보

PAGE 1

90.08.11   02:16 FC

외신 1과 통제관   0142

주 영 대 사 관

충 22대
(22-기

번 호 : UKW(F)- 0232   DATE: 90. 8. 10. 17:05
수 신 : 장 관 (통밀, 중근동) 사본 : 상공부
제 목 : 걸프사태 [영국의 제재조치 시행법령
        및 동설명자료)

연: UKW-1494

S T A T U T O R Y   I N S T R U M E N T S   (22-2)

1990 No. 1651
UNITED NATIONS

THE IRAQ AND KUWAIT (UNITED NATIONS SANCTIONS) ORDER 1990

Made	8th August 1990
Laid before Parliament	8th August 1990
Coming into Force	9th August 1990

At the Court at HM Yacht Britannia the 8th day of August 1990

Present,

The Queen's Most Excellent Majesty in Council

Whereas under Article 41 of the Charter of the United Nations the Security Council of the United Nations have, by a resolution adopted on 6th August 1990, called upon Her Majesty's Government in the United Kingdom and all other States to apply certain measures to give effect to a decision of that Council in relation to the situation between Iraq and Kuwait.

Now therefore Her Majesty, in exercise of the powers conferred on Her by Section 1 of the United Nations Act 1946(a), is pleased, by and with the advice of Her Privy Council, to order, and it is hereby ordered, as follows:-

Citation and Commencement, Extent and Interpretation

1.- (1) This Order may be cited as the Iraq and Kuwait (United Nations Sanctions) Order 1990.

(2) This Order shall come into force on the 9th August 1990.

(3) This Order shall extend to the United Kingdom and the Isle of Man.

(4) In this Order the following expressions have the meanings hereby respectively assigned to them, that is to say:-

---

(a) 1946 C.45.

(22-3)

(b) make or carry out any contract for the sale of any goods which he intends or has reason to believe that another person intends to export from either Iraq or Kuwait; or

(c) do any act calculated to promote the exportation of any goods from either Iraq or Kuwait.

(2) No person shall deal in any goods that have been exported from Iraq or Kuwait after the 6th August 1990, that is to say, shall, by way of trade or otherwise for gain, acquire or dispose of such goods or of any property or interest in them or any right to or charge upon them or process them or do any act calculated to promote any such acquisition, disposal or processing by himself or any other person. Provided that the aforesaid prohibition shall not apply, if a licence has been granted under paragraph (1) of this Article, to any dealing authorised by the said licence.

Supply of goods to Iraq and Kuwait

3.— Except under the authority of a licence granted by the Secretary of State under this Order or under the Export of Goods (Control) (Iraq and Kuwait Sanctions) Order 1990(a) no person shall—

(a) supply or deliver or agree to supply or deliver to or to the order of any person in either Iraq or Kuwait any goods that are not in either country;

(b) supply or deliver or agree to supply or deliver any such goods to any person, knowing or having reasonable cause to believe that they will be supplied or delivered to or to the order of a person in either Iraq or Kuwait or that they will be used for the purposes of any business carried on in or operated from Iraq or Kuwait; or

(c) do any act calculated to promote the supply or delivery of any goods to any person in Iraq or Kuwait or for the purpose of any business carried on in Iraq or Kuwait in contravention of the foregoing provisions of this paragraph.

(a) S.I. 1990/1640.

0145

(22-4)

"commander", in relation to an aircraft, means the person designated as commander of the aircraft by the operator thereof, and includes any person who is for the time being in charge of command of the aircraft;

(.c.   "land transport vehicle" includes a barge;

"master", in relation to a ship, includes any person (other than a pilot) for the time being in charge of the ship;

"operator", in relation to an aircraft or to a land transport vehicle, means the person for the time being having the management of the aircraft or the vehicle;

"owner", where the owner of a ship is not the operator, means the operator and any person to whom it is chartered; and

"person in Iraq or Kuwait" includes any body constituted or incorporated under the law of Iraq or Kuwait and any body carrying on business (whether within Iraq or Kuwait or not) which is controlled by persons or bodies resident in Iraq or Kuwait or constituted or incorporated as aforesaid.

Exportation of Goods from Iraq or Kuwait

2.-(1) Except under the authority of a licence granted by the Secretary of State under this Order or the Imports of Goods (Control) Order 1954(a), the Control of Gold, Securities, Payments and Credits (Iraq) Directions 1990(b), the Control of Gold, Securities, Payments and Credits (Kuwait) Directions 1990(c), the Hong Kong (Control of Gold, Securities, Payments and Credits: Kuwait and Republic of Iraq) Order 1990 or the Caribbean Territories (Control of Gold, Securities, Payments and Credits: Kuwait and Republic of Iraq) Order 1990(d) no person shall:-

(a) make or carry out any contract for the exportation of any goods from either Iraq or Kuwait;

(a) S.I. 1954/23, amended by S.I. 1954/627, S.I. 1975/2117 and S.I. 1978/806.
(b) S.I. 1990/1616.
(c) S.I. 1990/1591.
(d) S.I. 1990/1615.
(e) S.I. 1990/

Application of Articles 2 and 3   (22-5)

4.—(1) The provisions of Articles 2 and 3 shall apply to any person within the United Kingdom or any ~~country or~~ place to which this Order extends and to any person elsewhere who:

> (a) is a British citizen, a British Dependent Territories citizen, a British Overseas citizen, a British Subject or a British protected person; or

> (b) is a body incorporated or constituted under the law of the United Kingdom or the law of any other ~~country or~~ place to which this Order extends.

(2) Any person specified in paragraph 1 of this Article who contravenes the provisions of Article 2 (1) or (2) or Article 3 shall be guilty of an offence.

Carriage of certain goods exported from or destined for Iraq or Kuwait

5.—(1) Without prejudice to the generality of Article 2 of this Order, no ship or aircraft to which this Article applies and no land transport vehicle within the United Kingdom shall be used for the carriage of any goods if those goods are being or have been exported from Iraq or Kuwait in contravention of Article 2(1) of this Order.

(2) Without prejudice to the generality of Article 3 of this Order, no ship or aircraft to which this Article applies and no land transport vehicle within the United Kingdom shall be used for the carriage of any goods if the carriage is, or forms part of, carriage from any place outside Iraq or Kuwait to any destination therein or to any person for the purposes of any business carried on in or operated from Iraq or Kuwait.

(3) This Article applies to British ships registered in the United Kingdom or in any other country or place to which this Order extends, to aircraft so registered and to any other ship or aircraft that is for the time being chartered to any person who is—

> (a) a British citizen, a British Dependent Territories citizen, a British Overseas citizen~~, a British subject~~ or a British protected person; or

> (b) a body incorporated or constituted under the law of the United Kingdom or the law of any other ~~country or~~ place to which this Order extends.

(4) If any ship, aircraft or land transport vehicle is used in contravention of paragraph (1) of this Article,

(22-6)

... then each of the following persons-

    (a) in the case of a British ship registered in the United Kingdom or in any other ~~pountry or~~ place to which this Order extends or any aircraft so registered, the owner and master of the ship or, as the case may be, the operator and the commander of the aircraft; or

    (b) in the case of any other ship or aircraft, the person to whom the ship or aircraft is for the time being chartered and, if he is such a person as is referred to in sub-paragraph (a) or sub-paragraph (b) of paragraph (3) of this Article, the master of the ship or, as the case may be, the operator and the commander of the aircraft; or

    (c) in the case of a land transport vehicle, the operator of the vehicle;

shall be guilty of an offence against the Order unless he proves that he did not know and had no reason to suppose that the goods were being or had been exported from Iraq or Kuwait in contravention of Article 2(1) of this Order.

    (5) If any ship, aircraft or land transport vehicle is used in contravention of paragraph (2) of this Article, then-

    (a) in the case of a British ship registered in the United Kingdom or in any other country or place to which this Order extends or any aircraft so registered, the owner and the master of the ship or, as the case may be, the operator and the commander of the aircraft; or

    (b) in the case of any other ship or aircraft, the person to whom the ship or aircraft is for the time being chartered and, if he is such a person as is referred to in sub-paragraph (a) or sub-paragraph (b) of paragraph (3) of this Article, the master of the ship or, as the case may be, the operator and the commander or the aircraft; or

    (c) in the case of a land transport vehicle, the operator of the vehicle,

shall be guilty of an offence against this Order unless he proves that he did not know and had no reason to suppose

---

    :) 1894 c.60,

0148

(22-7)

that the carriage of the goods in question was, or formed part of, carriage from any place outside Iraq or Kuwait to any destination therein or to any person for the purposes of any business carried on in or operated from Iraq or Kuwait.

(6) Nothing in this Article applies to goods in respect of which a licence granted by the Secretary of State is in force under:

    (a)   Article 2(1) of this Order; or

    (b)   Article 3 of this Order.

(7) Nothing in this Article shall be construed so as to prejudice any other provision of law prohibiting or restricting the use of ships, aircraft or land transport vehicles.

Investigation, etc. of suspected British ships and aircraft

6.—(1) Where any authorised officer, that is to say, any such officer as is referred to in section 692(1) of the Merchant Shipping Act 1894(a), has reason to suspect that any British ship registered in the United Kingdom or in any other country or place to which this Order extends has been or is being or is about to be used in contravention of paragraph (1) or paragraph (2) of Article 5 of the Order, he may (either alone or accompanied and assisted by persons under his authority) board the ship and search her and, for that purpose, may use or authorise the use of reasonable force, and he may request the master of the ship to furnish such information relating to the ship and her cargo and produce for his inspection such documents so relating and such cargo as he may specify; and an authorised officer (either there and then or upon consideration of any information furnished or document or cargo produced in pursuance of such a request) may, in the case of a ship that is reasonably suspected of being or of being about to be used in contravention of Article 5(2) of this Order, exercise the following further powers with a view to the prevention of the commission (or the continued commission) of any such contravention or in order that enquiries into the matter may be pursued, that is to say, he may either direct the master to refrain, except with the consent of an authorised officer, from landing at any port specified by the officer any part of the ship's cargo that is so specified or request the master to take any one or more of the following steps:-

    (a) to cause the ship not to proceed with the voyage on which she is then engaged or about to engage until

0149

(22-8)

the master is notified by any authorised officer that the ship may so proceed;

(b) if the ship is then in a port in the United Kingdom or in any other country or place to which this Order extends, to cause her to remain there until the master is notified by any authorised officer that the ship may depart;

(c) if the ship is then in any other place, to take her to any such port specified by the officer and to cause her to remain there until the master is notified as mentioned in sub-paragraph (b) of this paragraph; and

(d) to take her to any other destination that may be specified by the officer in agreement with the master;

and the master shall comply with any such request or direction.

(2) Without prejudice to the provisions of paragraph (8) of this Article, where a master refuses or fails to comply with a request made under this Article that his ship shall or shall not proceed to or from any place or where an authorised officer otherwise has reason to suspect that such a request that has been so made may not be complied with, any such officer may take such steps as appear to him to be necessary to secure compliance with that request and, without prejudice to the generality of the foregoing, may for that purpose enter upon, or authorise entry upon, that ship and use, or authorise the use of, reasonable force.

(3) Where any officer of customs and excise or any person authorised by the Secretary of State for that purpose either generally or in a particular case has reason to suspect that any aircraft registered in the United Kingdom or in any other country or place to which this Order extends or any aircraft for the time being chartered to any person specified in paragraph 3 of Article 5 of this Order has been or is being or is about to be used in contravention of paragraph (1) or paragraph (2) of Article 5 of this Order or of Article 8 of this Order, that authorised person or that officer may request the charterer, the operator and the commander of the aircraft or any of them to furnish such information relating to the aircraft and its cargo and produce for their or his inspection such documents so relating and such cargo as they or he may specify, and that authorised person or that officer may (either alone or accompanied and assisted by persons under his authority) board the aircraft and search it and, for that purpose, may use or authorise the use of reasonable force; and, if the aircraft is then in the United Kingdom any such authorised

0150

person or any such officer (either there and then or upon consideration of any information furnished or document or cargo produced in pursuance of such a request) may further request the charterer, operator and the commander or any of them to cause the aircraft to remain in the United Kingdom until notified that the aircraft may depart; and the charterer, the operator and the commander shall comply with any such request.

(4) Without prejudice to the provisions of paragraph (8) of this Article, where any person authorised as aforesaid or any such officer as aforesaid has reason to suspect that any request that an aircraft should remain in the United Kingdom that has been made under paragraph (3) of this Article may not be complied with, that authorised person or that officer may take such steps as appear to him to be necessary to secure compliance with that request and, without prejudice to the generality of the foregoing, may for that purpose—

    (a) enter, or authorise entry, upon any land and upon that aircraft;

    (b) detain, or authorise the detention of, that aircraft; and

    (c) use, or authorise the use of, reasonable force.

(5) A person authorised by the Secretary of State to exercise any power for the purposes of paragraph (3) or paragraph (4) of this Article shall, if requested to do so, produce evidence of his authority before exercising that power.

(6) No information furnished or document produced by any person in pursuance of a request made under this Article shall be disclosed except—

    (a) with the consent of the person by whom the information was furnished or the document was produced:

    Provided that a person who has obtained information or is in possession of a document only in his capacity as servant or agent of another person may not give consent for the purposes of this sub-paragraph but such consent may instead be given by any person who is entitled to that information or to the possession of that document in his own right; or

    (b) to any person who would have been empowered under this Article to request that it be furnished or produced or to any person holding or acting in any office under or in the service of the Crown in respect

0151

(22-10)

of the Government of the United Kingdom on under or in the service of the Government of any other ~~country on~~ place to which this Order extends; or

(c) on the authority of the Secretary of State, to any organ of the United Nations or to any person in the service of the United Nations or of the Government of any other country for the purpose of assisting the United Nations or that Government in securing compliance with or detecting evasion of measures in relation to Iraq or Kuwait decided upon by the Security Council of the United Nations; or

(d) with a view to the institution of, or otherwise for the purposes of, any proceedings for an offence against this Order or, with respect to any of the matters regulated by this Order, for an offence against any enactment relating to customs or for an offence against any provision of law with respect to similar matters that is for the time being in force in any ~~country on~~ place to which this Order extends.

(7) Any power conferred by this Article to request the furnishing of information or the production of a document or of cargo for inspection shall include a power to specify whether the information should be furnished orally or in writing and in what form and to specify the time by which and the place in which the information should be furnished or the document or cargo produced for inspection.

(8) Each of the following persons shall be guilty of an offence against this Order, that is to say:-

(a) A master of a ship who disobeys any direction given under paragraph (1) of this Article with respect to the landing of any cargo;

(b) A master of a ship or a charterer or an operator or a commander of the aircraft who, without reasonable excuse, refuses or fails within a reasonable time to comply with any request made under this Article by any person empowered to make it or who wilfully furnishes false information or produces false documents to such a person in response to such a request;

(c) A master or a member of a crew of a ship or a charterer or an operator or a commander or a member of a crew of an aircraft who wilfully obstructs any such person (or any person acting under the authority of any such person) in the exercise of his powers under this Article.

0152

(22-11)

(9) Nothing in this Article shall be construed so as to
prejudice any other provision of law conferring powers or
imposing restrictions or enabling restrictions to be imposed
with respect to ships or aircraft.

Obtaining of evidence and information

7. ~ The provisions of the Schedule to this Order shall have
effect in order to facilitate the obtaining, by or on behalf
of the Secretary of State or the Commissioners of Customs
and Excise, of evidence and information for the purpose of
securing compliance with or detecting evasion of this Order
and in order to facilitate the obtaining, by or on behalf of
the Secretary of State or the Commissioners of Customs and
Excise, of evidence of the commission of an offence against
this Order or with respect to any of the matters regulated
by this Order, of an offence relating to customs.

Penalties and Proceedings

8.~(1) Any person guilty of an offence against this Order
shall be liable -

    (a) on conviction on indictment to imprisonment for a
term not exceeding two years or to a fine or to both;
or

    (b) on summary conviction to imprisonment for a term
not exceeding six months or to a fine not exceeding
~~£20,000 or to both~~ the statutory minimum or to both.

(2) Where any body corporate is guilty of an offence
against this Order, and that offence is proved to have been
committed with the consent or connivance of, or to be
attributable to any neglect on the part of, any director,
manager, secretary or other similar officer of the body
corporate of any person who was purporting to act in any
such capacity, he, as well as the body corporate, shall be
guilty of that offence and shall be liable to be proceeded
against and punished accordingly.

(3) Summary proceedings for an offence against this
Order, being an offence alleged to have been committed
outside the United Kingdom, may be commenced at any time not
later than twelve months from the date on which the person
charged first enters the United Kingdom after committing the
offence.

(4) Proceedings against any person for an offence against
this Order may be taken before the appropriate court in the
United Kingdom, or in any ~~territory~~ to which this Order
extends, having jurisdiction in the place where that person

0153

is for the time being.   (22-12)

(5) No proceedings for an offence against this Order shall be instituted in England, Wales, Northern Ireland or in the Isle of Man except by the Secretary of State or with the consent of the Attorney General or, as the case may be, the Attorney General for Northern Ireland or the Isle of Man

Provided that this paragraph shall not prevent the arrest, or the issue or execution of a warrant for the arrest, of any person in respect of such an offence, or the remanding in custody or on bail of any person charged with such an offence, notwithstanding that the necessary consent to the institution of proceedings for the offence has not been obtained.

Exercise of powers of the Secretary of State

9.— (1) The Secretary of State may to such extent and subject to such restrictions and conditions as he may think proper, delegate or authorise the delegation of any of his powers under this Order (other than the power to give authority under Schedule 1 to this Order to apply for a search warrant) to any person, or class or description of persons, approved by him, and references in this Order to the Secretary of State shall be construed accordingly.

(2) Any licences granted under this Order may be either general or special, may be subject to or without conditions, may be limited so as to expire on a specified date unless renewed and may be varied or revoked by the authority that granted them.

Miscellaneous

10.—(1) This Order applies to or in relation to any ship or aircraft or any body corporate that purports to be registered in any particular place or, as the case may be, that purports to be incorporated or constituted under the law of that place as it applies to or in relation to any ship or aircraft that is so registered or any body corporate that it so incorporated or constituted.

(2) Any provision of this Order which prohibits the doing of a thing except under the authority of a licence granted by the Secretary of State shall not have effect in relation to any such thing done in a ~~country of~~ place other than the United Kingdom to which this Order extends or done elsewhere outside the United Kingdom by a person who is ordinarily resident in, or by a body incorporated or constituted under the law of, that ~~country of~~ place, provided that it is so done under the authority of a licence or with permission

0154

(22-13)

granted, in accordance with any law in force in that ~~country or~~ place (being a law substantially corresponding to the relevant provision of this Order), by the authority competent in that behalf under that law.

G. I. de Deney
Clerk of the Privy Council

0155

Article 8

SCHEDULE   (22-14)

EVIDENCE AND INFORMATION

1.- (1) Without prejudice to any other provision of this
Order, or any provision of any other law, the Secretary of
State (or any person authorised by him for that purpose
either generally or in a particular case) or the
Commissioners of Customs and Excise may request any person
in or resident in the United Kingdom to furnish to him or
them (or to that authorised person) any information in his
possession or control, or to produce to him or them (or to
that authorised person) any document in his possession or
control, which he or they (or that authorised person) may
require for the purpose of securing compliance with or
detecting evasion of this Order; and any person to whom such
a request is made shall comply with it within such time and
in such manner as may be specified in the request.

(2) Nothing in the foregoing sub-paragraph shall be
taken to require any person who has acted as counsel or
solicitor for any person to disclose any privileged
communication made to him in that capacity.

(3) Where a person is convicted on indictment for
failing to furnish information or produce a document when
requested so to do under this paragraph, the court may make
an order requiring him, within such period as may be
specified in the order, to furnish the information or
produce the document.

(4) The power conferred by this paragraph to request
any person to produce documents shall include power to take
copies of or extracts from any document so produced and to
request that person, or, where that person is a body
corporate, any other person who is a present or past officer
of, or is employed by, the body corporate, to provide an
explanation of any of them.

2.- (1) If any justice of the peace is satisfied by
information on oath given by a person authorised by the
Secretary of State or the Commissioners of Customs and
Excise to act for the purposes of this paragraph either
generally or in a particular case -

(a) that there is reasonable ground for suspecting
that an offence against this Order or, with respect to
any of the matters regulated by this Order, an offence

0156

(22-15)

against any enactment relating to customs has been or
is being committed and that evidence of the commission
of the offence is to be found on any premises specified
in the information, or in any vehicle, vessel or
aircraft so specified; or

(b)   that any documents which ought to have been
produced under paragraph 1 of this Schedule and have not
been produced are to be found on any such premises or
in any such vehicle, vessel or aircraft,

he may grant a search warrant authorising any constable,
together with any other persons named in the warrant and any
other constables, to enter the premises specified in the
information or, as the case may be, any premises upon which
the vehicle, vessel or aircraft so specified may be, at any
time within one month from the date of the warrant and to
search the premises, or, as the case may be, the vehicle,
vessel or aircraft.

(2)   A person authorised by any such warrant as
aforesaid to search any premises or any vehicle, vessel or
aircraft may search every person who is found in, or whom he
has reasonable ground to believe to have recently left or
to be about the enter, those premises or that vehicle,
vessel or aircraft and may seize any document or article
found on the premises or in the vehicle, vessel or aircraft
or on such person which has has reasonable ground to believe
to be evidence of the commission of any such offence as
aforesaid or any documents which he has reasonable ground to
believe ought to have been produced under paragraph 1 of
this Schedule or to take in relation to any such article or
document any other steps which may appear necessary for
preserving it and preventing interference with it:

Provided that no female shall, in pursuance of any
warrant issued under this paragraph, be searched except by a
female.

(3)   Where, by virtue of this paragraph, a person is
empowered to enter any premises, vehicle, vessel or aircraft
he may use such force as is reasonably necessary for that
purpose.

(4)   Any documents or articles of which possession is
taken under this paragraph may be retained for a period of
three months or, if within that period there are commenced
any proceedings for such an offence as aforesaid to which
they are relevant, until the conclusion of those
proceedings.

(5)   In the application of this paragraph to Scotland
any reference to a justice of the peace includes a

0157

reference to the sheriff.   (22-16)

3.   A person authorised by the Secretary of State to
exercise any power for the purposes of this Schedule shall,
if requested to do so, produce evidence of his authority
before exercising that power.

4.   No information furnished or document produced
(including any copy of extract made of any document
produced) by any person in pursuance of a request made
under this Schedule and no document seized under paragraph
2(2) of this Schedule shall be disclosed except -

> (a)   with the consent of the person by whom the
> information was furnished or the document was
> produced or the person from whom the document was
> seized:
>
> Provided that a person who has obtained
> information or is in possession of a document only in
> his capacity as servant or agent of another person may
> not give consent for the purposes of this
> sub-paragraph but such consent may instead be given
> by any person who is entitled to that information or
> to the possession of that document in his own right;
> or
>
> (b)   to any person who would have been empowered
> under this Schedule to request that it be furnished
> or produced or to any person holding or acting in any
> office under or in the service of the Crown; or
>
> (c)   on the authority of the Secretary of State, to
> any organ of the United Nations or to the Government
> of any other country for the purpose of assisting the
> United Nations or that Government in securing
> compliance with or detecting evasion of measures in
> relation to this Order decided upon by the Security
> Council of the United Nations; or
>
> (d)   with a view to the institution of, or otherwise
> for the purposes of, any proceedings for an offence
> against this Order or, with respect to any of the
> matters regulated by this Order, for an offence
> against any enactment relating to customs or for an
> offence against any provision of law with respect to
> similar matters that is for the time being in force in
> any country or place to which this Order extends.

5.   Any person who -

> (a)   without reasonable excuse, refuses or fails

0158

(22-17)

within the time and in the manner specified (or, if no
time has been specified, within a reasonable time) to
comply with any request made under this Schedule by
any person who is empowered to make it; or

(b)   wilfully furnishes false information or a false
explanation or otherwise wilfully obstructs any person
in the exercise of his powers under this Schedule; or

(c)   with intent to evade the provisions of this
Schedule, destroys, mutilates, defaces, secretes or
removes any document;

shall be guilty of an offence against this Order.

0159

EXPLANATORY NOTE
(This note is not part of the Order)

(22-18)

This Order imposes restrictions pursuant to a decision of the Security Council of the United Nations in Resolution No. 661 of 6th August 1990, on the exportation of goods from Iraq and Kuwait and on supply of goods to Iraq and Kuwait as well as certain related activities and dealings, including the carriage of such goods in British ships or aircraft. ~~It authorises the imposition of restrictions on the transfer of certain property if this might facilitate the evasion of the Order.~~ The Order also makes provision for the investigation of ships and aircraft that are suspected or contravening the Order.

0160

(22-19)

Summary

1. Measures under UK domestic law to implement SCR 661 came into force 00.01 9 August. A European Community regulation covering aspects of the Resolution was adopted on 8 August and came into force with effect from 7 August.

Detail

2. Two measures made by the DTI as follows:
I) An amendment to the open General Import Licence to give effect to the import ban:
ii) An order under the Import.Export and Customs Powers (Defence) Act 1939 to give effect to the export ban. The effect is to ban the import into the UK of all goods (including crude oil and petroleum products) originating in Iraq or Kuwait except under an individual licence issued by the DTI. Any unused import licences issued by the DTI before 6 August for goods originating in Iraq or Kuwait have been revoked. Licences will not normally be issued except for goods in transit. Applications for goods in transit should be made to Import Licensing branch of DTI by 5 September. The export of all goods to Iraq or Kuwait without a licence is also banned.

III) The Iraq and Kuwait (United Nations Sanctions) Order 1990 prohibits the following activities:

a) Making and carrying out contracts for the export of goods from Iraq or Kuwait and any other act calculated to promote the export of goods from Iraq or Kuwait:

b) Dealing with goods exported from Iraq after 6 August 1990:

c) Supplying goods not in Iraq or Kuwait to, or to the order of, a person in Iraq or Kuwait:

d) Supply of goods to, or to the order of, an Iraqi or Kuwaiti company or Iraqi or Kuwaiti controlled company:

e) Any act calculated to promote the supply of goods to, or to the order of, a person in Iraq or Kuwait, or an Iraqi or Kuwaiti company or Iraqi or Kuwaiti controlled company.

These prohibitions apply within the UK and to UK companies and British nationals worldwide. The order also prohibits the use of UK flagged ships and aircraft and the use of those chartered by UK companies and British nationals for such purposes. Within the UK, the use of land transport vehicles for such purposes is also prohibited.

0161

- 2 -   (22-20)

Exports under existing contracts are prohibited under the
provisions of the order.

IV)   Article 4 of the Resolution concerning funds and
finance is covered by the directions issued by the Treasury
on 2 and 4 August freezing certain Kuwaiti and Iraqi assets.

V)   A further Order in Council implements the mandatory
provisions of the Security Council Resolution in UK dependent
territories.

3.   In addition, the European Community adopted a regulation
on 8 August which will apply as from 7 August throughout the EC
member states. The Regulation provides for a total ban on the
import or export of all commodities or products originating
in or coming from Iraq and Kuwait. It follows closely the
terms of the Security Council Resolution and in effect covers
the same ground as the UK legislation.

4.   The guidance set out above may be drawn upon in briefing
businessmen and companies on the effects of the various orders.
You may also wish to pass on the following telephone numbers
to be used by enquirers. DTI will answer questions on all the
orders except the two Treasury Directions which are for the
Bank of England.

        Export Licencing: 071-215-8070
        Import Licencing: 0642-364 333
        DTI General Enquiries:
                Iraq: 071-215 4365/4367/5376/4395
                Kuwait:071-215 5491/4388
        Bank of England: 071-601 3764/5463/4768/3309/3250/3848

Supplementary Questions and Answers
follow:
Iraq and Kuwait (United Nations Sanctions) Order 1990
Questions and Answers

Scope of Order
- Complements the measures taken to ban the import and export
of goods (i.e. the amendment to the Open General Import Licence
and the Order under the Import, Export and Customs Powers (Defence
Act 1939) by covering activities within the UK or by British
companies or individuals which might promote imports or exports
or the supply of goods to Iraqi or Kuwaiti controlled companies.

0162

- 3 -

(22-21)

How would this operate?
- These activities are prohibited without a licence.

Is the scope of this Order unprecedented?
- No. It follows the precedent of the Order giving effect
to the Security Council Resolution imposing mandatory
sanctions on Rhodesia in 1968.

What kind of British company is covered?
- Any company incorporated in the UK which carries on
prohibited activities. (If necessary: a separate order covers
companies incorporated in the dependent territories).

What is a definition of a British national?
- The Order covers all categories,i.e. British citizen,
British Dependent Territories citizen, a British Overseas
citizen, or a British Protected person.

Does this just apply to British companies and nationals in
the UK?
- No. It applies to British companies and nationals wherever
they may be found who are in any way promoting the export/import
of goods from/to Iraq and Kuwait.

How would a British company trading with Iraq or Kuwait be
affected or any of its British workforce?
- Continuation of such trade without a licence would be in
breach of the Order and the UN Resolution. Any of the workforce
directly involved in promotion of such trade would similarly be
affected.

What about e.g. British nationals working for Kuwaiti or Iraqi
oil companies?
- The export of oil products from Iraq or Kuwait is covered by
the terms of the Resolution. Any activities by a British
national which might serve to promote any Iraqi or Kuwaiti
exports would be covered by the terms of the Resolution and the
Order.

What about consultants?
- The same applies. A consultant helping to develop agricultural
yield in Kuwait is not directly concerned with the promotion of
exports. Someone advising on trade promotion or advertising
would be.

0163

(22-22)

Does this not present considerable difficulties of definition?
- There are bound to be difficult cases and we are mindful of
the particular problems of individuals in the current
circumstances. When companies or individuals are in doubt
about their particular position they should approach DTI for
a licence. In practice we are already in touch with many
companies about the position of their employees.

Are services covered by the Order?
- Services which serve to promote the export of goods from
Iraq or Kuwait or the supply of goods to an Iraqi or Kuwaiti
controlled company or person worldwide are covered.

Can HMG be made liable for any losses sustained by companies?
- No. We are acting under the United Nations Act 1946 to
give effect to a mandatory Security Council Resolution binding
on all member states of the UN. HMG would be under no legal
liability to pay compensation.

Are existing contracts covered?
- Yes. Exports and imports under existing contracts are
prohibited under the provisions of the Order.

What is the combined effect of the measures taken by the UK?
- Taken together the UK measures implement the mandatory
provisions of Security Council Resolution 661.

0164

외 무 부

종 별 : 지 급

번 호 : USW-3692　　　　　　　　　　일 시 : 90 0810 1730

수 신 : 장관(봉일,중근동,<u>미북</u>)

발 신 : 주미대사

제 목 : 미국의 대이락 경제 제재 조치

　　1.금 8.10 미 백악관은 미국의 대이락 교역을 전면 금지하는 시행령(EXECUTIVEORDER) 을 발표하였음.

　　2.동 시행령에 따르면 미 행정부는 미국 시민뿐 아니라 <u>영주권자, 미국법에 의해동록된 법인(외국 지사)과 기관,</u> 미국적선등 모든 미국인(US PERSON) 이 이락과의 상품,용역, 재정 거래에 개입하는것을 금지하고 있음(수수한 인도적 물품의 기증은 별도 고려).동 시행령 발표문 전문별전 FAX 송부함.

　　첨부: USW(F)-1772

　　(대사 박동진-국장)

통상국　　1차보　　　미주국　　중아국　　안기부

THE WHITE HOUSE
OFFICE OF THE PRESS SECRETARY

EXECUTIVE ORDER

BLOCKING IRAQI GOVERNMENT PROPERTY
AND
PROHIBITING TRANSACTIONS WITH IRAQ

FRIDAY, AUGUST 10, 1990

By the authority vested in me as President by the Constitution
and laws of the United States of America, including the
International Emergency Economic Powers Act (50 U.S.C. 1701 et
seq.), the National Emergencies Act (50 U.S.C. 1601 et seq.),
section 301 of title 3 of the United States Code, and the United
Nations Participation Act (22 U.S.C. 287c), in view of United
Nations Security Council Resolution No. 661 of August 6, 1990, and
in order to take additional steps with respect to Iraq's invasion of
Kuwait and the national emergency declared in Executive Order No.
12722,

I, GEORGE BUSH, President of the United States of America,
hereby order:

Section 1.   Except to the extent provided in regulations that
may hereafter be issued pursuant to this order, all property and
interests in property of the Government of Iraq that are in the
United States, that hereafter come within the United States, or that
are or hereafter come within the possession or control of United
States persons, including their overseas branches, are hereby
blocked.

Sec. 2.   The following are prohibited, except to the extent
provided in regulations that may hereafter be issued pursuant to
this order:

(a)   The importation into the United States of any goods or
services of Iraqi origin, or any activity that promotes or is
intended to promote such importation;

(b)   The exportation to Iraq, or to any entity operated from
Iraq, or owned or controlled by the Government of Iraq, directly or
directly, of any goods, technology (including technical data or
other information), or services either (i) from the United States,
or (ii) requiring the issuance of a license by a Federal agency, or
activity that promotes or is intended to promote such exportation,
except donations of articles intended to relieve human suffering,
such as food and supplies intended strictly for medical purposes;

1772
-- 1 --

0166

(c) Any dealing by a United States person related to property of Iraqi origin exported from Iraq after August 6, 1990, or property intended for exportation from Iraq to any country, or exportation to Iraq from any country, or any activity of any kind that promotes or is intended to promote such dealing;

(d) Any transaction by a United States person relating to travel by any United States citizen or permanent resident alien to Iraq, or to activities by any such person within Iraq, after the date of this order, other than transactions necessary to

effect (i) such person's departure from Iraq, (ii) travel and activities for the conduct of the official business of the Federal Government of the United Nations, or (iii) travel for journalistic activity by persons regularly employed in such capacity by a news-gathering organization;

(e) Any transaction by a United States person relating to transportation to or from Iraq; the provision of transportation to or from the United States by any Iraqi person or any vessel or aircraft of Iraqi registration; or the sale in the United States by any person holding authority under the federal Aviation Act of 1958, as amended (49 USC 1301 et seq.), of any transportation by air that includes any stop in Iraq;

(f) The performance by any United States person of any contract, including a financing contract, in support of an industrial, commercial, public utility, or governmental project in Iraq;

(g) Except as otherwise authorized herein, any commitment or transfer, direct or indirect, of funds, or other financial or economic resources by any United States person to the Government of Iraq or any other person in Iraq;

(h) Any transaction by any United States person that evades or avoids, or has the purpose of evading or avoiding, any of the prohibitions set forth in this order.

Sec. 3. For purposes of this order;

(a) the term "United States person" means any United States citizen, permanent resident alien, juridicial person organized under the laws of the United States (including foreign branches), or any person in the United States, and vessels of US registration.

(b) the term "Government of Iraq" includes the Government of Iraq, its agencies, instrumentalities and controlled entitites, and the Central Bank of Iraq.

Sec. 4. This order is effective immediately.

1772
-2-

0167

Sec. 5. The Secretary of the Treasury, in consultation with the Secretary of State, is hereby authorized to take such actions, including the promulgation of rules and regulations, as may be necessary to carry out the purposes of this order. Such actions may include prohibiting or regulating payments or transfers of any property or any transactions involving the transfer of anything of economic value by any United States person to the government of Iraq, or to any Iraqi national or entity owned or controlled, directly or indirectly, by the Government of Iraq or Iraqi nationals. The Secretary of the Treasury may redelegate any of those functions to other officers and agencies of the Federal Government. All agencies of the Federal Government are directed to take all appropriate measures within their authority to carry out the provisions of this order, including the suspension or termination of licenses or other authorizations in effect as of the date of this order.

Sec. 6. Executive Order No. 12722 of August 2, 1990, is hereby revoked to the extent inconsistent with this order. All delegations, rules, regulations, orders, licenses, and other forms of administrative action made, issued, or otherwise taken under Executive Order No. 12722 and not revoked administratively shall remain in full force and effect under this order until amended, modified, or terminated by proper authority. The revocation of any provision of Executive Order No. 12722 pursuant to this section shall not affect any violation of any rules, regulations, orders, licenses, or other forms of administrative action under that order during the period that such provision of that order was in effect.

This order shall be transmitted to the Congress and published in the Federal Register.

George Bush

END

/772
-3-

0168

암호수신

종   별 :

번   호 : ARW-0522   일   시 : 90 0810 1700

수   신 : 장 관(중근동,미남,정일,기정,국방)

발   신 : 주 아르헨티나 대사

제   목 : 이락-쿠웨이트사태관련 주재국 입장

이락의 쿠웨이트 침공관련 지금까지 취한 주재국입장을 아래 보고함.

1. 외부부 8.2. 성명을 발표, 이락군의 쿠웨이트 침공이 국제평화와 안전을 파괴하는 행위라고 하고 이락군의 쿠웨이트로부터 즉각적이고 부조건적인 철수 요구

2. CAVALLO 외무장관은 8.8. 유엔 안보리 결정으로 평화군 파견 요청이 있는 경우 평화군 파견을 검토 할것이라고 기자회견에서 언급 (군대 파견이 아닌 OFFICER 파견)

3. 안보리 결의 601 에 따라 이락과의 봉상 전면 중단을 결정하고 8.9. 당지 이락대사에 통보

4. 8.2. 외무부 성명관련, 당지 주재 이락대사는 이러한 아르헨티나의 조치가 아르헨티나에 손해를 줄것이라고 경고하는 유인물을 배포하였는바, 아르헨티나 정부로부터 강력한 반발을 받고 주재국 외무부를 방문 사과를 하였으며 메넴 대통령도 동 대사의 경솔을 지적, 너무 말이 많다고 8.9. 기자회견에서 언급한바 있음.

(대사 이상진-국장)

중아국   차관   1차보   2차보   미주국   통상국   정문국   정와대   안기부
국방부

PAGE 1

외 무 부

원 본

종 별 :

번 호 : CSW-0379

일 시 : 90 0810 1740

수 신 : 장 관(통일,중근동,미남)

발 신 : 주 칠레 대사

제 목 : 대이라크 조치

연:CSW-0369

연호에 이어, 주재국 외무성은 8.8 성명을 통하여, 주재국 정부는 유엔안보리 결의
661 호를 지지하며, 동 결의의 내용(대 이라크 및 쿠웨이트 무기수출 금지 포함)을
국내적으로 시행하기 위한 제반 조치를 강구중이라고 발표 하였음. 끝

(대사 이용훈-국장)

예고: 90.12.31 까지

통상국   차관   1차보   2차보   미주국   중아국   정와대   안기부

외 무 부

종 별 :

번 호 : UKW-1498

일 시 : 90 0810 1910

수 신 : 장 관(봉인, 중근동,구일,미안)

발 신 : 주 영 대사

제 목 : 대 이라크 제재

대 WECM-0020

대호 관련, 주재국의 대이라크 쿠웨이트 교역및 부자현황을 아래 보고함.

0 대이라크 교역(1989)

수출: 450 백만 파운드(전체수출의 0.5 프로) 발전설비, 비료공장 건설등 대형 프로젝트용 기자재가 주수출품임.

수입: 55 백만 파운드(전체수입의 0.04 프로)

0 대 쿠웨이트 교역(1989)

수출: 229 백만 파운드 (전체수출의 0.2 프로)

수입: 150 백만 파운드(전체수입의 0.1 프로)

0 쿠웨이트의 대영국 부자는 BP, MIDLAND BANK 등 석유, 금융, 보험, 관광,호텔, 부동산 분야에 11 건(부자금액 미상)임.

0 이라크의 대외채무는 약 7 백억 달러에 달하는 것으로 추정되며 그중 상당액이 중동국가로 부터 차입인것으로 알려짐.끝.

(대사 오재희-국장)

예고:90.12.31 일반

통상국   차관   1차보   2차보   미주국   구주국   중아국

90.08.11   08:30   0171
외신 2과   통제관 DL

외 무 부

종 별 :

번 호 : COW-0289   일 시 : 90 0810 1800

수 신 : 장 관(중근동, 미중, 통일)

발 신 : 주 코스타리카 대사

제 목 : 이라크 규탄

1. 주재국 외무부는 아래 요지 성명을 발표함.

'무력 비행사 원칙을 신조로 하는 정부는, 이라크의 용서할 수 없는 정당치 못한무력 전개를 개탄하며 쿠웨이트에의 침략을 단호히 규탄함. 이라크군이 철수하고, 세계 안정과 평화에 대한 심각한 위협을 해결할 때까지 가능한 모든 외교, 경제조치를 취할것을 국제사회에호소함.

2. 주재국 국회는 동일 만장일치로 훗세인 이라크정권의 쿠웨이트 침공을 규탄하고, 군대 철수를 주장하였음.끝.

(대사 김 창근-국장)

중아국   미주국   통상국   정문국

PAGE 1   90.08.11   09:51 WH

외신 1과 통제관   0172

외 무 부

종 별 :

번 호 : AVW-1166 　　　　　　　　　일 시 : 90 0810 1900

수 신 : 장 관(봉일,중근동,구이)

발 신 : 주 오스트리아 대사

제 목 : 오스트리아의 대이라크 제재조치

1.오스트리아의 조치 내용

가.오스트리아 정부는 유엔 안보리의 대이라크 제재 결의를 전면 이행하기로 8.7. 결정하였음. KLESTIL 주재국 외무차관은 동 결정에 따라 오스트리아의 모든 대이라크 거래관계(ALL BUSINESSCONTACTS)가 중단된다고 설명하였음.

나.오스트리아 국립은행은 8.9. 이라크 및 쿠웨이트의 모든 자산에 대한 처분과양국에 대한 은행의 모든 자금이전(ALL BANK TRANSFERS TO IRAQ AND KUWAIT)은 국립은행의 특별허가(SPECIAL PERMISSION)가 없는 한 동결한다고 발표하였음.

2.오스트리아-이라크 경제관계

-주재국의 이라크 및 쿠웨이트로 부터의 원유수입은 전체의 2퍼센트 미만으로서금번 사태로 원유수급에 큰 타격을 받지 않을 것으로 전망되고 있으며, 전체 경제적으로 FEE 대한 이라크의 중요성은 미미한 것으로 평가되고 있음.

-이라크는 오스트리아에 대해 약 9억불의 채무를 지고있음.

3.이라크의 반응

-이라크는 오스트리아의 유엔안보리 결의 이행결정에 대해 '심심한 유감과 놀라움'(DEEPREGRET AND SURPRISE) 을 표명하였음.

-이라크 대사관은 8.8. 성명을 통해 오스트리아의 태도는 현재는 물론 장래 오-이라크간 무역관계에 손상을 초래할 것이라고 하면서, 이라크는 특히 오스트리아의 이러한 입장이 중립(NEUTRALITY) 정신에 반한다는 사실 때문에 이를 놀라움으로받아 드린다는 입장을 발표하였음.

(끝)

통상국 　구주국 　중아국

PAGE 1 　　　　　　　　　　　　　　　　　90.08.11　　12:06 DA

외신 1과 　통제관

0173

외 무 부

관리번호 90-438

종 별 :

번 호 : POW-0403

수 신 : 장관(통일)

발 신 : 주 폴투갈 대사

제 목 : 대 이라크 제재

일 시 : 90 0810 1900

김

1990. 12. 31 예고문에 의거 일반문서로 재분류됨

대:WECM-0020

1. 주재국 정부는 EC 각료회의에서 8.7 승인한 표제규정(8.9 EC 관보 게재)을 검토하기 위하여 8.9 국무회의를 개최하고 이락의 쿠에이트 침공사태를 재평가 하였음

2. 동 국무회의는 이미 폴투갈 정부가 이락을 강력 규탄하였음을 상기시키고 EC 의결과 유엔 안보리 의결에 따라 폴투갈은 이락과 쿠웨이트에 대하여 전면금수조치를 이미 시행중에 있으며, 바그다드와 리야드는 자국 상주공관을 통하여, 상주공관이 없는 쿠에이트는 영국, 이태리 공관을 통하여 각각 자국민을 보호하고 있다고 부연함

3. 동 국무회의는 동 규정중 -이들국가(쿠에이트, 이락)와의 모든 군사협력의 형태- 에는 군수품과 군장비의 판매는 물론 경제, 기술 및 과학에 관한 모든 협력 활동이 포함된다고 언급하고 의약품과 식료품을 제외한 모든 물품을 동 국가로부터 수입하거나, 수출하는것이 금지됨은 분명하나 조선수리등 서비스 제공에 대하여는 구체적 규정이 없어 브라셀에 유권해석을 요청, 그 지시에 따라 조치키로했다고함

4. 추가보고 사항

가. 교역량

-대이락

89 년(대미환율 1:145): 수입(FOB) 144,834 천 미불(전교역량 대비 0.77프로)

수출(FOB) 12,379 천 미불(전 교역량 대비 0.09 프로)

-90 년 1-5 월(대미환율 1:142)

수입 86,211 천미불

수출 1,190 천 미불

-대 쿠에이트

-89 년: 수입 21,897 천 미불(전교역량 대비 0.12 프로)

통상국	장관	차관	1차보	2차보	중아국	정문국	청와대	안기부

수출 6,676 천 미불(전 교역량 대비 0.005 프로)

-90 년 1-5 월 수입 35 천 미불

수출 3,099 천 미불

나. 투자현황

-쿠에이트 대 폴투갈

88 년 75 백만에스쿠도(517 천 미불상당)

89 년 2 백만에스꾸드(14 천미불 상당)

-이락 대 폴투갈 투자없음

다. 외채

주로 유로시장이나 런던, 뉴욕에서 조달하고 중동시장에서는 거의조달하지 않음

라. 체류국민

-쿠웨이트 20 명

-이락 50 명. 끝

(대사 유혁인-국장)

예고:90.12.31 일반

주 핀 랜 드 대 사 관

핀정 20730 -152

1990. 8. 10.

수신 장관

참조 중동 · 아프리카국장, 구주국장

제목 이라크, 쿠웨이트 사태 관련 주재국 반응

　　　　이라크, 쿠웨이트 사태에 관한 주재국 외무장관의 성명 및 경제제재 조치에 관한
관계자료를 별첨 송부하오니 참고하시기 바랍니다.

첨부 : 동 자료 각　1부 (핀어및 영역본).　끝.

　　　　　　주　핀　랜　드　대

45112

영사기관

0176

LEHDISTÖ TIEDOTE PRESS MEDDELANDE PRESS RELEASE

2.8.90 klo 11.00
no. 207

ULKOASIANMINISTERIÖN LAUSUNTO KUWAITIN TILANTEESTA

Kansainvälisten uutistoimistojen tiedot toteavat Irakin
joukkojen tunkeutuneen Kuwaitiin, Kuwaitin hallituksen kaa-
tuneen ja uuden Irakin tukeman hallituksen mahdollisesti
tulleen valtaan.

Ulkoasiainministeriö on saanut omia kanaviaan pitkin saman-
suuntaisuuntaisia tietoja. Niiden mukaan Kuwaitin keskusta
on suljettu ja tiedonvälitys katkennut. Sodan äänet ovat
lähestymässä parhaillaan keskusta-alueita. Tietoja liikkuu
myös joidenkin Kuwaitin omien joukkojen vallankaappaus-
yrityksestä.

Suomen hallitus ei voi hyväksyä voimatoimien käyttöä
missään tilanteessa kansainvälisten ristiriitojen ratkaisemiseksi. Kuwaitin tilanne on parhaillaan esillä
Turvallisuusneuvostossa, jossa Suomi tulee ottamaan
lähemmin kantaa tilanteeseen.

Kuwaitissa on tällä hetkellä 22 suomalaista. Suurlähetystö
on saanut yhteyden käytännössä kaikkiin. Tarkoitus on koota
suomalaiset suurlähetystöön, johon on jo saapunut
6 suomalaista.

0177

MFA PRESS RELEASE

2.8.1990 at 11:00, No. 207

THE STATEMENT OF THE MINISTRY FOR FOREIGN AFFAIRS ON THE
SITUATION IN KUWAIT

The information of international news agencies state that Irak's
troops have penetrated Kuwait, Kuwaiti government has been
overthrown and a new Iraqi supported government has possibly
taken over.

Through its own channels the MFA has received similar kinds
of information. According to that, the center of Kuwait has
been closed and communication ended. The noises of war are at
the moment approaching the center areas. There are also some
rumours about a coup attempt of some of Kuwait's own troops.

Finland's government cannot accept the use of force in any
situation for solving international conflicts. The situation
of Kuwait is at the moment discussed in the Security Council,
where Finland will make a more detailed statement about the
matter.

At the moment there are 22 Finns in Kuwait. In practise, the
Embassy has been able to contact all of them. The purpose is
to gather the Finns to the Embassy where 6 Finns have already
arrived.

LEHDISTÖ   P R E S S   P R E S S
T I E D O T E   MEDDELANDE   R E L E A S E
STT:LLE   3.8.1990
Toimituksille   no. 208

ULKOASIAINMINISTERI PERTTI PAASION LAUSUNTO 03.08.1990

Suomen hallitus ei voi hyväksyä voimatoimien
käyttöä missään tilanteessa kansainvälisten ristiriitojen ratkaisemiseksi.

Turvallisuusneuvoston eilisen yksimielisen päätöksen mukaisesti Suomi tuomitsee Irakin invaa-
sion ja vaatii välitöntä vetäytymistä sekä vetoaa
osapuoliin neuvottelujen aloittamiseksi.

Turvallisuusneuvostolla on päävastuu kansainvä-
lisen rauhan säilyttämisessä ja ristiriitojen
ratkaisemisessa. Siihen pääsemiseksi Suomi osal-
listuu asian jatkokäsittelyyn turvallisuusneuvostossa.

0179

ULKOASIAINMINISTERIÖ UTRIKESMINISTERIET MINISTRY FOR FOREIGN AFFAIRS

MFA PRESS RELEASE

3.8.1990, No. 208

STATEMENT OF MINISTER FOR FOREIGN AFFAIRS PERTTI PAASIO 3.8.90

Finland's government cannot accept the use of force in any
situation in order to solve international conflicts.

According to the unanimous decision of the Security Council,
made yesterday, Finland is condemning Irak's invasion and demands
immediate withdrawal as well as appeals to the parties in order
to start negotiations.

The Securitity Council bears the main responsibility for
maintenance of international peace and solution of conflicts.
In order to reach that aim, Finland will participate further
talks about the matter in the Security Council.

0180

L E H D I S T Ö   P R E S S   P R E S S
T I E D O T E   MEDDELANDE   R E L E A S E

7.8.1990
no. 212

STT:lle
Toimituksille

IRAKIN TALOUSSAARTO

YK:n turvallisuusneuvosto hyväksyi myöhään maanantai-iltana
6.8.1990 lähes yksimielisesti laajat ja kaikkia valtioita
sitovat Irakin vastaiset talouspakotteet. Päätöslauselman
puolesta äänesti 13 neuvoston jäsentä, niiden joukossa kaikki
viisi pysyvää jäsentä.

Vain Kuuba ja Jemen pidättyivät äänestyksessä. Aikaisemmin
sitovia talouspakotteita on sovellettu vain kaksi kertaa,
Etelä-Rhodesiaa ja Etelä-Afrikkaa vastaan.

Turvallisuusneuvoston päätöslauselmassa toistettiin 2.8.1990
hyväksytty vetäytymiskehotus Irakille ja todettiin sen nou-
dattamatta jättämisen takia neuvoston päättäneen peruskirjan
pakotetoimia koskevan VII luvun nojalla seuraavista toimista:

    Kaikkien valtioiden on estettävä
    - Irakista tai Kuwaitista peräisin olevien
    tuotteiden tuonti sekä tällaisten tuotteiden vientiä
    em. maista tai kauttakuljetusta edistävä toiminta;
    - tuotteidensa, ml. aseiden ja muiden sotilastar-
    vikkeiden, vienti Irakiin tai Kuwaitiin,
    lukuunottamatta lääkintätarvikkeiden ja erityisissä
    humanitäärisissä tapauksissa elintarvikkeiden
    vientiä.

0181

ULKOASIAINMINISTERIÖ   UTRIKESMINISTERIET   MINISTRY FOR FOREIGN AFFAIRS

MFA PRESS RELEASE

7.8.1990, No. 212

ECONOMIC BOYCOTT OF IRAK

Late on Monday night 6.8.1990 the UN Security Council accepted
almost unanimously extensive and binding economic sanctions
towards Irak. 13 members of the council voted for the resolution,
among them all the five permanent members.

Only Cuba and Yemen refrained from voting. Earlier, binding
economic sanctions have been applied only twice, against Southern
Rhodes and South Africa.

The resolution of the Security Council repeated the request
for Iraqi withdrawal accepted on 2.8.1990 and stated that as
the request was not obeyed the council decided to take following
measures on the basis of the UN charter's chapter VII:

All countries must prevent

- the import and export of products that originate from Irak
or Kuwait or activities that promote to their transit conveyance;
- the export of their products and export of weapons and other
military equipment to Irak or Kuwait, excluding the export of
medical equipment or in special humanitarian cases the export
of foodstuffs.

All countries must refrain from giving money or financial assets
to the Iraqi government or a company operating in Irak or Kuwait.
Countries must also prevent their citizens from practising this
kind of activities. An exception are the payments for the goods
that were not included in the export ban.

All states, also states outside the UN, are requested to take
proper actions to realize the sanctions accurately, regardless
of whether the business transactions have been agreed on before
the resolution of the Security Council.

The sanctions accepted by the Security Council became binding
to Finland at the same time they were accepted in the Council.
The government has already taken up measures to bring them into
effect immediately and in full.

The government in Finland will prescribe more detailed
regulations for carrying out the sanctions by a decree given
on Thursday 9.8.1990. The procedure is based on law on Finland
realizing some its obligations as a member state of the UN given
on 29.12.1967.

All activities against the resolution of the Security Council
should be stopped immediately.

0182

Kaikkien valtioiden on pidätyttävä antamasta Irakin
hallitukselle tai Irakissa tai Kuwaitissa toimivalle
yritykselle tai viranomaiselle rahavaroja tai muita
taloudellisia voimavaroja. Valtioiden on estettävä
myös kansalaisiaan harjoittamasta tällaista toimin-
taa. Poikkeuksena ovat maksut edellä mainituista
vientikiellon poikkeustapauksista.

Kaikkia valtioita, ml. YK:n ulkopuoliset valtiot,
kehotetaan toimimaan tarkasti pakotteiden toimeenpanemiseksi riippumatta siitä, onko kaupallisis-
ta hankkeista sovittu ennen turvallisuusneuvoston päätöksen tekemistä.

Turvallisuusneuvoston hyväksymät pakotteet tulivat Suomea
sitoviksi samalla kun ne hyväksyttiin neuvostossa. Hallitus
on jo ryhtynyt toimenpiteisiin niiden saattamiseksi voimaan
välittömästi ja täysimääräisinä.

Tarkemmista määräyksistä pakotteiden toimeenpanemiseksi
Suomessa hallitus säätää torstaina 9.8.1990 annettavalla
asetuksella. Menettely perustuu 29.12.1967 annettuun lakiin
eräiden Suomelle Yhdistyneiden Kansakuntien jäsenenä
kuuluvien velvoitusten täyttämisestä.

Kaikesta turvallisuusneuvoston päätöslauselman vastaisesta
toiminnasta olisi pidättäydyttävä välittömästi.

외교문서 비밀해제: 걸프 사태 28

걸프 사태 쿠웨이트, 이라크 및 각국 경제 제재

초판인쇄 2024년 03월 15일
초판발행 2024년 03월 15일

지은이 한국학술정보(주)
펴낸이 채종준
펴낸곳 한국학술정보(주)
주 소 경기도 파주시 회동길 230(문발동)
전 화 031-908-3181(대표)
팩 스 031-908-3189
홈페이지 http://ebook.kstudy.com
E-mail 출판사업부 publish@kstudy.com
등 록 제일산-115호(2000. 6. 19)

ISBN 979-11-6983-988-4 94340
       979-11-6983-960-0 94340 (set)